The Making of an
Ink-Stained Wretch

Jules Witcover

The Making of an
Ink-Stained Wretch

Half a Century Pounding the Political Beat

THE JOHNS HOPKINS UNIVERSITY PRESS | BALTIMORE

The Johns Hopkins University Press
2715 North Charles Street
Baltimore, Maryland 21218-4363
www.press.jhu.edu

Library of Congress Cataloging-in-Publication Data
Witcover, Jules.
    The making of an ink-stained wretch : half a century pounding
the political beat / Jules Witcover.
        p. cm.
    Includes index.
    ISBN 0-8018-8247-8 (hardcover : alk. paper)
    1. Witcover, Jules. 2. Journalists—United States—Biography.
I. Title.
    PN4874.w6824A3 2006
070.92—dc22   2005009012

A catalog record for this book is available from
the British Library.

To all the boys,
and the girls,
on the bus

The feverish atmosphere was halfway between a high school bus trip to Washington and a gambler's jet junket to Las Vegas. . . . There was giddy camaraderie mixed with fear and low-grade hysteria. . . . [But] when it came to writing a story, they were as cautious as diamond-cutters.

TIMOTHY CROUSE
The Boys on the Bus: Riding with the Campaign Press Corps

Contents

19 One More Campaign 311

20 The Way We Were, and Are 324

    Index 333

    Illustrations follow page 152

Preface

PERMIT ME TO INTRODUCE MYSELF. I'm a political reporter, but I don't, as seems to be the fashion these days, play one on TV. So unless you're an old political junkie who knows the difference between H. L. Mencken and Walter Lippmann, you've probably never heard of me.

I'm not complaining, because for the last fifty years and more I've had a lively time being a fly on the wall at some of the great and small scenes of contemporary American history and politics. I've witnessed assassination attempts against presidents and presidential candidates, elections and defeats of great men and rogues, political campaigns at every level in just about every state and more than a score of national party conventions, and backroom conversations with giants and pygmies of both major political parties. And I've spent thousands of hours sitting, drinking, singing, writing, and only occasionally sleeping on whistle-stop trains, press buses, and planes from New Hampshire to California.

From the era of manual typewriters, carbon paper, dictationists in the newsroom, Western Union teletypers, and booze in the back of the bus, to the current days of laptop computers, the Internet, e-mail, cell phones, and Diet Cokes, what follows is one account of how it was, and how it is now.

Starting as a jack-of-all-trades at a new small weekly in New Jersey in 1949, I found my way toiling as a sports copy editor at the *Providence Journal* and a general-assignment reporter at the *Newark Star-Ledger* before eventually landing in Washington in 1954. There I worked, in turn, for the Newhouse Newspapers chain, the *Los Angeles Times,* and the *Washington Post* as a political writer, until, after years in the trenches, I finally became a columnist at the *Washington Star* and then the *Baltimore Sun* in the 1970s.

The journey has been marked by much more, however, than changes in the mechanics of political reporting and in the dissipations and tastes of its practitioners. Those of us who over the last half a century have told in print the story of the election of public officials at every governmental level have seen our role expand well beyond the reporting of who has won and who has lost and by how much. The task of digging deeper into the whys and where-fores of campaigns and elections, and the political philosophies pursued, now rests in the hands of better-educated reporters and editors of all gen-ders, races, and ethnicities, to the point that we're all now known as "jour-nalists," practicing not a craft but a profession. Where once a novice at best finished high school and then started in the newsroom, newcomers these days usually have college degrees, many from journalism schools.

In the less-charted waters of analysis and opinion in which I now swim, the dictates of speaking one's own mind necessarily require some departure from the old newspaperman's axiom that he should be neither seen nor heard, at least not in his own voice. But I have learned that in spouting off one's opinions, as in straight reporting, it is vital to remain rooted in careful and thorough fact-finding and research and to have a practiced wariness toward rumor and conspiracy theories, which seem to abound these days.

This book, rather than delving too much into what's right and wrong about how politics is reported, focuses on the delights of doing it, on the sat-isfaction, the fun, and the folly encountered in a lifetime of laboring at every level of newspapering, from covering small-town council meetings to long days and nights on the presidential campaign trail, as an "ink-stained wretch." Maybe it will give you a laugh or two, and along the way possibly a better sense of a craft so many Americans love to hate. I hope so, anyway. If this chronicle seeks to make one point beyond others, it is that you can't beat having a front seat at the great events of your time, and getting paid to write about them.

Acknowledgments

IN RECORDING THE OFTEN-RAMBUNCTIOUS DASH down the lane
of more than fifty years in the newspaper business, I have relied first
of all on my memories and the many boxes of clippings I have accu-
mulated over that period. They have helped me recall my feeble beginnings as a sports reporter in college, my slow trek from a small weekly newspaper to some of the best and not-so-best larger dailies, and
eventually to my playpen in Washington. Along the way, I have benefited from the professionalism, the wisdom, and maybe most of all
the good humor of the traveling companions, in the press and in politics, who have shared the long journey with me. I come away from all
those memories and associations with an undiminished zest for the
work of political kibitzing, tempered only by a certain nostalgia, as my
generation of reportorial brothers (and in the later years sisters) on
the campaign trail gradually vanishes. Everything related here, good
and bad, happened to me, and the opinions expressed about what
is right and wrong with American journalism today are my own, but
the interplay I have enjoyed with this band of happy warriors has
provided the framework. Knowing and working with them has been
the greatest reward, and the reader will be introduced to them in the
course of this narrative. Special thanks go to one of them, my old colleague and good friend John Mashek, for reading the manuscript,
jogging memories, and offering constructive advice. A few others who
have not accompanied me on the trail, however, require mentioning
here for their boundless support: my longtime able and enthusiastic

agent, David Black; my daughters, Amy and Julie, and my sons, Paul and Peter; my nephew, Wayne Nicolosi, for some photographic magic; above all, my wife and indomitable fellow author, Marion Elizabeth Rodgers. Also, I am indebted to the Johns Hopkins University Press team headed by Bob Brugger, especially manuscript editor Anne Whitmore, for turning out this offering in grand style and record time.

The Making of an
Ink-Stained Wretch

1 An Unlikely Beginning

HOW I GOT THE NOTION of getting into the political-writing racket is beyond me. Nobody in my family had ever worked for a newspaper or had anything to do with writing. My father, Sam, was an auto mechanic par excellence who ran a one-man shop in Union City, New Jersey, directly across the
Hudson River from Manhattan. And my mother, Sadie, was a hard-working
housewife before, during, and after the Great Depression, when no self-
respecting woman would be caught dead calling herself a homemaker.

Sam and Sadie; their names sounded like the title of a radio soap opera
about a Jewish couple on Delancey Street, but "Abie's Irish Rose" would
have been more appropriate. My father was Jewish all right, but by birth
rather than practice, and my mother was Irish Catholic—a fact that led to
her ostracism from the Witcover clan for the first year of their marriage,
until the others discovered what a sweetheart she was and embraced her
with open arms. The Jewish side of the family even forgave the fact that she
brought up her two kids Catholic—my sister, Marilyn, and me, four years
her junior.

My parents generally only glanced at our local newspaper, the *Hudson
Dispatch,* now in the graveyard of local journalism. They didn't have to read
about politics to decide how to vote because where we lived made our family automatically Democratic. On election days, my mother asked my father
which Democrat to vote for, and he told her.

In Hudson County, it was an easy call. The famed (or infamous) Democratic boss Mayor Frank Hague of Jersey City presided over an unofficial
board of mayors from Union City and the other surrounding towns—all

Democrats and all under his thumb. Hague's fiefdom thrived on his largesse all during the Franklin D. Roosevelt years and beyond. For me as a kid, about the only thing that stirred awareness of his political power was the fact that on opening day of the baseball season for the Jersey City Giants, the New York Giants' prime farm team, all public schools in Hudson County were closed. Free tickets and buses were provided to students to assure a full house at the stadium.

Maybe this had something to do with my early ambition to be a sportswriter, but I doubt it. That came later, after years of playing pickup baseball in a vacant lot in Union City, next to the abandoned Schultz Brewery, a very profitable enterprise of the gangster Dutch himself in pre- and post-Prohibition days, and basketball on nearby Brown Street, where we kids strung a basket and backboard onto a telephone pole. Like many other youthful pleasures in Union City in those days, this defilement of private property was illegal. We overcame the problem by securing heavy rope to the backboard so it could be quickly lowered and hidden from view whenever a cranky neighbor called the cops to bring us lawbreakers to justice.

The neighborhood cops had more important duties, though. Among them was the task of keeping an eye on the brewery, where on rainy days we often took refuge and had races on the conveyor belt rollers of the bottling assembly line. Seated in empty wooden beer cases, we sped down the rollers from the second floor to the first, with only minor casualties. That this took place in Dutch Schultz's old stamping grounds provided a romantic touch, as did the reinforced steel door to his former apartment across the street, where one of our gang now lived, to the envy of the rest of us. Those in the kid's special favor might be treated to a tour inside, complete with the bullet holes on one wall.

But I digress. It was the vice of gambling, not bootlegging, that set my course in life. Every Thanksgiving, my extended family of aunts, uncles, and cousins gathered at the home of a clan elder for the traditional turkey dinner. My cousin Edward and I, schemers even at the early age of seven or eight, rigged up a game of chance for which older members of the family were asked to ante up a nickel. They were shown a board into which twenty or more rolled-up slips of paper had been inserted, each bearing a number—or a zero—written by us. A player poked one slip out of the board. If you got a "10" you won a dime, a "5" a nickel, a "1" a penny. The trouble—from the point of view of the gamblers, not us proprietors—was that there was only one "10" and maybe two "5"s, and the rest were ones and zeroes. Our ingenuity netted us about eighty cents of each dollar wagered. We called the game Poke-a-Winner, but it was quickly renamed Poke-a-Sucker by a perceptive aunt, obliging us to come up with a less transparent moneymaking enterprise.

We hit upon a family newspaper, which we printed by hand on a single sheet of paper, bearing all manner of family fact and gossip. We coerced adult relatives into buying ads extolling their businesses and then charged each customer a nickel to read the only copy of the paper, which had to be handed back when read. We gave our readers their money's worth with extravagant praise for our advertisers, and we titillated all with modestly scandalous rumors about their kin—some present, some absent. Our maiden exercise in freedom of the press met with a warm and profitable success, there being no overhead, and two budding Walter Winchells were on their way. Well, one, anyway; Edward wound up doing honest work as a successful school teacher, but I persevered.

Soon I was turning out a series of neighborhood newspapers, the first of which was *The Brown Street Rag,* printed in multiple copies by using one of those gelatine pads with which operators of neighborhood diners produced their daily menus in purple ink. Next came a toy printing press operated by hand, with stories set in rubber type, letter by letter with a tweezers. The result was no threat to the *Hudson Dispatch,* but as a legitimate revenue-enhancing endeavor it was a far cry beyond the discredited Poke-a-Sucker.

The business side of newspapering, however, did not in the long run appeal to me. I was never among that hardy crew of young boys who rose at dawn's crack to deliver the *Dispatch,* or after school brought the rival *Jersey Observer* to Union City doorsteps. The lot next to the brewery and the asphalt of Brown Street, which in addition to basketball provided the venue for everything from touch football and stickball to roller-skate hockey and boxball, proved greater lures. Then, with Pearl Harbor and the outbreak of World War II, when I was a freshman in high school, my father drafted me to keep his gas station open in the late afternoons while he was off working the night shift at a nearby defense plant.

The station, with its three gas pumps right on the sidewalk, became a hangout for my buddies. I practiced on an old saxophone there while the family dog, Buster, howled in discomfort at my dismal efforts. My pals and I wiled away the time discussing sports and our fictional successes and real failures with the fairer sex, and listening to Martin Block's radio program, *The Make-Believe Ballroom* as he spun the latest Miller, Goodman, Shaw, and Dorsey records. Sometimes we would amuse ourselves by writing new lyrics to tunes of the day, an affliction from which I suffered and later inflicted upon others in the back of press buses, trains, and planes in my life-long adolescence.

No member of my family had ever gone to college, and although my grades in high school were good—except for penmanship, that bane of the left-handed—I didn't give college much thought as I approached graduation in 1945. I knew I did not want to follow in my father's footsteps, having no mechanical ability, a major embarrassment as the son of a man who could fix anything and invented all manner of devices when need demanded.

In my senior year at Union Hill High School, our class valedictorian, a basketball teammate, informed me that he was going to New York that afternoon to inquire about applying to Columbia. I went along for the ride, picked up an application myself, and after conferring with my parents filled it in and sent it off—the only such application I submitted anywhere. All I knew about Columbia at that time was that it didn't have a very good football team. (Although later Columbia would score the biggest upset in its history by ending an Army winning streak of twenty-six games, back to the glory days of Glenn Davis and Doc Blanchard.) Had I known of the school's high academic standing, I probably would have been scared off, but somehow I weathered a tough, all-day intelligence test and got in. With some savings and help from my folks, I scraped up the $300 (only $300!) for the first semester's tuition and off I went—by bus and subway daily, returning home each night.

I struggled, in competition with better-prepared students from New York and elsewhere. At the same time, the shadow of military service hovered over me. Rather than waiting to be drafted into the Army, I decided to enlist in the Navy before my eighteenth birthday. The Navy seemed more romantic—and safer. The day I marched down a street in midtown Manhattan behind a salty old sailor with stripes clear up his left arm to take my physical examination, I was suddenly engulfed in confetti pouring down from skyscraper windows. At the same time, young girls streamed out of their offices and smothered me and my fellow recruits with hugs and kisses. The news had just been flashed that the Germans had surrendered. It was V-E Day and my fellow Navy enlistees and I were being mistaken for recruits headed off to war that very moment. We did not resist, and after our physicals we went home to await the call and, in my case, to finish my first semester at Columbia.

During that first term, I entertained the notion of going on to law school after graduation. But courses like British Constitutional History caused my eyes to glaze over and I began casting about for alternatives. In August of 1945, I was finally called to active duty, and after a dreary all-night train ride on the dingy Lehigh Valley Railroad, I arrived at Sampson, a Navy boot camp near Geneva in upstate New York. As my new buddies and I got off the train, grimy and disoriented, newly sheared skinheads shouted at us from the platform: "Go home! The war's over!" It was V-J Day.

It didn't occur to me then what a charmed military career I was embarking on—reporting on V-E Day and starting service on V-J Day, thus spared anything worse than a brief detour from my as yet uncharted civilian life. The war was, indeed, over but I wasn't going home quite yet. The term of my enlistment was the duration of the war plus six months, but because the end was not officially declared for some time, I spent just about a year in uniform before being discharged. Fresh out of boot camp, I was assigned to the USS *Apollo*, a submarine tender tied up at the sub base in New London, Connecticut. I was put to work in the ship's carpentry shop, fashioning plain wood boxes about the size of coffins in which mustered-out officers packed their personal belongings for shipment home. Said personal belongings in fact consisted of all useful objects that were not nailed down—and some that were. When the boxes were full of loot, my fellow amateur carpenters and I would obligingly hammer them shut for the officers on the spot, the contents thus escaping inspection.

I might have spent a lot longer in the Navy, or more accurately in a Navy brig, as a result of my most interesting experience in uniform, but again I got lucky. I was happy to be stationed so close to home, because my sister was getting married to her longtime fiancé, who had just returned from army service in Europe, and I was to be best man. I was about to depart the ship one late November day when word passed that it was being quarantined because a few of my shipmates had come down with scarlet fever.

I was frustrated, because I had had that very illness as a kid and saw no reason why I should be kept aboard. Naturally, my appeal for liberty was summarily rejected and I seemed certain to miss the biggest family celebration in years. My mother sounded heartbroken when I phoned to say I wasn't going to be there. Most of my shipmates, however, were old salts who had spent years in dismal Guam, and a good number of them were not going to let a little quarantine keep them aboard when they were only a couple of hours by train from New York or Boston. The first night of the quarantine, I watched as they dropped a long line from the *Apollo*'s deck to a submarine tied up next to it. One by one, they slid down onto the sub's deck and joined the unquarantined submariners in small rowboats (called punts) that took them around the stern of my ship to the dock, from whence they headed into New London and beyond.

The next night I joined these adventurers, armed with a phony pass cooked up for me by a veteran shipmate. I got to Union City by train and bus with no trouble. My mother, surprised and ever the strong Catholic, proclaimed my appearance "a miracle." I didn't bother to give her the details and risk shaking her faith. A great time was had by all at the wedding reception, and late that night I headed back to New London, a bit nervous but fortified by the numerous libations of the affair.

I got to New London and onto the base without incident, my phony weekend pass doing its job. I joined a group of submariners on the dock, boarded the little punt with them and climbed onto the deck of the sub, where by this time the enlisted men on watch were familiar with the route of my returning shipmates. They paid little attention to me as I started my climb up the line, but when I got about halfway up I slipped and slid all the way down. As my foot hit the sub's deck my ankle buckled and into the frigid waters of the Thames River I plunged. It was so cold that I found myself unable to pull myself up onto the deck of the sub, and only the quick thinking of one of the submariners on watch saved me. He leaned his leg over the side and told me to grab onto it. Others hauled me aboard, my teeth chattering.

These good submariners took me below, gave me warm work clothes, and assured me sincerely that I was no doubt headed for the brig. The fall had severely sprained my ankle and a second try up the line was out of the question. I would have to go over to the dock in the morning, limp up the *Apollo* gangplank, and turn myself in. The fact that I had been in the Navy only a few months, some old-timers told me, guaranteed that my ship's officers would throw the book at me for going AWOL when the vessel was under quarantine. I awaited daybreak like a man facing the gallows.

At first light, I was rowed to the dock, where the miracle my mother had proclaimed proved to have a second act. Coming down the dock were some of my shipmates toting trash cans to be emptied there. As they carried out their task and headed back, I fell in with them, walked up the gangplank behind them, smartly saluted the officer of the day, and swiftly disappeared into the bowels of the ship. Later, my submariner friends hoisted my wet clothes up the escape line to me and I was in the clear. This caper, which scared holy hell out of me, naturally made me a hero with the old salts, who previously had had nothing but contempt for the new rookie who was also a "college boy."

This episode convinced me, if I needed to be convinced, that a Navy career was not for me. Nevertheless, my year in Harry Truman's fleet proved to be a most beneficial one, because it qualified me for the G.I. Bill of Rights, which made it possible for me to reenter Columbia and graduate three years later. By that time I had decided that a law career was not for me either and that I wanted to pursue my fantasy of becoming a sportswriter.

At Columbia, I had had a taste of it, writing for the daily *Columbia Spectator*. The first couple of winters I drew crew as my assignment, and it was not exactly what I had in mind, after my Navy experience with boats. Each afternoon after classes I repaired to a dreary room in the bowels of the campus gymnasium where a stationary shell sat in low water in a pool barely long enough to hold it. There, the worthies of the boat-racing fraternity sat and stroked methodically to the barking of an undernourished coxswain for an hour or more as I watched, pencil and pad at the ready, for something to write about. I seldom found it, but I persevered each year until spring, when the boys would take to the Harlem River, below the old Polo Grounds, to experience a series of shellackings at the hands of Ivy League foes. Columbia being then essentially a school of subway strap-hangers who commuted daily and seldom even saw a decent stretch of water, its helmsmen (as I always incorrectly called them) were pitiful if persistent.

Crew did not offer a very wide range for my large repertoire of sports clichés, but in time I was assigned to, so to speak, greener fields to cover baseball and football. The latter enabled me to write, after a loss to Penn in 1948, "Columbia's Lion is licking its wounds and at the same time sharpening its claws for two vital Ivy League tilts" ahead, and that the team was "still completely capable of assuming the position of spoiler in the scrambled loop race." In a short time, I had polished my style sufficiently to scribble about the Dartmouth game, "The incomparable Lou Kusserow once more galloped himself into Columbia history by cuddling Bill Dey's soaring kickoff five yards in his own end zone and chugging down the middle, through a swarm of green jerseys, over to the left and down the sideline amid deafening shrieks from the capacity crowd to paydirt, 105 yards from his point of embarkation."

Such restrained prose earned me a chance to cover Columbia basketball during a historic season in which the Lions won twenty-six straight, including the snapping of a similar streak by Holy Cross led by the legendary Bob Cousy. We had a very short guard named Sherry Marshall whom I always described as—what else?—a "diminutive speedster." I also upheld Columbia tradition, in my fashion, by collecting splinters on the J.V. bench, scoring my only and meaningless point in three years on a foul shot against Princeton in the final moments of the lost game.

Astonishingly, for all this, no call came from the *New York Times, Daily News, Mirror,* or even the *World-Telegram,* demanding that I abandon my academic pursuits and start covering the even greener fields of Gotham's professional teams for them. The closest I came was a part-time, minimum-wage gig for the *Daily News,* sorting the paper's weekly football forecast contest entries. Every Thursday, Friday, and Saturday nights during the college season, about twenty sports nuts would gather in a small room at the Daily News offices on East 42nd Street and sift through scores of mail bags full of entries. To facilitate the sorting, pushover games were listed at the top and bottom of the list of fifteen to be played that Saturday. On Thursday and Friday nights, as instructed by a burly drill-sergeant type incongruously named "Sonny," we separated out all entries that had these two games "wrong," on the theory that entries that had no more than thirteen winners out of the fifteen games would be losers.

On late Saturday afternoon, as the results started rolling in, the more serious sorting took place. It lasted until all the thousands of entries had been examined and the winner of the $500 first prize, usually with fourteen or fifteen games right and one or more actual scores predicted, was identified. Lesser prizes were awarded to the next-best entries. It was boring and tiring work, but I could console myself by thinking that at least I was working "in sports." I was kind of like the guy who had a job in the circus shoveling up manure behind the elephants. Asked why he didn't quit such a disgusting assignment, he replied: "What? And get out of show business?"

While thus getting a questionable foothold on my chosen career track, I continued to put in my classroom time and finally received what I'm sure at the time I called my "sheepskin." It was handed to me by a retired army general named Dwight D. Eisenhower, who had returned from Europe and taken over as Columbia's president. Although himself an avid sports fan, he bestowed on me no word of commendation for my scintillating accounts in the *Spectator*, or my labors for the sports department of the *Daily News*.

My first real full-time job out of Columbia was as a pamphlet writer for a large insurance company in New York. My principal task was "writing" small booklets outlining insurance benefits for employees of insured corporations; more specifically, I selected already written texts, modifying them to conform with the insurance plan offered, choosing the ink and paper colors to be used, and then proofreading them. I didn't kid myself that Grantland Rice had started out this way, but the job kept me in movie money for a year.

I also had a gig five nights a week and all day Saturday across the Hudson in Hackensack, on a new weekly newspaper first called the *Star* and then the *Star-Telegram*. For this learning experience, which included the privilege of selling ads, I was paid ten dollars a week and was allowed to write a sports column. Depending on the season, it was most imaginatively called "Touchdown Talk," "The Hot Corner," or "Court Comments," and it chronicled the exploits of Jersey boys on college teams or in the pros. I sprinkled the columns with sports celebrity names of the time, from Joe DiMaggio and Pee Wee Reese in baseball to Sammy Baugh and Sid Luckman in football and Bob Cousy and Dick McGuire in basketball. I used the column principally to reassure myself, if nobody else, that I was on the right career track.

At the same time, I had the opportunity to cover other exciting fare, including the installation of one Calvin Weber as the Master Councillor of the Hackensack DeMolay; the rescue of Mary Haley, 82, from a "blaze" at 79 Main Street that had spread to Charlie's Shoe Shine Shop; rejection by the Fourth Ward Democratic Club of a proposal to build "a pool for negroes only in the Second District"; and a host of human interest stories with snappy leads, such as "When Royal Massie got in the way of a heavy truck that was backing up in the Brewster Construction Company's S-3 project several weeks ago, it looked like the end of the road for him."

I even got my hand in on writing inspirational editorials like the one urging citizens to support their struggling local merchants that summoned up

Abe Lincoln ("united we stand, divided we fall") and Franklin D. Roosevelt ("the only thing we have to fear is fear itself") to make the case that "there's nothing to fear from a word like 'depression' if you knock it into a cocked hat with simple business sense and a little of that old-fashioned element called community pride." There was plenty more where that came from, but still no calls, not even from the *Wall Street Journal.*

Around this time, I applied for admission to three schools of journalism: Columbia, Northwestern, and Syracuse. I was offered a place at the second two but not at the first, on grounds that I was one too many that year from the Columbia undergraduate program, and besides I was already (theoretically anyway) getting good journalism experience in Hackensack. But I was promised that if I were to apply the next year I would be accepted. Wanting to work in New York after graduate school, I decided to wait a year, and entered the Columbia Graduate School of Journalism in the fall of 1950.

I never regretted the choice. My year there gave me the opportunity to make many mistakes without being fired and, more important, to make friendships in the reporting racket that have lasted through the years. My chief faculty mentor was John Hohenberg, a former United Nations and foreign correspondent for the *New York Post* when it was a more respectable sheet and for other publications. Hohenberg was a super-enthusiast and romantic about newspaper work of the old school. The "J School" functioned more in the fashion of a newsroom than a lecture hall, with student reporters being dispatched into the city several days a week to gather and write news stories. Other students then edited the stories under the watchful supervision of pros from the *New York Times, Daily News,* and other real papers of the city.

Hohenberg was a cheerleader for vivid writing under deadline pressures. His most famous admonition to the slow and hesitant reporter was "Go with what you've got." My favorite Hohenberg story involves a classmate and pal, Juan deOnis, whose father was the longtime head of the Spanish Department at Columbia. Juan was American-born and had grown up in an apartment a block off the Columbia campus before going to Williams College for his undergraduate work. He was fluent in Spanish and English but unfortunately had never learned to touch-type, a J School admissions requirement he had finessed on his application. So when it came to turning in his story after a day of reporting off-campus, Juan invariably was one of the last to do so.

After a series of Juan's tardy submissions, Hohenberg, unfamiliar with his personal background, attached a sympathetic note to one of his stories. It went something like this: "Juan: I realize how difficult it must be for you to write in a second language. Just take your time and I'm sure you'll get the hang of it before long." Juan, continuing to hunt and peck at his typewriter keyboard, didn't bother to straighten Hohenberg out on the matter of his supposed handicap. He eventually overcame it and became an outstanding correspondent in South America for the *New York Times* and the *Los Angeles Times*.

One of the assignments each member of the Class of 1951 drew was a long investigative piece, and mine was to explore the emerging phenomenon of the television soap opera at the New York–based networks. Skeptics argued that American housewives, who could listen to radio soaps while scurrying about doing their household chores, would not allow themselves to be frozen in place watching television melodramas. After weeks of exploring the new experiment, I firmly concluded in my piece that maybe daytime television soap opera would survive and maybe it wouldn't. I was rewarded for my decisiveness with a ho-hum response from the faculty.

Even at this early stage in my newspapering, I was wary of making predictions—wariness I continued to practice when eventually I got into political reporting, leading me to shy away from saying who would win approaching elections. Not having a crystal ball, I concluded early on that I would only diminish what little credibility I might have with readers by calling the finish of the horse race before it was over. With a few exceptions, I've kept my hunches, however informed I might persuade myself they were, out of my copy—if not out of barroom speculations.

My Columbia J School classmates and I also often devoured lectures from working journalists in New York, many of them headliners of the time. The one I remember most clearly and has served me best in later years, was a talk by Leonard Lyons, the man-about-town syndicated columnist of the *New York Post*. One of the first questions put to him was how many papers carried his column. He replied: "Syndicated columnists are notorious liars about how many papers they have. They'll say they have a hundred or two hundred, when they only have seventy or eighty. Me, when I'm asked, I say sixty-six. And when I say sixty-six I don't mean sixty-seven and I don't mean sixty-five . . . I mean thirty-four!"

Lectures notwithstanding, Columbia was essentially a trade school and conveyed the notion that journalism—mostly the print variety, having only embryonic television courses—was a craft, not a profession, with clear, simple writing its prime tool. The few television news shows we produced, after venturing downtown to watch Douglas Edwards do his nightly stint on CBS, used still photos, especially mug shots, to go along with the written text. Somehow, one of my classmates, Phil Scheffler, managed to overcome this primitive instruction and became a senior producer of CBS's *Sixty Minutes.* But in those days most of us were aiming for jobs in print and started out there after our year on the Columbia campus and in the laboratory of New York City.

With my G.I. Bill money running out, I managed to get through journalism school with a weekend job that encouraged me to stick to the print side of the business. I was hired by Helen Worden Erskine, a one-time society and feature writer for the old *New York World,* as a combination nurse, companion, and editorial aide to her bedridden husband, author John Erskine. After a long and distinguished career as a writer, newspaper columnist, and essayist, and eventually a concert pianist, John Erskine was gravely injured in an auto accident on a rainy night as he was returning from a concert in Detroit. He could no longer walk and his speech was seriously impaired, but his mind and wit remained intact. I spent long hours reading to him and going over his mountains of papers, ostensibly with an eye to the publication of his memoirs but more as therapy for him.

In the process, I became acquainted not only with his best-selling novels of the 1920s based on mythology, the most famous of which were *Helen of Troy* and *Galahad,* but also his columns in the *Brooklyn Eagle* and elsewhere. He was, most of the time, a patient and pleasant man but could display a huge temper when his condition, or my mispronunciation of words or names, got the better of him. Then he would emit a roar of disapproval and exasperation that would shake the Erskines' stylish Park Avenue apartment.

A highlight for him was the Saturday afternoon visits his adoring wife arranged from other literary figures of the time, the most memorable of whom for me was Fanny Hurst, by then a dynamic and exotic old lady dressed and heavily made up in the fashion of Gloria Swanson in *Sunset Boulevard.* An Erskine son-in-law was Russell Crouse, co-author with Howard Lindsay of *Life With Father* and other long-running Broadway shows. Most Saturdays, the Crouses would arrive in the late afternoon for an hour with Erskine, who was delighted to see his grandson and granddaughter, who cavorted around the large apartment until his eroding patience dictated their departure. About twenty years later, my path again crossed that of the grandson, Timothy Crouse, by then a writer for *Rolling Stone* magazine covering the 1972 California presidential primary campaign.

During the J School's Easter recess, about half a dozen of us got tryouts at the *Providence (Rhode Island) Journal* and got our first daily newspaper jobs there upon graduation. My first real city editor, a gruff, portly gent named Elliot Stocker who was right out of central casting, in assigning me to my first story actually said, "Kid, I'm going to kick you off the dock and see if you can swim!" After covering a routine speech by the mayor, I managed to paddle my way back to shore. I was shunted to the state staff, where I was rotated from one small Rhode Island town to another covering police, the town hall, and all other aspects of the local scene, and only occasionally sports.

I spent a summer at the old resort town of Newport, interviewing the likes of local celebrity and English Channel swimmer Shirley May France and discovering the wonders of the New England clambake, described in the same gee-whiz style it took me eons to shake: "Only his close friends attended the clambake for Dan Coggleshall at the Colt Farm, Bristol, yesterday. But when the dust had cleared, more than 250 plates, piled with empty clam shells, lobster skeletons and other assorted casualties of a hungry crowd, lined the tables in evidence of how many close friends a man can have."

My most exciting story was about an irate male driver, stuck behind a slow woman driver, who got so exasperated that he rammed into the rear of the offending vehicle, then pulled out and hit it from one side, then steered around to the other and rammed it again. I forget what *he* got for this, but I got a byline—although well inside the paper.

Newport being the locale of a famous summer theater, I reveled in the free passes that came my way in return for reviews and interviews with such moderately famous movie stars as Basil Rathbone (Sherlock Holmes), Ruth Hussey, Constance Bennett, and Donald Woods. But the experience didn't make me want to be a theater critic. I still yearned for sportswriting. Finally a spot opened up on the *Journal's* sports desk and I grabbed it, working nights editing copy and writing headlines, and hoping to break into reporting. By this time, I was a newlywed and my bride from my hometown, Marian Laverty, was working days as a local editor for the American Mathematical Society, which made for a sort of revolving-door relationship in Providence. A former reporter herself for the *Hudson Dispatch* and a New York University graduate, Marian was most supportive, while longing to get back into the newspaper business, which she later did.

Sitting around the rim of the *Journal* sports copy desk each night, we editors vied to outdo each other with clever heads and photo captions. One snapshot of a Yankee shortstop taking the throw from first ahead of a Red Sox runner and completing a double play was memorably labeled "Washing Out a Pair of Sox." Or our sharpened black pencils would convert such sportwriter monstrosities as "The Splendid Splinter, an ace with the ash, swatted a brace of round-trippers" to "Ted Williams, the league's best batter, hit two home runs."

Although the subject matter we handled was sports, the veteran green-eyeshade types I sat beside were sticklers for proper English usage, which helped me deal with such niceties as the difference between "that" and "which" and "who" and "whom." One old grammar crank named John Davis pounded into me the "infinitive of purpose" rule—using an infinitive only to convey why an action was taken. Example: Never write "Jim Thorpe ran eighty yards for a touchdown to end the scoring" when ending the scoring was not his intent. Instead, write "Jim Thorpe ran eighty yards for a touchdown that ended the scoring." With such distinctions did we wile away the postmidnight hours around the sports copy rim. They made me all the more eager for the fresh air of a stadium press box.

At the same time, I had a mild interest in politics, it being after all a first cousin to the world of games with its scorekeeping, winning and losing, and all that. It was in Providence in the fall of 1952 that I saw my first live president, when Harry Truman, having decided not to seek another term, made a rousing speech for Adlai Stevenson downtown. On election night, I wasn't working on the sports desk, so I was drafted as a temporary United Press political reporter working for peanuts for the wire service's one Providence staffer, my friend Tom Gerber.

Tom was badly outstaffed by the Associated Press, which had a large operation based right in the *Journal's* wire room, and he had a critical task for me. Every half hour or so, I would saunter into the wire room, copy down the AP tallies for key Rhode Island precincts, and more or less surreptitiously phone them to Gerber. He would then do some fancy "rounding" of the numbers and report them to the UP office in Boston. Thus was the smallest of the then forty-eight states "covered" by one of the nation's great wire serv-ices. I didn't get a byline—and God knows didn't want one. There wasn't all that much room for ethics in the UP election-night operation at that time, at least not in the Providence "bureau."

After about a year of frustrating labors on the *Journal* sports desk, which my editor, Barney Madden, knew were not close to my heart, he passed along a tip to me: the *Quincy Patriot-Ledger,* a small but energetic daily out-side Boston, was looking for a sportswriter. I hastened the hour's drive north to the Hub, as our sports scribes always called it, for an interview. The sports editor, Pres Hobson, impressed by the *Journal* if not by me, said he was interested and the job would probably be mine, pending resolution of one complication that he could not confide to me.

I returned to Providence buoyed but anxious, and waited. A week passed and then two, and there was no word. One morning when I hadn't been on the sports desk the night before, I picked up the *Journal* at my doorstep, turned out of habit to the sports section, and read the headline: "Boston Braves Sold to Milwaukee." There went my sportswriting job. The "compli-cation," it turned out, was the pending deal to move the team that I would have been covering for the Quincy paper. In later years, I often reflected on the close call that, had it gone the other way, might have found me sitting year after year in some press box scribbling away about boys' games played by men.

So it was back to the *Journal* night sports desk, a sentence that was not without its personal rewards. They included the friendship of Mike Thomas, a grizzly old boxing writer who had discovered Rocky Marciano of nearby Brockton, Massachusetts, and Steve Cady, a Yalie with an untypical zeal for horse race handicapping, both of whom were my occasional companions at the local tracks, Narragansett Park and Lincoln Downs. Mike was a heavy bettor who would start the day expressing the hope that he would "break even because I need the money," and could not bear to watch the race after making a particularly heavy wager. Steve wound up in his dream writing job: covering racing for the *New York Times.*

Sportswriting on the *Journal* and the companion *Evening Bulletin* was such fun for those who did it that there was little prospect that any of them would be stepping aside anytime soon to make room for me, so I continued shopping around. It so happened that a customer at my father's gas station was a circulation man for the *Newark Star-Ledger.* Learning of my interest in moving back to the New York area, he got me an interview with Philip Hochstein, then the paper's editor and also the chief editorial executive for the whole S. I. Newhouse chain.

Armed with recent clips from the *Providence Journal* and old clips from the *Hackensack Star-Telegram* (I was playing the local angle), I made my pitch. Hochstein, a rather strange and intimidating bird, gave them a look and promptly bowled me over by asking whether I'd be interested in going to Washington. Without hesitation, and also without grasping what I might be getting myself into, I said yes. He countered by saying that he would try me out for six months there at the *Star-Ledger* and if I did well he would ship me off to the chain's Washington bureau. It wasn't sportswriting, but what the hell, it would be writing and it would get me out of Providence. And after all, covering politics was a game much like sports, and I did have a passing interest in it. I grabbed the offer. Marian and I moved back to New Jersey, and she proceeded to get an editing job at the *Wall Street Journal*. One of us had made it to New York.

My six months at the *Star-Ledger* would stretch out to nearly a year before I was finally transferred to Washington. During that trial period, I got a close-in education on tabloid journalism, although the paper was a broadsheet in format. Typical was my story about a machinist named David Dickman who swallowed his false teeth, went to four different local hospitals for help without success, then finally reached down his gullet and retrieved them himself. "I was pretty worn out by this time," he told me, "so I decided to do something. Fingers were invented before instruments, so with my fingers I got my teeth up."

The city editor was a raucous Irishman named Art Heenan who was a tough-talking taskmaster who didn't mind his reporters cutting corners to get the story and was a sucker for a gimmick. For example, to herald the opening of the hunting season, he rented an old open touring car, put a moosehead behind the steering wheel and tied a comely young female reporter named Googie Grossman to the right front fender. The photo ran on page one.

Heenan introduced me to the valuable newspaper reporter's axiom "Don't cheapen the beat." When I submitted a very conservative expense account with every penny spent itemized, Heenan threw it back at me. "Kid, don't ruin it for the rest of us," he growled, ordering me to add several nonexistent taxi fares and another meal or two with a phantom, or at least unfed, source.

Heenan's chief flaw, however, was a weakness for Senator Joseph R. McCarthy of Wisconsin, the right-wing Republican demagogue who was terrorizing Washington with his make-believe claims of evidence that communists were infiltrating key branches of the federal government, and particularly the State Department. In Heenan, fellow Irish Catholic McCarthy found a pliable ally in the distant outpost of Newark. McCarthy would feed tidbits to Heenan, who would pass them on to his reporters to pursue, with little provable result. The Heenan-McCarthy connection gave me an early introduction to the Wisconsin wild man prior to my reassignment to Washington.

My assignments at the *Star-Ledger* included the night rewrite desk. My buddy there was a suave middle-aged gent named Lester Abelman who resembled Fred Astaire in his dress and walk. He strode around the newsroom, his shoes clicking on the floor as if he were about to break into the Continental, looking distinctly out of place in the broken-down old relic on Halsey Street, around the corner from Minsky's Burlesque. The linotype machines were on the floor above the newsroom, their roar inhibiting soft conversation, threatening at all times to fall through the skimpy floorboards onto us. It was not exactly a heart-wrenching experience when I left the *Star-Ledger*.

On January 1, 1954, Marian and I arrived in the nation's capital amid springlike weather. Still not having lost my interest in sportswriting but eager to give the political version of games-playing a whirl, I settled into the Newhouse Washington bureau to tell the world about the second year of the first administration of President Dwight D. Eisenhower. I reflected that it was a small world after all. Five years earlier Eisenhower had signed my bachelor's degree and held forth at my graduation at Columbia. Now I would have a chance to say in print what I thought about him. I was soon to discover, however, that as a regional reporter—a very small fish in a very big pond—my focus would by necessity be on considerably lesser targets.

2 Destination Washington

FROM THE FIRST MINUTE I WALKED into the Newhouse Washington bureau in the then-dismal National Press Building at Fourteenth and F Streets, I realized it was not going to be the way it was in the movies. The bureau occupied about four tiny, cramped rooms stretched railroad-car style one floor below the National Press Club, where the bureau chief, an unschooled but streetwise hack named Andy Viglietta, ruled with an iron hand over four young wet-behind-the-ears reporters. Ours was strictly a regional bureau, with each of us assigned to one or more of the Newhouse newspapers, then a mostly motley collection of second-rate sheets that were milked for every penny they could be made to yield by Samuel I. Newhouse, the miniature impresario of the chain.

Actually, we were never allowed to refer to the collection as a chain. The old man insisted that each paper should have its own identity, and as long as it made money, he didn't care much about whether its quality as a purveyor of news was good, bad, or indifferent. In the 1950s and for a long time thereafter, there were no or few Newhouse papers in the first category; they fell into the second and third. S.I., as he was called, knew little about news and cared less. He referred to his newspapers as "properties," and treated them as such. Personally, he was a deferentially polite little man who, on his rare visits to the bureau, comported himself in the manner of an embarrassed intruder, always asking if he could use a phone or sit at a desk.

His work week consisted of traveling from one of his newspapers to another, checking on the business operation and, legend had it, collecting cash receipts in a brown paper bag. When I joined the bureau, he owned about a dozen newspapers, in such places as Long Island, Newark, Staten Island and Jersey City in the New York metropolitan area, and Syracuse, Harrisburg, St. Louis, Birmingham and Huntsville, Alabama, and Portland, Oregon, in the hinterlands. The flagship was the *Long Island Press,* a rather wretched local sheet, where the old man and others who passed as executives hung their hats. By the time I escaped, seventeen years and a few bureau chiefs later, newspapers in Springfield, Massachusetts, Cleveland, Denver, Mobile, Alabama, and other cities had been added. A tired joke about the old man was that one morning he left his apartment on Park Avenue, telling his wife Mitzi he was just going out to buy a paper, and came back with the *Cleveland Plain Dealer.*

The publishers and editors of all these "properties" ran their own shops, and for many years there was little or no editorial connection among them. They used the Washington bureau to churn out stories about their local congressmen and about local issues that came before Congress or any federal department or agency. The three other reporters and I routinely produced four or five short stories a day, punching them out ourselves on a rickety teletype machine in the office, reporting early in the morning, and often not heading for home until seven or eight o'clock at night.

Viglietta was out of the office most of the time schmoozing with the congressmen from Long Island, whose care and feeding seemed to be his main responsibility. He was, in fact, much more a Newhouse fixer than a working journalist, although he occasionally turned out a story or two glorifying his Capitol Hill buddies. He "wrote" a Sunday column in the *Long Island Press* with the imaginative title, "Long Islanders in Washington," which essentially was a regular puff piece for the boys on the Hill. Every day he would remind us he needed "short items" about the Long Island delegation, and in addition to our other duties, we had to troll for them, write them, and give them to the column's "author." Naturally, the diminutive S.I. Newhouse acquired the nickname "Short Item" among us grunts in the bureau.

In Viglietta's tireless efforts to suck up to the Newhouse family and to carry its water for important members of Congress with responsibilities in the legal area, he did not hesitate to stretch geography so as to qualify certain key legislators for coverage as locals. One such Capitol Hill kingpin was Emanuel Celler, chairman of the House Judiciary Committee, from

Brooklyn. We minions were instructed by Viglietta always to refer to Celler in a particular way in the *Long Island Press:* "Chairman Celler, whose district in Brooklyn borders on the Rockaways" (on Long Island).

One of my chief chores in my first few years in the bureau was to keep track of the Long Island congressional delegation's (and Viglietta's buddies') effort to secure permanent status for the U.S. Merchant Marine Academy at Kings Point. Every twist and turn in the saga to "save Kings Point" had to be duly (and, often, dully) reported in the *Long Island Press* and *Star-Journal,* with quotes from the local congressmen about what they were doing to protect the academy from the budgetary ax. President Eisenhower finally signed the enabling legislation in 1956. The fight provided me with the material for the first magazine article I ever "sold," which ran in a trade sheet called the *Marine News.* To the best of my recollection, my only reward was the satisfaction of seeing it in print.

The interest of the *Press* and *Star-Journal* in alleged communist infiltration into American newspapers in 1955 gave me my first crack at a national story, when I covered the hearings of the Senate Internal Security Subcommittee at which CBS correspondent Winston Burdett told of his brief membership in the Communist Party in the late 1930s and early 1940s. He named about a dozen former co-workers on the *Brooklyn Eagle* as party members at the time. I also covered the testimony of Clayton Knowles, a *New York Times* reporter formerly of the *Long Island Press* who also had been a party member briefly, and the testimony of a Long Island man before Joe McCarthy's Senate Investigations Subcommittee. Later, Senate investigations into labor racketeering gave me my first close-up exposure to Senator John F. Kennedy and his sidekick brother, Robert, who was then a rather obnoxious young committee aide who could not be bothered with local-angle inquiries such as mine.

Viglietta's care and feeding of the Long Island delegation sometimes made him more an adversary than a colleague. When Governor Nelson Rockefeller in 1959 started flirting openly with challenging then Vice President Richard Nixon for the 1960 Republican nomination, I discovered in conversations with members of the New York congressional delegation, both upstate and on Long Island, that a number of them were already committed to Nixon. They now felt themselves in a most uncomfortable squeeze, with their own governor making noises about competing against him. I didn't have to be hit over the head to realize that here was a pretty good story, and I wrote it. Viglietta was so shaken that he ordered me to write him a long memo explaining the genesis of the story and why I had written it. I had to work hard not to point out that only an idiot would ask the question. I suggested that had I been writing for a California paper and found that members of that state's delegation were thinking of backing Rockefeller, I would have been obliged to let my paper's readers know about it. A distinct coolness toward me followed for weeks thereafter.

Needless to say, my colleagues and I in the Newhouse Washington bureau toiled for coolie wages, but the big-hearted Viglietta would take each of us aside at the end of one of our sixty-hour weeks and whisper: "You'll find an extra five bucks in your paycheck this week. Don't tell the other fellas." (I didn't get that message the week I wrote the Rockefeller-Nixon story.)

For the huge bonus given us, we had to endure not only the long hours but also Viglietta's insufferable name-dropping of Washington figures we came to learn he did not know, and his temper over our indiscretions, such as occasionally going upstairs for lunch or a beer at the National Press Club, which he did not permit us to join. (When such historic figures as Winston Churchill and Fidel Castro spoke at the club, we underlings had to sneak up the back stairs to get a peek.) Viglietta had a penchant for coming up with the looniest story ideas, and when things didn't go the way he wanted, he would proclaim, "I don't know, maybe *I'm* crazy!" Which of course we all believed he was.

For many years, we bureau slaves labored with only minimal benefits—two weeks' vacation a year—and no health insurance. In time, the management began to spring for a tiny Christmas bonus, starting at about twenty-five dollars and shooting up an astounding five dollars a year after that. At one point, we found included with the bonus a printed card, which I still cherish, that said: "It is not to our taste to offer any expression on this occasion except our very best wishes of the season, but our lawyers insist that it is necessary for the record to note, in respect to this and future years, that this is a wholly voluntary offering on the part of the management and not the result of any agreement or understanding." It turned out that there had been a case somewhere in which an employee had been receiving a bonus from his employer for so long that he came to consider it part of his salary. When it didn't come through one year, he sued and won. So much for the Newhouse season's greetings.

The one bright light for me in those early years was that I was assigned to work the Washington beat for the two Newhouse papers in Syracuse, the morning *Post-Standard* and the afternoon *Herald-Journal.* The morning paper didn't want much, but the afternoon sheet, to my good fortune, was edited by a former *Washington Post* managing editor named Alexander "Casey" Jones, an exile from the big time.

My daily routine required that I make the rounds of the congressional offices from the central (upstate) New York region, particularly that of the House member from the Syracuse area, a gentlemanly Republican named R. Walter Riehlman, a moderate and a straight shooter who provided me an uplifting introduction to official Washington. He was open, cooperative, and without a devious thought in his head. Riehlman was a refreshing contrast to the bunch of self-serving hustlers who represented Long Island at the time and who also were part of my beat in my function as a Viglietta legman.

For several years I worked the Long Island and upstate New York beats on Capitol Hill, at the same time scouring the bureaucracy for other stories, to broaden my scope. In my first month in Washington, I was thrilled to stumble upon a fellow from the Syracuse area working in the bowels of the Department of Agriculture who had created "Smokey Bear," the cartoon character on government posters who warned that "Only You Can Prevent Forest Fires." I reported—cleverly I thought then—that the gentleman "spends his time taking care of a teddy bear. But it's no child's play. Lives depend on it." Such were the first heights I attained in my quest for journalistic stardom.

I had been in the capital only two months when Puerto Rican terrorists shot up the House of Representatives. Although eager to get a piece of the story, the best I managed was an account of how Congressman Riehlman narrowly missed being in the line of fire, having been delayed from going to the House floor by a committee report on racketeering on his desk. I had to settle for Riehlman's eyewitness of the after-the-shooting scene on the floor, which, I consoled myself (but not my editors), was better than nothing.

My early days were filled with slow congressional machinations relating to the St. Lawrence Seaway, the threatened and actual closings of upstate military bases, Agriculture Department fights over milk-pricing orders, the plight of the Onondaga Indians, Mohawk Airlines route hearings, and the like, which were not very exciting. Ever in search of the local angle, and often frustrated by the effort, I seized the occasional opportunity to get in on a national story when a celebrity of hometown origin made the news. I was able, for example, to write this lead in 1960 about a one-time favorite on local radio station WOLF: "Former Syracusan Dick Clark, 31, who has made a name for himself talking to teen-agers on radio and TV, fought a day-long war of words yesterday with the House subcommittee investigating 'payola.' When the battle recessed until Monday, the nation's best-known disc jockey was still insisting he had never taken any payoffs for playing records."

When Representative Leo O'Brien of Albany (far across upstate from Syracuse) as chairman of the House Territories Subcommittee engineered statehood for Hawaii in 1959, eight months after having done the same thing for Alaska, I got the story on page one. I observed high up that he was "the *Syracuse Herald-Journal*'s Albany reporter until he defected to 'the other side'—politics—in 1952."

No stretch was too long in my quest to escape provincial reporting. When in early 1959 Governor Nelson Rockefeller of New York bowed out of the running for the 1960 Republican presidential nomination, I quickly took it upon myself to inject Senator Kenneth B. Keating of neighboring Rochester into speculation for the vice presidency. Not only did the notion never get off the ground; Keating found himself out of the Senate four years later, courtesy of carpetbagging Robert Kennedy.

Another avenue for me out of the provincial toward the big picture was the small Newhouse paper in Alabama, the *Huntsville Times,* which was booming in the late 1950s along with the missile and space programs that were importantly engaged in the small northern Alabama town. Assigned as the *Times'* man in Washington in addition to my duties for the Syracuse papers, I got to visit Huntsville, interview some of the top scientists, including former German rocket wizard Wernher von Braun, and pretend in print that I knew something about our race with the Russians into the great beyond.

I also periodically found relief from my local angle search by interviewing such famous folks as comedian Danny Kaye, a United Nations Ambassador-at-Large for UNICEF, the UN's international children's fund, who told me, "I learned young in life that any adult can communicate with a child if he makes an idiot of himself." Thereafter I sometimes tried out the theory with adults as well, with mixed results.

Through the 1950s, from time to time I sneaked over, without Viglietta's awareness, to Eisenhower press conferences in the Indian Treaty Room of the Old Executive Office Building. There I watched the old pros like Merriman Smith of United Press, Jack Bell of the Associated Press, Scotty Reston of the *New York Times* and Bob Donovan of the *New York Herald Tribune* confront the great man with questions of the day. For a long time, I satisfied myself with sitting quietly with my mouth shut and staying out of the way as "Smitty" said the traditional "Thank you, Mr. President" and the old-timers dashed to the few available phone lines outside the room.

Eventually, however, I was obliged to shed my inferiority complex and ask Eisenhower a question myself. In those early days of televised presidential press conferences, they were taped and aired only after White House Press Secretary Jim Hagerty had satisfied himself that Ike had not revealed any state secret or his own misinformation about a particular subject. Editors back home watched with interest and many took pleasure in requiring their correspondents to pose queries to the president for them. More often than not, the questions were inane and embarrassing to those who had to ask them, so it became ritual that a reporter thus burdened with an editor's inquiry would begin by saying, "Mr. President, I have been requested to ask you the following question." That was the tipoff to fellow correspondents and White House sources that he was posing it with a gun to his head.

It so happened that the aforementioned Philip Hochstein in my first months in the Newhouse bureau instructed me to ask Eisenhower about what was to me a complicated and obscure situation. I boned up on it as best I could the night before, wrote out the question, and after much trepidation got recognized. To my horror, the president did not have the faintest idea what I was inquiring about, and he asked me to elucidate. Before I could mumble anything halfway coherent, he mercifully cut me off by saying he would have an aide look into the matter and get back to me. I was ready to vote for him for a second term right then and there. (By 1956, though, I had changed my mind and cast my ballot for Adlai Stevenson, again demonstrating my talent for picking winners.)

In time, Casey Jones recognized my frustration with the local angle and helped me start climbing out of the dungeon of regional reporting. He gave me a weekly column of my own in the *Herald-Journal* in which I could comment on national political matters, and he expanded my duties to writing a series of national takeouts, requiring occasional travel that accorded me relief from Viglietta's clutches. Under Casey's wing I was able to take on in-depth pieces and series on a variety of subjects. They ranged from farm problems in the Midwest and the failed experiment with private, segregated academies in southern Virginia during Dixie's "massive resistance" to school integration, the peace movement, the peacetime draft, and the growing anti-Vietnam protest.

Thanks to Casey, a sometimes cantankerous volcano but a solid newsman who often grew restless in Syracuse, I got the most personally satisfying story of my life in December 1956, at the time of the Hungarian revolution. The United States having backed off from military intervention in the Soviet Union's quashing of the street revolt, the Eisenhower administration sought to make up for it by launching a massive refugee resettlement exercise. I flew to Austria with other reporters on an Air Force plane, helped some Hungarian escapees cross into Austria, and eventually brought back a young Hungarian couple for resettlement in Syracuse.

A few days before Christmas, Marian and I picked them up from the camp where they were staying in central New Jersey and drove them to my parents' house in Union City, where they enjoyed their first American holiday. We then flew on to Syracuse. I recorded their odyssey from East to West in daily stories that Casey plastered all over the front page of the *Herald-Journal,* and that led to the resettlement in Syracuse of scores more Hungarian refugees. The couple, Martin Tornallyay, a young minister, and his wife Klara, became our lifelong friends.

As a result of that assignment in 1956, I applied for and received a one-year fellowship from the Reid Foundation of the old New York Herald Tribune family to study further the refugee problem in Europe. The amount was $5,000 for the full year, including travel, but we managed. Marian, then pregnant, and I packed up and left in early 1958, setting up house in Zurich, Switzerland, as a convenient location from which to visit the post–World War II refugee camps, most of which were in Austria and Italy. I augmented that vast sum by writing more than seventy stories for the Syracuse paper, for which I was paid $600 total—at the end of the tour, which, according to my math then and now, came to slightly over eight bucks a story. For this price I delivered a range of gems including interviews with actress Brigitte Bardot in Geneva, Anne Frank's father in Amsterdam, and exiled mobster Lucky Luciano in Naples, coverage of an Atoms-for-Peace conference in Geneva, and a running commentary on the lives and foibles of Europeans wherever my main topic of interest, life in the camps, took me.

To my dismay, I soon learned that the camps—many of them old German concentration camp barracks—had become the permanent home for thousands of refugees from World War II and the Cold War, as well as Hungarians who had not been resettled after the 1956 revolution. By this time, most of the professional and other highly trained Hungarians had been snapped up by the United States and other Western countries, leaving those who were ill, ill-educated, or both behind. Hundreds of thousands of other people from the East had been living in the camps ever since the end of World War II, trapped by their illnesses and other detriments to emigration. Many children of war had been raised within the camps and were now raising families of their own there.

The highlight of our year in Europe had nothing, however, to do with refugees. It was the birth of our first child, Paul, in Zurich, on a sunny August day. As was commonplace in Switzerland, I was permitted to observe the natural delivery, which Marian had trained for and at which I had been a somewhat queasy coach. It was an amazing and emotional experience, and afterward I rushed to contact my only American friend in town, to invite him for a celebratory drink or two.

Bill Rutherford, the director of the International Press Institute based in Zurich, had welcomed us to the city, was an oasis of good cheer and company for us, and hence the obvious person I would call. The episode proved to be more revealing about the state of my professed liberalism toward human relations as a born and bred white American at the time. When I placed the call, Bill's female cousin, married to an American serviceman based in West Germany, answered the phone and informed me that Bill was out of town. Although I had met her several times, all I did was tell her the news and hang up, disappointed that I would have to drink to this great occasion alone, which I did that night. Only later did it occur to me that I should have invited her to join me. I had not, I belatedly recognized, because she was a black woman. Although I considered myself to be without racial bias, and certainly without gender bias, and although I was in Switzerland, I might as well have been a white redneck in Mississippi for all the obtuseness of my behavior. It was an unintentional self-taught lesson I haven't forgotten to this day.

Upon our return near year's end, with new son Paul in tow, I spent much time trying to sell magazine pieces on the terrible plight of the refugees, to no avail. The huge publicity given to the immediate escapees from the Hungarian revolution apparently had satiated editors on the subject of refugees. It was not until the United Nations declared a World Refugee Year for 1959–60 that some resettlement resumed, but the camps continued to house thousands of these forgotten victims of war. So it was back to the quest for the local angle in Washington. All this while, I kept knocking on the doors of the likes of Scotty Reston, Bob Donovan, and lesser lights, while the "N" for Newhouse I imagined on my chest grew larger, as did my frustration.

I continued to occupy myself between chores for Syracuse and Huntsville with writing long series and take-outs on important issues of the day. For all the complaints I had about the Newhouse operation being cheap and disorganized, I was pretty much given my head and was able to spend weeks on some assignments. I undertook investigations of such groups as the political arm of the American Medical Association, the National Rifle Association, an anti-drug shock therapy group called Synanon, the peace movement, Students for a Democratic Society (SDS), French separatism in Quebec, and so on.

The Synanon movement was centered on the West Coast, with a live-in facility on the beachfront at Santa Monica led by a reformed alcoholic named Chuck Dederich, who had an almost mystical effect on the inmates. In the early 1960s it became a pet project of Hollywood types, who used to attend regular Saturday night sessions, rubbing elbows with young junkies trying to reform, and feeling very hip doing so. Synanon had an impressive track record of keeping the kids free of drugs as long as they were living in the house, but too often they fell back into their habits upon leaving.

The shock therapy consisted of small groups of residents sitting in a circle and unloading verbal abuse on each other. The idea seemed to be that one had to hit rock bottom before starting back up. The assignment also took me to the Nevada state prison in Carson City, where similar sessions of inmates exchanging invective were held. It being Nevada, the most intriguing thing I saw behind the prison walls was an inmate-run gambling house, complete with roulette wheels and card tables where the residents could wager cigarettes and other desirable commodities. It being Nevada, there also were rumors that a brothel functioned in one of the prisons, but I was never able to verify its existence.

Thanks mostly to Casey Jones, these years were not all grim and in fact had some light moments. In 1962, the fact that I had been a city boy all my life led him to send me to Kansas to take a fresh look at the nation's huge grain storage problem, the result of massive overproduction. Before departing I checked in at the Agriculture Department and was directed to a Commodity Credit Corporation office in the farm town of Salina. There I met one of the most intriguing of the many characters I've encountered in my years as a reporter, and I will never forget the manner of our meeting.

On a hot summer afternoon, I introduced myself to the head of the Salina office, and we sat at a long conference table as I told him the things I hoped to see. He listened for a while, then nodded. "Yes, they told me you were coming," he said, "and I've arranged to have my best man take you around." Whereupon he picked up the phone on the table. "Shorty," I heard him say into it. "Can you come in here for a minute?" Presently a clumping sound came down a hallway and into the room, but I saw no one. Suddenly, however, Shorty appeared at the far end of the conference table, as if he had materialized out of thin air. It turned out that my guide was a smiling, good-natured gentleman who somehow had lost the lower half of both his legs and had propelled himself into the room on wooden blocks attached to his knees.

After a thorough briefing on what I would be shown the next couple of days, Shorty hopped down from his chair and I followed him down the hall-way and a steep set of stairs to his car. Motioning me to get in the front seat on the passenger side, he went around to the driver's side and boosted him-self in behind the steering wheel. The car was equipped with shifting and braking mechanisms on the wheel and he used them expertly as we sped out of Salina onto the open road, which he proceeded to traverse at a breakneck speed. I had to admit it was nerve-wracking to look down on the floor on the driver's side and see no foot brake, especially as we rolled into the next town well over the speed limit. But he always brought the car to a halt for every red light and stop sign, and in short order I was able to relax.

Shorty was good, light-hearted company. As he took me around Kansas to visit Agriculture Department outposts, we would enter each office togeth-er, whereupon the officer in charge would ask me if he could help me—until Shorty out of his view from below the counter would call out the name of our host and receive a hospitable greeting in return from the officer peering down. Shorty proved to be an expert and most congenial guide as the mys-teries of grain storage and associated farming functions were revealed to me. To my chagrin but his apparent unconcern, bystanders repeatedly stared at Shorty and a few even asked him point-blank and insensitively how he had lost his limbs, but he just ignored them. I was relieved at least that nobody asked him how he got his nickname, and I didn't either. After several days, we parted with my heartfelt thanks, and respect for him.

I was grateful for these occasional reprieves of a merciful editor during my long stint as a regional reporter, and was eager for liberation from the regular round of upstate New York congressional offices. After about a decade in Washington, it finally came, in an unexpected way.

3 Covering the Center Ring

CONDITIONS IN THE NEWHOUSE WASHINGTON bureau, both financial and professional, improved somewhat in 1962 when a congressional committee began looking into ownership of multiple newspapers as a possible antitrust violation, and whether such acquisitions improved the acquired newspapers. In what seemed to us grunts obviously a response to this legal threat, the Washington bureau was expanded into a sort of national wire service for all the Newhouse papers. For the first time, the bureau started covering national news not related to the individual local papers. One motivation clearly was to superimpose quality on the papers being examined by the committee. The problem was, individual editors resented this "intrusion" and made only sparse use of the copy filed by the national reporters in the bureau, one of whom I had become.

Nevertheless, I welcomed this development, in part because it effectively pushed the zany Viglietta to the sidelines. But primarily it got me, after more than a decade, away from mostly local coverage, which was like watching a sideshow at the circus while others were spectators under the big top. Now the senior reporter in the bureau, I hoped for one of the prime assignments, either the White House or the State Department. Instead, as a result of internal politics and the installation of a new bureau chief, I wound up in what I considered Siberia—the Pentagon.

The bureau boss was a kindly Texan named Arthur Laro from the *Houston Post* who brought along a buddy to cover the White House. Philip Hochstein, the Newark editor who had sent me to Washington in 1954 and hired Laro, continued to oversee the expanded Washington bureau. He installed his son, a bright young guy but a Washington neophyte, at State and I was shuttled over to the Defense Department. I knew next to nothing about military affairs, my most memorable experience on that front being the time I was fished out of the river at the New London Submarine Base on that frigid November night in 1945. I survived at the Pentagon by focusing on the politics of defense and managed to get a fair share of stories in competition with what was probably the most entrenched major press corps in Washington. I arrived at the Pentagon only weeks before the Cuban missile crisis of 1962, and when it hit, the tension was immense as the whole town and the country watched in shock and, not to put too fine a point on it, fear.

By this time we had three small kids—Paul, Amy, and Julie—and were living in a northern Virginia suburb. I had become so nervous amid the general Cold War missile buildup, felt most intensely at the Pentagon, that I had built a fallout shelter myself in the basement of our house. When it came to manual labor, I was not my father's son, and I was particularly glad that my handiwork never got put to a survival test. On the critical weekend of the missile crisis, one of our next-door neighbors picked up his family and headed for the West Virginia hills—after calling in sick so as not to lose vacation time!

At the Pentagon each morning I attended tense briefings by Secretary of Defense Robert S. McNamara. Security was especially heavy, but, incomprehensibly, the Soviet reporters for the Tass news agency were able to sit in on the briefings, which often covered American strategic thinking and tactics as the U.S.-Soviet face-off headed toward a possible Armageddon. During those days, I wrote some ominous pieces from what I humorlessly called "ground zero," certain that in any nuclear exchange the Russkies would no doubt hit the bull's-eye that was the courtyard in the center of the nation's Military Command Central.

It all ended safely after the famous confrontation in which President Kennedy and Soviet President Nikita Khrushchev figuratively stared at each other and Khrushchev blinked. The Russian ships bringing missiles toward Cuba turned around in the ocean, and missiles already in Cuba were shipped back to the Soviet Union. I was a pool reporter on one of the Navy planes that observed and photographed the removal at sea, an unforgettable experience for the manner in which it took place.

The whole affair was carefully staged between the American and Russian governments and forces. It was agreed that the U.S. planes at an appointed place would fly low over the ships as Russian seamen on deck would pull back the heavy tarpaulin covering the missiles so their presence could be verified and filmed. But when our planes reached the rendezvous it was too dark for the photographers, who included still and film news crews, to do their best work. The mission waited while our planes were detoured overnight to Puerto Rico, where we caught a few hours' sleep. Before dawn we headed back for the intercept in clear morning light.

The long hours of waiting for action had by now exhausted the subjects of conversation favored by the news photographers—sports and sex—and the animals were getting restive. The Navy planes were sonar-equipped for submarine detection and there was only one small window on each side from which to witness and photograph the staged pullout. So as our plane swooped down over the missile-laden Russian ships to be photographed, the camera boys rushed into the cockpit where the view was better, shooting either over the shoulders of the pilot and co-pilot or even in front of them if they couldn't "make" the shoot properly. Warren Rogers, then of the Associated Press, and I managed to cop a look when the cameramen pulled back to reload, all the while wondering whether we were going to crash and make it a bigger story. But the pilots coped with the interference, and all ended well. For years afterward, whenever footage of the air inspection of the withdrawn missiles showed up on my television screen during anniversary stories of the missile crisis, I remembered that thrill-packed ride.

One offshoot of the Cuban missile crisis was an order in the midst of it by the Assistant Secretary of Defense for Public Affairs, former *Newark News* Washington correspondent Arthur Sylvester. It required that a public information officer (PIO) sit in on all reporters' interviews with Pentagon sources. If not, the source had to submit a written report to Sylvester's office covering what had been said. The Pentagon press corps at the time was one of the most senior of all Washington beats, led by the legendary and courtly Mark Watson of the *Baltimore Sun*. To the reporters—except for me as a newcomer—the order was a joke because they had spent years building reliable sources, but it was burdensome nevertheless. It made for all-out war between Sylvester and the press room, and it was compounded soon after when Sylvester declared that a government official had "the right to lie" if national security was involved.

The requirement that all interviews be monitored threw a monkey wrench into shoe-leather reporting. Sometimes a request for an interview was intercepted by a counter-request for written questions, followed hours later by written answers, often unresponsive, that precluded the possibility of follow-up inquiries. Sometimes the monitor would inject himself into the interview, "explaining" what the source meant to say. On one occasion, a monitor even started to sum up the interview by telling me: "Well, I think this will be your lead . . . ." End of interview. The practice of monitoring eventually fell of its own weight.

A preoccupation of my three and a half years at the Pentagon was the effort to get assigned to another beat. But the assignment did have some interesting interludes, including coverage of an earthquake in Chile and visits to the Berlin Wall to examine new Soviet refinements in repression. In my first weeks on the beat, I stumbled onto a national story that, for once for any Newhouse grind, was picked up by the national wires. Scouring the bowels of the Pentagon for anybody in the building from Syracuse, or anybody working in an office with an intriguing job description on the door, I came upon a gentleman who had been working for years on the psychological problems of military personnel assigned to guard or trained to fire nuclear missiles. Nobody from the outside had talked to him in years and he was only too happy to tell me all about some of the more unusual cases in his files.

The best of them concerned an Air Force sergeant stationed at a missile base in England. Distraught over suspicions that his wife had been unfaithful, he had climbed up onto the superstructure of a missile and threatened to detonate it with his firearm. After hours of tension, he was finally talked down—by his wife. There were similar incidents, documented by my newly discovered source. These threw the Pentagon brass into a tizzy. In Pentagon briefings, missile experts were trotted out to deny that a nuclear explosion could be caused in that way. In response, some nuclear energy scientists at MIT and elsewhere disagreed. The result was a full-blown debate in which the Pentagon disclosed new details about its missile security procedures and safeguards.

I had just gotten lucky with the story. As a neophyte in the Puzzle Palace who barely knew my way to the nearest men's room, I was "that kid from Newhouse" to the grizzled veterans in the press room. I had no illusions that I would ever come close to any of them in knowledge of the complicated defense beat, and I continued to scratch for stories while plotting my escape back "across the river."

Unschooled in the niceties of weapons systems, budgets, and defense strategies, I concentrated on the politics of the Pentagon, particularly the rivalry among the services for money and roles. At the time, the Air Force was in the ascendancy and Secretary McNamara and his "Whiz Kids" were grappling with a military laboring in a dark tunnel called Vietnam at the end of which there seemed to be no light.

One reward of covering the Pentagon was the chance to observe first the arrogance and then the torment of Robert McNamara, a man of extreme intelligence but severely limited political judgment. He had come to the job as an auto industry efficiency expert bent on getting a handle on the huge defense budget and bureaucracy. A man of strong religious background, he found himself gradually being transformed into one of the world's most powerful warlords by virtue of the huge military arsenal he was deploying against tiny North Vietnam. As the frustrations of that effort grew, so did his doubts about its wisdom and justice. He began to spend much time and resources in the effort to "win the hearts and minds" of the Vietnamese people, and on using the military to conduct good works, called "civic action," in the war zone and other troublespots. I always thought this focus conveyed McNamara's gnawing conscience over his warlord role—a self-doubt much later confirmed in his own *mea culpas*.

One day, as I labored on at the Pentagon with one eye on the exit, to my astonishment I got a phone call out of the blue from Ben Bradlee, who was busy assembling an all-star cast for the *Washington Post* newsroom he had just taken over. My hopes jumped, but alas he wanted to talk strictly about my covering the Pentagon. When I told him I was single-minded in trying to get out of the place and yearned to cover politics, he noted that he had already hired a top man for that beat—Ward Just, a colleague from *Newsweek*. That was the end of my aspirations to cover politics for the *Post*, or so I believed at the time.

A cataclysmic event on November 22, 1963, took precedence over everything else. I was scanning the wire in the Newhouse bureau office around lunchtime when a United Press International flash jolted me: President Kennedy had just been shot in Dallas, maybe fatally. Stunned, I shouted the news to colleagues and then, in a state of shock, ran downstairs and out onto Fourteenth Street, where traffic was stopped and drivers were getting out of their cars conveying the news to anyone at hand. I raced to the White

House, a few blocks away, where all was in confusion, and then back to my office, where I watched the chaotic scene outside the hospital in Dallas unfold on television. I was pressed into rewrite duties most of the afternoon but broke away to go to the White House back lawn in time to witness in the gathering darkness the arrival by helicopter of the already sworn-in new president, Lyndon B. Johnson. Through the plane's large picture window I could see Johnson in animated discussion with Secretary McNamara as the whirring blades slowed and the aircraft settled onto the lawn. LBJ wordlessly came down the steps and moved quickly inside, grim-faced and head down, stopping briefly only to shake hands with an old Johnson friend and colleague of mine, John Cauley of the *Kansas City Star*, who had covered him in the Senate.

Like millions of other Americans, I spent the rest of the weekend glued to a television set until it was time for Kennedy's body to be moved to the Capitol Rotunda for public viewing. My young family was walking across the Mall to watch the funeral cortege and listening to a small portable radio when the news suddenly came that Lee Harvey Oswald, held as the suspected assassin, had been shot as he was being moved out of his jail in Dallas. In the solemnity of the occasion, I resisted an impulse to tell others in the crowd, and we walked on in shock to Pennsylvania Avenue, which was lined with onlookers. The horse-drawn carriage with large wooden wheels, pulled by six sleek horses, soon rolled by in a silence broken only by the mournful and incessant roll of drums. I remember the trancelike scene to this day.

That afternoon and into the night, thousands of Americans inched slowly in single file across the Capitol Plaza, up the Capitol steps, and into the Rotunda, where JFK rested on a catafalque like the one that had borne the body of Abraham Lincoln ninety-eight years earlier. With my press credentials, I was able to gain admittance to the Rotunda directly, and inside I stood for hours and watched the procession past the casket as the line crept forward amid whispered prayers and silent tears from the viewers.

On the day of the burial, I stood just off the front portico of the White House as a solemn but controlled Jacqueline Kennedy emerged and greeted some of the world's great: President Charles de Gaulle of France—tall, now rotund, but erect in his plain World War II general's uniform; Prince Philip of the United Kingdom, fairy tale handsome in his Admiralty uniform; Emperor Haile Selassie of Ethiopia, resplendent in his kingly robes;

Anastas Mikoyan, the short, somber deputy premier of the Soviet Union, faintly oriental in appearance with a stubby mustache that gave him a slight resemblance to Charlie Chaplin.

After a college chorus sang a hymn, Mrs. Kennedy in a simple black dress, flanked by Robert and Edward Kennedy, took her place behind the carriage bearing her husband's casket and stepped out as it rolled down the White House driveway onto Pennsylvania Avenue, with the new president and his wife behind. Trailing them was a ragged band of the most illustrious leaders on earth, with de Gaulle's expressionless but noble countenance dominating the group. Secret Service and security guards from other countries mingled with the notables in an attempt to provide whatever safety was possible in a situation that, on its face, was fraught with potential peril. The marchers appeared oblivious to it, consumed in the solemnity of the occasion.

As the procession made its way to nearby St. Matthew's Cathedral for the funeral service, I boarded a press bus to Arlington Cemetery and positioned myself on the hillside just above the gravesite, on a direct line to the Lincoln Memorial across the Potomac River below. From there, after listening on a radio to the service at St. Matthew's, I was able to watch the long procession winding around the memorial and across Memorial Bridge to the cemetery amid lines of spectators. As it approached, you could hear the familiar drum roll and the slow creaking of the caisson's wheels.

At the burial place, Mrs. Kennedy stood hand-in-hand with Robert Kennedy, who was dressed in morning coat and tails. The assembled notables gathered randomly around, with President and Mrs. Johnson practically lost in the crowd about five rows back and to one side at the foot of the grave. Mrs. Kennedy, red-eyed but unyielding, looked up briefly as a squadron of jet planes roared overhead in tribute, then watched as an Irish drill team went through its maneuvers. At this point, under a gray sky, a flurry of autumn leaves suddenly floated down on the scene in the clearing far from any tree, an inexplicable phenomenon. After simple remarks by Richard Cardinal Cushing of Boston, a family friend, about "this wonderful man, Jack Kennedy," the strains of Taps, with a single broken note at the start, filled the air. The flag was lifted from the coffin, folded with swift precision into the prescribed triangle and handed by the honor guard of four enlisted men, one to the next, and finally to the young widow. One of the soldiers then gave her a torch and with Robert Kennedy's assistance she lit the eternal flame of propane gas she had instructed be placed there. After bestowing a light kiss on the cheek of General Maxwell D. Taylor, chairman of the Joint Chiefs of Staff, who had walked in the procession despite a bad leg, she turned, stumbled for a second, was steadied by her brother-in-law, and walked down the hill to her awaiting limousine.

It was an unforgettable scene, marked by gestures of grief by the mighty and the common folk alike, many kneeling at the gravesite before moving off. I stayed to watch a while. I remember a photographer standing next to me, usually brash and loud, whispering to me, "Do you think it's okay to smoke?" I told him, "It's up to you." Whereupon he lit up, took one puff, then threw the cigarette down and stepped on it. "What's the matter with me?" he muttered. Red-faced, he continued to berate himself in a whisper. Back on the press bus, the only conversation was about the stoic manner of Mrs. Kennedy. Of all the demonstrations I have ever witnessed of her husband's definition of courage—grace under pressure—this was the most striking and memorable.

For most of the unfinished presidential term completed by Lyndon Johnson, I continued to toil at the Pentagon. In early 1965, I was treated to a brief stint in Vietnam, courtesy of the Defense Department. Uncle Sam decided to fly regulars on the Pentagon beat there. We suspected it was an attempt to counter all the negative reports about the quagmire of American involvement being filed endlessly by the veteran U.S. correspondents on the scene. We weren't there long enough to learn much, and certainly nothing to contradict what the excellent in-country reporters were sending back home.

In visits by military helicopter to such garden spots as Can Tho, Pleiku, Kien Binh, and Rach Gia (pronounced "rockjaw" in Americanese), I got the expected optimistic reports from U.S. officials on the ground about the ongoing "oil spot" pacification program of the time that was supposed to spread across the Vietnamese terrain but didn't. I sat in on interrogations of Viet Cong prisoners, observed the South Vietnamese junk fleet on patrol in the Mekong Delta and listened to GIs who thoroughly bought into the domino theory, complaining about home-front pessimism and lack of moral support.

The only halfway decent story I wrote as a result of the trip reported that "in the struggle to keep ground transportation routes open through Viet Cong–dominated areas north of Saigon, the United States in effect is bribing the enemy." I had learned that American truck drivers transporting airplane fuel without military escort between Qui Nhon and Pleiku on Highway 19 were routinely paying off Viet Cong "tax collectors" for safe passage. The explanation for this rather strange transaction was that the enemy needed the money to finance his guerrilla campaign and felt that U.S. airpower wasn't hurting him all that much.

One uneasy experience during the visit was flying from Da Nang to Saigon on a plane that bore the remains of a newly arrived U.S. Marine encased in an olive green body bag with the word "Head" stenciled at one end. Another was haplessly wandering out of the Caravelle Hotel in deserted downtown Saigon after curfew one dark night and taking a fearful hour finding my way back. Also, while awaiting an interview with General William Westmoreland at his headquarters one afternoon, I innocently wandered up a staircase and stumbled into a meeting of CIA spooks, causing a monumental uproar as they fell all over themselves trying to convince me they were something else. So much for my vast catalog of war stories.

On the way home, I stopped off in Manila for an interview with presidential candidate Ferdinand Marcos at his home. I was met at the door and ushered in by his glamorous wife, Imelda, who, I wrote, "has given him three photogenic children and campaigns among the women for him. She doesn't hurt him with the men's vote either. She is tall, dark and svelte—a former Miss Philippines." If I took note at the time of her footwear, which became famous in later years, I didn't mention the subject in my dispatch home.

While at the Pentagon, I went on other interesting trips: to the Panama Canal and tours of the NATO countries, with a couple of sidetrips to Berlin to witness the building and then refinement, so to speak, of the onerous wall. In Panama, we reporters were helicoptered into the jungle for what was to be a taste of survival training. But what we got a taste of was a delicious lunch parachuted in by military aircraft, along with a keg of cold beer, after which we were guided out by native tribes in picturesque costumes and canoes.

Back in Panama City, a group of us hired a local guide one night to take us to see the infamous local sights, which included a grotesque "exhibition" not recommended for the queasy of stomach. We ended with a quick drop-by at one of the city's most popular brothels, a stop that infuriated the madam because none of us cared to buy the raunchy wares. When our driver-guide apologetically explained to her only that "the boys are having themselves what they call 'a night,'" she immediately chased us out the door amid much shrieking and amused applause from her employees.

In Germany, on another trip, we had a very scary helicopter ride in heavy smog over the Main River one afternoon as we were being ferried from Frankfurt to an Army outpost for a cocktail party. The pilot had no foul-weather instruments, so an electronic beam had to be sent up for him to sit the chopper on and come straight down, lest he hit high-powered lines in the vicinity. Aboard were such Pentagon veterans as Mark Watson of the *Sun,* who gripped his seat with white knuckles like the rest of us as we made a successful descent.

My mentor in many of these tribulations was the genial Jack Raymond of the *New York Times,* who added to my very limited knowledge of Pentagon journalistic tradition by instructing me in the nose-wheel game, wherein the plane's front wheel was chalked with numbers clockwise before takeoff. Bets were made aloft, and on landing the wheel was checked for the winning number, which was where the wheel stopped. I never had it.

In these years also, given occasional furloughs from the Pentagon beat, I had the good fortune of a rewarding apprenticeship in the politics of social change, covering the latter phase of the civil rights revolution in the American South. In Atlanta in 1963, I interviewed Dr. Martin Luther King Jr. at the ramshackle headquarters of his Southern Christian Leadership Conference (SCLC). I found him to be earnest and low key, hardly the rabble-rouser he was painted to be by his southern white detractors, but unabashedly committed to taking to the trenches of the war against racial discrimination and injustice.

"We are no armchair organization," he said concerning SCLC, often criticized at the time by such more orthodox groups as the NAACP and Urban League. "I do have to confess that I am head of an organization that believes in action, and I am in jail sometimes when heads of some other organizations can sit in a chair and direct things over a phone." Of criticism that he was a poor administrator, King smiled and answered: "I can't always keep up on correspondence from a jail, that's true. But if that's a weakness, it's strength for a larger cause." In subsequent years, he validated that view with his actions, cut short by his assassination outside his room at a Memphis motel in 1968.

My civil rights coverage also took me to Harlem in 1963, where in the rear of a restaurant I interviewed the man who then called himself Malcolm X Shabazz. The large, strapping man who, as "Big Red," had served a long prison term in the 1940s after a sordid underworld career, and at this time had become a disciple and spokesman for Elijah Muhammad, "Messenger of Allah and Sole Prophet of the Lost-Found Nation of Islam in the West," popularly known as the Black Muslims. He recited the Muslims' creed: "Never be the aggressor, never look for trouble. But if any man molests you, may Allah bless you!" To my surprise, like King he spoke in a modulated, temperate voice, and in the end like King became the victim of an assassin's bullets.

In the fall of 1965, through much of 1966, and into 1967, I wandered around the Deep South observing and reporting on the ramifications of the Voting Rights Act of 1965, pushed through Congress by Lyndon Johnson. After one such trip through Georgia and Alabama, scheduled in advance, I decided to swing by Jackson, Mississippi, as well. I had just checked into my hotel room when the phone rang. It was the switchboard telling me I had an urgent message to call home. Baffled, since my wife did not know I had decided to come into Mississippi, I called her and learned that my father had taken ill. She had phoned my previous hotel, in Birmingham, and after a brief delay was connected to the Jackson hotel. Such was the surveillance of Yankee reporters by police in the Deep South. Happily, my dad improved, enabling me to continue my Dixie trip.

In Jackson, I visited the headquarters of the Mississippi Freedom Democratic Party, which had challenged the status quo at the Democratic National Convention in Atlantic City two years earlier and was now working to register the 42 percent of the state's population designated on a wall map as "Black Mississippi." Chester Taylor, who ran the headquarters, talked earnestly about the limited effectiveness of Dr. King's nonviolent principle. "Nonviolence plays on the conscience of the people," he said. "But people are getting tired of being beaten over the head. Here, to express nonviolence seems to bring only contempt. The tactic should work in a Christian society, but it hasn't. This will make more Negroes lose faith in nonviolence in the next few years. I don't believe that the white man is going to give the Negro political power as a result of the nonviolent tactic."

Barely a month after enactment of the Voting Rights Act, I was in Natchez, Mississippi, where more than a thousand blacks marched in support of NAACP demands for more black jobs in the city, in the wake of the car bombing of one of the organization's local leaders. The event was tense but peaceful as the Mississippi Grand Dragon of the Ku Klux Klan, E. L. McDaniel, constrained by a federal injunction, watched sullenly from his parked car. Chārles Evers, whose brother Medgar, the state NAACP field secretary, had been slain two years earlier, used the Voting Rights Act to help the NAACP counter the growing influence of "black power" as advocated by the Student Nonviolent Coordinating Committee (SNCC).

In June 1966, James Meredith, the young man who integrated the University of Mississippi and became its first black graduate, embarked on a solitary walk down the state's main north-south highway, Route 51, to the state capital, Jackson, to encourage black voter registration. Three miles north of the town of Hernando, Meredith was shot in broad daylight and seriously wounded, triggering a protest march of hundreds of blacks and some whites the rest of the way to Jackson.

A coalition of the leading civil rights groups sponsored the march, and federal observers were rushed into the state to oversee the placing of black Mississippians on the voting rolls at county courthouses along or just off Route 51. Marchers, under the watchful eyes of state highway police, urged blacks along the way to "come over now and get your freedom" by joining them. Only a relative handful along Route 51 did. At one point, as the marchers strolled by chanting, "What do we want? Freedom!" an unsmiling, tight-lipped white farmer shook his head and said to me: "They want freedom. What do they mean when they say they want freedom? You ask 'em and they can't tell you." He was wrong, because at the end of each day's marching they held "freedom rallies" in black sections of the town where they bedded down, their leaders patiently explaining why local blacks needed to "conquer fear" and register to use political power as their salvation.

It was a time when white Yankee reporters such as myself were no more welcome in the state than were the white and black civil rights workers who intruded on the pervasive racial segregation that governed every aspect of life there. The march's organizers posted unarmed sentries of their own each night around the campsites. "Don't forget you're in Mississippi," they reminded each other, although no reminder seemed necessary amid the hostile eyes of white locals.

In Greenwood in the Delta, I had an illustrative experience in what being an outsider in Mississippi meant in those days. When I asked at my hotel where I could find the local SNCC office, I was met with dead silence. Only when I was riding up the hotel elevator to my room did the black operator halt the car between floors and whisper the instructions to me. As I drove my rental car along a deserted dirt road toward the civil rights group's office, I spied a young black man apparently headed there. I offered him a ride and he hopped in, but we had gone only a very short distance when a police car came out of nowhere and stopped us. We were both pushed over the hood of the car and frisked, and I was told I would be jailed if I was still in Greenwood the next morning. Needless to say, my passenger had to walk the rest of the way. It was no small wonder that in Mississippi black churches were the sanctuaries of choice.

One evening, after a mass arrest of mostly elderly blacks on the lawn of the Leflore County courthouse during a voter registration drive, I sat in on a combination prayer and politics meeting at the First Christian Church. About a hundred congregation members linked hands and sang "We Shall Overcome" and then settled into the familiar ritual of preaching and response that runs deep in the Delta tradition. They were led by an elderly black minister, his thumbs hooked in wide black suspenders:

"Time's about running out, brothers and sisters."

"That's right, preacher."

"We cleared the land around here forty years ago and now we can't even stand around the courthouse."

"You said it, brother."

"It's awful, but we ain't gonna stop. We too close. Work and sufferin', we used to it. Castro and Khrushchev wouldn't treat you as low as they do. It's awful. You can't even walk around the courthouse."

"Amen."

"Well, let's go along to the courthouse. We have God on our side. I want you to tell him to move in Greenwood. Because when he move, he dangerous. Tell him to move tonight and in the morning when you get up. Keep on telling God. Complain to God. We can't complain to Kennedy."

Seated on the front of the stage between the preachers, nodding and saying "That's right" and "Amen" along with the rest, were a number of young blacks who were removed at least a generation from the rest of the congregation. One was a Yale Law School student; others were undergraduates from southern all-black colleges. Between the traditional preachings, from time to time one of them would get up and make the practical pitch:

"All right now. I've been sitting here listening to you saying 'Amen' and clapping your hands, and I've been doing it right along. But is that all you're gonna do? Do you really believe in God?"

"Yes, indeed!"

"But are you willing to trust him and sacrifice? You say, 'I got my children. I got to go down to Miss Sally's kitchen.' Or, 'Mr. Charlie told me I got enough freedom already.' You're scared. You stay home and watch TV instead of going down to the courthouse. You got the key. Now tomorrow you go on down there and get your freedom!"

After a local judge named C. C. Williamson had sentenced nineteen blacks to from four to six months in jail for the misdemeanor of refusing to leave the courthouse lawn when ordered, I asked him why. "The only reason it wasn't more," he said with a straight face, "is that's all the statutes call for."

At SCLC's tenth annual convention in Jackson in the summer of 1966, King challenged the black power movement, calling for a "coalition of conscience" among whites and blacks. He argued that "even a cursory analysis of power will reveal to us that Negroes are not the only ones who are deprived of the right to decide in our society. . . . At a time when some are thinking black exclusively," he said, "we are becoming more aware of the fact that we are bound together black and white in a single garment of destiny."

On the heels of the Meredith march, SCLC workers moved into Grenada, Mississippi, along the line of the march, with a goal of "breaking" the town in what was SCLC's first real commitment in the state. A drive was undertaken, assisted by federal voting examiners, to register most of its 49 percent black population, and an economic boycott was invoked by blacks against its white businesses to force more hiring at better pay for local blacks.

Nighttime marches in support of the boycott ran into local white obstruction. On one night, about 500 raucous white demonstrators jammed the town square, obliging highway police to form an anti-riot line and move toward them with the safety catches off their tear-gas shotguns. Some demonstrators, armed with slingshots, lit cherry bombs and hurled them into the marchers. When the trouble finally was quelled and marchers and demonstrators had dispersed, I found myself alone in the deserted town square. A highway patrol car drove up and the driver ordered me to get in. He told me I was in peril and drove me back to my motel.

In Grenada after the march, four federal registrars helped put nearly 1,200 unregistered blacks on the voting rolls and soon were adding more at a rate of 300 a day. In twenty-four Mississippi counties, they registered 42,400 by the end of July, and local registrars added another 82,000. According to the Justice Department, black registration in Mississippi rose from 8 percent before passage of the federal Voting Rights Act in 1965 to 37.6 percent.

In neighboring Louisiana as well, new voting rights for blacks were slowly prying open the political process despite the efforts of the legendary segregationist boss of Plaquemines Parish, Leander Perez, to hold the line of white dominance. "For God's sake," he told me in explaining a counter-registration drive of whites he was directing, "we can't let these Congolese take over, can we? What would the South be?"

In East Feliciana Parish, District Judge John J. Rarick, another staunch segregationist, expressed no trepidation about an expanding black vote. Telling me he intended to "ignore the Nigra vote," he dismissed new black registrants, saying "they're just like children. They get something to show up the white people and they play with it awhile, and then they get tired of it." The real threat was not black voters themselves, he said, but white liberals "who will buy the Nigra vote just like they've always done."

Vail M. Delony, speaker of the Louisiana House of Representatives, had the same attitude. He allowed that new black registrations gave blacks an edge of about 500 among the 5,000 registrants in the town of East Providence: "Yes, it's gonna hurt us. [But they] don't have the capacity to take over. If the nigger is left alone, he will not vote in a bloc. We've had some niggers vote here before. I remember one came in and said, 'Mr. Delony, we want to know if we can vote for you.' I told him I'm not gonna solicit anybody's vote. Like I say, the nigger respects me, but I've got a white skin and I'm gonna keep a white skin. I won't stoop to entice the niggers. They either vote for me or they don't."

Such comments were made without the slightest hostility or self-consciousness. They reflected the traditional attitude of Deep South whites in the 1960s, even as moderation was making some progress in the Democratic Party in Dixie. Atlanta, for example, had one of the South's strongest voices for civil rights in a white man, Congressman Charles Weltner.

Yet it was also a time of contradictions. In Georgia in the fall of 1966, the Democrats nominated for governor Lester Maddox—"Ol' Lester," the owner of Atlanta's Pickrick Restaurant, who once physically barred blacks from his eating establishment by brandishing a pickax handle and pistol. His candidacy was such an affront to party moderates that Weltner withdrew from his own race for reelection rather than run on the ticket with him, saying "I cannot compromise with hate." At the same time, in Tuskegee, Alabama, voters elected Lucius D. Amerson as sheriff of Macon County, the first black ever to hold such an office anywhere in the Deep South.

Maddox was the most unlikely bull ever to shatter a political china shop when he rode racial unrest to election, beating Bo Callaway, Georgia's first Republican congressman in the twentieth century. Maddox, who dressed in black suit and skinny black tie and wore rimless eyeglasses and a look of righteousness, had the appearance of a country preacher, or of a dime-premium insurance agent out on door-to-door collections, toting a fat book stuffed with papers under his arm. He deferentially called everyone "sir," including newspaper reporters, and on the surface seemed the most inoffensive of creatures. When I asked him before his election whether he would make concessions to moderates in his party for unity's sake, he replied: "No, sir. I've got a mandate from the people, sir, and I intend to live up to it."

As governor, however, he proved to be much more bark than bite, focusing more on rhetoric than action, holding an open-door "Little People Day" every week, and trying not to appear too incompetent. "Why, sir," he told me after taking office, "the way I'm conducting myself is the way I've always conducted myself. The image of Lester Maddox that some folks had was the image my opponents in the news media, politics, and business wanted to build. I think the people today are seeing the real Lester Maddox." But an Atlanta lawyer told me: "His background is so appalling, and he is so totally unqualified to be governor, that everybody is amazed that he's been able to strike a few responsive chords, and that the blatant racism that has marked his past hasn't asserted itself." In any event, Maddox managed to muddle through with no permanent damage to Georgia or the Republic, and some good laughs were had by all.

Sheriff Amerson was by far the more interesting of the two newly elected public officials. His election in the town that is home to Booker T. Washington's Tuskegee Institute came in the wake of the shooting of a young black civil rights worker and the acquittal of the accused white man by an all-white jury. Furious blacks splashed black paint on the statue of a Confederate soldier before the Macon County Courthouse and added a bright yellow streak down his back, along with the words "Black Power" over the dedication by the United Daughters of the Confederacy. This was desecration of the highest order in Dixie.

Yet Amerson was not supported by civil rights groups in his election bid, nor did he embrace black power as the vehicle to the sheriff's office. Rather, he ran and won as a moderate who happened to be black, not surprising in a town dominated by the predominantly black but basically conservative institute. Maddox's victory demonstrated how deep racial attitudes remained in the South; Amerson's showed how they were slowly evolving.

The expansion of the Newhouse bureau provided another bonus for me. I met and developed a long personal and professional relationship with one of the best newspapermen I've ever known, Erwin Knoll. Erwin, a veteran of the *Washington Post,* was brought into the bureau as its education expert, but his talents and sources soon dictated his use on a much wider range of interests. He eventually was switched to the White House beat, and we soon teamed up to do political stories and long series on aspects of the two wars being fought by President Johnson—the one in Vietnam and the one at home against poverty. We examined at length the peace movement in this country and the efforts not only to combat poverty but also to encourage grass-roots participation in politics at the neighborhood level.

I spent a fair amount of time examining a new organization working largely in the North called Students for a Democratic Society, known as SDS. It had held a founding convention at Port Huron, Michigan, in the summer of 1962 with a manifesto seeking to create "a democracy of individual participation" in which each person would "share in those social decisions determining the quality and direction of his life." The chief drafter was a young University of Michigan graduate named Tom Hayden. I first met him in Newark, New Jersey, where he was running a community organizing project in the poor black neighborhood of Clinton Hill, using the SDS technique of guiding rather than leading the local people in deciding what actions they wanted to take to better their lot.

In Chicago, I watched as SDS organizers in a poor North Side neighborhood simply observed for a long time as the local people debated how they could get the infamous Mayor Richard J. Daley to let them clear a lot as a playground for their kids. This exchange ensued:

"Wait a minute. You gotta get permission."

"Why?"

"Because it belongs to the city."

"So what? Who is the city, the people or Daley? Let them arrest us. Then we can say Daley won't give us a play lot for our kids and he won't let us build our own either."

After it went on a while like that, the SDS organizer spoke up: "Wait. Maybe we can work out a compromise. There seems to be a majority who don't want to risk arrest. We could start clearing the lot, and if the cops come and ask us to get off, we just get off. It still would make Daley look bad." The lot was cleared with no police interference. To the SDSers, the exercise was successful, even in the failure to provoke the cops. The poor had acted and had seen what could be done themselves.

Hayden and his colleagues didn't just talk "democracy," they sought to encourage it in the most basic sense. I'll never forget attending a conference of the SDS national council at a state park near Bloomington, Indiana, late in the summer of 1965 and listening to the two dozen or so members, lounging in the grass, discussing how they should go about their SDS business. There being only a temporary chairman of sorts, the dialogue went like this:

"Look, can I call for a vote on how we want to discuss this? Should we sit as one committee, or break up into smaller workshops, or what?"

"Well, everybody who wants to break up into workshops raise his hand."

"Wait a minute. How would the workshops be divided? By subject?"

"We could do that, or we could break up and everybody could kind of drift off into any group he wanted to, and talk."

At one point, an emissary from the mess hall came running up.

"We've got corn to husk for dinner. How about two or three volunteers?"

"Let's get this over with first."

"How about bringing the corn down here? That way we won't waste time."

"Or we could all go up to the kitchen and continue this there."

"That's a good idea. That way, the people working in the kitchen can get in on this. They have a right to vote, too."

The scene tended to trivialize the seriousness with which the SDS members went about their deliberations. Over the rest of the 1960s, as the organization grew and involved itself more deeply not only in fighting poverty through these efforts at pure democracy but also in fighting the American involvement in the Vietnam war, it became a major force.

The work of generating grass-roots political activity at the neighborhood level brought Erwin and me into contact with one of the most colorful and effective street organizers of the time, Saul Alinsky. He was best known for creating the Back of the Yards organization in Chicago, working for the rehabilitation and self-government of a slum section near the stockyards. Alinsky, whose slogan in organizing low-income people to challenge City Hall was "Rub raw the sores of discontent," was an irascible, secretive operator who came into greater public view as a result of LBJ's creation of the Office of Economic Opportunity in 1964. Alinsky was recruited by local communities in such places as Syracuse and Rochester, New York, to help poor neighborhoods, using OEO funds, organize to improve their lot and strengthen their voices in managing their own community affairs.

When Alinsky moved into Syracuse, where there were two Newhouse papers, Erwin and I were dispatched to find out what he was up to. We located him in an obscure apartment and called on him one afternoon. When he declined to open the door, we identified ourselves through the closed door and explained our mission. He again refused to talk to us, but Erwin persisted. In Rochester, the notorious company town of the Eastman Kodak film and camera empire, which had a very high black unemployment rate, Alinsky had turned the city upside down with a new neighborhood organization called FIGHT, an acronym that abbreviated nothing until Alinsky and local volunteers decided it stood for "freedom, integration, God, honor, and today." After much arguing through the closed door, Alinsky said he would see us the next day if we could produce a copy of the Rochester newspaper, so he could see what was going on there in his absence. Like Dorothy ordered by the Wizard of Oz to fetch the Wicked Witch's broom, we left with no immediate plan, Rochester being about eighty miles to the west of Syracuse.

However, Erwin and I, both veterans of small-town journalism, wherein bus drivers often were used to send copy back to the home office, hit on the answer. We went to the Greyhound station and talked a driver headed for Rochester into buying the latest edition of the local paper and handing it over to us at the end of his return run. On receipt, we raced to Alinsky's apartment, where this conversation ensued, still through the closed door:

"Mr. Alinsky?"

"Yeah?"

"Knoll and Witcover."

"Have you got it?"

"Yes."

"Slip it under the door."

We did so, and after a few minutes, while presumably he read the story about his project in Rochester, he opened the door and invited us in. It was the beginning of a long, fruitful, and fascinating relationship with perhaps the most famous and successful social worker of his time—a relationship that lasted long after he had left Rochester and Syracuse, where local government officials bore the political scars of his combative technique. In Syracuse, his effort included community voter registration drives that made Republican mayor William Walsh, facing reelection, apoplectic. "These people go into a housing project," he told us, "and talk about setting up a 'democratic organization—small 'd'—but it sounds just the same as Democratic—big 'D.' In a close election it could be decisive."

Erwin was the most gregarious individual I've ever met. He knew everyone and everyone knew him. Walking down the street with him in Washington was like being with one of those Mafia dons in *The Godfather,* except nobody kissed his ring. It was maddening for me after a while, particularly when it also happened when we were on assignment out of town. Even on airplanes, strangers (to me) would come up and start talking with him. I finally got my revenge at a party in my home when, near the end of the evening, all the other guests broke out buttons that said "Who is Erwin Knoll?" (though of course they all knew him).

Unknown to Erwin, I collected the buttons after the party and over the next several years would plant them on people he encountered under unexpected circumstances. For example, when he went to Nova Scotia on a family visit, he was greeted at the door with relatives wearing the button. When he called on a cabinet member for an interview, his subject sported the button. When he had to undergo surgery on his knee, the first thing he saw when he came out of the anesthesia was the surgeon leaning over him wearing the button. When he went on a presidential trip to the Pacific and disembarked from the press plane on Pago Pago, standing at the foot of the stair was a native dressed in not much else but the button. I was frustrated, however, in what would have been my crowning achievement; the masterminds of Neil Armstrong's "one small step for man" onto the surface of the moon gave me thumbs down on having him make Erwin Knoll part of outer space history.

If it hadn't been for Erwin, I probably would not have survived the Newhouse years. He and I shared a small office, and as the bureau became zanier and zanier, we as the in-house veterans doctored one of those signs that said "The Doctor Is In" to read in the plural and hung it on our door. Frustrated fellow staffers paraded in and out regularly, except when a deadline obliged us to change the sign to read "The Doctors Are Out." Our diagnoses and prescriptions seldom cured anybody. And the old adage "Physician, heal thyself" weighed heavily on both of us as we continued to toil in that particular insane asylum.

4 Politics at Last

THROUGH ALL THE VARIOUS DIVERSIONS of covering the Pentagon and civil rights and playing house psychiatrist for other Newhouse inmates, my ardor and ambition for covering politics never cooled. The summer of 1948, when as a twenty-year-old college student I hopped a train from Newark to Philadelphia with a high-school buddy and hung around outside the Republican National Convention that nominated Thomas E. Dewey for the second time, I was bitten by the bug. With no tickets to the hall, we waited for the day's session to end, then slipped inside and picked up discarded banners and buttons to prove we had been there for what most of the world then believed was the nomination of the next president.

Except for my aforementioned one-night stand as a "reporter" for the UP at the *Providence Journal* in 1952, however, I was still a virgin in the political-writing racket when I got to the Newhouse Washington bureau at the start of 1954. More than two years passed before I got my first real (and legitimate) taste of presidential politics. My rabbi, Casey Jones, agreed to give me a small bite in the fall of 1956 by letting me join the White House press corps accompanying President Eisenhower to Philadelphia by train for his speech at a party fund raiser. The event itself, at the old Bellevue Stratford Hotel, left less of an impression on me than being part of the allegedly elite gaggle of reporters on the train. I watched and kept my mouth shut as such newspaper icons as Merriman Smith sat in their compartments tapping out copy on portable typewriters or smoking and playing cards. Western Union runners would come through the train calling for copy as

Eisenhower aides busied themselves with all the mundane tasks required to keep a president of the United States functioning on the move.

Rather than returning with the Eisenhower entourage, I spent the next day interviewing local politicians for a Sunday piece on Republican Senator Hugh Scott, seeking reelection. I returned to Washington that night with enough information to justify the cost of travel to this distant outpost. On subsequent brief news-gathering trips for the Newhouse chain, I always operated on the understanding that I was to come back with several stories in hand, to justify the expense. It was like doing piece work at a shirt factory, only for less money.

Before such trips, Viglietta would take me aside and explain the drill. On getting off the train or plane, the first thing I was to do was find the local telephone Yellow Pages and open to the "Hotels" section. Then I was to call around to a dozen or more establishments, find the cheapest, and reserve a room. This unscientific method guaranteed overnight stays in some of the crummiest hotels in some of the dreariest sections of the host cities, because the prime objective was to demonstrate frugality, not taste. Failure to do so would result not only in a sharp rebuke from Viglietta but a hiatus in further expense-account traveling for weeks or months ahead.

It was largely because Casey Jones had toiled in the big time before his move from the *Washington Post* to the *Syracuse Herald-Journal*, that he understood my travails in chronicling the minutia of local members of Congress and responded to my endless pleas for broader assignments. In 1960, Jones dispatched me to West Virginia to cover my first presidential primary, the Democratic contest between Senators John F. Kennedy and Hubert H. Humphrey. Kennedy had run virtually unchallenged in New Hampshire and had beaten Humphrey in Wisconsin, but he had not yet convinced the party power brokers that he could be a national winner.

West Virginia was a bare-knuckles affair, with Humphrey accusing Kennedy of spreading "political payola" around the state and Kennedy through a surrogate questioning Humphrey's lack of military service in World War II. "I don't have an open-end checkbook," I remember Humphrey declaring at one point from the steps of the Mingo County courthouse. "I don't have any daddy to pay the bill." He told voters at other stops that Kennedy was traveling around the state "carrying a little black bag" and "with a checkbook in his hand," and charged that Kennedy was spending $250,000—a lot of money in those days—to buy West Virginia votes. Meanwhile, Franklin D. Roosevelt Jr., whose father was an icon in the state, was busily casting aspersions on Humphrey's lack of war service. Kennedy finally disavowed the attack, but not without observing of FDR Jr.: "Nobody's word is more highly regarded."

It was possible in 1960 to stroll down the main street of Charleston, West Virginia, with Kennedy and two or three other reporters as he dropped into shops and introduced himself to customers who had never heard of him. It was possible, too, to ride in the candidate's private car with just the driver and another aide or two and talk about how the campaign was going. I have a clear memory of Kennedy visiting a working coal mine at shift change with his gaily frocked sisters in tow, and the senator in an expensive suit sitting on a rail track heading into the mine and chewing the fat with the coal dust–covered, awestruck miners.

Another keen recollection was a brief encounter in the Kennedy press room one night with Robert Kennedy, then running his brother's campaign. The room was empty and Kennedy, who often had stiffed me when I sought answers from him in his capacity as a Senate committee aide looking into labor rackets, strolled over and began to engage me in idle conversation about the West Virginia campaign. I was pleasantly surprised but suspicious. The Kennedy clan was notorious for using people, but I couldn't figure why a reporter from an obscure chain of newspapers would be considered usable. I remained skeptical, especially when I saw my new friend having breakfast with press secretary Pierre Salinger the next morning and naïvely asked whether I could join them. The freeze I got chilled my bones and sent me off to eat my bacon and eggs at another table.

Senate Majority Leader Lyndon Johnson, while not competing in the primary, was also flirting with the Democratic presidential nomination and hoped that his Senate colleagues would deliver it to him. On the weekend before the primary, he flew into Clarksburg for a party dinner and while there learned that an American U-2 spy plane had been shot down over the Soviet Union and the pilot, Gary Francis Powers, captured. LBJ held a press conference before the dinner, sitting at a long table with perhaps twenty reporters around it. Sitting next to him at one end were two veteran Senate reporters, and Johnson proceeded to discuss the situation with them in almost a whisper, while the rest of us strained to hear. Polite requests for him to speak louder were ignored in what was my first introduction to the Imperial Lyndon. Another fairly junior reporter from the *Washington Star* named Mary McGrory sat next to me and kept asking loudly, "What did he say?" That was my introduction to her, too.

West Virginia, whose Catholic population was reputed to be only 5 percent, was an ideal laboratory for testing Kennedy's contention that a Catholic could be elected president. He was the first to make a serious effort since Democratic New York governor Al Smith was trounced by Republican Herbert Hoover in 1928. The Kennedy campaign played on West Virginians' desire not to be seen as prejudiced, and it worked. It was there that I got a real taste of national political reporting and set my sights on doing it full time. But that was not to happen quite yet.

In 1964, I attended my first national political convention, the Republicans' in San Francisco. There I witnessed Barry Goldwater's famous "extremism in the pursuit of liberty is no vice" speech and experienced the wrath of GOP delegates shaking their fists and hurling epithets at the press section. There also my future good friend John Chancellor won journalistic immortality by being arrested on the convention floor. As he was escorted from the hall, he informed his television audience that he was reporting from "somewhere in custody."

Also that year I covered the Democratic convention in Atlantic City, where Robert Kennedy introduced a moving film about his slain brother, but not before a seemingly endless floor demonstration of cheers and tears that left him wan and disarmed. But in the fall, while the spotlight was on Johnson's landslide romp to a full presidential term in his own right, and on Robert Kennedy's election to the Senate from New York, I was limited to pulse taking in California, Illinois, and heavily Republican counties in Ohio in search of Goldwater voters who weren't there. Goldwater's hawkish rhetoric about pursuing the Vietnam war scared many fellow Republicans, and his zany statements on other matters made him a laughingstock.

My only escape came late in the campaign when I was assigned to cover a five-day Goldwater swing by whistle-stop train through Ohio, Indiana, and Illinois. Although the Republican nominee sought to focus on GOP areas of each state, he nevertheless encountered raucous hecklers at nearly every stop, responding to his reputation as a trigger-happy Cold Warrior who also wanted to kill or at least maim Social Security by making it voluntary. Signs held aloft for him to read said such things as "Help Barry Stamp Out Peace," "I'm Too Young to Die," and in Appalachian Ohio, "Don't Stop Here. We're Poor Enough."

Goldwater's comebacks, such as chiding Johnson's vice-presidential nominee as "Humpty Humphrey, one egghead who's headed for a great fall," and accusing LBJ of a strategy of "lie, lie, lie and elect, elect, elect," fell lamely on Democratic ears. Yet for the most part the senator from Arizona remained in good spirits and was a favorite personally of many of the accompanying reporters, even while they thought his views were crazy. When he would come out with a particularly bizarre observation at a rally, and we reporters would scribble it in our notepads, one of his faithful in the crowd would become irate, asking, "Why are you writing that down? You're not going to put it in the paper, are you?"

At each whistle stop, we had to get off and run alongside the tracks to the rear to hear Goldwater speak. When he was finished, we had to race back to the press cars and climb aboard before the train pulled out. At a stop in Athens, Ohio, five of us didn't make it, and Goldwater stood on the rear platform signaling forlornly to us that there was nothing he could do about it. We quickly hailed the only taxi in sight and the driver took us on a wild ride over hill and dale to the next train stop, at Chillicothe forty miles away. We arrived just as Barry was going into his speech windup, which by now we knew by heart. Expecting to have to pay the driver at least fifty bucks apiece, we were astonished to hear him say we owed him only forty total. He enjoyed the excitement of the chase, he told us. We gave him a good tip—but not as good as he deserved, expense accounts being not as liberal for some of us as for others.

After the Goldwater debacle of 1964, I spent time observing the Republican attempt to put the party together again. I remember well a GOP National Committee meeting in Chicago at which Goldwater accepted blame for his defeat and turned off the talk of a third-party movement that was being bruited about by frustrated conservative supporters. The party was at rock bottom, and its master mechanic of the time, Ray Bliss of Ohio, was chosen as the new national chairman, to focus on his specialty, nuts-and-bolts organizing. The chairman of the National Republican Congressional Committee at the time, Congressman Bob Wilson of California, well described the GOP plight and the determination it required to resuscitate itself: "If I was in hell, with one leg gone, and one arm gone, and one eye gone, I'd still be thinking: 'How can I get out of here?'"

Another presidential loser, Richard Nixon, always with the good of the party foremost in his mind, had the solution. He called for a moratorium on presidential politicking until after the 1966 congressional elections, at which time the party could restore itself. Nixon pledged to do none of it himself, an act of self-sacrifice that didn't much impress the party faithful, because after his loss for governor of California in 1962, few thought he had any political future. But the moratorium he proposed would have the practical effect of freezing the race for the 1968 Republican nomination for two years, to the benefit of guess who.

In 1966, after considerable in-house lobbying on my part, I was finally given time off for good behavior, relieved of my Pentagon assignment, and handed a newly created national political beat. Fortune at last was smiling on me, and I embarked on the endeavor with undisguised zeal, joining a small fraternity of reporters—and it was pretty much a fraternity at the time—who devoted full time to national politics, and not just in election years either.

Most of us were in our early or middle thirties and very competitive but also most congenial, thanks to the generous flow of alcohol on the back of press buses and trains of the time. It helped that for most of the day we were unreachable, in that era when the cellular phone was not even a twinkle in a demanding editor's eye. On the campaign trail, we were free to cover our stories as we wished, relaxing on the bus or train between events. It made for nonstop camaraderie within our small band of brothers, which included in those days Bruce Biossat, Dave Broder, Jim Dickenson, Jim Doyle, Pat Furgurson, Jack Germond, Bob Healy, Paul Hope, Ted Knap, John Lindsay, Loye Miller, Walter Mears, Bob Novak, Tom Ottenad, and Warren Weaver— all print reporters, and all guys. A handful of television types, like Jack Chancellor, Roger Mudd, and Herb Kaplow, also were part of the club— none of them of the posturing, blowhard and blow-dried Larry Largelungs variety.

Occasionally a clean-fingernails columnist would show up, such as Joe Alsop, Mark Childs, Jack Kilpatrick, or Joe Kraft, to give us the benefit of his long-distance wisdom about the campaign we were covering daily. And during the presidential primaries we could count on an appearance from the always cordial Teddy White, to tell us how it was in the Jack Kennedy days. Alsop, a walking American version of a British fop, when favoring one of us, would always address him, in full noblesse oblige, as "dear boy."

The majority of us, however, were unrecognizable grunts traveling the campaign trail in happy obscurity and a carefree climate of fraternal togetherness. The only regulations we observed were self-imposed, the most prominent of which were the Germond Rule and the Weaver Rule.

The first, created by the group's prodigious-expense-account author, dictated that when two or more members dined together, the bill was divided equally, regardless of anybody's consumption. The inevitable corollary was "Eat and drink defensively," that is, consume and imbibe as much as Germond did or pay the price when the tab was settled up.

In this regard, one of the most impressive participants in conforming to the rule was the late Tom Ottenad of the *St. Louis Post-Dispatch*. Tom was a small, wiry, soft-spoken fellow of most tenacious nature in pursuit of a story, and he demonstrated a similar tenacity in making sure he was never out-eaten or out-imbibed at our group tables. His alcoholic intake especially was impressive, with never a trace of the inebriation that others often exhibited. As for myself, I made the mistake during one trip to San Francisco of abstaining from booze for a spell, to lose weight. The sauce consumption of Germond and Ottenad obliged me to double-up on desserts to break even, thus sabotaging my effort to diet.

The second rule, authored by the alert-of-mind if often slow-of-foot *New York Times* reporter Warren Weaver, required that the man sitting next to the taxi driver pay the fare for all. Weaver had to hustle to avoid being victimized by his own rule, and we all learned to dash from the dinner table to the awaiting cab and pile into the back seat. Anyone shunted to the front seat who refused to pay received a reprimand from Weaver. Bob Novak was a frequent loser. Once, in Denver, he retaliated by renting a car for himself when we went to a minor-league baseball game, rather than suffer another humiliation within the fraternity.

Germond and I, working as we did in those days for obscure newspaper chains, found ourselves shut out of the traditional press breakfast of the day, run by the *Christian Science Monitor*. In response, we founded what we so cleverly called the Political Writers for a Democratic Society. Most members of the above band were included, and we held frequent private dinners in the home of a member, at which we consumed much food and drink with some invited politician, the better to know him.

The PWDS dinners were on deep background, meaning nothing said was to be attributed to the guest. The rule produced few hard news stories but usually gave us an excellent sense of our guest for future evaluation in print.

When stories did come out of a dinner, gleaning the identity of the source did not pose much of a challenge for a moderately discerning reader. For example, after one lively four-hour session in 1966, I wrote: "Vice President Hubert H. Humphrey is known to be boiling mad over the rising criticism from liberals that he has abandoned them out of political expediency. The idea that he has been dragooned by President Johnson into distasteful positions, especially concerning the Viet Nam war, has put the Vice President in a fighting mood. He is insisting that he is not only an enthusiastic supporter of the President's policies but an innovator of some of them and an active consultant on virtually all of them."

The congenial and loquacious Humphrey was one of our favorite dinner guests. Among the many others hosted by this and successor groups over the years were Barry Goldwater, George Romney, Gene McCarthy, Howard Baker, Bob Dole, Ted Kennedy, Jack Kemp, Ed Muskie, Pat Robertson, Gary Hart, John Connally, and Bill Clinton, as well as many leading political consultants of both parties.

Perhaps the most memorable dinner was one we held with Muskie at the time he was struggling to make up his mind on the Vietnam war. We had heard of his terrible temper and some of us had experienced it, and as we pressed him on where he stood on the war, he erupted, threatening to get up and leave. We calmed him down and the conversation continued, until the subject was raised again and he erupted again. The dinner prepared us for his later public display of anger when William Loeb, the publisher of the *Manchester Union Leader* printed derogatory remarks about Muskie's wife Jane, and Muskie got so exercised he went to the paper and berated Loeb, bringing himself to the point of tears—or so some reporters concluded as they watched snow roll down Muskie's cheeks.

Affairs like our cozy dinners were sometimes criticized by other reporters as evidence that we got too close to our sources and gave them a free ride, not reporting something they said or did at the dinners that could hurt them politically. Admittedly, that was a trade-off for the intimate access, but we operated on the premise that it was more helpful and fruitful in the long run to see and hear these people with their guard down than to be able to use one damaging quote. At the same time, in those days we followed an accepted rule that if you learned something of a derogatory nature about a source, you reported it only if it appeared to hinder his ability to do his job. Thus, heavy drinking or womanizing generally went unreported. In later years, obviously, and with the advent of "gotcha" journalism after Watergate, that standard crumbled.

Most of the time, however, for all of our hijinks, we all operated independently in a fierce competitive atmosphere. In the fall of 1966, I undertook coverage of several key gubernatorial races, including George Romney's campaign for a third term in Lansing, Nelson Rockefeller's bid for the same in Albany, the campaign of a Grade B movie actor named Ronald Reagan for a first term in Sacramento, and George Wallace's successful effort to put his wife, Lurleen, in the governor's chair in Montgomery when he was term-limited out of it.

At this time, Governor Romney of Michigan was regarded as a hot Republican property. He was a self-styled citizen-politician driven by his self-discipline and religious fervor as an elder in the Mormon church. He had a remarkable record in business as head of struggling American Motors, introducing the low-priced Rambler sedan and elbowing his company into a competitive position against Detroit's Big Three automakers, General Motors, Ford, and Chrysler. Turning the same zeal to politics, he had built an enviable record as Michigan's governor; and in 1966 he hoped, in the process of winning a third term, to qualify himself for the Republican presidential nomination in 1968. I went along for much of the ride.

One late winter morning I met him for an early breakfast at his home in the stylish Bloomfield Hills suburb of Detroit. I found myself chasing him as he ran—not walked nor rode—around a local golf course getting in eighteen holes to start the day. With a full work schedule ahead, he had his own typical, time-saving solution. On the first tee, he hit three balls, one after the other. Then he set off at a trot, pulling his golf cart behind him, to the first ball, hit it, then ran to the second and hit it, and the same with the third. In this way, hitting three balls over six holes, he managed to play the eighteen holes in about an hour. He was an awful golfer—his swing resembled a man trying to kill a snake with his club—but he got his day's exercise in the process.

Romney approached everything with the same grim determination. In his reelection campaign, he was hounded with questions from me and other out-of-state reporters about his presidential ambitions, but he steadfastly declined to be drawn into discussions of national affairs, and particularly the Vietnam war. He was running for governor, he said, "and that's all I'm running for. There isn't anyone who can foresee what's going to happen two months or two years from now." At the same time, however, he declined to say flatly that he would serve out his full four-year term if reelected. So the pack stayed on his heels, and our focus on him intensified after he scored a solid reelection victory in November.

Rockefeller, after having failed to catch fire in his first attempt at the presidency against Goldwater in 1964, nevertheless campaigned with his old, famous energy for another term as governor of New York. He was plagued as always by voter unhappiness with the high taxes he imposed for various state improvements, including in public education. At one stop in upstate Endicott, as Rockefeller was holding forth on his campaign against water pollution, a heckler came out of a nearby bar, weaving unsteadily, and shouted: "What are you going to do about the state income tax?" Rocky shot back: "First, let me tell you about pure water. I know you don't bother with it. But let me tell you about clear water and then you can go back to your scotch." That got the crowd's attention more than all the dry statistics he had previously been imposing on them.

For all of Rockefeller's shortcomings as a national candidate, in New York State he still was a force of nature. He campaigned as if he, like Romney, had his eye on the 1968 Republican presidential nomination, but he steadfastly denied it. When I asked him on this particular trip whether in spite of his denials circumstances might change his mind, he said flatly, "No, I'm finished." Did he mean "categorically, absolutely," I asked? "Yes." It was a response I had cause to remember later.

It was this Rockefeller campaign, against Democrat Frank O'Connor, that produced one of my all-time favorite quotes in politics. Mario Procaccino, a one-time Democratic candidate for mayor of New York City campaigning for Rocky's rival, stood before a Democratic audience and tried to convince his listeners of the worthiness of O'Connor. "I know that when you first meet Frank O'Connor you may not think much of him," Mario said earnestly. "But when you get to know him, he grows on you—like a cancer!"

Rockefeller's money allowed him to travel like a sitting president, and he just about did. In that 1966 reelection campaign, he had five advance men smoothing his way and a large research and public relations staff as he toured the big state in his own turbo-prop plane. For intermediate stops, he chartered a nine-passenger helicopter. Reporters trying to keep up with him rode in a comfortable campaign bus more than amply supplied with refreshments, both solid and liquid.

After one morning of public events in New York City, Rockefeller had a couple of hours of private meetings. His press secretary, Leslie Slote, directed the press bus to Sardi's, the famous celebrity restaurant in the midtown theater district, where a sumptuous lunch was awaiting the dirty-fingernail press grunts. Our ethical standards took a holiday as we dug into the feast, washing it down with the house's best libations. Such was the profligate atmosphere generated by the Rocky campaign. The governor himself seemed at times slightly embarrassed about his huge wealth, and instead of saying "Thanks a million" to folks, he would invariably say "Thanks a thousand!" Nor did that wealth dissuade him from wearing ancient brown double-breasted suits out of the Roaring Twenties.

Reagan too was taken with big-shouldered brown suits and had the same geniality as Rockefeller, but he was campaigning as a political novice against Democratic governor Pat Brown in 1966. The most notable aspect of traveling with him was listening to him recite his favorite political fables with all seriousness as he flew around California aboard an ancient DC-3 prop plane. It was known as "The Turkey" because its pilot-owner was a turkey farmer who used it to haul his gobblers to market when he wasn't ferrying a candidate. Reagan would sit in the first row of the passenger compartment with his long legs braced against the wall to the pilot's cabin and regale you with such fables, as well as old movie yarns and jokes.

One such political fairy tale was about how racial segregation had ended in the armed forces. As Reagan told it, when the Japanese attacked Pearl Harbor, a black steward's mate came up out of the galley, grabbed a machine gun and shot down a kamikaze plane. That act, he said, immediately led to the integration of the military. The armed forces were in fact not desegregated until 1948, nearly seven years after Pearl Harbor, by President Harry Truman.

Reagan, in criticizing government welfare assistance, liked to conjure up the picture of what would happen, absent welfare, if your neighbor's house burned down one night. Everybody in the neighborhood, he told me with the deepest conviction on one flight, would be there the next day rebuilding the house and feeding the victimized family members until they could move back in—a few days later. In this way were the hours passed traveling with the future president of the United States.

It is an old ritual for the passengers to applaud when a campaign plane makes a safe landing. On The Turkey, we reporters instead would gobble loudly, at first baffling Reagan but afterward causing him to throw his head back in laughter, his own turkey-like wattles shaking merrily.

What I remember most about that election, however, was Pat Brown, a warm and chatty man, sitting in his own campaign plane on the final weekend, peering out the window at the Golden State below, then at his wife, Bernice, sitting across the way, and sadly saying to me: "I can't believe I'm going to lose to a movie actor. I've been a good governor. Poor state. Poor governor. Poor wife!"

Brown did lose to Reagan in spite of efforts to save him from leading fellow Democrats in and outside California. One was actor Gene Barry, who played Bat Masterson on television and campaigned with Brown, assuring voters that Reagan was not the choice of the movie and television industry. "All Reagan has is John Wayne and Buddy Ebsen on his side," Barry would tell crowds. "We know Ronnie Reagan and that's why we can't vote for him. I'm known for always getting the girl. Ronnie never got the girl. Why the hell should we turn the state over to him?" That appeal to the intellectual vote did not, for some reason, work on election day, and Reagan was on his way.

George Wallace, unlike Pat Brown, did not surrender the governor's chair in his state in 1966; he simply saw to it that his wife was elected to succeed him and then, as he continued to run Alabama, she was sent off to handle ceremonial chores or just stayed home. He used her in the same way he used others he encountered, including Yankee reporters like me, to make political hay with the Alabama faithful and advance his national ambitions.

I well remember when, in the fall of 1966, George was taking Lurleen around the state to get her elected over a weak Republican challenger, Congressman James Martin, the state legislature having declined to change the law so the incumbent governor could run for another term. The Wallaces were touring Jacksonville State College, which he had established, and when I introduced myself he invited me to board the campus bus with them, asking me how I liked Alabama. As the bus pulled out, he stood in the aisle and announced to the assembled educators aboard that there was a newspaper reporter from Washington with him who, he said with a grin, "came here to write a lot of distortions and lies about me." I smiled back and told him I would try not to disappoint him.

From then on, it became a little game. At every campaign stop, Wallace would tell the crowd about the Yankee reporter with him, "writin' down all them things about how we talk and dress in Alabama." The revelation would always bring catcalls and menacing looks at me from the assembled, until he would make a humorous remark about the misguided press and the sharp edge would melt into laughter. Whenever I would encounter him thereafter, he would invariably ask me whether I lived in the (black majority–populated) District of Columbia, and would half-smile, half-sneer when I told him I lived in northern Virginia. Every conversation ended with, "Y'all come and see us, y'heah?" and he seemed to mean it because he was starved for recognition outside Alabama.

Inside his own state, however, there never was any dispute that he was king. He acted the part and expected to be treated accordingly. Once he was sitting in the cafeteria of Troy State College with a table of his cronies, including a man whom he addressed and referred to only as "Adams," though he was at the time the president of the college, appointed by Wallace as an old faithful hanger-on. The governor was eating a hamburger, one of his favorite foods, when he looked around for ketchup, a Dixie staple that he was known to put on anything that did not move. A bottle sat idly at a nearby table. "Adams," Wallace commanded, "get me the ketchup." A pained expression came over Ralph Adams' face. "Aw, Governor," he complained, "I'm a college president now." Wallace snapped back: "Yeah, and I'm the governor of Alabama. Now get me the ketchup." Adams sheepishly complied. Such amusing scenes did not make George Wallace any more or less a demagogue, but they made observing him in his native habitat sheer entertainment. It was always fun to be around him, while maddening at the same time.

With the home folks around campaign time, Wallace was always the epitome of graciousness and friendship. One warm Friday night I accompanied him and his wife to the Alabama State Fair in Birmingham. As a wanly smiling Lurleen tagged along, George worked the crowd compulsively, grabbing every extended hand, chattering cordially with fairgoers whose names and "kinfolk" he unfailingly recalled in a tour de force of old-time local politicking: "Hello there, sure is good to see y'all. Where y'all from? Gadsden? What's your daddy's name? Oh, sure, your daddy's got the gas station up there. Didn't he carry you over to see me when I was runnin' for governor? You be sure to tell him hello for me, y'heah?"

As the Wallaces campaigned across Alabama that fall, although Lurleen was the candidate she was reduced to a prop, or at best to mistress of ceremonies introducing her husband. They would swing into town like a small traveling circus, with a replica of the Liberty Bell mounted on an open truck, and Sam Smith and his Alabamians would twang out country tunes to warm up the crowd. From the town of Oxford on a typical campaign day, I described

Mrs. Wallace—pretty, but wooden in her delivery—reads a short speech in a monotone, recites some statistics on Alabama progress, pledges that existing "policies will be continued and promises fulfilled" . . . Then, as necks in the crowd stretch for a first glimpse, she introduces "my husband and your governor, George C. Wallace!" On cue, "Dixie" and the Liberty Bell ring out across the gathering, and the star comes forth to perform. For the next twenty minutes or so, it is pure mesmerism.

George Wallace—short, solid, cocky and much more clever than most Yankees give him credit for—boosts the citizens' egos. He paints colorful word-pictures of their Yankee enemies and then proceeds to stomp on 'em, one by one, to the utter glee of the assembled. "Millions all over this country say, thank goodness for Alabamians," he tells them. The rallying cry against federal domination he sounded in his 1964 Democratic primary forays into three Northern states, he says, has been picked up everywhere.

"Everybody is watching," he assures them, "because these things we predicted are coming true. Wherever we go, people say, 'We're so proud of what's happening in Alabama.' You go to Europe and they might not can call the name of any state in the union, but they know Alabama!" When he goes to the annual governors' conference, George tells them, "I don't sit in no back row. I sit right up there in the front row with the governors from California and New York. Maybe even a little in front. Because I represent people just as good as any of 'em. You can be proud to be an Alabamian."

George tells them about an article written for a national magazine by "the wife of Governor [Robert] Smylie of Ide-ee-ho entitled 'Why I Feel Sorry for Lurleen.' Well, I wrote another one for them—I don't know if they'll print it— entitled 'Why I Feel Sorry for Governor Smylie of Ide-ee-ho,' because he got beat in the primary. Maybe he can get a job in the poverty program. . . . They sent down Bobby Kennedy, who wants to give blood to the Viet Cong Communists who are killing Alabama boys, to talk against my wife. . . . Any place you see the Confederate flag you won't see anybody giving blood to the Communist Viet Cong enemies of ours. . . ."

Later, in Anniston, Wallace joked about how as a gubernatorial spouse he intended to be "head of the beautification program [as Lady Bird Johnson was] and plant magnolias up and down the highways." More seriously, he

hinted about how electing Lurleen would free him up for another presidential bid in 1968, a bid necessary to spread "the Alabama movement" nation-
wide, because all the others in both parties likely to run offered voters no
real choice. What followed was classic Wallace, which we reporters soon
could recite by heart:

> Now you take a big sack and you put LBJ in there, and you put Hubert Horatio
> Alger Humphrey in there, and you put Bobby Kennedy the blood-giver in there
> and you shake 'em all up. Then you put this Richard Milhous Nixon who with
> Eisenhower put bayonets in the back of the people of Little Rock and in your
> backs, and you put in Earl Warren, who doesn't have enough legal brains in his
> head to try a chicken thief in my home county, and you shake 'em up. And then
> you put that socialist Nelson Rockefeller from the most liberal state in the
> country, and that left-winger George Romney who was out in the streets with
> them demonstrators, and that Clifford Case of New Jersey and that wild Bill
> Scranton of Pennsylvania and that radical Jacob Javits of New York, and you
> shake 'em all up. Then you turn that sack over, and the first one that falls out,
> you pick him up by the nape of the neck and drop him right back in again,
> because there's not a dime's worth of difference in any of 'em, national Dem-
> ocrats or national Republicans!

Needless to say, the Alabama crowds loved this litany, and as I stood in
the crowd and scribbled it all down, I drew looks of animosity. Wallace
always made a point of informing his audiences that we "distorters" on "a
distortin' trip" were among them. At first, he would say, "you could spot
them easy, with the long hair and the beards. Now they make them get a
haircut before they send them down, and they blend in better in the crowd.
But they're out there with you."

One on one, though, he was invariably friendly and could be most amusing. After Lurleen was elected, I called on him at the state capitol in
Montgomery and found him sitting in his old chair in the governor's office,
Lurleen having been sent out on one chore or another. He held forth as of
old, puffing and chewing on his ever-present wet stogie, flicking ashes into
and around the gubernatorial spitoon. During our chat, he barked orders
into his phone, leaving no doubt that he was still running things.

The subject was his national ambitions, now that he had Lurleen installed as his stand-in and was free to test the waters beyond the state whose
denizens still clearly adored him. Dismissing criticism that the most he
could hope for was to be a spoiler in the 1968 presidential race, Wallace

straight-facedly invoked the history of Abraham Lincoln in arguing that he could win the White House. "Lincoln was a plurality winner and I'll be a plurality winner," he insisted. "In a four-man race he didn't get a majority of the people's votes, but he had enough to get a majority of the electoral votes. Well, if I run, this will be at least a three-man race and the same thing can happen." He clearly enjoyed the irony in comparing himself to Lincoln to a Yankee reporter.

Wallace had already demonstrated in 1964 his pulling power in three northern states, winning a remarkable 43 percent of the Democratic primary vote in Maryland, 34 percent in Wisconsin, and 30 in Indiana. The only reason he lost in Maryland, he was fond of saying thereafter, was that when election officials early on election night saw him running so strongly, they "recapitulated" the vote to his disadvantage. "When they say they gonna recapitulate on you," he would warn, "watch out!"

In any event, in the spring of 1967, when Wallace set out on a short northern swing from Dartmouth College in New Hampshire to Syracuse, Pittsburgh, and Cleveland, I went along. Although he hated flying, in those days he used a small state-owned propeller plane, a DC-6 if memory serves me, and was always accompanied by a corps of plainclothes state police. Unlike the overwhelmingly supportive crowds he routinely met in Dixie, his crowds on this swing ran from polite to raucously hostile, with picketing protesters at each stop. The most frenzied night was at Syracuse University, where he was so heavily heckled that at one point he stopped and audibly wailed, "Man, this is tough."

At the outset of his speech, a group of black students wearing white sheets marched up the aisle pulling another along with a rope around his neck. "Hey, George!" one of the captors called out to him. "We got one!" Wallace was rattled but he pressed on, and as the crowd settled down, he remarked: "There's a hot time in the old town tonight." It was not a complaint; Wallace thrived on such scenes, and he would jut his jaw out in defiance, while nevertheless revealing some personal trepidation as an air of violence filled the hall. At one point I heard him say softly, almost to himself, "I wish everybody could remain in a good humor until we get away."

Wallace soon found campaigning in the North was not the same as it was down home, where few blacks joined his crowds of adoring whites and he played the cheerleader to the hilt. In alien northern territory, he encouraged and thrived on racial division, often baiting his crowds until fights broke out and he would shout, "Let the police handle it!" It was Wallace's conviction throughout that there was just as much racial unease and potential for racial violence in the North as in the South, and just as much resentment toward the federal government in Washington, and he was determined to tap into it. Throughout 1967, he explored his chances in further trips to the Midwest and West Coast, stirring up the animals wherever he went. At the same time, he labored diligently to achieve ballot position in all fifty states, which he eventually succeeded in doing.

I got an unusual glimpse of the hard edge of Wallace's political ambitions one night when I went to interview him in Houston. Lurleen, who after her election as governor had undergone three operations for cancer, was now receiving outpatient radiation treatments at the Texas Medical Center. The Wallaces were just sitting down to dinner with their daughter, Peggy Sue, in the coffee shop of the gaudy motel where they were staying, when I walked over just to say hello and inquire whether he would have a few minutes to talk to me later.

Unhesitatingly, Wallace jumped up and led me to another table, leaving his wife and daughter behind. He proceeded to regale me at length with the success of a trip to California he had just completed to get his new American Independent Party on the ballot there. My repeated suggestions that he rejoin his family and meet me later were to no avail as he pressed on. Finally, when Lurleen and Peggy Sue had finished their dinner, the wan-looking Lurleen came over to our table and told her husband she was going to her room. He looked up, slightly irritated at the interruption, and with a half-smile, half-sneer as if he were responding to a heckler, said: "All right, *Governor*, you go right on up, *Governor*. I'll be on up in a while now." Her illness was clearly putting a crimp in his third-party campaign. However, the next time I saw him, in Montgomery after Lurleen had endured yet another surgery, he seemed genuinely shaken. He dwelled on her ordeal and her courage in meeting it, and spoke of what he said was her concern that her health was forcing him to keep his campaign on hold. She died soon thereafter.

His wife's death freed him to resume campaigning in full intensity, but without the full apparatus of the state of Alabama behind him. He did not lose all the privileges. The lieutenant governor, Albert Brewer, became governor and shortly after being sworn in announced that he would instruct the state police to continue to provide Wallace with security wherever he went, which he definitely needed, as he continued to preach his politics of resentment and division. But Wallace's entitlement to the governor's chair in Montgomery was not yet over, of which more later.

Another prominent politician I got to know in the fall campaign of 1966 was the man who in Chicago a year earlier had urged fellow Republicans to observe a moratorium on presidential politicking until after the 1966 congressional elections. When I next encountered him, he was enforcing the moratorium in his own way—by campaigning frenetically for Republican candidates and putting himself squarely in the national spotlight again. For a week I was the only reporter accompanying Richard Milhous Nixon; it was an education and, as things turned out for me, a career opportunity.

5 Nixon and Me

OF ALL THE POLITICAL FIGURES I have encountered in half a century of
reporting, none was as baffling, intriguing, and maddening as Richard Milhous Nixon. Upon his death in 1994, I was asked, as the author of *The Resurrection of Richard Nixon*, an account of his remarkable political comeback
and election as president in 1968, to appear on C-SPAN and comment on
him. I conveyed the above sentiment by observing that I had always thought
that when he passed away, his brain should be willed to science. My reason-
ing was that, for all his political success, rising to the American political
peak, he had a colossal inferiority complex that dominated his personality,
and it would be revealing to determine what made him tick.

It so happened that, as I was offering this and other candid observations
about Nixon, unbeknownst to me C-SPAN was showing to viewers scenes of
his bereaved family's arrival for the approaching funeral and of the grieving
and the curious public passing by his casket in display of respect. Immediately the C-SPAN switchboard lit up, and the studio's fax machine started
spewing out protests and all manner of condemnation of me. C-SPAN officials told me later that no guest commentator had evoked a public reaction
to match the one my remarks about Nixon had triggered. So much for my
career on television.

Actually, a few discerning (Democratic) folks wrote me saying they were
pleased, or at least amused, to hear what I had said in contrast to the extensive revisionism about Nixon that was spoken and aired at that time. My
favorite was the observation of President Bill Clinton in his eulogy. In an obvious reference to Nixon's Watergate scandal, he intoned that a man should

not be judged by one incident in his life, but by his whole career. To that comment I could only say, Amen.

From my years as a young reporter in Washington, my clearest personal recollection of Richard Nixon is a reference to him made in 1960 at an Eisenhower press conference in the old Indian Treaty Room of the Executive Office Building. That was the famous occasion when a senior colleague asked Eisenhower what decisions of his administration Nixon had been involved in. Eisenhower paused, then said, "If you give me a week, I might think of one." The answer brought unbelieving looks throughout the room. I showed up again the next week to hear if he'd come up with any, but to my astonishment, nobody asked the question. As a junior in the press corps, I was still too intimidated to pose that one to the president of the United States, and it never occurred to me that I might raise the matter.

I didn't see much of Nixon in 1960 when he ran against John F. Kennedy and lost, or in 1964, when he made a little-recognized effort to throw a monkey wrench into Barry Goldwater's march to the Republican nomination, in the hope that the party would turn to him again.

It was early in 1966 when Nixon, at a Republican National Committee meeting in Chicago, called on all Republicans to declare a moratorium on campaigning for the 1968 presidential nomination until after the 1966 congressional elections. After the fiasco of Goldwater's rout by Lyndon Johnson in 1964 and the acrimony that followed, Nixon argued, the party had to restore harmony and unity if it was to have any chance of regaining the White House in 1968. He didn't bother to mention that such a moratorium would freeze other prospective candidates and give him time to reestablish himself as a selfless foot soldier in the GOP ranks, which he then proceeded to do. He publicly predicted that the party would make a record comeback in the fall elections, and he set out personally to see that it happened.

In late June, convinced that Nixon was positioning himself for another presidential run, I spent a week with him as he traveled the country campaigning for Republican congressional candidates. At this time, after his presidential defeat in 1960 and his failure to win the California governorship in 1962, he was widely regarded as a hopeless loser. After his infamous "last press conference" on the night of that latter defeat, in which he promised the assembled press corps, "You won't have Nixon to kick around anymore," it was taken as gospel that he was finished as a national candidate.

I barely knew Nixon, but I had some acquaintance with his press secretary and coat-carrier at the time, a young fellow named Pat Buchanan, who was part of the small Nixon entourage. The first thing I did on arriving at the Sheraton Cadillac Hotel in downtown Detroit on the appointed Sunday night was to seek him out. Pat had been an editorial writer at the *St. Louis Globe-Democrat*, a Newhouse newspaper, and he had dropped by the Washington bureau from time to time before joining Nixon. I knew him as a flaming conservative but personally a pleasant and often funny guy, not above trading wisecracks about the man he always called "The Boss." Occasionally I had shared a radio microphone with him in Washington for Station KMOX in St. Louis and later on for what was a very calm forerunner of his combative *Crossfire* program.

As I got off the elevator on Buchanan's floor, there was Nixon, waiting for a down car. I introduced myself, saying I would be following him around on his campaign swing that week. It was an awkward moment, but he smiled and we shook hands. For some reason, he felt he had to explain to me what he was doing there. "I just got in from the airport," he said. "I've just met with five or six of the boys, from what you would call the Establishment." He obviously abhorred a conversational vacuum. We discussed the week's travel schedule and when I said I hoped I would have a chance to have a conversation with him along the way he assured me we would talk one night before the trip ended. The elevator door opened, he stepped in and pushed the down button.

The next morning on the sidewalk outside the hotel, Pat reintroduced me to Nixon as four or five of us piled into his car for the day's campaigning around Michigan. Nixon said hello but little more to me, clearly wary. Sizing up the situation, I kept my trap shut all day, satisfied just to observe the great man up close. At the end of the day, he said goodnight as he headed for his hotel room and, according to another aide on the tour, former California congressman Pat Hillings, an exciting fare of milk and cookies before turning in.

It went like that through the succeeding days, Nixon nervously glancing at me out of the corner of his eye from time to time. Reporters in 1966 were not exactly breaking doors down to cover a two-time loser, and I was able to sit in on all breakfast, lunch, and dinner meetings at which he spoke, as well as press conferences and hurried conversations with local pols shuttled in and out of his car from airport to hotel and back again. On the small private planes used from city to city, I sat just behind him as he worked and reworked his speeches on a yellow legal pad, leaving off occasionally to read the sports pages of local newspapers. He was, as often reported, an extremely disciplined man.

In his many press conferences along the way as we went south to Alabama, west to Oklahoma, and finally winding up in Roanoke, Virginia, Nixon was ever cautious behind an overdone cordiality. I remember that at the first such encounter, at Cobo Hall in Detroit, where he was to address a convention of the U.S. Junior Chamber of Commerce, he was all smiles and apologies for being late. He shook hands with the reporters in the first row, much to their surprise, saying, "I'm sorry I held you up. I understand we had a camera crew late. . . . It wasn't my fault." He apologized again for not having a printed text of his remarks: "You'll have to cover me live. I'm not equipped with staff [to prepare] texts."

When Nixon wasn't being cordially apologetic, he was busy reassuring his listeners that he was a man motivated only by a desire to resurrect his party, not himself. He turned away all questions about his own future, insisting he would abide by his own call for a moratorium on presidential politics until the November congressional elections. "You can't make up the winter book on the presidency," sports enthusiast Nixon would say, "until you get past the 1966 elections." He would point out that he had no political staff, adding, "if I were concerned only about 1968, why would I be making three fund-raising speeches in Michigan?" Why, indeed?

After each press conference, Nixon would go out and make a speech of half an hour or more, a panoramic lecture on the domestic and world scene with nary a note. His grasp of the subject would always wow the crowd, but first he would play the stand-up comic, showing that for all the bad press he had received in the past about being a cutthroat political hatchetman, he was really a good guy with a great, self-deprecating sense of humor. He was, he would tell the audience, "a dropout from the electoral college." He would stop to let photographers arrayed in front of him do their work. "I want to be sure these people get their pictures," he would say, pausing. Then, "I've had trouble with pictures." Another pause. "I've had trouble with television, too."

When the laughter died down, he would continue in the same vein: "A little girl came up to me on the street in New York the other day with a copy of *Newsweek* opened to a picture of me, and asked me to autograph it. I did, and then she said, 'Mr. Nixon, that's a wonderful picture. . . . It doesn't look at all like you.'" He could tell this story a hundred times and still, after each time, throw his head back with his eyes wide, as if he himself was hearing it for the first time, then grinning happily.

There was always a snappy review of his world travels, including the recollection that "I got stoned in Caracas. I'll tell you one thing, it's a lot different from getting stoned at a [providing the name of the host organization] convention!" But it was the serious, experienced Richard Nixon that sold best with his audiences. His speech always included a seminar on Vietnam, "a war that had to be fought to prevent World War III," and a rallying cry for the Republican Party, which he was selflessly continuing to serve. After the Goldwater debacle, he predicted, a Republican tide would sweep the country in the 1966 congressional elections, because the Democrats were in disarray over the war. But the Republicans would have a chance to regain the White House in 1968 only if they rebuilt their own party in 1966.

In smaller party fund-raising receptions, Nixon was more intimate and confiding of political strategy with the insiders. He always liked to make them feel that they were getting a special peek into the expert political mind he possessed. At such affairs he was the performer and others pitched for money, often without guile. At the home of a big Oklahoma oil man in Tulsa, for example, the host stood on a chair on his crowded patio and instructed: "This is real low pressure. We don't want anybody to give more than five thousand dollars—that's the limit. As you go [inside] you'll see some blank checkbooks. Just think now of what you want to give and then write it right out, while you still have a chance. You may not get the chance again." The guests chuckled, and Nixon with them.

Each night after the final speech, Pat Hillings and I, not being addicted to milk and cookies, went down to the hotel bar or elsewhere in the environs where one could find a drink. Hillings told me later that each morning Nixon would get him aside and ask: "What does he want? What's he going to write about me?" But that was only for openers. After a day or two, the questions became more personal: "Where did you go last night? Did you pick up any girls? Did you score?" Hillings got a big kick out of it. "He lives vicariously," he told me one day after one of the Nixonian interrogations. "He doesn't have the nerve to do anything himself, but he likes to hear about it." Unfortunately, Hillings had little of a titillating nature to report, but that didn't stop Nixon from asking him every morning.

As the week wore on, I got nervous. Nixon's distance made me fear I would never get an interview—essential to the long story I had been assigned to do beyond daily reports. But Buchanan kept reassuring me: "Don't worry, he'll talk to you. Just be patient." So I continued being a fly on the wall, sharing cars and airplanes with Nixon and his aides as he diligently pitched Republican House candidates.

He didn't exactly snub me; it was more that my presence seemed to make him uncomfortable. It wasn't the Nixon hostility toward reporters that had flared up in the 1962 "last press conference" and later was revealed in spades in the Watergate tapes. On this trip he was always courteous to me and other reporters encountered along the way. One morning in Birmingham, Alabama, because of a scheduling mix-up, I had to hail a taxi and race to the airport, fearing I had missed the Nixon plane. When I arrived, I saw it sitting out on the runway. It was a sleek six-seat Lear jet loaned to Nixon by Bill Lear, the World War II aviation electronics pioneer. I got a ride out and scrambled aboard, mortified to see Nixon sitting patiently in his regular seat. I apologized profusely for holding him up, but he waved me off and kindly changed the subject. I was impressed with his generosity, and told Hillings so. He smiled and told me: "The rest of us wanted to take off without you, but he said, 'No, he's the only reporter we've got.'"

The last stop on the tour was Roanoke, for a speech at the Virginia Republicans' state convention. After it was over, we headed for the airport and the final leg, back to Washington, and still I hadn't had my interview with Nixon. The Lear jet was gone and in its place was a tired-looking old propeller-driven Beechcraft. Besides Nixon and myself, the only other passengers were Hillings and John Whitaker, a Washington advance man. Hillings sat in the back with Nixon and I took a seat up front. Well, I thought, there goes my interview, after a week of waiting.

The ancient plane rumbled and groaned down the runway and took off. As soon as it leveled off, Hillings came forward and motioned me back to a seat next to Nixon. He greeted me in a relaxed way, apologizing for not having had a chance to talk with me sooner. Whitaker broke out a bottle of scotch and some ice and we had a drink all around. The plane's engine was so noisy I was afraid no one could be heard over the drone, but Nixon talked over it in a strong voice, showing no hesitation except declining to discuss his own political future. He was still the party soldier toiling selflessly in the trenches.

Surprisingly, what came out over the next hour, captured on tape, was a self-appraisal that was remarkable in a man who had a reputation for guardedness about himself. It was surprising mostly, however, because the picture he painted of himself was greatly at variance with the Richard Nixon of his public reputation—as a pure political tactician, almost an anti-intellectual, and a hater of the press. One might have thought, in fact, that it was Adlai Stevenson talking:

> I wish I had more time to read and write. I'm known as an activist and an organizer, but some people [not identified] have said I'm sort of an egghead in the Republican Party. I don't write as well as Stevenson, but I work at it. If I had my druthers, I'd like to write two or three books a year, go to one of the fine schools—Oxford, for instance—just teach, read, and write. I'd like to do that better than what I'm doing now. I don't mean writing is easy for me, but writing phrases that move people, that to me is something.... My best efforts—my acceptance speech in 1960, my Moscow speech, my unity speech at the 1964 convention—all were dredged out by writing my head off.

Presidents today, Nixon argued, are kept so busy doing things that

> others have to do their thinking for them.... The president should have the luxury of several days just to think.... The danger today is that the American executive submits things to his highest advisers and then decides on the basis of what they tell him. In order to make a decision, an individual should sit on his rear end and dig into the books.... In this respect I'm like Stevenson. He was criticized as governor of Illinois because he always wanted to do his own work and research. Stevenson was a century late. He would have been more at home in the nineteenth century. He was an intellectual and he needed time to contemplate.

This self-comparison with Stevenson surely would have astonished the two-time Democratic presidential nominee, not to mention appalled him. Stevenson's revulsion from Nixon was well illustrated in a television talk he made on the eve of the 1956 election. "I must say bluntly," this normally temperate man warned, "that every piece of scientific evidence we have, every lesson of history and experience, indicates that a Republican victory tomorrow would mean that Richard Nixon would probably be president within the next four years. I say frankly as a citizen more than a candidate that I recoil at the prospect of Mr. Nixon as custodian of this nation's future, as guardian of the hydrogen bomb, as representative of America in the world, as commander-in-chief of the United States armed forces."

Nixon also insisted that he was unconcerned about the image he project-ed—in the face of much evidence that he was obsessed with what people thought of him. "I believe in never being affected by reports about me," he said. "I may read some selected clippings a week or so later, when somebody sends them to me, but never the next morning. I never look at myself on TV either. I don't want to develop those phony, self-conscious contrived things."

But on the trip that was just winding down, he seemed repeatedly unnat-ural and self-conscious, smiling at inappropriate moments, gesturing with his arms awkwardly as if he were somehow out of sync. He was always on guard for a trick question and careful not to give offense.

Regarding his well-known combat with the press, Nixon professed that his loss in the California gubernatorial race and that "last press conference" in 1962 had been a blessing in disguise for him. "The press had a guilt com-plex about their inaccuracy," he told me. "Since then, they've been generally accurate and far more respectful." Astonishingly, he said, "I like the press guys, because I'm basically like them, because of my own inquisitiveness." This answer strained my ability to keep a straight face, but somehow I man-aged.

The old Beechcraft by now was coming in for a landing at Washington National Airport over and past the White House, the occupancy of which Nixon was insisting was the farthest thing from his mind right then. He glanced at the Washington Monument, basking in spotlights, put down his drink, shook hands, and was off into the night, leaving me with much food for thought about this complicated and mysterious man who saw himself so differently from the way many others did.

That trip turned out to be an integral early part in a remarkable political comeback for the Republican Party for which he toiled that summer and fall, and for himself. Helped by President Lyndon Johnson, who singled him out as a partisan campaigner playing politics with Vietnam "in the hope that he can pick up a precinct or two, or a ward or two," Nixon suddenly found himself identified as Mr. Republican again. When the GOP fulfilled his pre-diction in gaining forty House seats, three in the Senate, six governorships, and 540 state legislative seats in November, he was widely credited as the chief architect of that victory. Two out of every three candidates for whom he campaigned won.

The trip yielded not only that exclusive interview but an assignment from the *Saturday Evening Post* to write a piece about Nixon's prospects for another presidential run in 1968. This assignment opened the door for a follow-up interview with him at his roomy, well-appointed apartment on Park Avenue in New York in which he offered further surprising revelations about how he saw himself. But he still displayed that same old trait of insisting he was a totally unstaged politician—while bending over backward to present himself in the best light. A photographer accompanied me to the apartment; we found Nixon dressed in jacket and tie, seated in a comfortable leather lounge chair, feet up on a matching ottoman, reading a book.

As the photographer made his preparations, Nixon launched again into a monologue about how much he loved to read, particularly histories of great men. He had one such book in his hands and held it as he was photographed. Later, when the photographer showed me some contact prints of his work, there was Nixon reading the book, which on close observation he was holding upside down.

Two days after the 1966 election, he and Mrs. Nixon left New York for a Florida vacation. Although he was still observing his no-presidential-politics moratorium, with the intercession of Pat Buchanan he agreed to let me ride out to La Guardia Airport to discuss the outcome of the off-year elections that he had predicted so accurately, his observations to be included in the magazine piece. Johnson's attack on him, he told me, was what had swung the elections so heavily for the GOP. "He played into our hands," he said, "by hitting us on the one issue he should have left alone—Vietnam. . . . I couldn't believe it. It was too good to be true. I disagree with Johnson," he said, "but I have great respect for his political skill. But you never build up a major spokesman on the other side. In my view, controversy builds up, not tears down. That's standard rule. There's an old saying: 'Never strike a king unless you kill him.' In politics, you don't hit your opponent unless you knock him out."

That ride to La Guardia with Dick and Pat Nixon, Buchanan told me much later, was instrumental in his voluntarily ending his own career as a press secretary. Adhering to Nixon's moratorium on politics, he had turned away repeated requests from my friend and colleague, David Broder, for an interview with Nixon. When Dave saw my piece in the magazine and it was clear I had talked to Nixon about presidential politics, Buchanan said, he hit the roof. "That did it," he told me. "I didn't want any more of that and I asked Nixon for another job." He eventually got it, became a policy adviser in the Nixon administration and, eventually, a presidential candidate himself.

The *Saturday Evening Post* article at the end of 1966 was the first in a major publication to treat seriously the notion of a Nixon presidential come- back. Thereafter he seemed to regard me without hostility but still with some wariness, as indeed he acted toward most other members of the repor- torial tribe. I saw him only occasionally over the next year, as he remained coy about his political intentions, and as conventional wisdom continued to dismiss him as a loser who might be able to help his party but whose own future was past.

Those experiences with Nixon, however, convinced me that he remained a politician to watch as the next presidential election approached. My opportunities to view that race from a front-row seat in the press section increased as I became the Newhouse man on national politics. The exposure to Nixon I now had under my belt would stand me in good stead, as he would soon openly abandon that deceptive, self-imposed moratorium on campaigning in his own behalf and set himself eventually on a comeback bid for the Oval Office once again.

The next time I encountered him up close for an extended period of time was in early February of 1968, when he dropped all pretense and threw his hat into the ring for the Republican nomination.

He made the announcement in an unorthodox way, by sending letters to all New Hampshire voters in advance of a formal declaration in a Man- chester Holiday Inn. In the question-and-answer period, it was as if that 1962 "last press conference" had never occurred. There he was, smiling and affable, responding to reporters' inquiries with the old self-assurance. As if to underscore that here was a New Nixon, he even held a small press party that night at the old Highway Hotel in Concord. Drink in hand, he circulat- ed among us, making small talk in a friendly way. At one point, he jumped onto a chair for a few informal remarks.

It had been a cold and windy day, and as was his wont, he assured his old adversaries that he hadn't ordered it up. It reminded him, he said, of a visit he had made as vice president to Morocco, which had been suffering from a severe drought. As he arrived, he said, the heavens opened with an onslaught of much-needed rain, and that night at the state dinner he was toasted as "the man with green feet," meaning, a translator told him, "Wherever you walk, grass grows."

Later that night, after Nixon had retired, several of us retired ourselves— to the hotel bar—and wrote an appropriate ditty to commemorate the rare overture from the man we had the chance to kick around again after all. To the tune of "The Wearing of the Green," the first stanza went:

Oh, your name is Richard Nixon, you're the newest ever seen,
You're speaking on the issues, but your feet have turned to green.
You're the party's elder statesman, there's no place you haven't been,
But who will buy a used car from a man with feet of green?

There was no more than the customary malice in the exercise, and I, at least, came away from the evening's merriment thinking that Nixon's gesture might be ushering in a new era of good feeling between the candidate and our traveling fraternity on the campaign trail. I based the hope on Nixon's promise in his remarks that he was going to run an open campaign, with more access and candor in dealing with the press than perhaps he had offered in the combative past. After all, he was making a new start in presidential campaigning and the old way had not served him particularly well.

The very next morning, though, my illusions went into the trash can with word upon my awakening that while we scribblers had slept in, Nixon, Buchanan and other aides had risen early and slipped out of the hotel for a "town meeting" of select New Hampshire supporters. In a carefully pre-packaged exercise, they posed softball questions that Nixon answered for the benefit of a hired camera crew, the exchanges to be used in a Nixon commercial. We reporters were not informed in advance so we could cover the event, Buchanan said, because it was feared that the town meeting participants would feel "inhibited" by the presence of reporters. We weren't notified "so that people would feel at ease." So much for the new open campaign—and the new Nixon.

Through the rest of 1968, the Nixon campaign proceeded pretty much that way—proclaiming a new accessibility and a new candor while remaining under extremely tight control. Meanwhile, events fell into place for him. Romney could never get off the ground in New Hampshire and dropped out even before the primary; Rockefeller vacillated and never posed a serious challenge; Johnson, embarrassed by McCarthy in New Hampshire and faced with an additional challenge from Robert Kennedy, decided not to seek reelection. Nixon sharply limited his public appearances, and almost always they were carefully orchestrated. Spontaneity was the enemy, as were frequent press conferences. One exception was a promise Nixon had made that night of the press party. He said those of us who represented specific local newspapers would be granted exclusive interviews when the primary campaign calendar brought us into one of our base cities or states, and he kept the promise.

I was still working in the Washington bureau of the Newhouse Newspapers, one of which was the *Portland Oregonian*. Thus, when the campaign trail wended into Oregon, it was my turn. I knew by now how the interview would probably go. There would be a minimum of idle chatter, Nixon would be serious, and time would be limited. Therefore, the night before, in my room at the Benson Hotel, I sat down and wrote the questions I wanted to ask. And knowing the precise and logical way Nixon's mind worked, I prepared the topics in logical sequence, so that I would not waste time in posing the questions, leaving most of the time for his answers.

At the appointed hour, I was ushered into his Benson suite by Dwight Chapin, one of his young coat-carrying aides, much later a figure in the Watergate scandal. Nixon walked over and shook hands, gesturing for me to take a seat on a sofa while he settled into an armchair, propping his feet up on a coffee table. As usual, he was dressed in jacket and tie. After just a few words of casual conversation, my written questions on a pad on my lap, I launched into the first of them. He answered it in detail and, without my asking, answered the second, which grew out of the first. Then he answered the third and fourth. He was not a man to leave loose ends, and before I knew it he had touched on most of my questions in a logical monologue.

As he provided this free-flowing panorama, I could not help but smile, and when he caught me, he seemed a bit unnerved. Recognizing his reaction, I tried to make light of what was going on. "Mr. Nixon," I said, "I believe you've peeked at my notes. I've written down my questions and you've answered most of them already." When I said that, he stopped and frowned. "Oh, no," he said with all sincerity, "I wouldn't do that." Realizing that he was taking my joke seriously, I quickly assured him it was only that. He had a moment of embarrassment for not having caught on, then he laughed awkwardly and the interview went on to its orderly and logical conclusion.

The most revealing aspect of the interview was the manner in which he volunteered, in spite of his frequent self-description as a fatalist who never wasted time revisiting the past and accepted what the future might bring, that he had scrupulously dissected his past failures in setting his current course. "Haunting this campaign," he admitted, "is the specter of 1960. . . . One-half of one percent made the difference." That meant, he said, he had to have better people, not be "saddled with first-rate second raters," his description of the Eisenhower administration team involved in his first presidential run. While saying that the 1968 campaign was proving to be too fluid for firm planning—citing the Romney collapse, Rockefeller's foot-dragging, and Lyndon Johnson's withdrawal—he said that the primaries had enabled him to test his organization and his campaign techniques.

"In 1960, there was a frenetic quality about my campaign," he acknowledged. "Promising to go into all fifty states. We aren't going to make that mistake again. I've learned that the candidate should take time to think. Every three weeks I go to Florida for a few days. That's how I keep the tan." By now, in May, it gave him a healthy, bronzed glow. "I take some of the boys with me," he went on, "and we mix it; on the beach for a while, and then hours of going over ideas." By this stage of the campaign, Nixon had no serious challenge in sight for the nomination, and the best strategy was to say as little as he could get away with. One of "the boys," John Sears, told me later, "We kept going back to Florida mainly so he could keep that tan."

One thing he had learned from his failed 1960 campaign, Nixon told me, was that in the developing television era, what he said on the stump was less important than what he said, and how he looked, on television. "In 1950, I felt the big speech was the most important," he said, "and I had to be up for it." Meeting with politicians, holding press conferences, and being on television came next in that order then, he said. "Now we've reversed the order. Now television and the press conferences are the most important, and that's why I won't do them on the run." That last was true enough. His press conferences and television appearances were now few and far between, and always very carefully staged, to avoid any careless missteps.

With the party's national convention approaching, Nixon said, he was going to continue going to Florida for a few days every two or three weeks to rest and do some heavy reading. Again he painted himself as a big thinker, lest anybody think otherwise. "I'm basically more of an intellectual than I ought to be." And what would he be reading, I asked? "No politics. No mysteries either. Some good philosophy that makes the mind work."

How his mind worked had always fascinated me, and no less after this interview. It was certainly logical and orderly, there could be no doubt of that after the way he had "stolen" my questions. But his penchant for protesting too much that he was a man of the mind more than a political tactician always screamed to me of a self-sense of inadequacy. He seemed driven to convey that he was no mere political hack, that he was a genuine "intellectual" of the Adlai Stevenson stripe—a man he had often demeaned in campaign speeches, but about whom he seemed to have a galloping inferiority complex.

Once Nixon was nominated, I saw him during the general election campaign against Hubert Humphrey only from a distance, at numerous campaign rallies and speeches. But these too were often very revealing about the way his mind worked. My favorite peek into it was the opening of a speech he made in a huge university gym on the night before the Oregon primary, which he won easily against only token opposition. He always cast himself as the principal player in a great drama, citing some special milestone, and on this night he observed that "in this final event of the Oregon primary"—and then he paused for a long moment before adding—"as far as nighttime events are concerned." He obviously remembered that there also was a breakfast meeting and speech scheduled for the next morning, and he didn't want to leave that loose end hanging. We in the press section chuckled at this mental tidiness.

My next personal encounter with Nixon was not until after his election, when I was covering his transition, being run from the plush Pierre Hotel in New York. Each day he would come down to the lobby to make announcements to the press about the formation of his cabinet. It so happened that a book I had just written about Robert Kennedy's 1968 presidential campaign was being published and the publisher pressed me to give Nixon a copy, in the obvious hope that he would make a favorable comment. I felt compromised by doing so but finally relented, putting the book in a plain manila envelope and slipping it to him as inconspicuously as I could as he was getting back on the hotel elevator after his afternoon briefing. I expected that he would tuck it under his arm or hand it to an aide, but instead he pulled it out of the envelope and waved it at the battery of photographers catching his every movement, as news photographers are wont to do. I was mortified but my publisher was elated, especially a day or two later when photographers were admitted to the Nixon suite to take pictures of where the great man was doing his heavy thinking about the new administration. There on his desk, in a prominent position, was my book, its presence generating some mentions in stories about what he was currently reading.

It may have been mere happenstance, but an aide told me later that it had been placed there intentionally on Nixon's instruction. If so, it was another gesture of the sort that had resulted in that jet on the Birmingham runway being held, waiting for the one tardy reporter covering him at the time. For all the shortcomings I perceived in the man over the years, I recognized that tendency for the generous impulse—or was that, too, calculated? With Nixon, you always found yourself wondering.

Weeks later, I had my last personal exposure to him before he was swallowed up into the cocoon of the presidency, and then later into his California exile after Watergate. When the Nixon family went to Florida for the Christmas holidays, reporters covering him took a charter plane ahead of him with our families, the plane landing at Homestead Air Force Base outside Miami. When his plane landed, a crowd had gathered and he walked to the fence and shook hands of well-wishers. Then, seeing the gathering of reporters standing to one side with our families, he came over and greeted us. When he shook the hand of my then-eight-year-old daughter, Amy, he was for the moment speechless. She looked back at him, also speechless. The awkward silence went on until at last he blurted out: "I guess you're glad I got elected president, so you could come to Florida for Christmas!" She just kept looking at him and he walked away. "Gee," she said in her eight-year-old perceptiveness, "he was embarrassed, wasn't he? He didn't know what to say to me."

It was incidents like these of which I was thinking years later in that C-SPAN interview that earned me a reputation as an insensitive slug for talking about Nixon's brain as he lay in state in California. Although I will say in all candor that I thoroughly disliked Richard Nixon for his behavior as a public man, from the time he was elected to the House of Representatives through his dark years as a political hatchetman and later as a corrupter of the political process itself when president, I did find him to be the most fascinating character study in politics in my fifty-plus years as an observer of public figures. I was not, obviously, an intimate of the man, but I did see enough of him during a critical period of his life to see in him the stuff of both high drama and comedy.

In his last years, the new stories about his political excesses that surfaced with each release of more Watergate tapes always inspired me to write more columns about him. My eventual colleague at the *Washington Post*, Bob Woodward, liked to call the tapes "the gift that keeps on giving." One day, an amateur cartoon came to my office showing a vampire-like Nixon rising out of a coffin as my column partner, Jack Germond, and I stood behind a crucifix for protection. Nixon seemed like that to me; each time a stake was driven through his political heart by new Watergate revelations, he managed to rise again and plague American politics with remembrance of his callous and foul behavior. I look back at times with disgust and anger, but I also see him as a pathetic figure, hounded by dark impulses and fears.

6 Reserved Seat on the Bus

ALTHOUGH I HAD COVERED parts of the previous four presidential campaigns, it was not until late 1966 that I got involved in the full cycle, which at that time started more than a year out from the election year itself. The Vietnam war by then had become the centerpiece of all American politics, with increasing questions about President Johnson's vulnerability as he approached what nearly everyone expected would be his vigorous bid for reelection.

At a National Governors Conference at the Greenbriar resort in White Sulphur Springs, West Virginia, Democratic governors got together and aired their gripes about LBJ so loudly that we reporters, hanging around outside their supposedly closed meeting, got an earful. When the governors came out, they were still so steamed about their party's leader over a variety of matters, from his failure to consult them on aspects of his Great Society proposals to his conduct of the Vietnam war, that they repeated their complaints to us on the record. It made a terrific story.

In an effort to gauge the degree of public disenchantment with LBJ, I made three trips that year, one to Canada to talk with young Americans who had fled there to escape the draft and two others, to Kentucky and Connecticut, past areas of strongest rural and urban support for the president. The draft evaders, obviously, had no love for Johnson, but the disaffection was clearly discernible as well among strongly Democratic voters in the two states.

With LBJ's 1968 renomination taken for granted, however, most political attention in 1967 turned to the competition in the Republican Party to be his challenger. I therefore spent much time going to GOP meetings and talking with party leaders, whose speculation centered on three men: George Romney, Richard Nixon, and Nelson Rockefeller. Nixon continued to say he was honoring his self-imposed moratorium on presidential politics and Rockefeller kept insisting he wasn't interested. But Romney, fresh from his solid reelection in 1966, was now openly assessing his presidential prospects. A Harris Survey right after the election indicated he was the only Republican who at that point would beat Johnson. Rockefeller, true to his word, urged Romney to go after the GOP nomination, and the Rockefeller family reportedly gave him $300,000 to get going.

In February of 1967, Romney's quest took him on a well-publicized trip to Alaska and down into the Rocky Mountain states, stronghold of his Mormon religion, hoping the jaunt would demonstrate his readiness to make a presidential bid. By now, the great literary success of Teddy White's *The Making of the President 1960* and its 1964 sequel had convinced newspaper editors with national political writers on their staffs that chronicling what we called the "inside baseball" of presidential campaigns should not be left to book writers.

About forty of us—most of the regulars on the national political beat and some others—signed on for the Romney trip, on the assumption that we were, or might be, getting in on the ground floor of the next making of the president. If not, we would surely be in position to answer the burning political question of the day: was George Romney, for all his energy and evangelical zeal, really up to being president? His early indecision about running and unwillingness to take a clear stand on the Vietnam war raised questions about his political savvy and intellectual smarts. So the pack set out to discover: Was the Rambler Man a lightweight, an empty suit?

From the very outset, we knew we were onto one of the most hilarious such junkets ever. Romney and his wife, Lenore, as devout Mormons, did not drink, and so they were scandalized by their traveling press companions on the very first leg of the journey, a Northwest Airlines commercial flight from Detroit to Seattle and on to Anchorage. The stewardesses on the plane were, to say the least, lax in holding to the two-drinks-a-customer airline rule, and in short order there was unabashed raucous singing and other revelry in the press section. It continued more or less unabated for the six days of the tour from Alaska to Idaho, Utah, New Mexico, and Arizona, by plane and chartered bus. In Alaska, the situation was not alleviated by the fact that the Anchorage bars stayed open until 4 a.m. and reopened at 6 a.m. Not all of our party availed themselves of this liberal policy, but enough did to keep the campaign entourage well-oiled throughout.

Romney kicked off his speaking tour at a fund-raising dinner for a Republican congressman who happened to have only one arm. In attacking Lyndon Johnson, Romney brought gasps from the partisan crowd, and guffaws from the press section, when he offered that LBJ was as effective "as a one-armed paper hanger." Romney was equally adept in ridiculing himself. In his boyhood hometown of Rexburg, Idaho, he regaled the students at Ricks Junior College with how he once had concluded a harrowing drive of a harvesting machine by crashing into a fence. "As you can see," he said, "I was really a stupid kid." As the students roared in appreciation of his candor, he added: "The national press here won't think these mistakes are unusual for me."

As a goody two-shoes, Romney's sense of the naughty ran mildly to the scatological. His idea of a big Halloween night in his youth, he reported, was tipping over "those little buildings out back." One morning on his charter plane he got on the intercom to explain he was so sleepy because he had to get up in the night to go to the bathroom and couldn't get back to sleep "because the toilet wouldn't stop flushing."

The preference seemed to be a family affliction. Lenore liked to tell dinner audiences that the life of a governor's wife was not all roses. "One day when our children were small," she would say, "something went wrong with the bathroom plumbing, so I called a man in. He adjusted a few pipes and gave me a bill for twenty dollars [remember, this was in 1967]. 'Twenty dollars?' I said. 'For two minutes work?' And he said to me, 'Lady, you ought to see where I have to put my hands.' Well, I led him right up to the nursery and over to the diaper pail. I opened it and said, 'See where I have to put my hands?'"

Romney himself was forever putting his foot in his mouth—hardly a recommendation for the presidency. In Pocatello, Idaho, after a rather noncommital introduction by conservative Republican Governor Don Samuelson, Romney seemed at a loss over how to reply. With their spouses sitting there, Romney finally blurted out that he and Samuelson "share a common asset—our wives."

Samuelson himself was not very quick on the uptake. At a joint news conference with the visiting governor of Michigan, Warren Weaver of the *New*

York Times in all seriousness asked him how he would assess Romney's chances for the presidency. Samuelson thought for a moment, then said, "Well, I'd stand on the street corner and as people came along I'd ask them about it." Thereafter we referred to him among ourselves as "Sam Dumbuelson."

More than such silly episodes, however, Romney's presidential aspirations were tarnished by his repeated inability or unwillingness to express his position toward the Vietnam war policy in lucid and decisive terms. He accused LBJ of "political expedience" but refused to provide any example, and he wound up his "exploratory" tour with his presidential aspirations considerably tarnished. One of his chief political lieutenants, Walter deVries, lamented the decision to bring the press along. "We wanted this to be off-Broadway," he told us on the plane one night near the end. "You take your soundings, and if your staff makes some mistakes or your candidate makes some mistakes, you correct them. Well, it's off-Broadway, but we've flown the critics in with us." Romney himself blamed it all on what he called "the Teddy White Syndrome," having a gang of reporters delving so deeply into the inner workings—and missteps—of campaign operations.

When Theodore H. White in 1960 got his nose under the tent of John Kennedy's campaign, he discovered a tremendously dramatic and interesting story involving other campaign figures and inside strategies, which he deftly told in the first of his highly successful "Making of the President" series. In presidential campaigns that followed, newspaper editors began demanding that their reporters do the same, on a daily basis. Many responded by bringing readers into hotel rooms and campaign headquarters by recreating critical meetings, though often concentrating on obscure details that lent intimacy or titillation but did not necessarily shed great light. Before long, not only the candidates but also heretofore obscure functionaries around them were undergoing more personal scrutiny and, thanks to television, achieving celebrity in the process. The intensified scrutiny certainly did raise the credibility bar, not only for Romney, but also for candidates thereafter. At the same time, however, many of them became more adept at finessing their shortcomings and controlling press access.

The Romney campaign that summer again invited the national political press corps to join him, this time on a tour of the nation's troubled cities, ostensibly to give him greater familiarity with the problems of urban America. First, however, he held a weekend party for the newsgatherers at

Michigan's Mackinac Island that was obviously designed to improve his relations with us. It turned out to be a journalistic version of a collegiate food fight, and although the Romneys were teetotalers, the booze flowed in the fashion of a Saturday night at a frat house. We reporters were billeted in the homes of Romney supporters on the island and, to the hosts' dismay, there was no curfew; the drinking and horseplay went on almost until dawn. One colleague who shall remain nameless was found fast asleep on the only seat in the guest bathroom and was aroused to resume the festivities. Others slumbered on lawns of the sedate community that so cherished peace and quiet that automobiles were barred and horses and buggies were the only permitted transportation.

During the Mackinac weekend, Romney gave out prizes of limited appeal, such as joining his foursome at golf—a particular torture. If nothing else, the comical interlude prepared the Romneys for the rigors of his urban tour. Over twenty days in September, they visited slum and ghetto sections in seventeen cities from coast to coast, starting in Detroit, west to Los Angeles and on to New York and Pittsburgh. Romney's aides billed the trip as fact-finding and nonpolitical, but the presence of the press corps assured daily coverage of a presidential aspirant working hard to learn about one of the major challenges he would face if he were to win.

In part the tour was an acknowledgment of how little he knew about inner-city life and inhabitants, and we reporters had trouble finding fresh daily copy, except on rare occasions. In Chicago, Romney was treated to a rough interrogation by militant blacks about racial exclusion in his Mormon church. In San Francisco, the Romneys had their street vernacular broadened in a "meditation" with Haight-Ashbury hippies and sandal-clad love children that we found hilarious as red-faced George and Lenore squirmed. When they asked him passionately what he intended to do about Vietnam, he offered to send them all copies of a speech he'd made some months before. Clearly, he did not lock up the hippy vote that day, but at least he gave us an amusing story to write.

My colleague and friend Jon Lowell, then of the *Detroit News*, summed up our dilemma one afternoon late in the tour as the Romney plane came in over New York City, the site of a then-popular television series based on stories of its inhabitants. Mimicking the announcer's weekly closing observation, Jon proclaimed as he gazed out the window: "There are eight million stories in *The Naked City*, and we're covering the dullest!"

But then the man whose story we were following stumbled decisively. Later that summer, referring to an earlier trip to Southeast Asia, Romney carelessly observed in a Detroit radio interview: "When I came back from Vietnam I just had the greatest brainwashing that anybody can get when you go over to Vietnam. Not only by the generals, but also by the diplomatic corps over there, and they did a very thorough job." The off-hand comment, heard in the context of his flip-flopping on what U.S. policy should be there, put his campaign into a free-fall he never was able to break.

The remark inspired Senator Eugene McCarthy to quip that with Romney, rather than a brainwashing, "I would have thought a light rinse would have done it." The gaffe also inspired us watchdogs on the press bus to write a song for him, to the tune of "Something Stupid," a tune in vogue at the time and sung by Frank and Nancy Sinatra:

> I know I stood ahead of all until I went and dropped the ball
> By talking too much.
> I tried so hard to satisfy the press request to clarify
> Vietnam and such.
> And then I went out in the cold to try to get a little vote or two,
> I had to go and spoil it all by saying something stupid like
> I'm brainwashed.

Romney's radio comment, and the public reaction to it, while Rockefeller stayed on the sidelines, probably did as much as anything to spur an eventual reassessment of the chances of my old traveling companion, Dick Nixon, to make a comeback. At the same time, speculation continued, especially in New York, that Rockefeller still coveted the White House himself and was using Romney as a stalking horse. One day, riding with Rocky in his limousine through the rush-hour streets of Fun City, I pressed him again on his interest and availability. "I can just tell you that under no circumstance will I be a candidate," he insisted, "and I will not go into any primary." He said it without irritation, but rather with resignation. Well, I pressed on, what if all others—meaning Romney—fell by the wayside? "I frankly feel that what you say is an impossibility," he answered. "I'm just not going to knock myself out thinking about it." Why then, I pursued, was his name still being mentioned? "I'll be darned if I know," he said. "All I know is these people weren't speaking out that way last time, when I was working like hell for it."

Meanwhile, one other Republican star was rising in California—newly elected governor Ronald Reagan, the old movie star who had mesmerized the Republican right wing in 1964 with a dazzling speech in behalf of Barry Goldwater. In the two years following, he had diligently worked what he called "the rubber chicken and mashed potatoes circuit" and was becoming the darling of GOP conservatism. Only two months after he'd taken office in Sacramento, I had called on him and inquired whether he had presidential ambitions—at a time when many people were still having trouble picturing him as a real live, functioning governor.

Ever genial and with an air of disbelief that his questioner could be serious, he went only so far as to say, "I'll probably be a favorite son, but only to maintain the unity in the state we have now, and to assure California a proper voice in the convention." He vowed he would do "anything I can" to discourage anyone's placing his name in the 1968 presidential primaries, but "how can I claim to be a favorite-son candidate in my own state and then turn around and say I'm not a candidate?"

That was enough, however, to keep him in the 1968 speculation, even as he was just getting his feet wet in the job of governor. The star quality he brought to the office retained its luster all that year, best illustrated at the Western Governors Conference in West Yellowstone, Montana. He breezed in flashing his famous grin, sporting a light tan western jacket and jeans, cowboy shirt and boots, and signing autographs for gaping tourists. A Republican colleague of distinctly more liberal bent, Tom McCall of Washington State, after watching Reagan work the crowd, observed: "It was like an operetta. All the lights go on and the great white charger comes in. There are just plain old governors, and then there's Reagan."

McCall, however, shared the view that the new California governor needed a little political seasoning before reaching for the White House. "We're going on the strength of charisma and lovability," he told me, "which begs the question of whether he knows what to do when he gets to the White House." Reagan would be better off, he said, passing up 1968 "just to get a little training," and "if he's around in 1972, he deserves a shot at it." That seemed to be Reagan's timetable as well, but as matters worked out on the Republican side and as President Johnson seemed increasingly vulnerable, Reagan would eventually show a bit more interest as the 1968 GOP convention approached.

In the fall of 1967, I went along as he made a sentimental journey to his alma mater, Eureka College in Illinois, and also to Milwaukee and Columbia, South Carolina. The trip, as I wrote then,

> stirred strong memories of the quixotic days of Goldwater's disastrous 1964 campaign.... Although it is easy to write Reagan off as a naïve movie actor, any exposure to him establishes that he is much better in making Goldwater's case than the candid but fumbling Arizona senator ever was three years ago. Not only is he handsomer than Goldwater, he is shrewder in politically dangerous give-and-take press conferences, and his benign appearance and manner give a veneer to strong views that sounded like madness coming from Barry. He can talk about sealing off or destroying the North Vietnamese port of Haiphong ... in a tone of voice suggesting it would amount to no more than temporarily closing a lane of highway traffic for repairs.

If that reads like a self-promoting advertisement for a clairvoyant's certificate, let me add that shortly after this Reagan swing I wrote the following: "Though the 56-year-old Ronald Reagan flashes his most modest grin and disavows interest when asked about presidential ambitions, there is little doubt that he has his eye on the White House and that 1968 is probably now or never for him. If he waited until 1972 he would be 61 years old in an era looking to younger men, and there is also the possibility he might not be governor of California at the time." So much for my crystal ball.

Around the same time, the nation's governors were preparing for their annual conference. In the year before a presidential election especially, such meetings are always magnets for political writers. But no further inducement for attending was necessary, because the organizers of the governors' association had had a brainstorm. In the fall, they chartered an old ocean liner, the SS *Independence,* for a work-and-play cruise from New York to the Virgin Islands and back. It turned out to be the junket to end all junkets, with the governors and their staffs frolicking like any carefree vacationers, clad in loud tropical shirts, lunching on lobster with Bloody Mary chasers each noontime on the ship's fantail, cavorting on the dance floor each night with their spouses, or somebody else's, and imbibing at the Bottle Bar until the wee hours.

George and Lenore Romney, costumed like Xavier Cugat and Carmen Miranda, and Ronnie and Nancy Reagan were among the more prominent hoofers, and everybody got into the swing of things at once—except for Georgia's segregationist governor, Lester Maddox. Whether in the air-conditioned committee meetings or out under the hot rays of the promenade deck (which he pronounced "pompade"), Maddox hewed to the standard uniform of the Dixie county courthouse—black suit with silver Shriners' pin in lapel, white shirt, narrow black tie, black shoes. The only time he broke down was one night at a huge beach party under the palms at Magen's Bay. As others crowded three torchlit bars and swigged rum punch, Ol' Lester played jump-the-waves for press photographers, his pants rolled up to just below the knee, a red sport shirt flapping with every leap.

Shipboard segregation, not of the sort championed by Maddox, created some early disharmony between governors and the press, when the two classes were assigned separate dining rooms. At a midnight caucus in the ship's bar, several of the 160-odd newsmen aboard worked up a fourteen-point declaration fashioned after the demands of black power leaders of the day, signed it "Press Power," and delivered it to the conference staff. The most significant demand was open occupancy of one bar previously reserved for the governors, and prohibition of "honky" governors in the press room. The bar was opened thereafter, but the governors rejected another demand by the press, who were mostly lodged in the lower decks of the *Independence*, that busing be provided from their "ghetto" to the upper decks where the governors were billeted. Governor John Love of Colorado, the conference chairman, appropriately appointed Maddox to investigate the press allegations of segregation.

The floating conference did, however, provide the huddled reporters yearning to breathe free ample opportunity for interviews with their betters, as well as dirt-cheap drinks in the ship's bars once we got outside the three-mile limit. With drinks being so cheap, and all meals included in the price of your ticket, my fraternity was sorely tested to submit expense accounts that would satisfy the traditional admonition not to "cheapen the beat." One of our number finally discovered "lighterage," the fee that had to be paid to small boats that brought to the ship passengers who had missed the sailing. Soon lighterage charges were appearing on so many expense accounts that if all the reporters who claimed them had actually used them, an armada of small boats reminiscent of Dunkirk would have streamed out to the *Independence* at every departure.

Needless to say, there was much revelry among us, there being not much to write about in terms of hard news and only limited means to transmit stories if we had them. So our chief interest for the first few days was ordering expensive wines at dinner, not to cheapen the beat. Jack Germond, who alleged a broad knowledge of wines that turned out to be limited to the produce of Wente Brothers, a California winery, always insisted on ordering for our table. But one night he relented and the waiter brought the bottle I had chosen. It had no label on it. Thereafter I was barred from making the selection.

The most memorable episode in the wining-and-dining department came when Walter Mears of the Associated Press brought his venerable colleague, Jack Bell, to our table one night. Bell was a famously irascible sort who got into so many arguments that the rest of us took to asking Mears not to bring him to dinner. Mears would reply, "Jack's not a bad guy," and would bring him anyway, thus assuring another mealtime row when Bell got going. One night when we had been at sea several days, Bell ordered a steak. The waiter informed him that there were no more aboard. Bell flew into a rage and sent the poor waiter back into the kitchen in search of one. Miraculously, he found one more steak somewhere and served it up to Bell, who bit into it, declared it overcooked, and sent it back!

Added to our revelry was the development of a hilarious news story at sea, when Lyndon Johnson, desirous of a strong endorsement from the governors conference for his conduct of the Vietnam war, sent a cablegram to his agent on the ship, former governor Price Daniel of Texas. He ordered Daniel to put heat on Republican governor Jim Rhodes of Ohio to back the war, and the cable was stolen or otherwise acquired from the radio room by Lyn Nofziger, an aide to Governor Reagan. Copies were made and handed out to the cruising press corps amid Republican cries of protest and Democratic laments of anguish. The story broke as various governors frolicked on the ship's dance floor with their wives or other partners. LBJ's closest ally on the ship, Democratic governor John Connally of Texas, hid in his stateroom until the firestorm passed.

Germond and I shared one minor scoop for our papers on what came to be known thereafter as "the Ship of Fools," when we cornered Rockefeller on deck one afternoon and asked him about the cover of the current issue of *Time*. It had a picture of Rockefeller and Reagan as possible GOP running mates, at a time when Rockefeller was staunchly in support of Romney. "I wouldn't be human if I didn't appreciate a nice remark," he told us, "but I'm not a candidate, I'm not going to be a candidate, and I don't want to be president." Did we hear him correctly? It was taken for granted he still lusted after the presidency but was facing political reality. We asked him again: Was he saying he didn't want the job? "You heard me loud and clear," he replied. We persisted. If nominated, he wouldn't accept? "I said," he answered with irritation, "I don't want to be president." We rushed to inform Romney and Maryland governor Spiro T. Agnew, who at the time was a one-man draft-Rockefeller committee. Romney was relieved; Agnew was puzzled, as we rushed to the ship's radio shack to get our mini-scoop out to the world via the Newhouse and Gannett newspapers. Such were our small triumphs in those days.

While all this was going on, a much bigger story was developing in Democratic ranks that would keep me busier than ever in the next year. Two young graduates of the University of North Carolina named Allard Lowenstein and Curtis Gans were shopping around a far-fetched idea. They wanted to dump Lyndon Johnson from the Democratic ticket in 1968 and were looking for a candidate. They approached some senators, including Robert Kennedy and George McGovern, but could not find a taker. They finally settled on Eugene McCarthy, and what followed was both the best and the worst year for me as a reporter still pressing to get my nose under the big tent.

McCarthy may have been the most unusual, interesting, and yet most frustrating candidate I have ever encountered. Essentially drafted to run by Lowenstein and Gans as the presidential candidate of the Vietnam war protest, he seemed totally devoid of the lust for the Oval Office that marked nearly every other politician who ever sought it. Indeed, he would never allow that he was going after it, only that he had agreed to be the candidate and would agree to serve if elected.

In that sense, he was the perfect vehicle for the war protest, embodying it and articulating it in an impersonal way that kept the purpose of his candidacy in the forefront at all times. As a result, the mostly young protesters who rallied around him saw him in iconic proportions and came to venerate his very aloofness—often directed toward them.

The little-known McCarthy at first was a sort of stealth candidate in what began as a shadow campaign. With Johnson remaining in the White House, the attention of the press corps camped out in New Hampshire often focused on George Romney, who hoped that goodness would bring him the

Republican nomination. His campaign slogan, proclaimed on billboards across the tiny state, was "Romney Fights Moral Decay" and made him sound like a new brand of toothpaste.

His off-hand confession to having been brainwashed in Vietnam had unfortunately characterized this intense but kind and well-meaning man as somewhat of a buffoon, and as often happens in politics, things began to occur on the campaign trail that appeared to confirm the impression.

Striding into a bowling alley one afternoon to shake hands with voters, he tried his luck at duckpins, the game of shorter pins in which the player has three turns to knock them all down. After he had rolled the allotted three balls and had left two or three pins standing, he gritted his teeth and kept going—another ball and another and another, to no avail. As we reporters watched, first amused and then astonished, Romney kept going, and going, and going, until he finally knocked over the last pin—on his thirty-fourth try! The television cameras, to his chagrin, recorded his marathon effort, including his concluding good-natured grin at his bowling ineptitude. Romney was nothing if not determined.

By this time, Nixon had thrown off all pretense of not running and had entered the race, and in the wake of Romney's "brainwashed" statement had shot ahead of him in all the main public-opinion polls. Two weeks before the primary, Romney, under pressure from his strategists, pulled the plug and withdrew from the race. Suddenly Nixon was converted from loser to winner, fortunate to have drawn the hapless Romney as his opponent for the GOP nomination. Romney's withdrawal put the spotlight in the closing weeks of the primary more squarely on McCarthy, running in New Hampshire against a write-in candidacy by establishment Democrats in the state on behalf of Johnson, who stayed home. In his absence, a remarkable political phenomenon unfolded.

Hordes of college students and drop-outs from New England and other campuses descended on the state, knocking on doors for McCarthy and for an end to the war. Often shedding the hippy style of the day, including their long hair, the McCarthy "kiddie corps," organized by a young Yale divinity student named Sam Brown, went forth "clean for Gene."

As the Minnesotan's crowds continued to build along with his student army, we reporters began to sense that he might make a respectable showing, though few of us were predicting how it would turn out. Five days before the voters went to the polls, I wrote for the Newhouse file:

NASHUA, N.H.—The quiet, almost clandestine campaign of Sen. Eugene J. McCarthy moves down to the wire in the New Hampshire presidential primary with a deceptively benign quality that could mark him as the sleeper in next Tuesday's voting. There are no bands, no placards, few cheers, little applause, and an unbelieveably self-effacing, low-key candidate in the effort to beat the write-in for President Johnson by Democratic regulars. Yet, in spite of McCarthy's almost surreptitious style on the stump, there are growing suspicions his support is building sufficiently to cause the White House to await Tuesday's balloting with some apprehension.

On election night, McCarthy won an astonishing 42.2 percent against the sitting president and captured twenty of the state's twenty-four delegates to the Democratic National Convention in Chicago that summer. At the Sheraton Wayfarer in Bedford, a Manchester suburb, the McCarthy campaign, with the college kids in the forefront, held a raucous victory celebration. Even the stoic candidate allowed himself some enthusiasm and praise for his followers. "People have remarked that this campaign has brought young people back into the system," he observed. "But it's the other way around. The young people have brought the country back into the system."

The mirth, however, was short-lived, because one of the Democrats who had spurned the Lowenstein-Gans invitation to lead their dump-Johnson movement was now poised to rain on McCarthy's parade by entering the race himself. Four days later, Robert Kennedy, rationalizing that McCarthy's showing meant that the party was already split and he hadn't done the splitting, jumped in.

Kennedy's entry followed weeks of private agonizing over whether to become a candidate, during which he consulted family members, longtime Kennedy political aides, and eventually favored members of the Washington and New York press corps. His deep dislike of Johnson and his desire to see him deposed were well known, but he was torn over whether he was the one to attempt it. He confided to associates a fear that a challenge by him would divide the Democratic Party and turn the country over to the despised Nixon. And he was afraid running against LBJ would be dismissed as no more than a personal political vendetta.

Once McCarthy demonstrated Johnson's vulnerability, however, Kennedy was able to convince himself that the party already was divided over LBJ's leadership and therefore he could not be blamed for it. So he plunged in, announcing his candidacy at a packed Senate Caucus Room where his older brother had declared his own bid for the presidency only eight years before. It was also the same room where the two of them earlier had interrogated suspected racketeers before the Senate Labor Committee, John Kennedy as a committee member, Robert as a staff counsel.

What I remember most about the event was Kennedy's staunch but ultimately ineffective effort to quash the notion that his entering the race on the heels of McCarthy's New Hampshire showing was another example of his much-advertised political opportunism and "ruthlessness." His insistence in his speech that his candidacy would be "in harmony" with McCarthy's, not in opposition, in their joint opposition to the war in Vietnam, brought snickers and guffaws from my fellow reporters. So did his statement, "My decision reflects no personal animosity or disrespect toward President Johnson." In the question-and-answer period, he was pounded with inquiries about why, if he wanted LBJ out so much, he didn't simply endorse McCarthy and work for him. It was a Robert Kennedy thrown on the defensive who left the Caucus Room.

Once outside, however, it was as if a great weight had been lifted from him, and from thousands of voters he would now encounter. Those of us reporters assigned to cover his hastily organized campaign raced with him to Washington's National Airport and boarded a commercial plane to New York for his participation in its St. Patrick's Day parade. Regular passengers were astonished to find themselves aboard a de facto campaign plane in a scene that was to be repeated often across the country in the dozen weeks ahead.

Although as a reporter I had covered Robert Kennedy off and on since the 1950s, I really had not had much opportunity to take a reading of him as a politician or as a man. That opportunity came now, over the eighty-five days of his frenzied and ultimately ill-fated dash for the presidency, and I learned that behind the ambition and the "ruthlessness" there was another man of other qualities. This helped explain to me why he came to be so admired and even cherished by millions of Americans, even as other millions continued to detest him.

7 Getting to Know Bobby

OF ALL THE POLITICIANS I'VE COVERED in fifty-plus years, none was more private and aloof yet ultimately more charismatic and appealing than Robert Kennedy. When, in the early 1950s, I was covering Senator Joe McCarthy's Permanent Investigations Subcommittee hearings, involving Long Island figures, for the *Long Island Press,* I found the minority staff counsel to be curt and cold-eyed. Whenever I ventured to ask him a question after one of the sessions, what I always got back was, "Who are you with?" In those days, long before he ever thought about running for the Senate from New York, Long Island meant about as much to him as Coney Island. I got the brush-off, but I didn't think much of it because I was used to getting the same from everybody who wasn't from one of the areas covered by the Newhouse papers.

I saw Kennedy on Capitol Hill over the next several years when he was chief counsel of Senator John McClellan's labor rackets investigating committee, bullying and browbeating witnesses and always seeming to have a chip on his shoulder toward reporters—unless you happened to work for the *New York Times* or the *Washington Post,* and sometimes even then.

That was why I was surprised when I encountered him in West Virginia that night during the 1960 presidential primary and he suddenly was talkative and almost chummy. When he became his brother's attorney general, I saw him occasionally at Justice Department press conferences, his feet up on the desk, shirt sleeves rolled up his arms, tie loose, his kids' drawings stuck to a wall with scotch tape. It was clear on such occasions that he didn't recognize me from Adam.

He was, during all this time, in the full-time service of the political career of his brother, the senator, the presidential candidate, and then the president. Over the sorrowful days in late November of 1963 when he lost and buried his brother, I saw him in the fullness of his grief—grim, lifeless, yet persevering at the side of the young new widow, the pillar on which she leaned.

Over the next nearly five years of his life, I was able to witness his transformation from his brother's brother to a man and political leader in his own right, as he pulled himself out from under the personal cloud that enshrouded him, into a public pursuit of the aspirations and goals of that brother. Many of his associates, infinitely closer to him than I as a reporter ever was, have denied there was any deep transformation in the man himself. But as one who earlier had occasionally been on the receiving end of his impatience and churlishness in that first role, I found him to be much more open-minded and tolerant toward the inquiries of the press after the loss of JFK. He remained to the end his brother's brother, but at the same time he increasingly charted his own course, fired by his burning opposition to social injustice at home and his late-blooming but finally relentless determination to end the killing in Vietnam.

At the Democratic National Convention in Atlantic City in 1964, shortly after he had resigned as Johnson's attorney general and announced he would run for the Senate from New York, rumors had stirred about a draft to make him LBJ's running mate. Such talk was a direct challenge to Johnson's earlier flat declaration that he would pick no one from his cabinet—a transparent gimmick to exclude Robert Kennedy. Kennedy had greeted it by joking that his only regret was that he "had to take so many nice fellows over the side with me." But the convention talk stirred renewed interest among some of Kennedy's most eager associates to force him on the then-despised usurper of the Kennedy White House.

I managed to get into Kennedy's hotel suite, perhaps because my *Long Island Press* credentials registered more with his entourage now that he was running for office in the Empire State. There I heard some of his aides pleading with him to go onto the convention floor to fuel the veep speculation. It was tempting, if just to irritate Johnson, and Kennedy toyed with the notion for a time before deciding not to go.

The idea of a draft from the convention floor to impose Kennedy on the president seeking election in his own right seemed far-fetched. A night or two later, when Kennedy appeared on the speakers' platform to introduce a nostalgic film about his fallen brother, however, it seemed less so. He entered the darkened hall unseen by the delegates as a film on LBJ was being shown, and stood on a rear walkway until it was over and the lights came on. As he walked forward to introduce his brother's film, the convention erupted in an emotional outpouring of admiration and nostalgia. For about twenty minutes, cheering, applauding, and singing brought the convention to a halt and kept it suspended as Robert Kennedy stood with moist eyes and a sorrowful gaze and let the demonstration wash over him. Each time he tried to start speaking, the din rose up louder as he smiled wanly, then surrendered to it.

Finally, when the convention was gaveled to order, he delivered a loving tribute to John Kennedy, ending with the lines from *Romeo and Juliet:* "When he shall die, take him and cut him out in little stars, and he will make the face of heaven so fine that all the world will be in love with night, and pay no worship to the garish sun." Many in the hall, including some reporters in the press section where I sat just below the platform, wept openly. But Kennedy himself stood stoically as the demonstration resumed, until the lights were dimmed again and the JFK film began. Then the younger brother sat silently behind a battery of small television monitors at the back of the platform, out of sight of the delegates but in my view, and watched the film somberly, alone. Only when a witty remark by the late president came from the screen did he laugh for a moment, and then he became silent and still again. That private moment remained with me thereafter, to this day.

After his election to the Senate, he threw himself with his old drive and determination into his duties, but always seemed somehow out of place and often rudderless, after all the years of being motivated single-mindedly in the service of John Kennedy's political ambitions. He was a freshman senator but was not seen as just that, even within the Senate. He drew more public attention than the most senior members but stood apart from his new colleagues, operating, I wrote then, in "a public climate of warmth and a private climate of coolness." His icy relations with President Johnson were not lost on them, particularly after Kennedy publicly broke with LBJ by suggesting that a coalition regime in South Vietnam might be the only way out of the situation there. Within the New York congressional delegation, which I covered as a Washington correspondent for the *Syracuse Herald-Journal* as well as the *Long Island Press,* I encountered considerable resentment toward him as a johnny-come-lately, and he didn't do much to counter it.

In the fall of 1966, I was one of about two dozen reporters, photographers, and cameramen who accompanied him on a swing through four midwestern states campaigning for congressional Democrats who had supported his brother's New Frontier agenda. It was an undertaking into which he could throw his enthusiasm, and slowly he was polishing his speaking style, which in his Senate race had often been halting and unimpressive. It was an opportunity for those of us traveling with him to get a better feel for the man. The press contingent was so large that his office had to charter a plane, as if the trip were a presidential campaign tour. From one stop to the next, he would stroll up and down the aisle joking and talking to reporters in a manner that was far different from those first days more than a decade earlier.

Everywhere we went on that weekend, Kennedy encountered extremely large crowds for an off-year congressional campaign when he wasn't running for anything. The young screamers and jumpers that marked his own later campaigning were already turning up, grabbing for him as he spoke or rolled by in an open car. He spoke repeatedly of "President Kennedy" but only three times in three days of "President Johnson," as in a rally at Carthage College in Kenosha, Wisconsin, when he mentioned the New Frontier program "we began with President Kennedy and was continued so ably by President Johnson." He also mentioned LBJ when he was asked about any presidential ambitions of his own for 1968, saying he supported the incumbent for reelection.

Most of the candidates he spoke for had served in Congress during the Kennedy administration and had supported his brother. In Wisconsin, however, the Democrat running for reelection to the House, Representative Lynn Stalbaum, had not been in Congress during Kennedy's term. Nevertheless, Robert Kennedy proceeded to praise him to the skies as a staunch backer of the New Frontier. Stalbaum beamed with unexpected pleasure as Kennedy spoke of him.

After the rally, we were all back on board the chartered propeller plane and rolling down the runway for takeoff when suddenly the pilot jammed on the brakes. He taxied back to the gate, the cabin door was opened, mobile steps were wheeled out and who came bounding onto the plane but a still-beaming Congressman Stalbaum. We wondered aloud why he had come aboard, because we were leaving Wisconsin to go on to a neighboring state. We learned later he just wanted to hitch a ride back to Washington that night. But Kennedy, sitting among the reporters, speculated that Stalbaum might be coming along "because he thinks I say those things about him at every stop!"

It was only 1966, but many in the crowds were already thinking of Kennedy for president in 1972, assuming LBJ would run and win a second term in 1968. A sign in the crowd at the airport in Cincinnati said, "Return Touch Football to the White House," and another in Milwaukee altered the Johnson campaign slogan to say, "All the Way with RFK."

Another trip to California, campaigning for Democratic governor Pat Brown against that Grade B-movie actor Ronald Reagan and on to the Northwest a few weeks later, brought the same response. I remember particularly a rally at Sacramento City College at which a student asked Kennedy for "some assurance that you will run for president in 1972." Haltingly, he replied: "Oh. Well, I—just quite frankly don't know what the future brings. I think one cannot plan that far in advance. . . . I'm going to continue, as long as I am around on this globe, and I'm going to continue in public life in some way. I don't know when that man way up there is going to take me, so I can't—" and he trailed off. "That's not a very satisfactory answer," he concluded, "but it's the best I can do."

Such early interest in him as a presidential candidate, expressed with high emotion most of the time, persuaded one of his young speechwriters, Adam Walinsky, to climb aboard the plane after one rally and proclaim: "The hell with 1968! Let's go NOW!" But Kennedy was still clinging to his intention, as personally distasteful as it might be, to support Johnson and Vice President Hubert Humphrey for reelection. In a speech on the same trip at the University of California at Berkeley, he rejected a call for him to "dissociate yourself" from LBJ over the Vietnam war, though his concern over the conflict and America's growing involvement in it was clearly deepening.

Such trips enabled me to see much more of Robert Kennedy in action at close range. The earlier stand-offishness I had witnessed was diminishing, as his role as a senator in his own right obliged him to be more of a public man than he'd had to be before. One Christmas he and Ethel had a party for the press to which our children were invited. I took my young son Paul, and when we arrived at Hickory Hill, all the kids were herded upstairs to play with the Kennedy younger set as we adults had drinks downstairs. On the way home, I asked Paul how he liked the Kennedy kids. "Fine," he said. Taking the opportunity to provide him with a little lesson, I told him the

Kennedy children's grandfather was a very rich man who had left each of them a million dollars so they could devote their lives to helping others when they grew up. I asked him what he'd do if I could give him a million dollars. He replied without a moment's hesitation: "Invest in real estate!" So much for that lesson.

In early February of 1967, I got a special insight into how much Kennedy was inhibited in expressing his concern over Vietnam by fear of having it perceived as no more than the product of his personal feud with Johnson. Kennedy had just returned from a European tour during which he had engaged in talks in Paris with President Charles de Gaulle and the French Foreign Office on Vietnam. The meetings did not sit well with Johnson, who saw them as meddling by Kennedy.

It so happened that the senator was scheduled to make a speech critical of U.S. policy toward China at the University of Chicago. A *Washington Post* reporter and I, who were accompanying him to Chicago, received advanced copies of his speech because we were going to be leaving Washington late and needed the lead time to make our deadlines. Reviewing the text in his Senate office before departure, the senator and aides decided to insert a phrase specifically saying he wasn't blaming past failures in China policy on "any one administration," adding that "there has been more growth in our awareness and knowledge of the problem in the past year than in the past decade." It was an obvious effort to deflect press reference to the feud. Kennedy's press secretary, Frank Mankiewicz, advised us two reporters of the insertion.

We joined Kennedy in his car for the drive to Dulles Airport and the early evening flight to Chicago. En route, he asked the *Post* reporter whether he had found anything in the speech to write about. He replied that he had written that Kennedy had attacked the China policy but had inserted a last-minute softener in the text. It was true enough, but the insert had been given to the two of us as a courtesy because of the time squeeze. The insert also had been included as part of the original text to be given later in general distribution to the press; hence the other recipients would have no reason to say the additional language had been "inserted" to avoid an interpretation that the speech was a knock at Johnson.

Kennedy, sitting in the front seat next to the driver, groaned and started arguing with the other reporter, who explained he thought there had been a general release and the insertion was a subsequent intentional softener. Kennedy continued to complain and got the reporter to phone in a correction before our plane took off from Dulles. But when we arrived in Chicago, a Kennedy aide was waiting with the story off the Washington Post–Los Angeles Times wire in hand, without the correction. As we walked to the hall for the speech, Kennedy continued his lament: "It will go out all over the country as just another attack on Johnson." In the question-and-answer period after the speech, Kennedy went out of his way to agree with LBJ's contention that he had "inherited" the Vietnam war. He said Johnson had handled the responsibility with "courage and determination" and that it would be "very unfair" to saddle him with the war. Nevertheless, many press accounts of the speech described it as another RFK attack on Johnson and more evidence of their continuing feud.

In my own follow-up piece, I noted, however: "When President Kennedy died, there were only a few hundred American advisory troops [in Vietnam]. Now there are an estimated 35,000 Americans, and U.S. air raids on North Vietnam are being conducted from there. Kennedy ought to be able to disagree with a clearly identifiable Johnson policy without having his criticism written off as mere personal sniping. He ought to, but as long as Washington and the nation remain fascinated by the spectacle of a juicy intraparty feud, he is going to have to endure the fact that whatever he says will be taken as more fuel for the RFK-LBJ fire."

The Chicago speech episode helped me understand later one of the main reasons Kennedy resisted the early overtures of Allard Lowenstein, the young New York lawyer and his liberal political ally, and Curtis Gans to take the lead in an effort to dump Johnson in 1968. It underscored that Kennedy felt his opposition to LBJ on the war would be widely dismissed as no more than a personal vendetta unworthy of him and of public support.

All through the spring and fall of 1967, I saw Kennedy only occasionally and learned only later of the Lowenstein-Gans efforts to get him to run for the Democratic presidential nomination against LBJ. Kennedy told Lowenstein he wasn't interested, and told anybody else who asked him that he intended to support the Johnson-Humphrey ticket for reelection. Lowenstein then approached Senator George McGovern of South Dakota, who said he was concentrating on winning reelection and suggested Senator Eugene McCarthy of Minnesota. McCarthy's first response, Lowenstein told me later, was, "I think Bobby should do it." When that wasn't going to happen, McCarthy finally agreed, culminating in another rivalry that soon was to become almost as bitter as Kennedy's feud with Johnson.

Not being a Kennedy intimate, I did not get wind of the Kennedy inner-circle conversations that went on from time to time about a candidacy. Neither, apparently, did others in the press corps, until Kennedy started agonizing openly with some of my colleagues about whether to enter the race, once McCarthy had demonstrated Johnson's political vulnerability in the New Hampshire Democratic primary of March 1968.

But once Kennedy put his doubts aside and did jump in, I was off and running with him, through the primaries in Indiana, Nebraska, Oregon, and California in search of sufficient public support to somehow bring him the Democratic nomination. From start to finish, criss-crossing the country, it was a phenomenon unmatched in all the years I have covered politics. After having held back so long against his strong feelings about the Vietnam war and LBJ, Kennedy threw himself into the campaign with a zeal and determination that ignited crowds everywhere.

Two factors differentiated that campaign from any other I ever covered. The first was the ad hoc, catch-up quality of it. Once Kennedy decided to enter the race, he just did it, putting together his organization and transportation on the run. His first flights to New York and Boston were on commercial planes. Reporters who were able to get seats tagged along, standing in the aisle trying to interview the new candidate as they went. Soon the Kennedy campaign was chartering jet planes—not the grungy prop planes of his earlier swings—to cope with the large traveling press corps, unprecedented for a primary candidate who was not an incumbent.

The second factor was the huge public outpouring of enthusiasm for him as he went from city to city and state to state. At first it seemed to reflect animosity toward Johnson and the war, personified by Kennedy; after LBJ announced he would not seek reelection, it continued to be fueled by Kennedy's urgency, coupled always with a public nostalgia for Camelot, the lost romance the country had experienced with John Kennedy.

Many young McCarthy supporters deeply resented Kennedy's late entry, but many other voters brushed that consideration aside. On one of the first nights, at the airport in Topeka, Kansas, I asked a young farmer named Stan Mitchell who had just excitedly shaken Kennedy's hand on the tarmac how he felt about the candidate jumping in on McCarthy's heels. "I don't care how he got in," the farmer said. "Just so he got in." Days later, when the Kennedy plane landed at the San Francisco International Airport, a woman defiantly held a sign that said, "Welcome Bobby-Come-Lately," and shouted: "Where were you in New Hampshire?" A woman next to her in the delirious mob turned and snarled: "New Hampshire is nothing! Look around you!"

The catch-up Kennedy campaign imposed exhausting hours on all concerned, and it became a familiar sight on the plane to see the candidate stretched out on the floor encased in a blanket, cat-napping. It was not just the packed schedule; at every stop the motorcade was obliged to inch through crowds of screaming teenagers and women, grasping to shake his hand or just touch his sleeve. He routinely had cufflinks torn from his shirt and even had a shoe removed on occasion and had to borrow the footwear of his chief lieutenant, Fred Dutton. Once, in expressing his appreciation to all the locals who had turned out, he ended, to the bafflement of the crowd, by thanking "Fred Dutton, for his shoe." For all his frenzied earnestness, there was always that playful side as well, which compensated for the ordeal of morning-to-night exhorting of the voters.

Kennedy was readily accessible to the reporters traveling with him, especially at the end of each day on the final leg of the trip. He enjoyed bantering back and forth, as long as it did not touch on John F. Kennedy, always referred to by him as "President Kennedy" or occasionally "my brother," never "Jack" in our presence. Any such familiarity by one of us would immediately draw a cold stare. Kennedy always wore his PT-109 tieclip, a talisman of the real insiders. Once on a trip in the West, another reporter removed his own tieclasp, handed it to Kennedy, and asked if he knew what it was. Kennedy looked at it, a strange pointed thing with wires. "It's a torpedo," the reporter said, intending it as a joke. "I wear it when I travel with you just to show I'm honest." Kennedy froze, handed it back and walked away.

From the moment Kennedy entered the race right after the New Hampshire primary, his eye was on Johnson, not McCarthy, and he looked for the first place he could challenge the president. The next primary was in Wisconsin, but the filing deadline had passed so he focused on Indiana. But McCarthy went into Wisconsin as a neighbor and with a full head of steam, and Johnson, who had not campaigned personally in New Hampshire and wasn't doing so in Wisconsin either, was in trouble there. A few days before the primary, I dropped by the LBJ headquarters in Milwaukee to talk to its campaign manager, Les Aspin, an analyst at the Pentagon whom I had known in my reporting days there (and later a Wisconsin congressman and then secretary of defense early in the Clinton administration). The place was deserted and he was downcast. Barring a miracle, he told me, Johnson was going to lose the primary, and badly.

Aspin was right, and that word had been passed to the White House before the president jolted the political world, and Kennedy, on March 31, the Sunday night before the primary, by closing his televised address to the nation with the declaration that "I shall not seek, and I will not accept, the nomination of my party for another term as your president." At that moment, I was standing in the rear of the auditorium of Carroll College in Waukesha listening to McCarthy address an overflow crowd. There was a stirring as some other reporters rushed up the platform and informed him of Johnson's withdrawal. McCarthy informed the crowd and there was bedlam.

Amid the cheering he left the hall and returned to his hotel in Milwaukee for a news conference. I rushed there as well, in time to hear a cool and unemotional McCarthy declaring that LBJ had "cleared the way for a reconciliation of our people." He said he didn't know whether Humphrey would now enter the race "but I think if you look closely, you might see a slight cloud on the horizon tomorrow morning." He was right about that, though Humphrey delayed his entry for weeks.

As he had done since Kennedy entered the race, McCarthy treated the man he had earlier suggested be the dump-Johnson candidate with a certain disdain. "I have not been seeking a knockdown, drag-out battle with him up to this point," he said. "On the other hand, I have not been seeking an accommodation."

Kennedy, startled by Johnson's decision, suddenly found himself needing a different rationale for his campaign. He heard the news as he was getting off a plane at Kennedy Airport. One of those in the car with him en route to Manhattan told me later that after a long silence, Kennedy had murmured: "I wonder if he would have done this if I hadn't come in."

Two days later in Wisconsin, where Kennedy was not on the ballot, having entered the race too late to meet the filing deadline, McCarthy won easily. The campaign headed into Indiana for the first direct confrontation between the two Democrats. Two more days later, on April 4, as Kennedy was about to speak to a black audience in Indianapolis, the political world was jolted again by the assassination of Dr. Martin Luther King Jr. in Memphis. As riots broke out in cities across the country, the Kennedy entourage returned to Washington, where on Sunday morning he walked through the ravaged streets of a black section with some of us in tow. A black woman came up to him, uncertain it was Kennedy, and asked: "Is that you?" He nodded. She grasped his hand and told him: "I knew you'd be the first to come here, darling." Such was the empathy blacks seemed to recognize in this white man of great privilege.

Around this time, I broke off from the campaign briefly to interview George Wallace in Montgomery about the likely impact of Dr. King's death and the resultant riots on his own campaign, predicated as it was on stirring up racial animosity. His wife was still living at the time but very near the end, and he held forth on the assassination, subdued, in the governor's chair at the state capitol. "I don't think about it in terms of how it helps or hurts in politics," he told me. "I just hope they catch the one who did it. I wish we could stop all this shooting." But he went on: "Of course, any breakdown of law and order is going to support the position of anybody like me who is against a breakdown. . . . Now, I don't want to be helped that way. I don't want to see any headlines that say Wallace is helped by the riots. All I say is they seem to be getting worse, and nobody wants to try to stop it. And that's all I want to say about that particular subject."

This response was a far cry from his earlier remedy for rioters, which was that if the first looter in a riot was shot, there would be no more looting. When he resumed campaigning shortly afterward, there was no appreciable difference in his message. While insisting that he could win the popular plurality in enough states to claim an electoral majority and the presidency in November, he suggested now that he might win enough electoral votes to persuade one of the major-party nominees to make a "covenant" with him—not a deal, he said; that sounded too harsh. It would be based, he said, on implementing some of his states' rights philosophy into the winner's administration. As he offered this notion, he flicked some cigar ashes into the gubernatorial wastebasket and let a tight, crooked little smile come over his face.

Back on the frenetic Kennedy campaign trail in Indiana, we in the traveling press corps maintained a generally genial relationship with the candidate, despite our customary criticism about campaign exaggerations, of which he was no freer than other hard-driving candidates. At nearly every stop, he had the habit of ending his remarks with a paraphrase from George Bernard Shaw's *Back to Methuselah*: "Some men see things as they are and say, Why? I dream things that never were and say, Why not?" When we heard him start, "As George Bernard Shaw once said," we knew it was time to dash for the press bus, lest we be left behind as the motorcade sped on. Finally, at one stop, Kennedy puzzled the crowd by concluding, "As George Bernard Shaw once said, run for the buses!"

Returning to Indiana after the King funeral in Atlanta, Kennedy one day whistle-stopped by train along the route of the old Wabash Cannonball. The song of the same name inspired several of us in the press car to write a seven-stanza parody we called "The Ruthless Cannonball," which chronicled Bobby's allegedly most prominent characteristic. The lyrics have been print-ed in full in my book, *85 Days: The Last Campaign of Robert Kennedy*, and elsewhere. My favorite stanza went: "Now good clean Gene McCarthy came down the other track, a thousand Radcliffe dropouts all massed for the attack. But Bobby's bought the right of way from here back to St. Paul, 'cause money is no object on The Ruthless Cannonball."

Kennedy and wife Ethel came into the press car to listen as we belted out all seven stanzas accompanied by Dave Breasted of the *New York Daily News* on guitar. When we finished, the Kennedys applauded but then in mock anger the candidate turned his famous laser glare on us and said: "As George Bernard Shaw once said—the same to you, sideways." I handed him a copy of the lyrics and said, "Forget where you got it." He gave me "the look" again and said, "Oh, no, I won't." He started toward his own car, then turned, grinned, and Ruthless Robert added: "See, it keeps slipping out all the time!"

While Kennedy sometimes encountered press criticism about his liberal credentials because of his law-and-order rhetoric, he wore them as a badge on other occasions, as when he addressed and engaged in debate with med-ical students at the Indiana University Medical Center. Some of them chal-lenged his call for more medical care for the poor and higher Social Security benefits, one of them asking him, "Where are you going to get all the money for these federally subsidized programs you're talking about?" He shot back: "From you." He noted the few black faces among the students and told them: "You are the privileged ones here. . . . It's the poor who carry the major bur-den of the struggle in Vietnam. You sit here as white medical students, while black people carry the burden of fighting in Vietnam."

When one of the students shouted, "We'll be going soon," Kennedy replied: "Yes, but you're here now and they're over there. The war might be settled by the time you go." And when a student asked him whether he would favor ending medical school draft deferments, he answered: "The way things are going here today, I'd say yes." He now understood, he said, why his campaign aides were having trouble "forming a doctors' committee for me in Indiana."

On the final day before the Indiana primary, Kennedy undertook a nine-hour marathon motorcade across the northwest tip of the state, from La Porte west through Porter and Lake Counties to the heavy industrial towns of Gary and Hammond and on across the Illinois line into Chicago. Riding most of the way in an open convertible, he stood or sat on the top of the back seat with his bodyguard, former FBI agent Bill Barry, clinging to him so he would not be pulled from the car by all the outstretched, grabbing hands along the way. Not only in the towns but also along the highways between, crowds lined the route, cheering and calling out to him. The motorcade rolled and often crept through side-by-side black blue-collar and white ethnic blue-collar neighborhoods, with the same frenzied reception everywhere. In all my years of covering campaigns, there was nothing like it before or after.

Young girls particularly jumped and screamed as he went by. At the start of the tour, I spotted two of them waving frantically as our press bus sped by, just behind Kennedy's car. As soon as we passed, they turned and dashed off, pushing their way out of the crowd lining the road. Several miles later, there were the same two, yelling and jumping again, and again about an hour later down the road. By actual count by my buddies and me that afternoon and night, we spotted the pair a total of thirteen times along the route. They leap-frogged the motorcade in their car, taking up positions in each town along the route. Finally a couple of photographers invited them into their own open car and they became part of the entourage. How they retrieved the car they left behind, we never found out.

In the town of La Porte, where the candidate spoke, he began to extol the virtues of one of my traveling colleagues, Dan Blackburn, an earnest and pleasant young reporter for one of the smaller radio networks. La Porte turned out to be Dan's hometown, and Kennedy made him sound like another Edward R. Murrow. The gesture was in keeping with the candidate's playful attitude toward the press accompanying him on the adventure—that is, unless something was said or written that got too close to the bone about his family or his motives. There was always the risk that in getting too close to him, or any of the Kennedys for that matter, the assumption would be drawn that you were on the Kennedy team when that was not professionally wise or possible.

After a final rally in the town of Whiting, the motorcade sped to Chicago's O'Hare International Airport around midnight for a flight back to Indianapolis. On arrival, Germond and I stopped in the bar of the Holiday Inn at Weir-Cook Airport for a nightcap. Kennedy came over and we invited him to sit with us, but he said he had to get to bed. Then he stood at our table and wearily reflected on the challenge of Indiana, a notoriously conservative state where he had struggled to connect by emphasizing law-and-order themes. For all the huge outpouring that day, he was subdued and seemingly resigned to bad news the next day. "Well, I've done all I could," he said. "Maybe it's just not my time. But I've learned something from Indiana. The country is changing."

He went on in that vein, talking of the common interest of blue-collar workers of both races and how a coalition on economic rather than racial lines had to be built in the northern cities. And he talked about the intensity of hate also encountered amid the adoration of the day's campaigning. One man in the crowd had held up a sign that said, "YOU PUNK," he told us, and grabbed his hand as his car inched by. "He squeezed my hand as if he were trying to break every bone in it," Kennedy said. We consoled him with the thought that he might be the man who could spur that coalition, and he smiled wanly and said he hoped so. Then he broke off, shook hands at a few other tables in the bar, and walked out.

The campaigning Kennedy had done in Indiana turned out to be enough. On primary night he finished first with 42 percent of the vote to 31 percent for Lyndon Johnson's stand-in, Governor Roger Branigan, and only 27 percent for McCarthy. From there it was on to the next primary in Nebraska, where McCarthy at first expressed optimism that he would beat Kennedy without an LBJ stand-in in the race. When he witnessed the wave building for Kennedy he decided otherwise.

A few of us were cutting into juicy steaks at the Blackstone Hotel in Omaha a few nights before the primary when McCarthy came over and joined us. He casually dismissed the Nebraska primary and told us he was leaving the next morning for Oregon, where he said the real test would come between him and Kennedy. He was right; Kennedy won Nebraska with 51.5 percent of the vote to 31 percent for McCarthy and single digits for Johnson and Humphrey. Kennedy hoped it would be enough to drive McCarthy from the race and enable him to concentrate on Humphrey, who by this time had announced his candidacy. But he was wrong about that.

McCarthy pressed on into Oregon, where he had a strong organization in place and the composition of the Democratic electorate was more favorable to him. Oregon was an anti-war state, and support had flowed naturally to him very early, before Kennedy was an alternative candidate. Just as important, Oregon was overwhelmingly white, relatively prosperous, and comfortable. With only 1 percent of the population black, Kennedy's black-and-blue-collar coalition was in short supply. When one out-of-state Kennedy strategist arrived and asked whether the ghettoes had been organized, Congresswoman Edith Green, the reigning Democratic power in Oregon, replied somewhat indignantly, "There are no ghettoes in Oregon." On top of that, much of organized labor was quietly lining up for Humphrey, who was not competing in the Oregon primary, a fact that undercut Kennedy.

His crowds in the state were not nearly as large nor as enthusiastic as they had been in Indiana and Nebraska. Near the end of the primary, Kennedy took a sightseeing boat on the Willamette River, basically a photo opportunity. It was flat and the candidate was gloomy, and as we walked off the pier I asked him how he assessed his chances in Oregon. "I've got a problem here," was all he would say. When I pressed him for what the problem was, he replied, without hostility, "You're a political writer. You can look around and see what it is. I don't want to play games. I have my own analysis, but I don't think it would be useful for me to go into it." And he walked off.

For the first time in the political history of the Kennedy family, one of them lost an election. Oregon went to McCarthy, with 44.7 percent of the Democratic vote to 38.8 for Kennedy and the rest split among Johnson, Humphrey, and others. Kennedy knew from the exit polls he would lose, and he made a gracious concession speech at the Benson Hotel in Portland and retired to his suite. There, the usual crowd of family members, campaign aides, friends, and some traveling reporters milled around, having a drink and quietly talking. Standing in his shirtsleeves, tie loosened, he held a watered-down drink in his hand as he exchanged small talk and accepted commiserations. He showed no bitterness, only resignation. At one point he moved into one of the two bedrooms and talked strategy for the next primary state, California, then returned to the living room.

We reporters peppered him with questions and he responded courteously, until the scene began taking on the aspect of a news conference. At last, he broke it off by saying he would be having a regular press conference the next morning and asking, "Can we hold off until then?" The other reporters walked off but I stayed, both curious and sympathetic. A tad unprofessionally, I asked him, "Why do you put up with all these questions at a difficult time like this?" He reached over and put his arm around me. "Because I like you," he said, and walked away. From the "ruthless" candidate, it was an unexpected gesture, but one whose sincerity you wanted to believe. That was how it was with Robert Kennedy; he had a side to him that defied his reputation for being tough and aloof. But the campaign, both the excitement of it and the disappointment, seemed to have a softening effect that showed itself in moments like this one.

It was on to California the next morning and the final chapter in Kennedy's presidential campaign, and life. On the flight south, Ethel Kennedy sought reassurance from reporters that the Oregon defeat didn't matter that much. "Such a small state," she reasoned to a few of us, "and only 15,000 votes" (the losing margin was closer to 20,000). "Do you really think it will make that much difference if we win in California? That's the important state, more like the rest of the country." The Oregon defeat had definitely set her husband back, but his black-and-blue-collar coalition was present in the Golden State and gave him an unforgettable reception. In downtown Los Angeles, immense crowds pressed against his open car, reaching for him, tearing away his cufflinks as souvenirs and any other part of his apparel that would come loose, including his shoes. It was as if the defeat in Oregon hadn't happened. It lasted that way for the next week as he raced from one end of the huge state to the other.

The final campaign day rivaled the one across northern Indiana weeks earlier in crowds and excitement. He was standing in the back of an open convertible, riding through San Francisco's Chinatown with his wife at his side, when half a dozen shots suddenly rang out. Ethel quickly slipped down into the seat, but her husband stood unflinchingly; they were only firecrackers going off among the festive mob. From there he went on to the Los Angeles suburbs, Long Beach, and finally San Diego. Falling behind schedule in Watts, the motorcade raced down side streets, either to make up time or to minimize television footage of the turnout of blacks and other minorities. As the press bus chased the candidate's car down one desolate street, Dick Drayne, Kennedy's press secretary, asked aloud to nobody in particular, "What is this? Are we going house-hunting?"

As the day wore on, Kennedy became ill but persevered, gulping down ginger ale to settle his stomach. Finally, at the day's last rally at El Cortez Hotel in San Diego, he raced through his remarks and then sat on the top step of the stage, head in hands. Bill Barry and Olympic decathalon champion Rafer Johnson hustled him into a bathroom where he composed himself, then returned and addressed the crowd again. We reporters, huddled to one side of the stage, could see he wasn't himself. When he finished, he turned to us and said: "For the benefit of my friends on the left I want to add, as George Bernard Shaw once said, 'some men see things as they are and say, Why? I dream things that never were and ask, Why not?'" It was his signal that the long primary campaign odyssey that had started in the Senate Caucus Room less than seven weeks earlier was at an end. Everybody wearily climbed aboard the chartered Kennedy plane for a quiet flight back to Los Angeles in a subdued atmosphere uncommon to the Kennedy campaign.

The Kennedys went off to a friend's house at Malibu for the night and a restful primary day of relaxation and waiting. Some of our press contingent and a few staffers repaired to Drayne's room at the Ambassador Hotel, which would be the campaign's headquarters on election night. There was more than a modest amount of drinking, which led to singing and general carousing. John Hart of CBS News provided the chief entertainment with a hilarious, ear-splitting imitation of Billy Graham in full cry, until protests from other guests drove us out and down to Kennedy's unoccupied suite, where we continued more of the same, developing some choice hangovers in the process. Before we left, we pinned a note of thanks to the candidate's pillow for use of the hall—and his liquor cabinet.

The next time I saw Kennedy was the next night, in the kitchen pantry of the Ambassador as he came down the hotel's service elevator to make his victory speech in the ballroom, having won a narrower-than-expected California success over McCarthy. A few minutes earlier, he had sparred on television with his old friend Roger Mudd, who playfully ribbed him about his reputation for being "ruthless" and tried to egg him into saying something about either McCarthy or Humphrey that would illustrate it. Kennedy artfully dodged, to the point of displaying mock horror at some of Mudd's suggestions of his behavior, until both candidate and questioner were grinning broadly.

Now, coming out of the service elevator into the kitchen pantry next to a long steam table, Kennedy shook hands with hotel workers until he spied Bob Healy of the *Boston Globe* and me observing him. We congratulated him on his California primary victory and he invited us to a postelection party later at a discotheque run by old Kennedy hand Pierre Salinger. I kidded him about the Mudd interview, telling him I thought he was "very ruthful" in his responses. He laughed, took a few steps down the corridor, turned and, with a big smile, said: "I'm getting better all the time!"

Healy and I followed him onto the ballroom platform and hung back, the better to beat a hasty retreat to the press conference room beyond the kitchen pantry when Kennedy finished his speech. Fred Dutton was standing there and said to me: "When I told the senator what went on in his suite last night, he was like a little boy who had missed out on something." We listened as Kennedy made all the usual thanks, starting with his brother-in-law Steve Smith for being so "ruthless" in running his campaign and ending with "my dog Freckles." Then he added: "I'm not doing this in the order of importance. I also want to thank my wife Ethel." He went on to praise McCarthy and to invite Humphrey to have "a dialogue or a debate, I hope" over direction of their party and the country, including moving in a "different direction" on Vietnam. When I heard him conclude by saying, "My thanks to all of you, and on to Chicago!" I turned and headed for the press conference.

Originally Kennedy was to go through the ballroom to another reception on a lower level. But the speech he had just made had been piped into the other room and it was already past midnight, with deadlines pressing on the writing reporters, so Barry and Dutton decided to go directly to the press room and they started clearing the way in that direction. But Kennedy was being mobbed by well-wishers chanting "We Want Bobby!" and the assistant maitre d'hotel led him through a back exitway into the dark corridor leading to the well-lit kitchen pantry.

I was walking quickly just ahead of him past a large ice-making machine and stainless steel steam tables as he came up to the point where Healy and I had joked with him about his lack of ruthlessness in the interview with Mudd. I heard a shot, then a quick volley of them, and by the time I turned,

Kennedy was already sprawled on his back on the pantry floor, his eyes open and his arms over his head in the pose captured by the photographers in the room and flashed quickly around the country and the world.

There were many versions thereafter about just how many shots had been fired and about who grabbed the assailant, Sirhan Sirhan, and wrestled the gun from his hand. I saw Roosevelt Grier, the Los Angeles Rams football star, and Rafer Johnson, bending him over the steam table directly in front of me, trying to get the gun. Other hands reached in, and I remember being astonished at how long it took these burly attackers to get the gun loose and subdue this young, frail, frightened-looking little man. "My God, he's been shot!" I heard somebody cry. Then others: "Get a doctor! Get the gun! Get the gun! Kill him! Kill him! Kill the bastard! No, don't kill him! Don't kill this one! Oh, my God, they've shot Kennedy!"

It was a scene of horror and incomprehension that is cemented into my brain, and after all these years I still sometimes revisit it in a nightmare. One thing I remember very clearly was a usually most competitive woman photographer so hysterical that she held her camera down and said to her male colleagues, "You can have it! You can have it!" Then she began pulling at one of them who was clicking away with his own camera, until he shoved her off, telling her, "Get away! This is history!"

I scribbled frantically in my own notepad as I observed the frenzied scene—scribbles I later could not make out. In a moment Ethel Kennedy pushed through and saw her husband on his back, eyes still open. As the photographers crowded around, she knelt by him in her short-skirted orange-and-white dress and urged the crowd to step back. "Please go, please go," I heard her say. "Give him room to breathe." One young press aide named Hugh McDonald was sobbing uncontrollably and later was seen wandering about aimlessly, clutching Kennedy's shoes.

After what seemed like an eternity, an ambulance crew came in, lifted Kennedy onto a stretcher and took him out and to nearby Good Samaritan Hospital. Grier let his massive head and shoulders fall to the steam table as he sobbed quietly. I walked out into the ballroom amid the dazed Kennedy supporters. I saw a woman standing on the edge of an ornate fountain dangling a set of rosary beads over her head and saying to no one and everyone: "Kneel down and pray! Kneel down and pray! Say your rosary!" Immediately about twenty people kneeled around the pool. One man holding a drink and a cigarette placed both down on the carpet and joined them.

I then went to the press room and began writing my story on my old Olivetti portable:

LOS ANGELES—I was walking about 30 feet ahead of Sen. Robert F. Kennedy through the kitchen of the Ambassador Hotel when I heard four or five shots ring out. I thought at first they were firecrackers, and it ran through my mind what an idiotic stunt, considering what had happened to President Kennedy.

Then, suddenly I realized what they were and turned. I saw Roosevelt Grier, the huge Negro lineman of the Los Angeles Rams, rushing at a man with black, bushy hair and dark complexion, wearing a blue shirt and grey trousers. Others came and helped Grier pin the man against a steel countertop.

Behind Grier, and to the left, Robert Kennedy lay on his back, his head covered with blood. His lips were parted, his eyes open and staring. I could see he was alive, and in another moment a crowd of aides and photographers were around him.

The room was filled with shrieks and obscenities. Women pulled at their hair and men rushed at the would-be assassin, pounding him with their fists. The man struggled wildly and the throng of men holding him, even the gigantic Grier, had trouble restraining him. I went up and saw he was still holding a pistol in his hand, and some of the men had his arm pinned to the countertop. It must have been several minutes before they got the gun away from him. . . .

About three full newspaper columns later, I ended by observing that Kennedy's hour of political triumph in California "became another hour of mindless tragedy in a nation that cannot or will not keep weapons of death from the hands of madmen who walk its streets."

I then joined the vigil outside the Good Samaritan Hospital for the next twenty-five hours. Quiet crowds stood behind police barricades and waited. In the late afternoon of the day after the shooting, black bumper stickers with orange lettering appeared in the crowd, reading simply "Pray for Bobby." A working press room was set up inside the hospital and many of us busied ourselves writing reminiscences of the candidate and the man. In mine, I recalled the "brash, even bratty young minority counsel" of the old Joe McCarthy committee I had first encountered in 1954. I wrote about our chance meeting in West Virginia in 1960 when "this already influential, coiled-spring of a young man came over and engaged you in a long and friendly conversation about nothing. You recall wondering, when he left, what his angle was."

I wrote about RFK at the side of his brother's widow at his gravesite in Arlington, about his reception at the Democratic convention in Atlantic City in 1964 and his recital of the lines from *Romeo and Juliet:* "When he shall die, take him and cut him out in little stars. . . ." I wrote about campaigning with him in 1966, about his torment in 1967 over challenging Johnson, about the Indiana motorcade, the Oregon defeat, and I concluded:

> Now, as he lies across the street after a bizarre repetition of history that even now seems too cruel and too incredible to be true, it is hardest of all to . . . keep Kennedy in perspective. But looking back over those 15 years, and remembering the personal little things that inevitably colored one's view of the impersonal big things, it helps one understand his own ambivalence toward Robert Kennedy, with the bitter diminishing and the sweet edging in as the years passed. You still guard against liking him too much, against getting caught up in the Kennedy mystique, what the reporters used to call "being soft on Bobby." But there is little else that can be done now but to think back.

Some others of my colleagues, in anticipation of the worst, started on Kennedy's obituary. The worst came at about two o'clock the next morning, when Kennedy adviser Frank Mankiewicz came in and read a short statement saying that Kennedy had died. It was announced that the funeral would take place in his adopted state of New York, at St. Patrick's Cathedral in Manhattan. I went back to the Ambassador, packed my things, and took the first flight I could get to meet the Kennedy plane when it landed at La Guardia Airport. To try to get the whole terrible scene out of my mind for a while, I decided to watch the in-flight movie. It was a spy drama in which, in the opening scene, the head of a very lifelike dummy was blown off in a hail of gunfire.

At St. Patrick's, as thousands of mourners passed the closed casket in a steady stream for all the daylight hours and into the night, I took a brief turn as an honor guard, as did many of my colleagues from the campaign entourage. The service the next morning, witnessed by a host of celebrities led by President Johnson, was marked by the emotional eulogy by Ted Kennedy, who struggled manfully through it, his voice breaking only as he said: "My brother need not be idealized, or enlarged in death beyond what he was in life, to be remembered simply as a good and decent man, who saw wrong and tried to right it, saw suffering and tried to heal it, saw war and tried to stop it."

The final act, the train trip from New York's Pennsylvania Station to Washington's Union Station and then the motorcade to Arlington National Cemetery across the Potomac River, was a logistical marvel with a special Kennedy flavor. From the cathedral, a fleet of thirty buses took 700 invited guests to the twenty-one-car train for the 226-mile journey. Crowds lined the entire route to catch a glimpse of the casket elevated in a special observation car. This trip too was marked by tragedy, when two people standing on the adjacent tracks at the Elizabeth, N.J., station failed to see or hear an approaching train and were killed when they could not get off in time. Later, near Trenton, a young man of 18 climbed on a boxcar, brushed against a high-voltage overhead wire and was also killed.

A most remarkable feature of the long trip came as son Joe Kennedy, then 15, walked through the cars greeting every single passenger, identifying himself and saying, "Thank you for coming." Later, his mother, Ethel, also came through, repeating the greeting to every passenger. As word of her approach reached my car, many hard-bitten reporters put down their drinks, slipped into their suit jackets, and straightened their ties. She consoled many with a word or two, or a pat on the shoulder, before they could console her.

On the motorcade to Arlington, the press bus was assigned twenty-third place in line, but in keeping with the Kennedy campaign dictum of the press staying up with the candidate, Frank Mankiewicz ordered the driver to pull out and move up to just behind the hearse and family cars. The summer night was pitch dark by the time the entourage reached the John Kennedy gravesite. Long candles were passed out and lit as the Harvard University band played "America the Beautiful" and a brief prayer was recited by Patrick Cardinal O'Boyle of Washington. At the end, we boarded the press bus again and headed back into downtown. As I got off near my office, Chuck Quinn of ABC News, who had been with Kennedy all the way and was going on to the hotel for the traveling press, looked at me with a pained expression and asked, "Aren't you going to the end with us?"

Two months later, about seventy Kennedy staff and traveling reporters met in a private room at Duke Zeibert's old restaurant in Washington to witness about two hours of color slides of the campaign taken by Stan Tretick of *Look* magazine and other regulars. We all sat and watched as the excitement and good humor of the campaign came back to us, laughter filling the room until near the end, when Tretick flashed on a series of pictures of the contemplative candidate. The room fell silent until it was over, Mankiewicz said, quietly, "Thank you," and the lights came on. We all walked wordlessly out into the August night.

That reunion of campaign workers and the usually adversarial press was a measure of the uncommon spell Kennedy wove over all who had accompanied him on that last, often joyful but ultimately tragic odyssey. Later, a group of us in the Kennedy press corps established journalism awards in his name for exemplary reporting that examines the plight of the disadvantaged, a central concern and target of Kennedy's political career. The RFK Journalism Awards now draw more applicants than any others except the Pulitzer Prizes.

Like all my colleagues, I moved on to other assignments, including coverage of the trial and conviction in Los Angeles of Kennedy's assassin, Sirhan Sirhan, and of many subsequent presidential campaigns. But the 1968 campaign of Robert Kennedy, and the man himself, remain the most vivid in my memory, and sentiments, to this day.

8 Surviving 1968, and Branching Out

WITH LBJ A SURPRISE LAME DUCK and Martin King and then Robert Kennedy gone, we boys on the bus (and a few girls) now hoped for a less frenetic and bumpy ride to Election Day 1968. Surely nothing else could occur to so jolt us. In those first six months of the year, one unexpected event after another had kept our fingers flying over our portable typewriter keys, turning out page-one stories from bouncing buses, swaying trains, and windtossed propeller planes.

Filing daily reports was much more challenging then than today, when reporters tote laptop computers and travel in style on swift and well-catered jet flights. My daily transmission drill then consisted either of giving hastily typed copy to a Western Union operator accompanying the candidate's party and hoping it would arrive at its intended destination by deadline time, or of grabbing a telephone on the run at a campaign stop and dictating to the Newhouse bureau in Washington or to one of the papers. Even when you laboriously spelled out names and punctuation marks, errors inevitably occurred, not to mention missing buses, trains, and planes when you were unable to complete the chore before they left you in Podunk.

By this time on the Republican side, Nelson Rockefeller had reconsidered his "I don't want to be president" proclamation to us on the Ship of Fools. He let the word be passed that, with Romney's collapse, he was not going to allow Nixon a free ride to their party's nomination. At a news conference in which it was now widely expected that he would enter the race, however, Rocky demurred, shocking his one-man draft committee, Governor Spiro T. Agnew of Maryland, and driving Agnew into the Nixon camp.

But when Johnson took himself out of contention, Rockefeller reconsidered yet again and declared his candidacy.

At the convention in Miami Beach, Governor Reagan also came out from behind his favorite-son posture and announced his availability, but by this time Nixon had the nomination locked up. Thereupon he sprung a surprise by choosing the relatively obscure Agnew as his running mate. The mood at the hotel press conference at which Nixon announced his selection was one of incredulity. I was told later by John Sears, a Nixon campaign insider, that a poll had been taken about various vice-presidential nominees and it found none would help Nixon. "Actually, we wanted to run without a vice president," he said, only half joking. Unable to do that, Nixon picked a nobody. Sears, I learned later, had contacted Agnew in March right after Rockefeller had disappointed him and bagged him on the rebound. At a press party at Nixon's Key Biscayne hideway after the convention, the nominee said about his choice of Agnew: "There is a mysticism about men. There is a quiet confidence. You look a man in the eye and you know he's got it—brains. This guy has got it. If he doesn't, Nixon has made a bum choice." He could have said that again.

Among the Democrats, Kennedy's ill-fated victory in the California primary had effectively erased any chance McCarthy had for the nomination. Humphrey, having avoided all primaries, had clear sailing to the party convention, but he wore the albatross of LBJ's Vietnam war policy around his neck. Eighteen days after the Republicans left Miami Beach, the Democrats converged on a Chicago that was in a state of siege over that policy.

From my room at the Conrad Hilton, I literally had a bird's eye view of hordes of protesters in Grant Park across Michigan Avenue. I was serenaded each night with chants of "Dump the Hump!" and "Hey, Hey, LBJ! How many kids have you killed today?" The debate on the convention floor over the party's Vietnam plank was loud and bitter. One night, shouts of "Stop the War!" disrupted the proceedings until beleaguered Mayor Richard J. Daley, by drawing his finger across his throat, signaled convention chairman Carl Albert to declare the convention in recess. When it resumed and beat back the anti-war plank after three hours of debate, choruses of "We Shall Overcome" rang out over the floor. Many delegates, wearing black armbands, spilled out into the streets, where Daley's men in blue were already engaged in what a commission report later dubbed a "police riot."

After Humphrey was nominated, a film tribute to Robert Kennedy was shown. It was introduced on tape by Ted Kennedy, who throughout the convention had turned back efforts by his late brother's backers and others to draft him for the presidential nomination. The scene was chillingly reminiscent of Robert Kennedy's appearance at the 1964 Democratic convention, introducing a similar memorial film of John Kennedy. Although this time no Kennedy brother was in the hall to receive the delegates' applause, it erupted anyway and lasted for nearly five minutes, bringing many of them to tears and finally, to the singing of "The Battle Hymn of the Republic." When Chicago political hacks in the galleries started chanting "We Love Daley!" voices rose from the convention floor in reply: "We Want Teddy!"

Later, as I made my way back into the Hilton, I felt the sting of tear gas. Stopping in the glass-splattered Haymarket Lounge for a beer, I suffered the lingering malodorous product of stink bombs tossed through the saloon's plate-glass window. In a while, I wandered up to the fifteenth floor to say good-by to some of the young McCarthy workers I had known ever since the New Hampshire primary. I found them quietly drowning their sorrows, reminiscing, and softly singing songs, as if it were the weary aftermath of a fraternity party. I subsequently learned that a few hours later, around five in the morning, police and national guardsmen had stormed the McCarthy staff room, clubbed many of its occupants and herded them into elevators for a roundup in the hotel lobby. McCarthy himself finally showed up and told the kids to go to their rooms, as the police stood helplessly by. It was a sad end to an inspiring effort by young Americans to work through the political system to end a war they despised.

During the general election campaign that fall, I alternated traveling with the Nixon and Humphrey campaigns, with occasional diversions to the adventures of George Wallace, which were by now in full swing. His American Independent Party had achieved ballot position in all fifty states, and the Wallace campaign was nothing if not diverting. For sheer entertainment, the Nixon and Humphrey juggernauts could not hold a candle to it. George simply took across the Alabama state line the same country road show that worked so well for him back home.

On every speaker's platform, it opened with Sam Smith's five-piece band twanging "Cheatin' Heart," a rather unusual choice for a candidate seeking voter confidence. Then the Taylor Sisters, Mona and Lisa (later Wallace's third wife), would lead the crowd in "God Bless America." Next, "Wallace Girls" in red and blue blazers and skirts circulated through the crowd with yellow plastic pails into which the faithful could drop their dollar bills or even loose change. An Alabama weekly newspaper publisher named Dick Smith, a rough-cut version of Wallace himself if that can be imagined, would make the pitch, at the same time berating the hecklers almost always in attendance, especially up north. He would warn them that they could make all the wisecracks they wanted but on election day, "You're through." Once, early on the fall swing, his rhetoric got away from him and he bellowed, "After November 5, we're gonna do away with you!" The crowd cheered the prospect. Wallace customarily would then pick up the message, with such genteel observations as, if any protesters tried lying down in front of his car he'd simply run over them.

The comic highlight of the fall campaign as far as I was concerned took place in Pittsburgh on the occasion of Wallace's introduction of his running mate. Presumably to demonstrate that as president he would be just as tough on Cold War adversaries as on campaign hecklers, he produced Curtis LeMay, retired Air Force chief of staff and former commander of the nuclear-toting Strategic Air Command.

The event unfolded in the ballroom of the Pittsburgh Hilton, as Secret Service agents poked their heads in and out of large openings in a wall of psychedelic art behind the stage, reminiscent of the old television show *Laugh-In*. Unintentionally, the presentation turned out to be a laugh riot in itself as LeMay, predictably, was peppered with reporters' questions about his views on the use of nuclear weapons. As Wallace stood by unsuspecting but soon mortified, the general, already dubbed by many in the press corps as "the Mad Bomber," with no early warning dropped a political nuke on his own candidate:

We seem to have a phobia about nuclear weapons. I think most military men think it's just another weapon in the arsenal. . . . The smart thing to do when you're in a war—hopefully you prevent it. Stay out of it if you can. But when you get in it, get in it with both feet and get it over with as soon as you can. Use the force that's necessary. Maybe use a little more to make sure it's enough to stop the fighting as soon as possible. So this means efficiency in the operation of the military establishment. I think there are many times when it would be most efficient to use nuclear weapons. However, the public opinion in this country and throughout the world throw up their hands in horror when you mention nuclear weapons, just because of the propaganda that's been fed to them. I don't believe the world would end if we exploded a nuclear weapon.

Off to the side, Wallace was beginning to see his own political world disintegrating, but he held his tongue as LeMay explained. Despite "propaganda" that nuclear weapons caused permanent and hereditary damage to human, animal, and plant life, he said, tests at the Bikini firing grounds had proved otherwise. "The fish are back in the lagoons," he reported, "the coconut trees are growing coconuts, the guava bushes have fruit on them, the birds are back. As a matter of fact, everything is about the same except the land crabs. They get minerals from the soil, I guess, through their shells, and there's a little question about whether you should eat a land crab or not." But he assured us that the rats on the tropical isle were "bigger, fatter and healthier than they ever were before."

Wallace was squirming now, and got more uneasy as LeMay went on to concede that while nuclear war would be "horrible," there really wasn't any difference between getting killed by a nuclear bomb or by "a rusty knife" in Vietnam. "As a matter of fact," he said, "if I had a choice I'd rather be killed by a nuclear weapon."

A frantic Wallace swung immediately into damage control. "General LeMay hasn't advocated the use of nuclear weapons, not at all," he pleaded. "He's against nuclear weapons and I am too." Then, turning to the general, he applied verbal respiration: "They said you agreed to use nuclear weapons. You didn't say it." But LeMay, his dander up now, wouldn't retreat. "I gave you a discussion on the phobia we have in this country about the use of nuclear weapons," he told another questioner. "I prefer not to use them. I prefer not to use any weapons at all. . . . If I found it necessary I would use anything we could dream up—including nuclear weapons if it was necessary."

Wallace again sought to come to the rescue, turning to the reporters who were trying with little success to contain their mirth. "I know you fellows better than he does because I've had to deal with you," he said. But before he could roll the Mad Bomber back into his hangar, LeMay offered his own defense. "I know I'm going to come out with a lot of misquotes from this campaign," he said. "I have in the past. And I'll be damned lucky if I don't appear as a drooling idiot whose only solution to any problem is to drop atomic bombs all over the world. I assure you I'm not. . . . But I'm certainly not going to stand up here and tell our enemies that I advocate that under all circumstances that I'm not going to use nuclear weapons. We might as well bury them out at Fort Knox."

Having cleared up that matter, LeMay went on to say a few helpful words about Wallace. Reading about him in the press, he offered, "you get the impression George Wallace is a bigot and a racist of the first order." After talking to him, he said, he found him to be "reasonable and practical" on racial issues. "I sometimes wonder what the real fuss is about," he mused, noting that the Air Force had been integrated smoothly by using "good solid-citizen colored people" to pave the way.

Wallace, to cut his losses if possible, put LeMay in storage from then on, seldom giving him a microphone and reducing the proud general to a prop. Mrs. LeMay, meanwhile, seemed to have developed a crush on Wallace. As her husband sat stolidly and silently through his speeches, she gushed repeatedly at the cocky bantam rooster from Alabama, himself a bit subdued in the aftermath of the LeMay rollout and takeoff. As Wallace's support plunged, "Bombs Away With Curt LeMay" became a favored slogan on the Wallace press bus.

Shortly afterward at the National Press Club in Washington, Wallace wailed that LeMay "was questioned by some folks who are on our campaign trip for one purpose, and that's to discourage and disgrade [sic] and slant and distort." Before crowds, he continued to invite his supporters to look around at all the reporters on "a distortin' trip." We became his favorite whipping boys, along with "pointy-headed bureaucrats who can't park a bicycle straight" and lawbreakers who deserve to "be put under a good jail."

The Wallace campaign that fall was a corking good sideshow, but that's essentially all it was. In a year in which all the major candidates faced heavy heckling, Nixon handled it basically by staying out of the line of fire as much as he could. He ran a very antiseptic campaign of a limited number of set speeches in venues designed to be friendly. Humphrey, seeking desperately to sell himself as his own man but unwilling until very late to break with Johnson on his Vietnam war policy, encountered angry protesters at every turn. Unlike Nixon, who by turns disliked reporters or was afraid of what we might do to him, the garrulous Humphrey generally liked the press and was comfortable with us, even as he squirmed under questions about his loyalty to LBJ and Vietnam.

Nixon would make occasional efforts to be friendly, at least once serenading us on a small piano brought onto his campaign plane. But these attempts were always strained, as were most encounters he had with any homo sapiens he met, other than on campaign rope lines where all he had to do was stick out his hand to be shaken. The up side for us was that when we spent a day or a week traveling with him, we could be fairly sure we would not be bothered either with impromptu and awkward chats in the back of the bus or plane, or press conferences devoid of any substance. We would be spoon-fed with position papers and could always count on getting to a good hotel chosen by the campaign in plenty of time for a leisurely meal. A then-obscure campaign aide named John Ehrlichman often was available to join some of us, but never another, named Bob Haldeman, who hated reporters and didn't mind our knowing it. Both went on to big things in the Nixon White House, as well as premature exits in the wake of the Watergate affair.

One of the few rewards for me in covering the tightly buttoned-up Nixon campaign was my developing friendship with John Sears, a refugee from the Nixon law firm in New York, who was then a campaign delegate hunter and personal aide to the great man. He had been aboard the infamous "Ship of Fools" governors' conference as Nixon's eyes and ears, and he shared neither Nixon's fondness for early bedtimes with cookies and milk nor his dislike and distrust of reporters. He helped me and others of the press corps close many a saloon around the country in the following years. He was a reliable compass for us on stories that needed confirmation or waving off, while remaining loyal to Nixon and his campaign.

Sears' own reward was assignment in the fall as keeper of Nixon's running mate, Spiro Agnew, who was already establishing himself as Nixon's Nixon—a hatchet man, and a loose cannon to boot. Agnew's characterizations of Humphrey as "squishy soft" on communism, of Polish-Americans as "Polacks," and of a snoozing Japanese-American reporter on his plane as "the fat Jap" kept Sears busy finding ways to keep Agnew out of hot water with the press.

"Ted" Agnew also provided material for Walter Mears of the Associated Press and me, seatmates on the Nixon and Agnew planes, as we offered advice in lyrical form for Nixon to give his vice-presidential choice, unsung by him but often by us on the Nixon plane. To the tune of "Can't Take My Eyes Off of You," the chorus went:

Squishy soft on communism, without much thought of realism,
Ted Agnew's got a way with words that Cabot Lodge did not.

I need you, Spiro, for putting Hubert down,
Keep swinging, Spiro, I'll try to calm them down;
You take the low road, I'll keep my moratoriums high.
So cool it, Spiro, don't knock the Polack vote,
And let the Jap sleep, he just got off the boat. . . .

That was one ditty, as I recall, that Nixon never plunked out on his little airborne keyboard.

Humphrey and aides like Ted Van Dyk, Bill Connell, Jim Rowe, and especially Larry O'Brien were generally available on the Humphrey campaign's buses and planes, in a much more free-wheeling and less disciplined entourage. Humphrey himself seemed unwilling or unable to break off a day's campaigning, which always started earlier and ended much later than Nixon's. He would keep going as long as there was another hand to shake, another politician to schmooze, or another reporter to argue or joke with. If there was a distinct preference for Hubert over Tricky Dick among the traveling press, it was more on a personal rather than an ideological basis. While the politics of most of us probably was more in tune with Humphrey, we never let him off the hook regarding his unwillingness to separate himself from LBJ on the war.

Humphrey finally did make a speech in Salt Lake City in which, in his fashion, he broke from Johnson by pledging as president "to stop the bombing of North Vietnam as an acceptable risk for peace" leading to negotiations. In an effort to get on the offensive, he went after Agnew, asking crowds to consider "the possibility of a President Agnew," compared to "the great possibility of a President Ed Muskie," his own running mate, thus seeming to predict his own demise if elected.

Humphrey would assure audiences that "my co-pilot, Ed Muskie, is ready to take over at any time." One of my colleagues and pals on the Humphrey plane, Jim Doyle of the *Boston Globe*, wrote a fake lead on that day's story that began: "Vice President Hubert H. Humphrey pledged today that if elected, he will resign immediately and let Senator Edmund S. Muskie become president."

Agnew came under such heat that Sears decided to play kill-the-clock. Later he described a typical campaign day to me thus: "We sat all day in the hotel until night, then we got into a motorcade and motored way out of town to a rally. Then we came back, we went to bed, and the next morning left and arrived in the early part of the afternoon at the Detroit airport, where we made a fast move in the cars, a distance of about 500 yards over to the airport motel, where we sat until night, then went to Cobo Hall for a rally, gave a speech, got out and came back. We spent the night and then flew home for the weekend on Thursday—to take some rest."

Once, the reporters on the Agnew plane learned it was headed for a non-event weekend in Texas with no access to the candidate, and we complained to Agnew's press secretary, Herb Thompson. A tongue-in-cheek Sears instructed him:

> Herb, you go tell those bastards that if they want to come along with us, there's good food and drink on the plane, and we'll drop down once in a while and get a night's sleep at a good hotel. Tell them we have a nice weekend planned in Corpus Christi. They'll have a nice fishing trip planned for them in the morning, and a picnic in the afternoon, and on Monday we may make a speech. Tell them that after the next stop we're going to get up in that plane and just fly around. If they want to come with the next vice president of the United States, okay. Tell them we'll land after a while and then we'll all go into town and take a nap.

While Agnew thus was keeping the lowest of profiles, Nixon made daily public appearances that were carefully controlled to avoid the spontaneous, which might risk political error. Unlike his frenetic fifty-state-or-bust schedule of 1960, he often made only one very deftly crafted and faithfully read speech a day, delivered at or near an airport with frequent connections to the East. It came early enough so that television film could be dispatched by plane in plenty of time to make the nightly newscasts in New York. Meanwhile, Humphrey was continuing his habitual frenzied pace and loquacious observations, often risking politically damaging comment. Network editors in New York thus had their choice of Humphrey speeches, but often only the one carefully crafted Nixon speech or event. Under this arrangement, Humphrey as a general rule did not come off well.

Once Humphrey made his break with Johnson on Vietnam policy, however, he rapidly began to close the gap with Nixon in all the polls. The election came down to the final weekend, with much riding on whether LBJ could bring the South Vietnamese regime to the peace table with the North Vietnamese in Paris. Johnson, through FBI and CIA surveillance and wiretaps of the South Vietnamese embassy in Washington, received strong indications that Nixon and/or his campaign at the last hour had derailed the talks by promising the Saigon regime a better deal under a Nixon presidency.

My friend and colleague, the intrepid Tom Ottenad of the *St. Louis Post-Dispatch* Washington bureau, at this time scared hell out of the White House. "Eyes Only" memos to LBJ from National Security Adviser Walt Rostow, when later unsealed, revealed Tom's urgent inquiries about the behavior of Nixon supporter Anna Chennault, the Chinese-born wife of the American commander of the famous Flying Tigers of World War II. She was in close touch with the Saigon embassy, and Ottenad pressed Rostow on whether she was conveying a deal from Nixon to South Vietnamese President Nguyen Van Thieu. Rostow wrote Johnson, "The lady is about to surface."

Astonishingly, I learned later, when writing a book about the incredible year of 1968, that Johnson had turned over incriminating evidence about Chennault's activities to Humphrey for use in the final days of the campaign. The idea was that such an act of treason would sink Nixon and elect Humphrey. But Humphrey declined to use it, partly because he felt he could not reveal the sources of the classified material, and—remarkably—he doubted that voters would believe Tricky Dick capable of such an act! Later, in his memoir, Humphrey recounted a memo of his own at the time: "I wonder if I should have blown the whistle on Anna Chennault and Nixon. I *wish* [his italics] I could have been sure. Damn Thieu. Dragging his feet this past weekend hurt us. I wonder if that call did it. If Nixon knew. Maybe I should have blasted them anyway."

One of Johnson's chief aides then, Joe Califano, told me later that Humphrey's refusal to use the information against Nixon, which would have charged him with a major criminal offense, "became an occasion for a lasting rift" between LBJ and Humphrey. "Johnson thought Hubert had no balls, no spine, no toughness," Califano reported.

Much later also, I tracked down Anna Chennault at a small office she kept in Georgetown, and while saying she could not talk because she was writing a book of her own (yet to appear), she insisted she had acted under instructions from the Nixon campaign in contacting the Saigon regime. "The only people who knew about the whole operation," she told me, "were Nixon, John Mitchell [Nixon's campaign manager] and John Tower [senator from Texas and Nixon campaign figure], and they're all dead. But they knew what I was doing. Anyone who knows about these things knows I was getting orders to do these things. I couldn't do anything without instructions."

In 1973, Rostow sent a sealed envelope to the LBJ Library in Austin containing "a file President Johnson asked me to hold personally because of its sensitive nature" that "contains the activities of Mrs. Chennault and others before and immediately after the election of 1968." Rostow recommended that the file be kept secret for fifty years. The embargo later was lifted and the file sent to appropriate federal agencies for clearance. But my repeated efforts to gain access have been turned down, with unofficial assurance that no "smoking gun" confirming intervention by the Nixon campaign is included. There the matter rests in what could be a story every bit as significant historically as the Watergate cover-up. The opening of the file apparently will have to await another Democratic administration, and might not happen even then. My efforts to get it continued through the Clinton years, to no avail, and again after Rostow's death in 2002.

In any event, Nixon squeezed through in 1968 and to the very end of the campaign played fast and loose with the truth, even on small matters. In a victory rally at the Waldorf-Astoria ballroom in New York, he recalled a sign he had seen from his campaign train, which I happened to be aboard. Some of the signs were friendly, some not, he said, "but the one that touched me the most was one that I saw in Deshler, Ohio, at the end of a long day of whistle-stopping—a little town, I suppose five times the population was there in the dusk—but a teenager held up a sign, 'BRING US TOGETHER.' And that will be the great objective of this administration at the outset."

Standing on the ballroom floor below Nixon as he spoke, several of us in the press section recalled the Deshler stop, but no such sign, and what he had said that day, hardly a message of togetherness: "In the 45 minutes it takes to ride from Lima to Deshler, this is what has happened in America: there has been one murder, two rapes, 45 major crimes of violence, countless robberies and auto thefts . . ." We were able to quote the message verbatim because Nixon had used the line at nearly every stop, simply changing the name of the town. Nixon speechwriter Bill Safire suggested in a subsequent book that Nixon may not have seen such a sign at all, but that another speechwriter, Richard Moore, had seen it, and a few days later it popped up as a clear recollection of the great man himself. It was a small thing, but it reminded me of Nixon's talent for recalling softball questions from invisible people in crowds and the self-serving answers he gave them—people and questions nobody else present at the time could seem to recall.

After the election, I next saw Nixon in New York when I covered the transition—the task of putting his new administration in place. The president-elect, staff, and press corps all stayed at the posh Pierre Hotel off Central Park East, where the exorbitant nightly room rate, sixty dollars at the time, made me glad that my old Newhouse slave driver, Andy Viglietta, was no longer reviewing my expense accounts. It was a relaxing time with usually only one or two briefings a day. Nixon, always grinning now, would descend from his suite to the Pierre lobby to introduce the members—the exclusively white, male members—of his cabinet, who exuded all the color, spark, and charm of the board of directors of a small bank.

After all those months of riding press buses and staying in crummy hotels in the Peorias of America, the change of venue was welcome. We scribblers could slip off for lunch and dinner at a wide selection of Manhattan eateries and even catch a Broadway show or two in that now long-past era when orchestra seats were going for less than a week's pay.

At Christmas, we reporters and our families dutifully trekked to Florida to keep an eye on the soon-to-be leader of the free world as he continued to work on his tan. The Nixon people usually kept a comfortable distance from the press corps, but I remember having breakfast one morning with Melvin Laird, the garrulous former Wisconsin congressman who was soon to become Nixon's secretary of defense. What remained with me was the vision of the huge gold cufflinks shooting out from Laird's coat sleeves as he ate his ham and eggs. I realized that they were miniature business cards bearing his name, address, and phone number. When I asked him where he got them, he simply replied, with a grin, "The special interests!"

Now that Nixon had won, he entertained his penchant for countering past failures with current victories. In 1960, he had met the man who had defeated him, John F. Kennedy, in Florida in a show of national unity. So when he learned that Humphrey was heading to the Caribbean on a post-election vacation, he invited his vanquished foe to meet him at an airport near Miami. Stepping to a microphone, Nixon with Humphrey at his side said to him: "I recall in 1960 after losing a very close election, President-elect Kennedy called on me when I was in Florida, and history repeats itself, so I know exactly how you feel." That no doubt made loser Humphrey feel much better.

In his inauguration address from the steps of the Capitol on January 20, the newly sworn president followed up on his remarks, in Deshler, on national conciliation, which were, or were not, inspired by the sign held by that teenager in the crowd. All the American people needed to do was simply to listen to each other. "In these difficult years," he said, "America has suffered from a fever of words: from inflated rhetoric that promises more than it can possibly deliver, from angry rhetoric that fans discontent into hatreds, from bombastic rhetoric that postures instead of persuading. We cannot learn from one another until we stop shouting at one another—until we speak quietly enough so that our words can be heard as well as our voices."

Yet, it could be said that listening was one thing he himself did not do, because in his winning campaign he seldom allowed himself, or his strategists seldom enabled him, to get close enough to average Americans to hear what was on their minds. I wrote later in *The Resurrection of Richard Nixon:*

> Perhaps the reason Nixon could make the kind of inaugural speech he delivered lies in the manner in which he traveled his long road to the White House. In the most antiseptic, controlled campaign in American history, he was a candidate in a glass booth. His smooth operation contrived for him appearances of enthusiastic support, and his own words attracted mostly those who already agreed with him. It was difficult for a candidate who had been so effectively sealed off from genuine dialogue with the public, and from debate with his opponent, to grasp the depth of the public passions of 1968 and the resoluteness of those who disagreed with him. Only one who had failed to properly gauge the intensity of the nation's dissent could ask, with any expectation of success, that its volume be modulated. . . .
>
> One of the striking things about Richard Nixon all along his determined road back was that he seemed so often to be traveling it by helicopter—hovering above, studying the route, but never absorbing anything emotionally from the pilgrimage. In public, he seemed often to be a spectator in his own drama, or a guest of honor at a series of testimonials. Spontaneity was avoided like a Viet Cong land mine. . . . And in the end, he did the one thing he had become so good at: he survived.

It had been quite a year, 1968, full of the unexpected and for many full of sorrow. But it was not without some personal compensation to me. My experiences in 1968 ushered me into the realm of book writing, first with that account of the breakneck and ill-fated presidential campaign of Robert Kennedy and then, the next year, with a chronicle of Richard Nixon's return from the oblivion of his defeat in the California gubernatorial race of 1962 to election to the presidency six years later.

Like many other reporters, I had always thought I'd like to write a book sometime, but I had no idea what I might write it about, not yet having encountered a story or experience that struck me as befitting a publishable book. As a grunt in the Newhouse bureau I worked off my frustrations by writing magazine articles and job applications. Most of the time my reward in both endeavors was the same—a pile of rejection slips and letters. Some were boilerplate, while others let me down easy with "This does not quite meet our needs" or "We're sorry this doesn't fit into our present plans, but keep trying."

I did so and eventually began to peddle articles to a number of obscure publications. My first "sale" was to *Marine News,* which printed a piece on the plight of the U.S. Merchant Marine Academy at Kings Point, New York, which constantly faced extinction despite the survival efforts of Long Island congressmen whose legislative labors I covered in my unending quest for "short items" for my demanding, bizarre boss, Andy Viglietta. My pay was the pleasure of seeing the piece in print, which believe it or not thrilled me at the time. From there I moved up to such other hot newsstand sellers as the *Magazine of Wall Street,* for which I wrote a sweeping assessment of the state of the Cold War, which I was about as qualified to do as was the Newhouse copyboy—or the bureau chief, for that matter.

In time, though, I attained the more rarified atmosphere of political opinion magazines like the *Reporter,* the *New Republic,* the *Nation,* and the *Progressive,* especially when my newspaper beat graduated from regional coverage for the Newhouse papers on Long Island, in Newark, and in Syracuse to national political coverage. Writing for such newspapers had the one advantage of allowing me to do spinoffs for these magazines. They didn't pay much, but I consoled myself with the notion that I was getting some visibility in my quest to escape from the newspaper chain that bound me.

Finally, my aforementioned long article on Richard Nixon in the *Saturday Evening Post* in late 1966 was a breakthrough for me, followed by another there on George Romney. I continued to do articles for the political magazines, on George Wallace, Hubert Humphrey, and other national figures I encountered, including Robert Kennedy. But it was not until I had covered Kennedy's unexpected and frenetic bid for the 1968 Democratic presidential nomination that ended so tragically that it occurred to me that I had the makings of a book.

In selling to the magazines, I had acquired a sympathetic agent in New

York named Carolyn Stagg. Days after I returned home from Robert Kennedy's funeral, I sent her a proposal, and in relatively short order she obtained a most modest advance of three thousand dollars from G. P. Putnam's Sons for a book on RFK's last campaign, on the condition that I could produce it in a few months. It was mid-June of 1968 and I set to work in a fever. I had two major advantages: good relations with many of the key players in that campaign, and my presence in the Ambassador kitchen on the night of Kennedy's shooting.

For openers, I did my best to recreate the atmosphere of self-doubt surrounding his decision first not to run and then to run, touching base with all the insiders I knew and adding my own observations as a reporter with my nose only slightly under the tent. Building on my daily notes and my own and others' newspaper clips of that amazing and ultimately heartbreaking campaign, I finished *85 Days: The Last Campaign of Robert Kennedy* in just a few days longer than the campaign itself. On the day after Labor Day, I turned in the manuscript to my editor, Arthur Fields, whom I had never met, and waited.

In about a week's time, he called me to his office in New York. I approached it with trepidation, and on my arrival his door swung open and a stocky man in a wheelchair bore down on me at top speed. My nervousness was pierced at once by the huge grin on his face as he expressed surprise that a novice had been able to turn out the manuscript so quickly. To my further relief, I found Arthur Fields to be a delightful and, most important, brilliant editor who spent time with me there and then. He offered highly constructive ideas on how to enliven the pace of the book and build to the ultimate eyewitness account of Kennedy's assassination and the aftermath, the climax of the narrative.

Thus began for me a fruitful relationship that was a far cry from the dismal stewardships of most of my newspaper editors up to then. At Arthur's encouragement, the next year I wrote *The Resurrection of Richard Nixon*, also published by Putnam, and in both books I employed a Fields technique that stood me in good stead in other books to follow. Whenever possible, he counseled, begin with a scene that either will in vivid terms set the stage for what is to follow, or describe a critical turning point in the narrative. It was advice I never forgot.

The events of 1968 and the Kennedy book also became my tickets out of the Newhouse organization. With the presidential campaign over and my rather strange friend Richard Nixon in the White House, I spent 1969 tracking his own tribulations with Vietnam, Ted Agnew's various assaults on press and television and the peace movement's protest against the war. I covered another round of governors' conferences and the grieving Ted Kennedy's return to active politicking.

In late April, I met up with Kennedy in Las Vegas for a weekend speech-making swing for fellow Democratic senators in Nevada and Missouri. It was low key all the way, with crowds warm and cordial if a bit more restrained than in the past for a campaigning Kennedy. His mood too was quieter than his usual glad-handing and backslapping; he was a man temperamentally more ebullient than his late brothers. I joined him at McCarran Airport as he deplaned from a commercial flight for the drive into town, accompanied by aide Paul Kirk, later a Democratic National Committee chairman, and a Las Vegas detective, who told me there had been a phone call that afternoon to Caesar's Palace, asking what room Kennedy would be occupying. When informed that the senator would not be staying there, the detective said, the man warned: "Well, I'm going to get him anyway." Extra security was added, but nothing happened. Yet the tenseness that often traveled with one or another of the Kennedy brothers was still present, maybe more so, though Kennedy himself seemed unaffected.

The political dinner was at the Sands, where he toyed with the partisan crowd about talk of his availability for the presidency in 1972. The fact that he was no longer shutting off the possibility, as he had done the previous year amid his grief, titillated the audience. At the time, there was speculation in Nevada about having an early presidential primary there in 1972, and Kennedy said: "I wonder if Ed Muskie has been here before me. There has been an awful lot of publicity about us and the presidential nomination, and we don't like it. . . . He doesn't like mine and I don't like his." The serious part of his speech included familiar quotes from his brother John about a rising tide lifting all boats, and from his brother Robert about the need to seek a newer world, but much of the old passion seemed missing.

Afterward, he slipped out the back way, inviting me to join him for a drink in his suite on the fifty-second floor of the nearby Sahara. Still dressed in a double-breasted tuxedo, he waved me onto the balcony where aide Dave Burke, later a top NBC executive, served us a couple of scotches. In a reflective mood, the senator reminisced about his work for John Kennedy in the western states in 1960, losing eleven of thirteen states, he admitted, and of piloting a small plane himself from state to state, and even taking turns at the controls of the *Caroline*, the family plane, from time to time.

He told of another occasion in West Virginia in 1960 when he tried to give a voter a Kennedy bumper sticker and the man refused, only to come back later, saying: "Yes, I want one—to wipe my ass with." He recalled having to stand in for his brother when the candidate's voice gave out there, and of joining him at factory gates in Wisconsin on frigid mornings. Later, at the White House, he said the new president remarked, "Eddie, last year we were out in front of those factory gates in Wisconsin in the mornings, and the workers would come by and wouldn't shake my hand." He said his brother told him the last thing he wanted to do was go there and do that again, but that in the next election he would be right out there doing it once more.

Clearly, it was going to take time for Ted Kennedy to put the past behind him and throw himself into political oratory as of yore. But his future was never far from the thoughts of many who came to see him in Nevada and later in Springfield, Missouri, where a man at the airport called out: "Hi, Senator Kennedy, see you in '72." Speaking at little Drury College, he allowed himself some of the dry, self-deprecating humor that always marked his family. "When I was a teenager and was looking around at colleges," he said, "I thought about coming to Drury. 'No,' my father said, 'Drury College is too big and impersonal, and you'd get lost.' So I went to Harvard."

Kennedy warmed to his task and before he was through he was giving the audience a full-blown critique of the war in Vietnam as "a tragedy for the United States but far more a tragedy for the people of Vietnam." When he finished, the crowd of about 600 rose and applauded at length. If he was not yet all the way back in political harness he was well on his way after this first unabashed political swing since the loss of Robert Kennedy had driven him to the sidelines.

Late that night we headed for the local airport amid dark and menacing clouds, flashes of static lightning, and rumbles of thunder not uncommon in that part of the country at that time of year. As the pilot pondered taking off, Kennedy was introduced to a local deputy sheriff, a standard obligation on the campaign trail. The man, wearing a gray Ozarks slouch hat, turned out to be Mickey Owen, the great Brooklyn Dodger catcher who unfortunately was best known for dropping a third strike on what would have been the final out for a key World Series victory over the New York Yankees in 1941.

It was not the best omen for a takeoff in such foul weather. But Kennedy climbed into a seat behind the pilot, and after the rest of us got aboard, we were airborne, rain beating fiercely against the plane, lightning flashing all around, and zero visibility outside as the pilot put the jet into a steep, bumpy, and scary climb. It was definitely a white-knuckle flight, but Kennedy, who had survived one small plane crash, sat quietly until we reached St. Louis and better weather. I asked him whether he had been sleeping en route. He just looked at me, as if I were joking. The flight to Washington was uneventful, tempered by large samplings of Chivas Regal all around. I went home that night more inclined to believe that if he were willing to endure such days and nights again, he probably was going to reach for the Democratic presidential nomination in 1972. On another night, on Chappaquiddick Island less than three months later, however, that expectation would be shattered.

The Chappaquiddick story and its political aftermath kept me busy most of the summer, and in the fall I focused on the mushrooming protest against the war in Vietnam. On Moratorium Day in mid-October, as hundreds of thousands demonstrated in Washington and around the country, I accompanied Al Lowenstein, "the man who dumped Johnson" and by this time a Long Island congressman, in a small plane on a fly-around to college campuses from the University of Connecticut, Yale, and Princeton to Villanova and Georgetown.

En route to Princeton, we flew over Shea Stadium where, along with 57,000 fans who were observing Moratorium Day in all-American style, I saw a fleeting bit of my first and only World Series game, between the New York Mets and the Baltimore Orioles, from about 15,000 feet up. I was fascinated, while the intense Lowenstein demonstrated only passing interest. At Princeton he demanded that President Nixon ask Congress for a declaration of war against North Vietnam, challenging the notion "that the President of the United States has a right to wage war unilaterally." I remembered the day more for that demand than for the flyover of the Mets' stadium, especially when thirty-four years later another president blatantly exercised that "right" in Iraq.

Also in 1969, I finally engineered a new political column for myself in the Newhouse papers, in which I wrote a host of interviews that ran the gamut from Lester Maddox and Barry Goldwater to Malcolm X. The column became my long-sought swan song to my seventeen years with the much-maligned chain. Its reputation as a collection of undistinguished papers, not always deserved, had nevertheless in all those years seemed to me a liability. I peddled my wares in various opinion magazines in the hope of overcoming the scarlet letter "N" tattooed—in my imagination anyway—on my chest. Yet at Newhouse I had made some very good friends and worked with some distinguished colleagues, Erwin Knoll foremost of them. In the process, I had a barrel of laughs and gained the extensive experience that had finally paid off.

Covering local congressmen for the individual papers had helped me immeasurably in learning Washington. Casey Jones in Syracuse had given me great opportunities to travel and cover national stories, including my first on the political beat. My difficult but eventually instructive stint as a Pentagon reporter when the Washington bureau was expanded to cover national events forced me to explore new fields, while heightening even more my desire to write politics. And finally, my assignment to do just that for all the Newhouse newspapers had put me on the path to greener professional pastures.

After all those years of knocking on the doors of the Washington bureaus of major papers, one finally opened for me, at the *Los Angeles Times*. Nobody ever said exactly why, but I have reason to suspect that the Kennedy campaign book had a lot to do with it. The national editor at the time, Ed Guthman, had been Kennedy's press secretary at the Justice Department and I knew him casually. I'm sure he put in a good word for me, as did my all-time journalistic idol and best boss, as bureau chief of the *Times*, Bob Donovan, and his chief deputy then, David Kraslow.

As 1970 dawned, I looked forward to the new challenge, though not without some trepidation at finally suiting up with one of the more prestigious papers. If nothing else, my good fortune showed that perseverance can make up for other shortcomings. I suppose I might have been able to "escape" the Newhouse papers sooner by leaving Washington for a newspaper elsewhere, but by this time I was hooked. The term "Potomac Fever" is usually applied to politicians who become afflicted with presidential ambitions. In my case it was just that I had come to enjoy breathing the same air as they did, and there was much more intake to come.

9 Escape to the *L.A. Times*

GOING TO THE *Los Angeles Times* after seventeen years with the Newhouse papers was like moving in baseball from the Toledo Mud Hens to the Yankees. The Washington bureau was a beehive of serious journalism with all the latest physical facilities to match. A teletype operator was on the staff to send stories instead of your having to pound them out yourself. And when you phoned a source for a story or to arrange an interview, you actually got your calls returned without having to explain whom you worked for.

More important for me was the bureau staff itself, headed with easy authority and the total respect of his peers by bureau chief Bob Donovan. When I arrived, the bureau was peopled with some of the best reporters I had ever encountered, including Bob's deputy, Dave Kraslow, Don Irwin, Ron Ostrow, Bob Jackson, Stu Loory, Murray Seeger, Rudy Abramson, Ted Sell and Bob Toth, and editor Bob Barkdoll. Soon after I joined the bureau, Jack Nelson from Atlanta also came aboard. Under the affable and professional Donovan, it was a most congenial and collegial group that worked and played together—and often shared the frustrations of dealing with editors a continent away.

Donovan himself was our icon—a journalistic luminary going back to his days as White House reporter in the 1950s and eventually Washington bureau chief of the *New York Herald Tribune*. Bob, a close friend and competitor of the *New York Times'* famed Scotty Reston, had authored the best-selling *PT-109*, the saga of John F. Kennedy's Navy service in World War II, and an authoritative account of Dwight D. Eisenhower's presidency.

Bob was the perfect boss, always encouraging and helping members of the bureau and running interference with the editors in L.A. Although he had a private office beyond the bureau's large bullpen, he kept a desk in it and spent about 95 percent of his office time there, among the troops. We were thus able to tune in on his conversations with the town's mighty as he invoked the Donovan Treatment to find out the lowdown.

I remember his frequent calls to Secretary of State William P. Rogers, a Nixon intimate. They typically would go something like this: "Hello, Bill? Bill, I'm in an awful fix. I wonder if you can possibly help me out. L.A. wants me to do an analysis of the situation in the Middle East. Bill, what do I know about the Middle East?"

Bob then would listen, scribbling away as he got a full rundown of the situation from the horse's mouth. When the secretary of state was finished, Bob would say something like: "Bill, you're a lifesaver," and with more profuse thanks would hang up. Then he would turn to whoever was sitting nearby listening with fascinated admiration and say: "I don't know whether I can do this piece. It's really over my head." His listener would dutifully reassure him that he was up to it, and Bob, shaking his head in doubt, would set himself to the task at his typewriter. Before you realized it, he had turned out the most lucid and tight analysis of the complicated situation any editor could ask for. Then he'd observe to one of his awestruck subordinates: "Could I ask you to take a look at this? I don't think it does it." But of course it did. It is not too much to say that Bob Donovan was inspirational, as much for his manner in going after a story as for his reportorial reputation and achievements.

Donovan ran a happy shop, and it stayed mostly happy after he was called to Los Angeles for a year as prelude to becoming the paper's editor—about which, more later. At Donovan's insistence, Kraslow took over as bureau chief, but in a manner that was strikingly different from that of his predecessor, often laughingly so. Kraslow was a mite less self-effacing and reveled in the trappings of high office, yet seemed to be inhibited from enjoying them after the everyman manner of Donovan.

When Donovan moved out, Kraslow felt obliged to occupy his desk in the bureau bullpen as one of the boys. But whenever a call came in for him from the L.A. office or he had to call L.A., he would jump up and stride quickly to his private office at the other end of the bureau. These frequent dashes caused much chuckling among the staff. Shortly into Kraslow's tenure as bureau boss, however, he suffered a mild heart attack that kept him out of service for several weeks, and on his return he was under orders to take it easy.

That caveat inspired Stu Loory and me to address the problem. Stu had a friend who worked at the D.C. telephone company, and he agreed to lend us a full-size, closed telephone booth to place next to Kraslow's bullpen desk, so he could (theoretically) take calls from his L.A. superiors or phone them in private without the mad dash to his private office. We had to go out to the telephone company's warehouse in the farthest reaches of the District to pick up the booth, so Stu rented an open truck and out we went. We laboriously loaded the giant booth onto the truck, drove back to the bureau, squeezed it onto the office elevator, and then toted it across the bullpen to Kraslow's desk.

The phone in the booth was not connected, and hence could not really be used for conversations between the bureau and L.A. It was just an elaborate prop for a gag. Nevertheless, we posted a sign on the booth that said "D.K. to L.A. Only" and attached a Times internal phone directory to the booth handle. It was worth all the effort to see the reaction from our bureau colleagues when they saw the towering booth next to our leader's desk and when Kraslow came strolling in the next morning and saw what was awaiting him. All we got out of him for our trouble was a mild chuckle. Apparently it wasn't quite as hilarious to him as it was to the rest of us.

Kraslow, as it turned out, served a rather short tenure as bureau chief, and the managing editor in L.A., a big and crusty turf-conscious man named Frank Haven, sent a business reporter with zero Washington experience, John Lawrence, as his replacement. The new man was distinctly a loner who did not fit in at all with the collegiality of the Donovan-Kraslow days. He had a noningratiating habit of quietly sidling up to people in the bureau to find out what they were up to. One second he would not be there, the next second he would be. He administered his coup de grace one morning at the Democratic National Convention in Miami Beach. Ed Guthman, Jack Nelson, and I, along with John Mashek, then of *U.S. News and World Report*, were taking an early dip in the Atlantic, all alone in the briny, when suddenly Lawrence materialized beside us. Henceforth I dubbed him "The Spook," and the name stuck (out of his earshot, of course) until he was recalled to Los Angeles.

The Great Telephone Booth Caper was, of course, frivolous. Loory, who was our White House reporter at the time, and I undertook intrigue of a more serious nature out of frustration over lack of accessibility to Nixon, and about his elusiveness even when there was some access. In December of 1971, on one occasion when a full-fledged press conference was announced, Stu and I concocted a mild scheme to make the conference more productive from the press's point of view. In advance, we organized a meeting of reporters at the old Washington Hotel near the White House to discuss how we could achieve that end.

Aware that the Nixonites would criticize such a meeting as a press conspiracy, we recruited the venerable John Osborne of the *New Republic* magazine to chair the meeting. Nearly thirty of our colleagues showed up, and after much palaver it was decided to ask Nixon at this press conference simply to hold them more often, and on our own to try to follow up each other's questions to pin him down when he was evasive, which was often.

Familiar with Nixon's paranoia about the press, we asked Osborne to go over to the White House afterward and tell press secretary Ron Ziegler of the meeting and what had been discussed. When Osborne arrived, Ziegler smiled and told him he had already heard about it. The upshot was an op-ed piece in the *New York Times* by Herb Klein, Nixon's director of communications and resident apologist, noting that the reporters "took pains to say they were not part of a cabal or conspiracy and that in no way did they discuss either the order or the subject matter of the questions that would be asked at the forthcoming conference. Whether or not they did, the timing of the meeting did nothing to enhance press credibility."

At the press conference in question, Nixon got some tough questions but not much follow-up, and he was tactfully asked by Herb Kaplow, then of NBC, about the possibility of more frequent press conferences. Nixon went into a hearts-and-flowers answer about his awareness of his responsibility to communicate with the public and invited suggestions on how he could do a better job. Shortly afterward, Peter Lisagor of the *Chicago Daily News,* as head of the White House Correspondents Association, responded with a list of suggestions, including the notion of weekly press conferences. That was the end of it. Loory and I were no more effective in achieving greater press access to Nixon than we were in getting Kraslow to curtail his dashes to his private office whenever the editors in L.A. phoned.

I was hired at the *Times* at first not as a full-time political writer but rather as a general reporter and sometime assistant news editor, responsible for overseeing the writing and editing of the paper's trademark lengthy exploratory articles, which ran from the front page well into the paper. These stories were the equivalent of magazine articles and were expected to be "non-duplicative," that is, to discuss matters not being written about elsewhere. They were known inside the Times as "non-dupes," and members of the staff, in Los Angeles and the various bureaus including Washington, vied for the great space given over to them and for the internal prestige they brought to their authors. At Newhouse, I had written scores of such long pieces or series on subjects ranging from grain storage problems in the Midwest and the gun lobby to the American peace and civil rights movements, so the editors figured I could guide others on non-dupe writing.

It was an interesting and educational task, mostly in teaching me why I didn't care to be an editor and was not particularly well-suited to be one. Many of the bureau staffers had been writing non-dupes for a long time and needed no kibitzing from me. With those few who were experiencing some difficulty, I too often had insufficient patience with making suggestions and found myself wanting to take over the piece and write it myself. That, of course, was not what the job called for, so I refrained from doing so, all the while wishing to get back to full-time writing myself.

One of my functions on the desk was to interview job seekers, a particularly unwelcome task, because the Times then seldom hired from outside the organization for positions in the Washington bureau. So, whenever anyone came looking for a job, I had to let the would-be applicant down easy, especially if he or she had little or no newspaper experience. For example, a young fellow came in one day, just out of the military, determined to land a reporting job in Washington. I told him the usual discouraging word, and when he persisted, I advised him to try his luck at one of the suburban Virginia or Maryland papers and meanwhile pester the local editors of the *Washington Post* and *Washington Star*. If he did well enough in the 'burbs, and was persistent enough, he might break through. He thanked me for the advice, with which in those days, along with a quarter, he could have bought a cup of coffee. More about him later.

Fortunately, I did have time in my first year at the *Times* to do some political writing along with my editing duties, and I soon worked my way into focusing on politics again. In a non-dupe of my own that jumped to two inside pages, I traced the slow descent back into relative obscurity of Gene McCarthy as he approached the voluntary end of his twenty-two-year congressional career. In his Senate office, I found the former presidential candidate, who in 1968 had liked to quote Dylan Thomas's admonition not to "go gentle into that good night," appearing to be going gently.

When I asked him why he wasn't still raging against the Vietnam war, which he had opposed so vocally in 1968, inasmuch as it remained on the front burner of Senate issues, he told me: "I don't know if there's anything to rage about in the Senate. There's no need in fighting to see who's standing over the front burner. I don't really care if I'm doing that or getting credit for it." With classic McCarthy derision, he added: "You kind of hate to give up the Senate. It's a good address."

In the congressional elections of 1970, in which President Nixon made a strong but ultimately unsuccessful effort to secure a Republican majority, I got back on the road, covering both Nixon and Vice President Agnew on trips that featured the Nixon-Agnew theme of law and order. As president, Nixon toned down the inflammatory rhetoric he'd used in the past, often mixing his attacks on candidates who were condoning "lawlessness and violence and permissiveness" with his ever-familiar references to sports. In the course of addressing the Republican faithful in downtown Columbus, he playfully chided one television network for failing "to make the Ohio State–Michigan game the game of the week so I could see it on TV." Later, on a visit to the Ohio State campus, a student told him: "We don't want to talk about Ohio State football. Just stop the war."

Agnew, for his part, wasn't kidding when he assailed the networks and any other critics of the administration. That included Republican senator Charles Goodell of New York, an intense critic of the war, whom he labeled a "radical liberal" or "radic-lib" for short. Late in the campaign, over lunch, a southern Democratic senator was discussing the excesses of the Agnew rhetoric. He compared it to the man standing at the ship's bar when the Titanic struck an iceberg who said: "I just asked for one ice cube." My favorite Republican line of the year came at a GOP governors' conference at Sun Valley, Idaho, where Agnew was dispatched to inform them, many of whom were coveting administration jobs, that Democrat John Connally was being appointed Nixon's next secretary of treasury. Governor Frank Sargent of Massachusetts asked simply, "Can he add?"

The Nixon-Agnew assault on radic-libs indirectly led to my first major political assignment at the *Times*. It so happened that as Democratic senator Ed Muskie, the 1968 vice-presidential nominee, was seeking election to a third term, the Republicans ran a newspaper ad that said, "The radicals want Muskie in the Senate," and accused him of links to them. The ad so angered Muskie that he agreed to give the Democratic Party's closing election-eve talk to the voters, passionately calling for a return to decency in politics. The speech was so well received, even as the Nixon bid to take over Congress was rejected, that Muskie was propelled into the front ranks of prospective 1972 Democratic presidential nominees. The *Times*, concluding that it would be good to have a reporter start shadowing him early, gave me the assignment.

Muskie's political strategists decided that in 1971 he ought to embark on a high-profile visit to Israel, Egypt, the Soviet Union, and West Germany to polish his foreign-policy credentials, and the *Times* sent me along. I found Muskie to be a cordial, reserved man and a pleasant traveling companion. He liked reporters—until they pressed him on some matter or issue about which he was unready or unwilling to respond. Then he would unfurl a fearful temper that kept his staff in awe and reporters at bay.

As the Democratic frontrunner, Muskie proved to be a most cautious globetrotter during the two-week trip, speaking only in generalities about his lengthy meetings with such leaders as Israel's Golda Meir and David Ben Gurion, the Soviet Union's Alexei Kosygin, Egypt's Anwar Sadat, and West Germany's Willy Brandt. Yet I managed to file at least one story a day, except when Muskie took a day off in Cairo to visit the pyramids and the Sphinx. I was amused to find young boys bouncing rubber balls off the steps of one of the pyramids in an Egyptian version of the American inner-city game of "off the point."

My old friend Dick Stewart of the *Boston Globe*, covering the local angle, and I also found time to take in a night club show in a desert hot spot somewhere in the Sahara, complete with belly dancers with whom the always game Stewart sought to frolic. In Moscow, our party went high-brow with a visit to the Bolshoi and afterward Stewart and I had the distinction of being stopped by the Moscow police in Red Square and questioned about the bottle of champagne we were toting in our taxi after a reception at the American Embassy. They judged, correctly, that we were unlikely spies and an international incident was avoided.

The main thing we learned about during the trip was the Muskie temper. The senator was having difficulty articulating his views on the Vietnam war. At the Tel Aviv Hilton during a very nice little party that he threw for the seven-member press corps traveling with him, some of us amiably broached the issue with him. Muskie suddenly unleashed a verbal thunderstorm of outrage over our inquiries, until the storm passed.

On my return, I wrote a memo to the national editor, Ed Guthman, with my impressions of the man, including the following: "He much prefers reflection to shooting from the hip, and he reacts with irritability and testiness when crowded by the press for the quick or short answer. His caution and prudence control a very quick temper that he reserves for private discourse with his staff, and occasionally with reporters. . . . I think we'll see more and more of the man's caution, together with increasing pressure from the press for more directness on issues and positions. If it reaches the point where it triggers his short fuse, it could be his Achilles heel." About a year or so later, the Muskie temper proved to be part of his political undoing when the senator, angered over a New Hampshire newspaper's remarks about his wife, blew his cork during the 1972 primary and was accused of "crying" his way out of the presidential race.

Muskie, however, was a volcano who erupted only occasionally, and from this trip I developed an admiration for him that grew into friendship over his remaining years, including service as secretary of state under President Jimmy Carter. The trip may have been short on news, but with the zany Stewart as a companion, it was a rare treat. He was a great mimic and impersonator, not especially given to protocol. Wherever we went, he made a point of imitating the local language, as on one Lufthansa flight, when he took a teaspoon, put it in his eye as a monocle and proceeded to spout harsh German gibberish to an astonished steward. (You had to be there.) We had such good times that on our return to Dulles Airport after the two weeks, I turned to Dick and said: "Oh, magic carpet, don't land!"

But it did land, and a few days later I was off again, on a much more orthodox campaign trip with Muskie to California. By this time I had been accepted as the bureau's political reporter, and through the rest of the winter and spring of 1971 I continued as the "body man" on the Muskie campaign, keeping an eye on him as his frontrunner status slowly eroded and other Democrats like Senators George McGovern, Scoop Jackson, and Birch Bayh moved into the race, making frequent visits to New Hampshire. Others, like Fred Harris and Harold Hughes, moved in and out.

Under new party rules, if party officials, members of Congress, and other officeholders wanted to become national convention delegates, they had to run for the honor in their states' primaries, usually in support of a candidate. Many such officials climbed aboard with Muskie, who through 1971 amassed an impressive list of endorsements in a misleading indication of his strength. I didn't know it at the time, but I had been saddled to a horse that had early foot but insufficient staying power for the stretch run.

In one telltale event, a dinner of the Pittsburgh chapter of the Americans for Democratic Action, Muskie made a limp appeal to its liberal members by recalling having recently told some high school students: "Don't abandon old values until you have new ones that are better." He counseled that "we must somehow put together a coalition of Americans to retain what should be retained, to change what should be changed, and to have the wisdom to know the difference." It wasn't playing with the liberal crowds.

Meanwhile, I had time to look in on other candidates. During a New Hampshire swing with McGovern, he allowed on a television show in Durham that "in a three-or-four-man race, if I got ten percent of the vote I'd say that's a very respectable showing." Few disagreed, and certainly not I. On one commercial flight from Washington to Boston, as a German television crew took footage of McGovern, I asked a young New Hampshire student what he thought of the man getting all the attention. "Well, I guess he's better than the last one we had," he said, mistaking McGovern for the state's Democratic senator, Tom McIntyre, in no way a look-alike. I also had the local-angle task of keeping an eye on overreaching Los Angeles mayor and long-shot presidential hopeful Sam Yorty. His pathetic flirtation in the state's primary inspired a cartoon by my friend Paul Conrad in the *Times* that summed up the Yorty bid. It showed a maple tree with a tap and bucket attached, captioned: "The Sap is Running in New Hampshire."

In the spring of 1971, I had another assignment that earned me no brownie points with Agnew in his running combat with the press. Along with Dave Kraslow, I was covering yet another Republican governors' conference, at Colonial Williamsburg, Virginia, when Agnew held a three-hour, late-night, off-the-record meeting in his suite at the Williamsburg Lodge, with nine reporters, none of whom was Kraslow or me. In it, as drinks flowed, he rather undiplomatically took sharp issue with the Nixon administration's decision to send an American table-tennis team to what was then called Communist China.

At that time, the administration was basking in favorable publicity for this decision, for piercing "the Bamboo Curtain" with what was being hailed as "ping-pong diplomacy." But Agnew, a staunch defender of Taiwan, had argued against the trip in the National Security Council, and he told the attending reporters so. They were sworn to secrecy by the Agnew aides, but I managed to learn the details of what the vice president had said.

Not having attended the meeting and thus not bound by any off-the-record caveat, I wrote in a front-page story for the *Times,* under a double byline with Kraslow, that Agnew had "complained that the United States took a propaganda beating" on the visit and had "expressed disappointment with some facets of the administration's policy of easing relations with the Peking [now Beijing] regime." The story said Agnew had "suggested that an administration policy that might seem to be too eager to embrace a longtime foe of the United States could adversely affect American public opinion regarding Taiwan." My good friend Tom Ottenad, who also got wind of Agnew's apostasy, filed a story to St. Louis in the same vein. Back in Washington the administration went bonkers.

In the diaries of Nixon's chief of staff, Bob Haldeman, published three years later, Haldeman wrote of Agnew: "The P[resident] wants him now to get off this wicket and say that he was completely misunderstood. K[issinger] had recommended that Ziegler say that the VP's expressing his personal view. But the P disagreed with that, and agreed with Ron's recommendation that he say that the VP's authorized him to say that there is no difference on the part of the VP with the P's policy on China." Unknown to Agnew at the time, Nixon's breakthrough visit to China was already secretly in the works, and he obviously feared that the Agnew outburst could scuttle it.

Also according to the Haldeman diaries, Agnew's gaffe fanned Nixon's feeling that his vice president might have to be kicked off the ticket in 1972. "The P got again to the point," Haldeman wrote, "that Agnew shows qualities here that are very damaging. He wants me to talk privately to Connally, and to move very, very slowly; but to start getting him with it, in this area of possible Vice Presidential candidate." In other words, Nixon was already thinking about replacing Agnew with Connally. The former Texas governor and Democrat, however, according to the diaries, wanted to be Nixon's secretary of state in the second term, as a better stepping stone to the presidency.

All this time, the diaries showed, Nixon was determined to get Agnew out of the line of succession to the presidency. Much later, Nixon's other chief aide at this time, John Ehrlichman, told me in a telephone interview that, as incredible as it sounds, Nixon toyed with the idea of getting Agnew out of the vice presidency by appointing him to—the Supreme Court!

In any event, as a result of the story on Agnew's rebellion against ping-pong diplomacy, Nixon and his top aides decided to put the vice president on ice, to make sure he would not gum up the president's planned trip to China. They sent him off on a trip around the world, notably skipping Taiwan, apparently to make sure he would say or do nothing that might interfere with Nixon's own planned trip to China. In the end, Agnew weathered the storm. Nixon and his political strategists decided that dumping him from the ticket in 1972 would make more trouble with the party's extreme right wing, which had come to worship the vice president, than it would be worth.

My modest role as a fly in Agnew's soup was only a brief interlude in my running assignment as the *Times'* Muskie-watcher through 1971. One episode in early November proved to be an education about the inner workings of my new employer. It so happened that the Muskie campaign took me to California as part of a West Coast swing, and I stumbled upon what I gauged to be a particularly juicy local political story. One Sunday, as we were flying on Muskie's chartered plane from San Francisco to Los Angeles, I spotted a new passenger closeted with Muskie in his private compartment at the rear of the plane. I had traveled with the Muskie entourage for some time by then, but I couldn't place the new arrival. When I asked Jack English, a key Muskie political adviser from New York I had known for years, who the newcomer was, English was uncharacteristically evasive.

On our arrival in L.A., the mystery guest accompanied Muskie to a meeting with prominent Democratic fund raisers at the Beverly Wilshire Hotel, further piquing my curiosity, and I leaned on English some more. Finally, conspiratorially, he filled me in. The new player was one William T. King, a prominent Los Angeles lawyer and Republican, who just happened to be co-sponsor of a huge GOP fund raiser scheduled at the same hotel two nights later, to be addressed via closed-circuit television by Nixon himself.

It seems that King had been outraged by a report that Nixon was about to nominate to the U.S. Supreme Court a woman on the California Court of Appeals who had been rejected as not qualified for the post by the American Bar Association. Meeting with English and other Muskie aides, King agreed to come over to the Muskie camp, but only after he had fulfilled his obliga-tion as a host at the dinner and a reception beforehand for Attorney General John N. Mitchell, the on-site dinner speaker.

I did not have to be Clark Kent to know I had a winner going. Gathering more details, I went to the Times building in downtown L.A., pounded out the story, turned it in, and headed back to the airport to rejoin the Muskie party, about to return to San Francisco for another dinner event that night. I boarded the Muskie charter and as we awaited takeoff, I used one of the plug-in phones aboard to check with the office on my story. Ed Guthman rather sheepishly informed me that the story was being held out. I couldn't believe my ears. When I asked him why, he told me that my story had been run by the paper's chief political writer, the formidable Dick Bergholz, who proclaimed that he knew King and the story could not possibly be true. King, after all, had been chairman of Nixon's Southern California citizens committee in 1968 and a strong supporter thereafter. A decision had been made not to use it unless Bergholz could reach King and confirm it.

The problem with that was, King by now was making himself as scarce as a cat in a dog pound, hoping to make it through the big Republican dinner he was co-chairing before word got out of his planned defection to Muskie. More shocked than disheartened, I brooded as the Muskie plane took off for San Francisco. On arrival at the Muskie dinner, I ran into Bob Walters, a crack reporter for the *Washington Star* and, still stunned and chagrined at my own paper's decision, told him about King. He checked the story out, verified it, and filed a story of his own in plenty of time to make the after-noon *Star*'s editions. The *Times* ran my own story on the day of the dinner, on page three. Thus did I learn of, and experience, the clout of Mr. Bergholz on the *Times*—a lesson that I was to experience on other occasions. For-tunately, it was one of only a few to jar my tenure at the best professional home I had found up to that time. I approached the 1972 presidential cam-paign in good spirits and high anticipation of the journey ahead.

Seaman First Class Witcover swabs the deck of the submarine tender USS *Apollo,* tied up at the U.S. Submarine Base, New London, Connecticut, after an adventure that nearly ended his Navy career (1945)

Marian Laverty Witcover and husband aboard the SS *Maasdam* of the Holland-America Line en route to a European vacation (1954)

The author on arrival in Syracuse, New York, with Martin and Klara Tornallyay, Hungarian refugees he brought from Andau, Austria, and resettled in Syracuse in the wake of the Hungarian Revolution (1956, *Syracuse Herald-Journal*)

Aboard the McGovern campaign plane, the author pounds out his story of the day on his Olivetti portable typewriter (1972, Annie Leibovitz, © 2002; by permission of Annie Leibovitz/Contact Press Images)

Senator Robert F. Kennedy and the author in the kitchen of the Ambassador Hotel in Los Angeles as Kennedy heads for the ballroom to make his victory speech on the night of the 1968 California Democratic primary. Less than half an hour later, Kennedy was shot only a few feet from the same spot. (ABC News, used by permission)

August 30, 1970

Mr. Jules Witcover
2505 Fowler's Lane
Reston, Va.

Dear Jules,

It would be easy for me, of course, to take a political approach to your book, to point out the factual errors, the gross distortions, the misleading statements, the faulty assumptions, and your total incapacity to shed the monumental biases that seem to envelop this entirely fictitious account of what in truth were my altruistic efforts to best serve the interests of all the American people. Nor do I wish to dwell on your irredeemable ineptness as a writer. Instead, let me say this, and I'm being very, very frank on this point regardless of how it may be interpreted by many of our so-called commentators: Jules, you did an excellent job on that title.

Very truly yours,

Richard Nixon

Letter on White House stationery and "signed" by President Richard M. Nixon commending the author on publication of his book *The Resurrection of Richard Nixon*, courtesy of Newhouse Newspapers White House correspondent, prankster, and pal, Erwin Knoll (1970)

The author (*left*) and sidekick Dick Stewart of the *Boston Globe* (*right*) with senator
and presidential hopeful Edmund S. Muskie returning from their "magic carpet"
trip to Western Europe, the Soviet Union, Egypt, and Israel, when Muskie was still
hopeful (1971, Burton Berinsky, used by permission of Helene Berinsky)

Fellow lyricist Walter Mears of the Associated Press (*center*) and the author serenading Senator George McGovern, the Democratic presidential nominee, with an original ditty, aboard the candidate's campaign plane, as Jim Naughton of the *New York Times* and McGovern aide Gordon Weil listen appreciatively (1972, photo by Stanley Tretick, used by permission of his estate)

Facing page

The author, then with the Washington bureau of the *Los Angeles Times,* justifying the lead on his story to his nemesis, Dick Bergholz, the *Times'* political writer in California, on the floor of the Democratic National Convention in Miami Beach (1972)

President Jimmy Carter in the Oval Office grins at the author's inscription on a copy of his book *Marathon: The Pursuit of the Presidency, 1972–1976,* chiding the peanut farmer from Georgia about some of his unkept campaign promises (1977, White House photo)

To Jules.
With best wishes — and respect —
George Bush

The author interviewing then Vice President George H. W. Bush in his office about his earlier "Take Sherman and cube it" vow not to accept the GOP vice-presidential nomination if offered it (1981, White House photo)

Holding former Vice President Fritz Mondale's empty wine glass for him at a
Democratic fund raiser in Los Angeles for his 1984 presidential campaign (1982,
Barry Levine, used by permission of the photographer)

Doonesbury cartoon signed by Garry Trudeau spoofing the author and his outrageous friend Dr. Hunter S. Thompson of the *Rolling Stone* National Affairs Desk (Doonesbury © 1975 G. B. Trudeau, reprinted by permission of Universal Press Syndicate. All rights reserved.)

Mutually cautious handshaking between Vice President Dan Quayle and the author, who in a book about the 1988 campaign, *Whose Broad Stripes and Bright Stars?* held the veep in minimum regard. The author's copy of the photo, on the wall of his study, carries the imagined repartee. (1989)

Author lectures and answers questions at the National Archives (1989, National Archives)

Lavish expense-account lunch at Galatoire's in New Orleans with the author's fiancée, Marion Rodgers, and old campaign traveling companion Curtis Wilkie of the *Boston Globe*. The reporters, as was customary, stuck their employers with the tab. (1996)

The author exchanging Christmas wishes with President Clinton at the White House, as Mrs. Clinton and the author's future wife do likewise. (1996, White House photo)

To Jack + Jules *Now I know where you get your news! It looks like you're waiting to see the dentist, not the President — a commentary on my economic plan?* Bill Clinton

Column partner Jack Germond and the author glancing through newsmagazines in the West Wing while cooling their heels before an interview with President Clinton. His caption, in barely legible Arkansas scrawl, says: "Now I know where you get your news! It looks like you're waiting to see the dentist, not the President—a commentary on my economic plan?" (1993, White House photo)

Facing page

Author's son and best man Paul gets a big laugh with his toast to the newlyweds: "On this joyous occasion, it occurs to me that this is as close as I'll probably ever come to fulfilling an occasional childhood dream of mine—that of giving my father away." (1997)

The author's son Peter, a computer whiz, tutors his old man on the difference between a Toshiba laptop and an Olivetti portable (2000)

Daughters Julie and Amy and son Paul (*left to right*) help the author celebrate an unspecified birthday at their hideaway in Bethany Beach, Delaware (1992)

10 Dirty Tricks and Disappointments

AFTER EXTENSIVE MUSKIE-WATCHING as the house expert on the man widely deemed to be the Democratic frontrunner, I was primed for a lively experience covering the 1972 race. Muskie's status was confirmed, as I wrote at the time, "by the strategy of the other Democratic hopefuls—to stop Muskie" by each "picking his spots in the early primaries in the hope of beating Muskie in one of them and simultaneously igniting his own campaign." The *Los Angeles Times'* editors wisely decided, however, on zone coverage rather than man-to-man, and that most of the primaries would be covered by a two-man team consisting of Dick Cooper, a crackerjack and ever-congenial correspondent from the Chicago bureau, and me.

I enjoyed getting back to New Hampshire, the site of my first sustained exposure to the presidential primaries with the hapless George Romney in 1968. My buddies and I set up shop at what was then the Sheraton Wayfarer Inn in Bedford, across the Amoskeag River from Manchester. The inn is a rambling affair with rooms clustered around a small but gorgeous waterfall, and with a comfortable bar that became the destination of most of us after the day's labors.

The waterfall often was frozen on frigid New Hampshire days and nights, which made it particularly beautiful. It was while gazing at this lovely sight one afternoon after lunch that a once-feared but later beloved colleague, Bill Lawrence of the *New York Times* and later ABC News, slumped over with a heart attack and prematurely left our congenial fraternity. I always thought that it was about as good a way to go as there could have been.

Bill was only 56 when he died. He had gone from being among the toughest of the print reporters to an amiable old shoe, as helpful to our younger generation as he had been cantankerous in earlier days. When Jim Hagerty, Dwight Eisenhower's press secretary, left the White House and took over the ABC news division, he signed the gruff-voiced Bill on as a commentator. The hire was Exhibit A of Hagerty's determination to bring solid news reporting to network television rather than pretty faces emitting dulcet tones.

The favorite story about Lawrence among his old print press buddies was about a phone call to the ABC News bureau in Washington. A deep and gravelly voice asked, "Is Bill Lawrence there?" When the caller was told he was not, the raspy voice said: "Okay. Just tell him his voice coach called." Political reporting lost a rare gem with Bill's passing.

In New Hampshire, Muskie, as a native New Englander, was a heavy favorite over a field that included George McGovern and several weak sisters, including Mayor Yorty, Senator Vance Hartke of Indiana, Representative Wilbur Mills, and a Hartford broker named Ned Coll, who memorably used a fake rat as a prop in one of their debates. Muskie, like George Romney in 1968, was having trouble clarifying his views on the Vietnam war, which McGovern opposed with supreme clarity, and it was one reason Muskie was already slipping in the polls. But something else contributed greatly to his undoing in the state, and possibly in the whole nomination contest.

It so happened that near the end of the primary, the rabidly conservative *Manchester Union Leader* published a letter purporting to have come from a Paul Morrison of Deerfield Beach, Florida, in which he alleged having heard a Muskie aide, not the senator himself, make an invidious comparison between blacks and "Canucks"—meaning New Englanders of French-Canadian descent, many of whom live in New Hampshire. When Muskie was asked what his aide meant, "Morrison" wrote, "Muskie laughed and said, 'Come to New England and see.'" The newspaper ran an editorial by famously vitriolic publisher William Loeb titled "Senator Muskie Insults Franco-Americans" along with the letter.

The Muskie temper with which I had become well-acquainted during the Middle East–Moscow trip soon entered the story. As Muskie's headquarters in Manchester began to be inundated with complaining phone calls, a young Muskie campaign coordinator named Tony Podesta hit on the idea of holding a press conference outside the *Union Leader* to complain about the "Canuck letter" and to disavow any slur. Muskie agreed.

On arrival in Manchester for the event the next morning, Muskie learned of another Loeb editorial based on a *Newsweek* magazine article that quoted his wife, Jane, as inviting women reporters on the campaign bus to trade "dirty jokes" and otherwise let their hair down. Muskie was enraged. Podesta told me much later that Muskie, often demeaned by Loeb, erupted: "That son of a bitch. I've been waiting twenty-five years for this. Tomorrow morning one of us is going to be destroyed." Muskie told me later he had no recollection of that comment but would not challenge it. But he did a slow burn. "The next morning I was goddamned mad," he told me. "You work yourself up to these things. You make up your mind to bring on a confrontation, and it has an effect on you."

That next morning, as a very heavy snow fell, Muskie mounted an open flatbed truck where a host of Franco-Americans stood to testify to his friendship. A man from Florida who had been with him at the time of the alleged incident avowed that neither Muskie nor anyone else had uttered a slur against "Canucks." Muskie himself denied it, but then, warming to his anger at Loeb, called the publisher a "gutless coward" and segued into an emotional complaint about the references to his wife. According to my old friend and colleague David Broder writing in the *Washington Post,* as Muskie read the editorial's title, "Big Daddy's Jane," his voice broke, "tears streaming down [his] face." Watching a television rerun of the scene, I could not tell whether tears or melting snowflakes were involved, but it was clear in any event that Muskie had lost control, and his image as a strong, Lincolnesque figure suffered in the numerous television replays thereafter.

Muskie told me later: "There were no tears. I was choked up because I was goddamned mad at that point. But that was all there was to it." But he said he was aware later that the scene had conveyed weakness. "I had no feeling of weakness," he said. "I just thought it was a display of anger. Maybe too much. I'm capable of that. It was a mistake to go. But I made the decision and I had to accept the consequences. The way it was written—tears in New Hampshire—that's the way it will live in history, and what I say won't change that."

It was revealed later that the Canuck letter that started it all had been an act of political sabotage by Nixon's Committee to Reelect the President, appropriately known as CREEP. But Muskie said he had no idea at the time who was behind it. "I felt it was a Loeb fraud," he told me. "It never occurred to me that it was related to CREEP."

Some reporters on the scene (I was not) never mentioned tears, and Dick Stewart, my old traveling companion on the magic carpet to Jerusalem, Cairo, and Moscow, by now Muskie's press secretary, argued that the senator's emotional defense of his wife would help him politically. And on the weekend before the New Hampshire primary, several reporters, including Broder, Ottenad, Germond, and me, had a meeting with Maria Carrier, Muskie's in-state coordinator. She was asked how she thought her candidate would do. "If he doesn't get 50 percent, I'll eat my hat," she said.

It's always a mistake for a politician to make a categorical prediction, as she soon learned. Muskie of Maine came out of his neighboring state's primary with "only" 47.8 percent of the vote, to 37 percent for McGovern and the rest spread among the also-rans. In the peculiar arithmetic of presidential politics, Muskie was marked down as a loser for having failed to meet Maria Carrier's prediction, and McGovern came out of New Hampshire with a head of steam. Muskie departed for Florida, the next important primary, where he would face George Wallace as well as McGovern and others, declaring "this is not a hundred-yard dash. This is a marathon." But he had stumbled out of the gate and had more hurdles to take. I headed for Florida too, to see whether he could clear the next one.

He couldn't. In fact, he ran a dismal fourth behind the winner, Wallace, Hubert Humphrey, who had entered the primary competition for the first time, and Scoop Jackson. Muskie had to contend with constant reminders of what was now routinely rendered his "crying in the snow" in New Hampshire. One Jackson aide circulated posters in the Tampa area that said, simply, "Vote for Muskie or He'll Cry."

Although he was the close runner-up in New Hampshire, McGovern ran a weak sixth in Florida; as a liberal, little had been expected of him there. He moved on to Wisconsin, prospectively more fertile ground for him, with the other candidates, who also included Republican-turned-Democrat Mayor John Lindsay of New York.

Muskie, looking for a lifeline, chose to enter a nonbinding primary in Illinois first, in which there was only one campaigning candidate, if you could call it campaigning. Gene McCarthy, on a quixotic effort aimed at changing the electoral college system, was there with little money but a lively imagination. One gloomy morning in late March I joined him for a day on the old North Central Airlines route from Chicago to St. Louis and back, with stops between. We bought special round-trip tickets that enabled us to stop over at each town, where McCarthy would hold a press conference in the local airport and then repair to the bar for a couple of martinis, awaiting the next flight. The round-trip ticket couldn't have cost more than a hundred dollars at the time, and we repeated the routine at each airport, McCarthy fielding questions from local reporters with his customary combination of aloofness, charm, and disdain.

Another time in Illinois he was invited to read his poetry at a small community college north of Chicago. It was another drab, rainy day and the site of the reading was an old World War II Quonset hut converted into a lecture hall, complete with galvanized tin roof. Just as McCarthy had been introduced by the college president and had begun to read, the heavens opened and deafening rain pelted the roof. The din became so great that it was impossible to hear him, but he droned on until the president stepped forward and said: "Senator, perhaps you should stop for awhile until this downpour lets up. The students can't hear you." To which McCarthy replied: "That's all right. I can hear me," and went right on reading.

In this low-budget campaign, he was staying on the campus of Northwestern University, and a student driver chauffeured us back to the campus. Throughout the fairly long ride, the student peppered McCarthy with pointed questions on such subjects as why he hadn't endorsed Humphrey sooner in 1968 and why he hadn't kept up his fight against the Vietnam war in the Senate instead of quitting it. Clearly miffed, McCarthy nevertheless answered the questions, providing little more response than he offered whenever professional reporters pressed him on the same inquiries. In spite of his rather unusual behavior as a lone-wolf candidate, McCarthy managed to win 37 percent of the vote in this meaningless "beauty contest" primary, far behind Muskie. Both moved on to Wisconsin for the next contest among all the major Democratic hopefuls.

For Muskie—or Edmund Sixtus Marciszewski, as three-foot-long bumper stickers now proclaimed him in this state with its large Polish-American population—Wisconsin was a make-or-break situation. It broke him, for various reasons, including the fact that he often campaigned as if he were already the nominee. His strategy of collecting big-name endorsements among Democratic governors, senators, and other bigwigs proved no substitute for the sort of ground organization assembled by McGovern under new delegate-selection rules written by a commission he himself ran. From the start, Muskie ran on "trust" but came across as fuzzy on the issues voters cared about, particularly how to extricate the country from Vietnam. And then there was that "crying in the snow" episode in New Hampshire that clung to him.

McGovern carried Wisconsin, and Muskie again finished fourth. After losing to Humphrey in Pennsylvania and to McGovern in Massachusetts, Muskie announced that he would suspend his campaign while remaining available for a lightning bolt that was never to strike him. At one point he appeared ready to endorse McGovern but decided otherwise, giving Humphrey a lease on life for a time.

Still in the picture at this time was George Wallace, winner of the Florida primary and now in quest of victories in states where, in 1964, he had amassed surprising support. I had continued to track his political ambitions on his occasional forays outside of Alabama, and there as well. I remember one night in the town of Midfield, Germond and I, friendly competitors, went to hear him make a speech before the local Chamber of Commerce. It was held in a big hall with an adjoining bar, where we sat out the dinner, waiting for Wallace to start speaking. Suddenly over the microphone came this summons in a deep Dixie drawl: "Is Jules Witcover of the *Los Angeles* [pronounced "Angelees"] *Times* in the room? Please come up to the head table. The governor wants to shake your hand." Aware of what was up, I dutifully trekked through the tables to where Wallace was sitting with a sly grin on his face. "Hi, Jules. I just wanted to welcome you to Alabama," he said, although Germond and I had seen him at lunch in a nearby town only a few hours earlier.

As I turned and worked my way back through the tables to the bar, a thoroughly used prop, the governor said to the crowd: "You see, he came all the way from Los Angeles to Midfield. The national press follows me everywhere, and tonight they followed me to Midfield." Nothing seemed to please Wallace's Alabama audiences more than evidence that their governor brought their state to the attention of the outside world, and he milked it for all it was worth.

Now, in 1972, on the eve of the Maryland presidential primary in mid-May, Wallace was venturing into the state where eight years earlier he had won 43 percent of the Democratic presidential vote in spite of having the Marylanders "recapitulate on" him. He was greeting voters at a shopping mall in Laurel when a would-be assassin shot him at close range and he was rushed off to Holy Cross Hospital, where I kept another vigil, amid expectations that the feisty little Alabamian wouldn't make it through the night. But he did; not only that, the next day he astonishingly won the Michigan primary, where school busing remained a hot issue, with 51 percent of the vote. But the victory came too late. The shooting left him confined to a wheelchair the rest of his life. That, however, was not going to end his political career or his quest for the presidency, as he later demonstrated.

Now the Democratic nomination came down to the California primary, at which 271 delegates would be awarded on a winner-take-all basis. This would be Humphrey's last chance to stop the surprising McGovern, riding the tail of a streaking anti-war comet in the Democratic Party.

Dick Cooper and I, having followed the campaign trail together through most of the key primaries, headed for the home state of our newspaper. Our first stop was the Times building, where we checked in with our boss, Ed Guthman. Before we could get into our plans for covering the California primary, Ed informed us that we wouldn't have to chase the candidates for the next couple of weeks because Dick Bergholz, Carl Greenberg, and other California-based staffers would be handling the story.

We were dumbfounded, and not consoled by being told we were free to continue covering whatever events we wanted, but not to write. Instead, we were given a leisurely if rather strange assignment. Each of us was to write a long postelection story on why the winner won—Dick about McGovern and me about Humphrey. The story about the eventual winner would go into the paper on election night for the big editions the next morning. The story about the loser would probably wind up on a copy desk spike.

Operating under this somewhat bizarre mandate, Dick and I occupied ourselves in a sort of limbo over the next days, drifting from one campaign to the other and trying our hands at what was not exactly fiction writing but wasn't Journalism 101 either. It so happened that a few days before the primary I found myself whistle-stopping through California's Central Valley with McGovern and his entourage. To kill time, I sat at my portable Olivetti and banged out possible leads explaining how Humphrey had upset McGovern, while not really believing it was going to happen. Meanwhile, Dick was going through the same exercise about McGovern, probably with a bit more confidence that his crystal ball was conveying the real outcome of the primary.

As I was thus engaged, a young writer for *Rolling Stone* magazine came through my train car. He had been assigned to write an inside account of the national press corps covering the 1972 campaign. He was going about stealthily eavesdropping on reporters' conversations and reading our copy as we wrote it while the train ricocheted along the tracks. Caught in the act, he was subjected to a stern warning that we would break his kneecaps if he continued his surreptitious ways, but that we'd be happy to talk to him about whatever if he asked straight out. That disagreement ironed out, he became one of the boys and thereafter a good friend.

He was, in fact, Timothy Crouse, the same young fellow I had met twenty-one years earlier when he was a small boy visiting the Park Avenue apartment of his grandfather, John Erskine, where I was working weekends as the distinguished old man's nurse-companion. Tim later expanded his magazine piece into the best-selling book *The Boys on the Bus*, and he autographed a copy to me: "In hopes you'll call off the lynching party."

In the book, he described me as "a tall but unprepossessing man of 45 with a weak chin, blank eyes and thinning hair" who "had the pale, hounded look of a small liquor store owner whose shop has just been held up for the seventh time in a year." He also chronicled me appearing "at a White House briefing in his black, funereal raincoat, looking like a cut-rate version of the bad fairy." Upon looking in a mirror, I couldn't argue with him.

Thus occupied with my imposed exercise in fantasy fiction, I dutifully finished the Humphrey piece, as Cooper finished his on McGovern. We turned them in, awaiting the outcome to find out which of us would have our long masterpiece featured prominently in the *L.A. Times* on the morning after the election. Election night proved to be a long, drawn-out affair with the issue in doubt into the early morning, and the paper went to bed without using either of our stories. It didn't matter much to me since I had written the losing version, but Dick, having told with great skill why McGovern had won, may have been perturbed. It was not recorded how Bergholz felt.

The California primary story, however, was not over, because the Humphrey camp as a last gasp decided to challenge the state's winner-take-all rule whereby McGovern had garnered all 271 convention delegates. Was this a California story or a national story? In the end, everybody pitched in to report what came to be called the ABM movement, for Anybody But McGovern. But it failed at the convention in Miami Beach in July, when the McGovern forces, led by his campaign manager, a dashing young fellow from Colorado named Gary Hart, outmaneuvered the Humphreyites. (I have a prized photograph on my wall at home that shows me talking to a stolid-looking Bergholz on the convention floor. I drew over my head a cartoon balloon showing me saying, "Maybe so, but we're not in California now.")

The big story after McGovern was nominated on the first ballot was his selection of a running mate. The fight over the California delegates had consumed most of McGovern's time and energy, and a throwback to the old smoke-filled room of yore resulted to pick the vice-presidential nominee. On the morning after McGovern was picked, a group of his aides gathered privately in a small dining room at the Doral Hotel and conducted a series of ballots, writing their choices on small slips of paper. My pal Tom Ottenad and I waited patiently outside until the meeting broke up and then went in. Ashtrays on the table were stuffed with the small slips ripped into smaller pieces. Tom and I spent the better part of an hour patching the slips together, without being able to determine a consensus choice. We learned later that Mayor Kevin White of Boston got the most votes but lost out as a result of a lack of enthusiasm from Ted Kennedy. Next, according to McGovern himself, was Senator Gaylord Nelson of Wisconsin, but he turned it down and recommended Senator Tom Eagleton of Missouri, who quickly snapped up the offer, brushing aside a perfunctory question from McGovern aide Frank Mankiewicz about whether he had any skeletons in his closet that might undermine the ticket.

In short order, however, it was disclosed that Eagleton had a major ghost lurking there, in having twice undergone electric shock treatment for mental depression, still a bugaboo to many voters. As the story was about to break, Eagleton met McGovern in Custer, South Dakota, where he was vacationing, and convinced McGovern that his medical problems were behind him. McGovern agreed to keep him on the ticket and through an aide declared that he was "one thousand percent" behind him, leaving himself no wiggle room when negative comments and calls for dropping Eagleton poured in from concerned Democrats.

At the time, I was in Custer covering the McGoverns' vacation, and the Eagleton flap was poisoning his postnomination glow. According to Dick Dougherty, his campaign press secretary and a former *L.A. Times* reporter, in his book on the campaign, *Goodby, Mr. Christian,* he asked the nominee if it might not be a good idea to signal Eagleton somehow that he wanted him to withdraw. McGovern replied: "Would it make any sense if I had a talk with Jules Witcover? I'll tell you why I'd like it to be Jules. A year or so ago when he was working on a book about Agnew he came to see me a couple of times to talk about the vice presidency. He was talking to me more as a historian than anything else. Anyway, I remember telling him that if, by some wild chance, I ever got the presidential nomination I would damned well avoid the messy way vice presidents had been picked in the past. I think Jules will remember that. I'll get hold of him and ask him up for a drink. If he wants to write something not-for-attribution, fine, if not . . . ." Dougherty concluded, "He let the sentence trail off. I assured him that Witcover would write something."

He was most assuredly correct. When a presidential nominee offers to drop a big story in your lap from his own mouth, you don't ask questions, even if it has to be on a nonattribution basis. I was not altogether baffled, however, as to why McGovern was singling me out from the reporters covering his vacation. It so happened that Eagleton was off in Hawaii at the time and was scheduled to return via California the next day. It seemed not a coincidence to me, nor would it to McGovern, that Eagleton likely would pick up the *Los Angeles Times* the moment his plane landed. A young McGovern aide phoned me in the campaign press room and told me the nominee wanted to see me in his cabin.

I showed up at the appointed hour and was greeted warmly by McGovern and his wife Eleanor in their Black Hills cabin hideaway, where he proceeded to discuss with regret the reality that Eagleton would have to go for the good of the ticket and the party. As I remember it, there was no mention of our previous conversations about the vice presidency; I was there as the designated reporter (or hit man?).

My lead story on page one of the *L.A. Times* the next morning was headlined: "McGovern Wants Eagleton Off Ticket," with the subhead: "Prefers to Let Running Mate Take Initiative." The lead said:

CUSTER, S.D.—Public and political reaction to Sen. Thomas F. Eagleton's disclosure of past hospitalization for nervous disorders has been so negative that Sen. George S. McGovern is convinced that Eagleton must withdraw from the Democratic ticket, The Times has learned.

At the same time, McGovern is determined to leave the initiative to Eagleton, convinced that when his running mate, just back from Hawaii, takes his own soundings he will reach the same conclusion.

But McGovern also is aware that the political dilemma is snowballing and must be resolved within the next few days if losses already suffered are not to mount even further.

After my interview, McGovern had tipped off other reporters in Custer, and there was no doubt that Eagleton would get the message on his return to the continental U.S. Yet on arrival he dug in his heels and asked McGovern for some more time to argue his case for staying on the ticket. McGovern decided to return to Washington, and on the flight home, as I sat in the press section to the rear of the plane, he walked back and took a seat next to me with a forlorn look on his face. "I guess Tom didn't get the message," I said to him as light-heartedly as I could. "No, he didn't," the Democratic nominee replied. As he began to discuss the situation, he looked up and saw a long boom microphone hanging over his shoulder, and that was the end of the conversation. He got up with another look of chagrin and walked back to his seat at the front of the plane.

That incident brought home to me as never before the intimidating aspect of recording equipment as a basic journalistic tool. A long and generally cordial relationship, very fruitful in terms of newsgathering, had been disrupted by this electronic intrusion into a private conversation. Similar interview hijackings were being perpetrated increasingly by the thrusting of microphones and hand-held tape recorders into other one-on-one conversations. Also vanishing was the courtesy of a reporter awaiting his turn with a source rather than barging in on somebody else's interview, especially in the close quarters of a plane, train, or bus.

The damage to communication in such circumstances was obvious. In this particular case, McGovern was not about to confide to me something he didn't want handled or mishandled by reporters he did not know or trust. While younger reporters might allege that a symbiotic relationship between a reporter and a news source co-opts the reporter's integrity, I have found over the years that you can get more information from a politician or other source who trusts you than from one who sees you as an adversary. Nor does having a friendly attitude toward a source mean you are somehow obliged to look the other way if you catch him with his hand in the cookie jar or learn of some other dishonest or dishonorable act.

Concerning Eagleton, the pressure became so great that he finally had to resign from the ticket. But the political damage had already been done, and it got worse as McGovern was obliged to go through a humiliating search for a sacrificial lamb willing to replace Eagleton. After talking to Muskie and getting another dose of procrastination, he finally settled on Sargent Shriver, brother-in-law of Ted Kennedy. In a version of the old gag response to the question "How's your wife?"—"Compared to what?"—McGovern matched his choice against Richard Nixon's decision to keep Agnew as his running mate. "If we have used valuable time in the selection of a vice-presidential nominee," he said, "the nation must wish the Republicans had made their choice with greater care."

The political focus now turned to Nixon and the Republicans, also holding their national convention in Miami Beach. Two months earlier, on the night of June 17, a mild stir had been created when the District of Columbia police discovered an attempt to break into the Democratic National Committee headquarters at the Watergate office and hotel complex along the Potomac River in Washington. Five men were arrested and were soon tied to the Committee to Reelect the President, CREEP. The *Washington Post* ran a front-page story the next morning, and the greatest political scandal of the century, or maybe in American history, was under way, though not thus perceived at the time the GOP met in Miami Beach.

The Republican convention was more a coronation of Nixon for renomination. It was so programmed that when Congressman Paul N. McCloskey Jr. of California won a single delegate seat in New Mexico in his fruitless challenge to Nixon on the Vietnam war, the convention ruled that the vote would be cast by a Nixon man. Managers of the convention controlled the program so tightly that chalk marks were laid down indicating where each speaker was to stand before, during, and after his presentation. Nothing was being left to chance in a campaign in which the Democratic nominee had already been hopelessly wounded.

As far as I was concerned, the most important event at the GOP convention was an invitation I received to have a private lunch with Ben Bradlee, Howard Simons, and Dick Harwood of the *Washington Post* at one of the convention hotels. They sounded me out on whether I'd be interested in joining the political team of the *Post* headed by my old and respected friend, Dave Broder. Back when I was covering the Pentagon for the Newhouse papers and Bradlee was looking for a new beat man there, I had said I was trying to escape the Pentagon to write politics, and that had ended the conversation. This time, I was eager to grab the chance, considering the *Post* to be the premier political newspaper in the country, but I said I felt obligated to stay with the *L.A. Times* through the 1972 campaign. Ben said we'd talk again after the election.

In the fall, I spent a good part of my time traveling with the McGovern entourage, listening to the candidate trying to make political hay out of the Watergate break-in story, which young *Post* reporters Bob Woodward and Carl Bernstein were steadily advancing, with occasional contributions from papers like the *New York Times* and the *Los Angeles Times*. The Nixon campaign stonewalled at every turn, and McGovern seemed unable to make the story stick in voters' minds. His efforts to nail Nixon on playing politics with the Vietnam war, which was now polarizing the country, also failed.

My fall stint with McGovern gave rise to another California moment for me. On one cross-country swing, the plane touched down in Iowa City for a major speech at the University of Iowa, a hotbed of protest against the war. Before the plane took off for the next stop I filed a story, and en route got hold of the text for the speech to be delivered at the next stop, which was Sacramento. It was pretty much the same speech McGovern had given in Iowa City, but knowing that the editors in L.A. would want the story updated, I wrote a new lead to file from Sacramento after the speech. As we landed and trooped into a large college gymnasium, I spied my old friend Dick Bergholz across the way. As soon as McGovern finished speaking, I found a phone and called the desk in L.A. to dictate my new dateline and lead. "Oh, don't bother," I was told. "Bergholz has already put a new lead on your story." He had just gone ahead and topped my story without a word to me. And so it went.

By now I was getting more frustrated with the *Times* for other reasons. I considered it a central part of political writing to provide analysis of what was happening on the beat, not simply who said what to whom. It seemed to me particularly imperative for the mainstream press to offer analysis at this time because advocacy journalism was on the rise, especially in what was called "the alternative press," trumpeting points of view that reflected little balance. But often an analytical piece of mine would be bounced back with the suggestion that I find someone else to express the analysis I had offered on my own, based on my reporting and observations. I argued that the viewpoint wouldn't be any more right or wrong if it came from somebody mouthing my view. Interviewing someone and recording what he or she said was reporting; assessing what it meant was analysis. More than once a piece of mine would get locked in purgatory until after a competitor had gotten his version into print.

I was also frustrated by the fact that too often I would file an exclusive story and it would be held for days on grounds of lack of space, until finally it was written by somebody from another paper, like the *New York Times* or the *Washington Post*. When I would point this out to an L.A. editor, I would be told that the *Los Angeles Times* was not in competition with either East Coast paper. That struck me as not the best way to generate drive for getting the story. We grunts in the trenches always considered ourselves to be competing with our colleagues wherever their stories appeared. I remember being called into the office of Frank Haven, then the managing editor of the *Times*, and warned to be careful about the Watergate story. I should not go overboard, he said, because the *Post* was getting itself pretty far out on a limb and might find it sawed off behind it.

In Tim Crouse's book, I was described by a colleague during the 1972 campaign as "a leashed tiger" who "can't get his stuff in the paper" and was on the phone arguing about it. "Chances are, he's having a go-round with some editor out there who's just shit-canned one of his articles," Crouse was told. That was about right. During the fall, I wanted to write a piece saying that Nixon's failure to campaign from elsewhere than the White House Rose Garden had reduced the election to a one-candidate campaign, with voters the losers. Wary of the reaction from L.A., I waited until McGovern accused the press of failing in its responsibilities by not forcing Nixon out into the open as he was. This was the hook I needed. Quoting McGovern's charge, I noted that while it was self-serving, it validly pointed out that Nixon was staying out of the line of fire, to the detriment of voters' ability to assess and compare the candidates. The editors killed the story, saying it was "opinion" and that I should find sources to say Nixon was ducking. So much for writing analysis.

Although the *L.A. Times* gave me a front seat for the 1972 campaign and other important stories, I was somewhat uncomfortable about an operation that was overseen from California with what I thought was a certain disconnect from reality. Some editors complained that too many stories filed from Washington were "downers"—not surprising, in that the nation's capital was a magnet for bad-news stories. In writing those lengthy non-dupes for page one, for instance, we in Washington were frequently asked whether anything upbeat ever happened that we could report. As one editor once put it to me, "Our readers don't want to wake up every morning to bad news at breakfast."

On a personal level, I was particularly chagrined at the paper's treatment of my idol, Bob Donovan. In my last year or so, Nick Williams, the brilliant editor who had taken the *Times* from being a weak regional sheet to earning a national reputation for excellence, was approaching retirement. A good part of his rebuilding had consisted of luring Donovan from the *New York Herald Tribune* to head up a revitalized Washington bureau. That goal had been achieved well before my arrival, by Donovan's ability to assemble an all-star cast of reporters and get the best out of them, both by setting an example of high standards and by his personal integrity. In some ways, I learned after my arrival, Donovan got so much credit for what he did in Washington that there was resentment in Los Angeles and a feeling that the bureau in some ways had gotten bigger than the paper.

Nevertheless, Donovan's reputation and performance led the powers in L.A. to make him a surprising offer. They would appoint him associate editor of the paper, bring him to Los Angeles to learn the ropes, and then, if all was well after a year, make him editor of the whole shebang. Bob had never run a newspaper, and his whole career, starting in Buffalo to New York and then Washington, was in reporting. He professed no interest in being an editor of anything, and beyond that his whole life and social circle were in Washington. He was perfectly happy staying where he was. But the powers insisted, and so Bob picked up and moved to California, replaced at his insistence by Dave Kraslow, who had been his right-hand man in the bureau.

All the next year Donovan proceeded on the understanding that he was the *L.A. Times* editor-in-waiting. But when the year was up, he was called in and told it wasn't going to work. They sent him back to Washington with some sort of editor's title, to our collective shock and dismay. We were overjoyed to have him back, but saddened at the shabby way he had been treated. True to form for Donovan, instead of saying on return that he had never wanted to go to L.A. in the first place and was happy to be back in familiar Washington, he told his old bureau buddies that he had loved it in California. Only Bob Donovan would have refused to make a silk purse out of the sow's ear of his treatment.

In any event, with all this as background, when the 1972 campaign ended and Nixon was reinstalled in the White House by a landslide, I decided to accept the *Washington Post*'s offer. I left the *Times* nevertheless with some regrets because my friends Bob Donovan, Dave Kraslow, and Ed Guthman had given me a breakthrough chance I had hungered for all those seventeen years I wore the Newhouse "N," and I had to walk away from the bureau congeniality that made it a pleasure going in there almost every day.

While all this was going on, my seatmate for most of the McGovern campaign, the AP's Walter Mears, and I decided that, after many years of writing amateur lyrics for songs about the candidates, we would turn pro. I found someone in New York who would compose original music for more than a dozen songs and in short order Walter and I penned the words. The result was a three-act musical based on the Watergate years and the Nixon-McGovern campaign that we called *Have I Ever Lied to You?* in honor of all the politicians who ever had done so. I then set out to find a producer, but although Mike Wallace set up an interview with Broadway's David Merrick for me, nothing came of it, not even an audition. Such catchy ditties as "Good and Evil," a duet sung by Evans and Novak clones, "The Wiretap Tap," a soft-shoe number for the Nixon buggers, and "Der Vorld ist Mine," a Henry Kissinger ballad, passed unperformed into the dustbin of musical history. The same fate befell the snappy "Sex Is Better than Politics," written a bit before its time.

Thus denied a radical career change, Mears and I resumed our old labors, he as the fastest wire-service gun on the campaign trail and I on my new assignment at the *Washington Post,* which to me had always meant the top rung in covering national politics. Washington has always been more of a political town than New York, and I had lost my lust for the Big Apple. I was pleased to be at the best political paper in the most political town, working for an editor and with a staff that was on the brink of journalism's highest laurels for their coverage of the Watergate scandal.

11 The *Post* | Watergate and Agnew

ON THE MORNING IN EARLY JANUARY 1973 when I got off the elevator at the Washington Post offices for my first day on the job, a familiar face greeted me. It belonged to the young fellow who had come by the *Los Angeles Times* bureau right out of the Navy looking for a job, and whom I had turned down and advised to try for a job on a suburban Washington paper, while pestering the *Post* and the *Star* to hire him. It was Bob Woodward, who by this time had left the Montgomery County *Sentinel* and, with Carl Bernstein, was part of the dynamic duo who had turned the Watergate break-in into the political story of the century.

His grin and handshake of welcome said it all. For years afterward, I lived off the story of how, in my matchless judgment of journalistic horseflesh, I had booted the chance to sign up the Joe DiMaggio, or at least the Mickey Mantle, of that era of American investigative reporting. Much later, as my Georgetown neighbor, Woodward always let me off easy by telling listeners how gently I had shown him the door at the *L.A. Times* Washington bureau on that day that will evermore live in my personal infamy.

Although I never had the opportunity to horn in on the dynamic duo's Watergate work, which won the Pulitzer Prize for the *Post,* I was soon given a piece on the periphery of the story, covering the Watergate hearings, chaired by Senator Sam Ervin of North Carolina, that eventually built the public case against President Nixon.

First, though, I was assigned to a rather dicey story in Florida, where television station licenses the Post owned in Jacksonville and Miami were being challenged before the Federal Communications Commission, amid suspicions that the Nixon administration was vengefully trying to influence the outcome. They were convoluted cases with which I wrestled for several days, finally writing a careful if boring piece full of denials of conspiracy against the Post. The story ran half a page inside the first section and was never heard from again, and the Post kept the stations, through, no doubt, no doing of mine.

The assignment by its nature put me, from the start, in the full scrutiny of the three most important people on the paper as far as I was concerned: the publisher, Katharine Graham, the executive editor, Ben Bradlee, and the managing editor, Howard Simons. On my return from Florida I was thoroughly grilled by Bradlee and Simons on what I'd learned. While I had not uncovered any smoking gun of White House complicity in the FCC's review, publication of the story did serve to show that the Post was not backing away from a politically sensitive matter in which its own corporate interests were heavily involved.

In this and in all subsequent matters, I found all three—Mrs. Graham, Bradlee, and Simons—to be straightforward and fair, and in Bradlee's case especially, inspirational in his quest for journalistic excellence. It was often said around the newsroom that Ben's one shortcoming was that he had "a short attention span," meaning he would get hugely excited and enthusiastic about a story but once it was launched would flit on to something else. To me, that was no rap but rather a description of his very effective leadership style—to stir up the troops, get them on the right path with encouragement and then get on with the next challenge, leaving them to do their jobs.

That spring, shortly after the Post won the Pulitzer Prize for its Watergate coverage (amazingly no prize went to Woodward and Bernstein, who also clearly deserved one), Ben came over one night and perched himself on the top of my desk. Winning the Pulitzer was a great achievement, he acknowledged, but now that the Post was on top of the heap, the test for the staff was staying there, not resting on its laurels but moving on to more great things. His own zest and his jaunty style, a combination of tough guy and fun lover, infused the Post with a dash and élan that put an indelible Ben Bradlee stamp on the paper throughout his tenure.

In my first months on the national staff, I was cast essentially as a general handyman, covering routine national political stories: Nixon's second inauguration, the burial in Texas of LBJ, the National Women's Political Caucus convention in Houston, and the forced demise of LBJ's Office of

Economic Opportunity, the headquarters of his War on Poverty. But in late March I got my first bite of the Watergate story, and it turned out to be a feeble one. I was assigned to survey Republican Party leaders in Congress and state party chairmen to determine the degree of concern over the Watergate revelations. I undertook it days after James W. McCord Jr., convicted of conspiracy in the case, had sent a letter to Judge John Sirica telling him there was much more to the story than had come out.

The result was this lead on a one-column page-one story: "They're talking nervously about the Watergate bugging in the offices and corridors of the White House these days—but apparently in few other places within the Republican family and America's living rooms." It went on to report the upshot of my survey: "growing anxiety within the White House about the latest Watergate developments is not yet shared by GOP pulse-takers around the country." Typical was a quote from Peter O'Donnell, a Republican National Committeeman from Texas: "I find no pressure on it from Republicans in Texas. It's hard to sustain interest." Pollster Albert Sindlinger said: "The general reaction on Watergate up to date is a big yawn. It is amazing the low priority people put on it."

It so happened that this story—one small ray of light in the cloud that was gathering over the Nixon White House—was brought to the attention of the great man himself, according to the Watergate tapes for the day the story appeared. His chief of staff, Bob Haldeman, seizing on the headline, "Watergate Indifference Cited by GOP," told Nixon in the Oval Office that "nobody has any interest in Watergate." I always wondered thereafter whether the story under my byline had anything to do with one of my big disappointments—never making Nixon's infamous "enemies list," a badge of honor among my colleagues at that time, and to this day.

However, any justification for Nixonian optimism was being rapidly erased by growing public questions about Watergate and his role in it. A week or so later, I teamed with Haynes Johnson of the *Post* national staff in interviewing a hundred voters in four Ohio and Michigan suburbs where Nixon had run very strongly in 1972. While the results yielded little sentiment that his presidency was in jeopardy because of the scandal, there was clear erosion in their confidence in him.

One man, Daniel Gower, 79, of Royal Oak on the outskirts of Detroit, did, however, speak the unspeakable at this early date: "I think the president should tell everyone to come clean. He keeps his silence and raises suspicion he knew something about it. He's not trying to clear the case up. If he isn't responsible, he's protecting those who were. I'd like to see him tell all he knows. If he is actively involved, he should possibly be impeached. [But] I don't know if that would be good for the country."

In the 100 interviews we conducted, impeachment was mentioned only three times. We wrote then: "These Middle Americans who helped elect Richard Nixon last November are not asking for his political scalp; what they want from him now is candor, and action, to clear the air. They are telling him, in effect, that they expected more of him as their president." Two days later, Nixon announced "major developments" in the Watergate case and, reversing himself, agreed to allow his aides to testify under oath before the Senate committee investigating the affair.

My new colleagues, Woodward and Bernstein, were not waiting for that testimony, though. They reported in a front-page exclusive that Nixon's former special assistant, Jeb Stuart Magruder, had already told federal prosecutors that campaign manager and former attorney general John Mitchell and White House counsel John Dean had "approved and helped plan the Watergate bugging operation," thus placing the scandal directly in the White House. At the same time, *Post* national staffer George Lardner Jr. and I wrote, "[Mitchell] made an effort earlier this month to persuade Democratic officials to drop their lawsuit over the Watergate break-in of party headquarters." The Democrats were seeking $6.4 million in damages, and named Mitchell a chief defendant. But such stories by us and a number of other *Post* reporters were mere appendages to the great work Woodward and Bernstein were continuing to do in blowing the lid off this extraordinary affair.

When Senator Ervin finally began open hearings on Watergate in mid-May, I was again teamed with another *Post* reporter, Lawrence Meyer, in covering them. Larry had the harder job of writing the daily factual account of what was said; I had the easier, and for me the more enjoyable, task of doing the daily color and analysis piece. The hearings started out rather dully, leading me to write: "If you like to watch grass grow, you would have loved the opening yesterday of the Senate select committee's hearings on the Watergate and related campaign misdeeds." I observed that the committee had spent five hours grilling "four secondary witnesses" through "mostly colorless and snail's pace testimony" to make the point "that the investigation doesn't intend to sacrifice thoroughness—or when necessary even bore-dom—for sensationalism just to hold the TV audience."

But that yawn-inducing tone didn't continue for long. The very next day, McCord, the former FBI agent and CIA security man, started blowing the whistle on White House bribes to the convicted but still mum perpetrators. "After an uneventful, methodical beginning," I wrote, "the man in the Watergate who wouldn't keep his mouth shut has got the Senate commit-tee's televised show on the road."

My assignment gave me not only a front-row seat for one of the great political scandals of American history but also a chance to stick a needle into some of the players who displayed their distorted sense of loyalty. About one of the first witnesses, I wrote: "It's a good thing for convicted conspira-tor Bernard L. Barker that his leader in the Watergate break-in, former White House aide E. Howard Hunt, never told him to jump off the top of the Washington Monument. Because the chances are, judging from Barker's testimony yesterday at the Senate's Watergate hearings, that he would have done it—and saluted all the way down."

In writing the daily commentary piece, I also had the opportunity to do a bit of portrait painting of some of the most nefarious villains in the annals of Washington chicanery. For example, I was able to write the following of Nixon's old friend, law partner, campaign manager, and chief law-enforce-ment officer:

John Newton Mitchell, former Attorney General of the United States, he of the curt and gruff—some would say arrogant—manner, sat there in the Senate Caucus Room yesterday afternoon like a fortress defying bombardment. Where other key Watergate witnesses had come fortified with interminable statements replete with dates, names and places, the jowly, placidly pipe-smoking Mitchell brought only backup papers and what he repeatedly called "my best recollec-tion. . . . In contrast to others whose tonsils had been lubricated by the sweet elixir of immunity from prosecution for their Senate testimony, John Mitchell sang a sad, slow song that had to be pulled from him. As a man already indict-ed [in another case], he testified involuntarily, under subpoena. But when it came out, although the words were different . . . the theme was pretty much the same: he did it out of loyalty, for the sake of the president, and therefore—through that tunnel-vision viewpoint common to all the involved Nixon admin-istration and re-election campaign officials—for the good of the country. . . . In the end, John Mitchell—like all those others in the loyalist ranks of Richard Nixon—"kept the lid on" to save the country from the worst of all fates—Sen. George McGovern.

The Ervin committee hearings went on all through that summer. The most memorable day for me, for reasons beyond the dramatic testimony given, was July 16, 1973, which happened to be my 46th birthday, but that was not one of the reasons I remembered it long afterward. It was the day when former White House aide Alexander P. Butterfield disclosed that for more than two years Nixon had been routinely taping his Oval Office and White House cabinet room conversations "to record things for posterity, for the Nixon library." My colleague, Larry Meyer, in the running story wrote that the Butterfield testimony indicated "that the White House may have in its possession the means to prove that President Nixon knew nothing about the cover-up of the Watergate affair until March 21, 1973, as he has maintained, or that former White House counsel John S. Dean III was correct in testimony that President Nixon knew about the cover-up well before March 21."

Fortunately for me, my assignment that day was to write not the commentary but rather about the White House response that the recording system was nothing unusual and that it was "similar" to one used in the Johnson administration. Former LBJ officials quickly said they knew nothing about such an arrangement in the Johnson White House, and a spokesman for the Secret Service, which had installed the system for the Nixon administration, said that if there was one there in the LBJ years, the Secret Service hadn't put it there. The LBJ Library in Austin confirmed, however, that it had "selective telephone conversations" between Johnson and others. Much later, those conversations became the subject of best-selling audio tapes and a book by historian Michael Beschloss.

The reason it was fortunate this was my assignment was because the night before, I had gone to a big party at McGovern's home, marking the first anniversary of his presidential nomination. Like others of my fraternity, I had overindulged and wound up with a humongous hangover. I covered much of the day's testimony lying on my back in the press room below the Senate Caucus Room, watching the proceedings on a television monitor on a nearby wall. It was not one of my finest hours, but I rebounded a few days later by leading the paper with an exclusive, under a banner across page one, that Nixon had ordered the deactivation of the automatic taping system. Considering the damage the existence of the system had already done, turning it off was a no-brainer, but getting the story made me feel a little better, as did the eventual passing of my hangover.

During the summer, I got occasional reprieves from Watergate coverage, such as a trip to Alabama with Ted Kennedy in which he used the occasion of sharing a platform with Governor George Wallace to skewer Nixon. While acknowledging his great political differences with the Dixie rabble-rouser, now in a wheelchair, Kennedy declared at a Fourth of July celebration in Decatur: "We have one thing in common. We don't compile lists of enemies whose careers and lives are to be shattered because of their disagreement. We don't use the tactics of a criminal or the power of the law in order to silence those whose ideas of politics are different than our own. For if there is one thing George Wallace stands for, it is the right of every American to speak his mind and be heard—fearlessly and in any part of the country. It is in that spirit that I come here today, for that is the true spirit of America." Score one for accentuating the positive.

The Watergate hearings themselves were not without comic relief. One day I was able to write:

> Sex tried—with only modest success—to rear its ugly head in the Watergate case yesterday. A self-styled New York call girl, attired in a black eye mask and blonde wig to hide her identity and in a plunging neckline and climbing miniskirt to reveal her anatomy, called a press conference at the Shoreham-Americana Hotel to tell all. "All" consisted of a rambling narrative of how she was recruited by a New York judge into high-priced prostitution and how she shuttled between New York and Washington plying her trade, with a little political espionage and blackmail on the side.

The lady in question named names of key Watergate figures, I reported, and told of "a New Year's orgy at the Watergate attended by 'a who's who, in the nude,'" but she offered no evidence to substantiate her claims. Her offer to testify before the committee in open session got nowhere, and about all she had to show for the caper, as far as I knew, was my story and a distinctly unfetching photo in the *Post*'s "Style" section.

The next big story to come my way that summer also was a serendipitous writing opportunity for me, in the paper and out of it. The previous year, my third book had been published, titled *White Knight: The Rise of Spiro*

Agnew. That fact may have been an element in my assignment by the *Post* to cover the sudden disclosure that the vice president was facing a Justice Department investigation into reports that as governor of Maryland he had taken kickbacks from government contractors. (Oval Office logs for April 3, 1972, that later found their way onto the Internet revealed that the book was the subject of a conversation between Nixon and aides about launching an "attack" on me. But if it occurred I was never aware of it.)

In the course of researching that book, I had come across some tantalizing tidbits of questionable behavior by Agnew and had written about them. In 1966, when he was running for governor, a story broke that his Democratic opponent, George P. Mahoney, had been offered a huge bribe by slot-machine interests in the state. He denied it, and for some reason Agnew revealed in an interview that on three separate occasions he had been offered up to $200,000 in campaign contributions by the same interests but had flatly turned them down. When a county attorney asked why Agnew hadn't reported the attempted bribes and who had offered them, he refused to say. In the same campaign, he was questioned about buying land near the construction site of the second Chesapeake Bay Bridge; he eventually sold the land, at the same time castigating his critics. But I found nothing at the time of the nature that brought the later charges.

During my own research in Maryland, however, I often encountered a bulldog investigative reporter for the *Wall Street Journal* named Jerry Landauer, who insisted that he knew Agnew was a crook and that he was determined to get the goods on him sooner or later. That time was now at hand. Landauer and a *Post* reporter covering Maryland for the Metro staff, Richard Cohen, simultaneously broke the story that federal investigators were charging that Agnew as governor of Maryland had taken bribes for government construction contracts.

With Cohen directly involved in the critical reporting of those investigation working out of Maryland, I was assigned from the national staff to handle the Washington end of the story. I had interviewed Agnew in the process of writing my book on him and had covered him from time to time as he ran for election and reelection to the vice presidency. After the Cohen and Landauer stories broke, I went over to the Executive Office Building next to the White House and at a televised press conference heard and saw Agnew straight-facedly label the allegations against him "false and scurrilous and malicious." He said he had "absolutely not" ever taken money for his personal use from any contractor doing business with Maryland or the federal government and had turned all his relevant papers over to his lawyers for their determination on possible release to the investigators.

Agnew said pointedly that he had no intention of resigning, a most pertinent matter in light of the continuing investigation of Nixon in the Watergate affair. While presidential impeachment was not yet very seriously in the air, Agnew as vice president was in direct line of succession to the presidency if such an outcome should eventually occur. In mid-August, I was in Denver for Agnew's first public appearances since disclosure of the investigation against him. At a labor union convention, he defended Nixon's decision to fight the Watergate charges against him and, by inference, his own right to soldier on himself. "Certainly every public figure must expect to draw some criticism for the way he handles his job," he said. "But just as each citizen has a right to criticize those in public office, so does every public official have a right to defend his actions, his honor, his integrity and his good name."

Agnew left no doubt he would fight the allegations against him. At one point he charged the Justice Department of his own administration with undercutting him with leaks to the press, and he dug in his heels. As Dick Cohen pursued the story through his excellent sources in Maryland, I concentrated on sources I had at Justice, where Agnew's fate increasingly occupied the deliberations of Nixon's new attorney general, Elliot L. Richardson, an independent moderate Republican of established integrity.

At the same time, I went back to covering the Watergate hearings. In the fall, I wrote a profile of Chuck Colson, the Nixon hatchetman who once famously owned up to saying, "I would walk over my grandmother if necessary" to assure Nixon's reelection. I also profiled Pat Buchanan, my sometime old radio partner for St. Louis station KMOX in Washington, now a Nixon speechwriter. Pat was one of the few Nixon insiders not enmeshed personally in Watergate and perhaps the only one who gave the Watergate committee as good as he got. I wrote then: "He was called as a key witness in the 'dirty tricks' phase of the Watergate hearings. For more than four hours he played the dirtiest trick a witness can perpetrate on televised senators—he made them look like a bunch of nitpickers. For every supposed political dirty trick they asked him about, he had either an explanation, a denial of involvement or a similar example from the lore of Democratic politics."

When asked what tactics he would have been willing to use to knock frontrunning Ed Muskie from the 1972 race, Buchanan replied: "Anything that was not immoral, unethical, illegal—or unprecedented in previous Democratic campaigns." He produced as Exhibit A tales of legendary Democratic prankster Dick Tuck, who once put on an engineer's cap and signaled the engineer to pull out the train from which Nixon was in the process of speaking. He revisited another time, when a group of black women said to be welfare mothers, all apparently pregnant, showed up at a Nixon event carrying placards with the campaign's slogan: "Nixon's the One."

Meanwhile, however, the tracks of the two investigations I was monitoring for the *Post*, the Watergate hearings and the bribe-taking allegations against Agnew, were beginning to merge. As the federal investigators built the case against the vice president and with Richardson about to present it to a grand jury, the question of presidential succession was taking on ever-greater significance, for both Agnew and Nixon. Some Nixon insiders calculated that as long as the highly controversial and now shady Agnew was in place as vice president, he might be seen as a sort of insurance policy for Nixon against impeachment and conviction. That is, as long as Agnew was next in line to succeed him, Congress would think long and hard about ousting the incumbent president. At the same time, Richardson was pondering the potential peril of having a man accused of taking bribes, now said to have continued to take place in the vice president's office, become president.

The president, for his part, at first tried to stay out of the sticky situation, but when Agnew began to go after his Justice Department and then threatened to take the matter directly to the House of Representatives, where it could drag on, Nixon decided that the vice president he had never wanted for a second term anyway would have to go. General Alexander Haig, the president's chief of staff, got the assignment to tell Agnew directly that Nixon wanted him to resign. Much negotiating between Agnew's lawyer and Richardson at first failed, and Agnew himself went to see Nixon, telling him he was determined to go to the House for "vindication." He apparently believed that in a case dealing with what he would say had been campaign contributions, the legislators, who lived off them too, would be more understanding. He also argued that he could not be tried in a criminal proceeding as long as he was in office—an argument that under the circumstances might have appealed to Nixon, himself possibly heading for the impeachment track.

In the end, however, Agnew overreached by attacking his prosecutors in a speech in Los Angeles and saying flatly that if indicted he would not resign. That tore it; the attorney general went ahead and filed for an indictment, with Nixon's acquiescence. Only then did Agnew's lawyers enter into plea-bargaining with the Justice Department, concluding with Agnew's agreeing to enter a plea of nolo contendere—no contest—on a single count of income tax evasion, based on net-worth calculations of his assets that went far beyond his regular income. The deal struck traded the vice president's resignation for a sentence without jail time, Richardson's principal objective being removal of Agnew from the line of presidential succession.

Although Agnew as part of the bargain affirmed to the judge that his nolo contendere plea was "an admission by you that the Department of Justice is possessed of sufficient evidence to prove its case beyond a reasonable doubt," he never ceased thereafter to contend that he was innocent and had been railroaded. In his statement before the judge, he said the "contributions" he had taken were "part of a long-established pattern of political funding" in Maryland and "at no time have I enriched myself at the expense of the public trust." In other words, he said he had only done what others before him had done, and that he didn't deny being paid off, only that the payoffs had influenced him.

Soon after Agnew's resignation, Cohen got a book offer on the case and asked me to join him in it. For five frantic weeks we pounded out the manuscript in an office at the Post. The result was *A Heartbeat Away: The Investigation and Resignation of Vice President Spiro T. Agnew*. My only reservation about how it turned out was the final paragraph, which I wrote. The paragraph started:

> For all his continued protestations of innocence, Agnew had to live with that realization [that he was the first vice president to have resigned in disgrace] in the quiet reflection of his own mind. In the first days of his exile from the Vice Presidency, he appeared to manage that very well. He seemed, in fact, more concerned with maintaining the high standard of living he had enjoyed at the taxpayers' expense than any remorse over what he had done. With Secret Service protection ordered by the President for months afterward, Agnew continued to live and travel in style. Indeed, he seemed to flaunt the decision that gave him his freedom in exchange for his high office, with neither his conscience nor any visible sense of shame inhibiting him.

Then came my naïve conclusion: "If, however, Spiro T. Agnew was really the introspective man he had always claimed to be, the knowledge that he was considered unfit and unworthy to be President could well become for him, eventually, a self-imprisonment as confining as any physical incarceration."

Ted Agnew in his remaining years proved that bit of speculation to be very much off the mark. He continued playing the wronged party, meanwhile consoling himself with posh living in the desert of Palm Springs. He even returned to Washington on one occasion in 1995, unrepentant as always, to observe the placing of a bust of him in the U.S. Capitol in a corner maintained for his vice-presidential colleagues. So much for my faith in the repentance of sinners.

Writing a 363-page book in five weeks at year's end was a test of collaboration that Dick Cohen and I undertook with diligence and good humor. The highlight of the latter aspect was an episode sparked by an innocuous Christmas Eve phone call to Cohen in our little sweatshop at the Post from Carl Bernstein, his good friend. It so happened that Cohen's wife was off visiting her parents over the holidays as Dick and I crashed the book project, putting in sixteen-hour or longer days. Carl was at Dick's house preparing a special holiday dinner of goose and he called to ask Dick to bring home some wine appropriate to the main course. Cohen confessed he had no idea what wine to serve with goose and he turned to me for advice. I had no idea either.

Then a light bulb went on in my head. An old friend and competitor from the *New York Times*, Johnny Apple, fashioned himself the world's greatest expert on wines and food and at the time was writing a column on the subject for the *Washingtonian*, a local monthly magazine. But it wouldn't do simply to flatter him by asking him to solve the problem. After conferring briefly with Cohen and positioning him to listen in on another phone, I dialed Johnny's number and, trying to disguise my voice and identifying myself only as a reader, I told him of the dilemma, using no names.

I risked the whole caper at the start by telling him I was a great admirer of his writing and particularly liked a recent column he had written in the *Washingtonian* on pizza parlors in the area. After he thanked me, I proceeded to tell him about the Christmas goose dinner and my appreciation that he was the one person who could advise me on the proper wine choice.

After thinking for a second, Apple came up with a long, fancy French label, saying it was the one best wine to serve with goose. I asked him where I could buy it and how much it cost, and he replied that there was only one shop in Washington that carried it. He gave me the name and said it would set me back about eighty dollars. After a pause, I told him that was a bit more than I intended to spend and asked for a less costly suggestion. He offered another long and fancy French name, a couple of shops that sold it, and a slightly lower cost. Again I informed him that his recommendation was beyond my price range. The conversation went on like that, with Johnny proposing cheaper and cheaper wines at more shops, each time eliciting my lament at the cost.

By the time Apple was mentioning ten-dollar wines that could be bought anywhere, and his patience was wearing thin, I went for broke. "Well, Mr. Apple," I said, "now that I think of it, I have a bottle of Manischewitz in the refrigerator. How do you think that would go with goose?" Only then did he ask, "Who is this?" as Cohen, still listening in, nearly fell off his chair holding his mirth in check. I never said, although I'm sure Johnny, the brunt of previous capers by me, knew. He never gave me the satisfaction of a response. In that, he was a soul brother of columnist Robert Novak, who over the years was the target of similar buffooneries but never owned that his tail had been twisted.

When our book on the Agnew resignation came out in April, Cohen and I, as members of the Washington Newspaper Guild, were engaging in what was known at the Post as "the Polish strike." We staffers, in a contract dispute with the paper, had elected, as the Guild put it, to "deny our excellence" to the Post by prohibiting use of our bylines. The executives promptly demonstrated how valuable our "excellence" was by taking over all editorial duties and squelching the strike in a matter of days, and the readers never seemed to notice. Anyway, our book was serialized in the *Post* during the strike, and the editors ran the pieces on page one under our bylines. In a lapse of sense, I called Bradlee's office at the paper and left word that Cohen and I were requesting, under the circumstances, that our bylines be dropped from the remaining installments of the series. Ben promptly relayed a two-word response that was both definitive and in character.

The Agnew resignation itself, however, opened another door for me professionally. Nixon, acting in accordance with the new Twenty-fifth Amendment, nominated House Minority Leader Gerald R. Ford Jr. of Michigan to fill the vice-presidential vacancy, putting him on track toward the presidency itself as a result of Nixon's Watergate woes. Upon his nomination I was assigned to write an explainer and eventually, as the impeachment case built, to function as the Ford "body man." I wrote basically that Ford got the job because he could be easily confirmed by his longtime friends in Congress, unlike two men who might have run into trouble on Capitol Hill, John Connally—the man Nixon probably wanted—and Nelson Rockefeller. Ford, hardly regarded as an intellectual giant by the legislators who had served with him for much of his twenty-five years in the House, also, like Agnew, seemed to offer the possibility of being a sort of insurance policy for Nixon against impeachment.

Even before Ford was confirmed, the specter of a presidential impeachment suddenly took on greater proportions on October 21 in "the Saturday Night Massacre." Nixon, trying desperately to block a move to subpoena the White House tapes, precipitously fired Watergate Special Prosecutor Archibald Cox and abolished his office. Immediately, Attorney General Richardson and his deputy, William Ruckelshaus, both resigned rather than carry out Nixon's dirty work, leaving that task to the Justice Department's willing solicitor general, Robert Bork, who himself would later be rejected as a Nixon nominee to the Supreme Court.

My page-one story in the next morning's *Post* said: "Demands for the impeachment of President Nixon mounted swiftly last night in the wake of his firing" of Cox and of the subsequent resignations. "Within the White House," my story continued, "sources reported an immediate reaction of 'shock' among presidential aides to Mr. Nixon's action, and an expectation that it was now inevitable that Congress would move to impeach him." A member of the House Judiciary Committee, Democrat Jerome Waldie of California, said he would quickly introduce an impeachment resolution, declaring that Nixon's move left no doubt that release of the tapes "would prove the President's complicity in the crime of obstruction of justice and would make him impeachable."

As the eventful year came to an end, talk of impeaching the president gained momentum, and in the first week of 1974 the *Post* sent a team of five seasoned reporters—Roy Aarons, David Broder, William Chapman, Stephen Isaacs, and Mary Russell—into a dozen congressional districts in ten states to take voters' temperatures on the burning issue of the day. Afterward, they digested nearly 250 in-depth interviews and I reported their findings in a banner story across the top of the front page that bore this lead: "America, at the start of 1974, is unhappy with its President, but doesn't seem to know quite what to do about it." Many voters, the story went on, "would prefer to have him resign rather than have impeachment proceedings instituted against him, a step they consider radical and destructive of national stability. Only slightly more than half of all those interviewed who went heavily for Mr. Nixon in 1972 want the President to stay in office and finish out his second term. About one in four says he should resign and turn the presidency over to Vice President Ford. About one in five says he should be impeached . . . and of those who say he should resign, about half say that if he refuses to do so, he should be impeached."

One citizen, however, who clung to the notion that Nixon would ride out the storm was Jerry Ford. All through the winter and spring of 1974, as a House impeachment inquiry got under way, the vice president who would be the direct political beneficiary of Nixon's removal continued to play the good soldier, insisting that he believed in the president's innocence and predicting that he would survive in office. Although friends in the House and in the Republican Party urged him to remain silent lest he be drawn into the vortex of the developing whirlpool, Ford continued to defend the man who had handed him an honor he had never expected.

Supporting the speculation that Nixon looked on the unimpressive Ford as an insurance policy against his own impeachment was a story in *Newsweek* in May later denied by Rockefeller but believed by many who knew Nixon. From behind his desk in the Oval Office, Nixon was said to have remarked to the New York governor, "Can you imagine Jerry Ford sitting in this chair?"

It was around this time that I was assigned by the *Post* to stay close to Ford, get to know him better, and thus be prepared to write the account of his elevation to the presidency if it were to come about. I traveled frequently with him thereafter and found him to be a congenial and uncomplicated man of strong party loyalty. Later, in my book *Marathon: The Pursuit of the Presidency, 1972–1976*, I wrote that "at a time when it might have been politically prudent to keep his mouth shut, the new Vice President stood in the front rank with the Republicans who insisted that the emperor was not naked. . . . Occasionally he would allow himself a criticism of the White House's editing of the Watergate tape transcripts or its refusal to turn over additional tapes to the House Judiciary Committee. But he held firm to the conviction that Nixon was 'innocent of any impeachable offense'—a notably limited exoneration—and he waited."

I occasionally covered Nixon out-of-town events as well, at which he got mixed receptions. At a speech in Miami, he was greeted with signs that said, "Impeach Nixon Now"; but at another gathering a few days later in Huntsville, Alabama, the message was "Hang In There, Mr. President." There, he alluded to his own problem by observing, "The American people are not a nation of quitters. We are a nation that will keep fighting on."

Through all this, however, the specter of impeachment hung over Nixon and fueled speculation about Ford's future. But the new vice president dodged it, standing four-square behind the man who had put him in that office. The most he would permit himself by way of criticism was to assault CREEP officials, calling them at one point "an arrogant, elite guard of political adolescents," and on another occasion to question the wisdom of the White House's editing of tape transcripts before release to the House Judiciary Committee, by now weighing possible impeachment. In an interview in his office next to the White House in early June, Ford also indicated that he disagreed with Nixon's adamant refusal to turn over more tapes to the committee, while continuing to declare his confidence in Nixon's innocence.

The noose nevertheless was closing more tightly around Nixon's neck. On July 9 the committee released a transcript it had made itself of one White House tape, and it included a quote that had been omitted from the White House version. Under a double byline with colleague Lou Cannon in the *Post*'s lead story, we reported Nixon's saying: "I don't give a shit what happens. I want you all to stonewall it, let them plead the Fifth Amendment, cover-up or anything else if it'll save it—save the plan. That's the whole point."

At this juncture, some of Ford's old and trusted friends, led by Philip Buchen, later his White House counsel, quietly and without informing the vice president began to look into some of the problems he would encounter if the presidency were suddenly thrust upon him. Meanwhile, he increasingly found reasons to get out of Washington and the line of fire, speaking at Republican party fund-raising events for the approaching congressional elections and, as I wrote in *Marathon*, "holding the clammy hand of a sick party."

I traveled with Ford in late July to Muncie, Indiana; Chicago; Canton, Ohio; San Francisco; Las Vegas; Reno; and San Diego for party meetings at which he reiterated his belief in Nixon's innocence. But he was being more guarded in his remarks, acknowledging in Chicago that defection among Republicans on the House Judiciary Committee "narrows the odds" on Nixon's impeachment.

Ten days before key Republican senators, including Barry Goldwater, went to Nixon with the bad news that he no longer had the votes in Congress to beat impeachment, I sat with Ford aboard Air Force Two on a postmidnight flight back to Washington. The House Judiciary Committee had just voted a third article of impeachment against the president. Ford sat in shirtsleeves, relaxed and cordial and puffing as ever on his pipe. He was reluctant to talk about the growing likelihood of his becoming president, as if doing so would be an act of disloyalty toward Nixon. But the evidence of what was happening was all around him: increased and more alert Secret Service agents, more reporters, and larger crowds, often bearing signs calling him "President Ford." Wherever he went, GOP pols elbowed their way to his side, another sign of approaching power.

As we chatted, Ford admitted that Republican friends were telling him he was hurting himself in continuing to proclaim Nixon's innocence. But, he said, Nixon had told him face-to-face that he was being falsely accused, and until he was convinced that the president was lying to him, that was good enough for him. He said he sincerely believed that the Judiciary Committee hadn't made a sufficient case against Nixon on a Watergate cover-up, and although he wasn't kidding himself about the gravity of the situation, he wasn't going to abandon the man.

Ford, however, up to this point had not only been defending Nixon but also attacking some of the president's Democratic accusers on the Judiciary Committee. Certainly he was aware that he might soon have to take over the leadership of the government and would need to work with them. He acknowledged that likelihood but felt that, having spoken up for Nixon, he couldn't simply fall silent. For the sake of the party, he said, he had to do what he could to help in its time of trouble.

Later, on the same flight, I asked Bob Hartmann, Ford's chief of staff as vice president, why he thought Ford had continued to attack some of Nixon's Democratic critics. Many of these Democrats, he replied, had voted against Ford's confirmation, and their action "had really hurt him because he really believes they opposed him out of pure partisanship, not on the facts. Sometimes politicans don't do the smart thing," he said, "even when they know what it is. Sometimes they just do what they want to do, or what they feel they have to do."

A few weeks earlier, Ford had come to the Post for lunch with Katharine Graham and some editors and political reporters. That morning the Supreme Court had ruled that Nixon had to produce the tapes being subpoenaed by the Judiciary Committee. Ford had conceded that he frankly didn't know what Nixon would do, although just before coming to the lunch he had been on the phone to Nixon's summer White House at San Clemente. That admission made clear that for all his loyalty he was not remotely on the inside of the strategies to save the Nixon presidency.

As we flew back to Washington that night, I reminded him of that open, friendly lunch and remarked on how it contrasted with Nixon's guarded, often hostile relationship with the press. He vowed that things would be different in a Ford White House, but he took care not to say anything critical of Nixon and he pointedly forbade me to use any observations that he may have made about how he would function in the office Nixon still held.

One thing that struck me particularly was that for a man facing the increasing likelihood of soon becoming president of the United States, he was remarkably relaxed. I wrote in the *Post* later:

> Jerry Ford is hardly the picture of the crashing student. He sits casually in his forward cabin, with aides . . . around him at a table. They chat idly as he autographs pictures, peruses the local papers or reads memos prepared for him on vice-presidential activities. There are on the table no books on the presidency, or on the burning domestic and global problems of the day. No heady theoreticians are aboard to brainstorm him on these and other subjects that may before long become his responsibility. . . . He is a man too much on the move to bone up for the presidency in that fashion.

Afterward I also wrote: "One senses a sense of personal sympathy, even compassion, toward Mr. Nixon that transcends Mr. Ford's best political self-interest." It was that sympathy, maintained through Ford's brief tenure as vice president, that nurtured the attitude that was to harm him severely in the first days of his presidency by producing his pardon of Nixon and imperiling his chances of election in his own right in 1976.

Before then, however, on yet another trip to Mississippi and Louisiana, in early August, Ford finally conceded the likelihood that Nixon would be impeached, while continuing to say he believed the president was innocent "of any impeachable offenses." After returning to Washington, however, he announced that he had "come to the conclusion that the public interest" was "no longer served" by his continuing to express that belief and that he would have nothing more to say about the impeachment matter. It was obvious from this that he knew the end for Nixon was in sight, and that he soon would have the responsibility of binding the nation's wounds over the whole affair.

Several nights prior to Nixon's decision to resign to escape certain impeachment, I was part of the press contingent obliged to camp out on the lawn of Ford's small and unpretentious house in suburban Alexandria, Virginia, waiting for the magic moment when he might suddenly, to paraphrase John Adams, the first vice president, go from being nothing to being everything.

On the evening of August 9, 1974, after watching Nixon announce via television that he would step aside the next day, Ford walked into the glare of lights on his front lawn and promised simply to govern "in a spirit of cooperation" with Congress and with the people. In the *Post* the next day, below a bold and screaming headline, "Nixon Resigns," and White House correspondent Carroll Kilpatrick's lead story, I noted in my off-lead the irony of the vice president's situation: "Gerald Rudolph Ford Jr., a Grand Rapids, Mich., lawyer who never aspired to national office but had it thrust upon him as a result of two of the greatest political scandals in American history, will become the 38th President of the United States at noon today."

The next morning, I was in the East Room of the White House as Richard Nixon bade farewell to the presidency in one of the more bizarre scenes I have ever been privileged to witness at close range. The room was packed with staff workers of all levels, waiting in solemn mood, when the president strode in wearing a forced smile and accompanied by his wife and two daughters.

After hearing his typically Nixonian maudlin farewell, I walked out onto the South Lawn to watch the Nixons' departure via helicopter to his awaiting government jet at Andrews Air Force Base in nearby Suitland, Maryland, for the long flight across the land he only minutes before had ruled, to exile in San Clemente. A long red carpet had been rolled out from the rear of the White House to the helicopter's stairs, and the Nixons and the Fords came out and stood for a few minutes chatting awkwardly as other staffers crowded around. Then, after quick good-bys, Nixon, his wife Pat, daughter

Tricia, and her husband, Edward Cox, walked down the carpet and onto the helicopter, private citizen Nixon being the last aboard. He climbed to the top stair, turned, and for one last time gave his familiar wave, sweeping over his head in a great arc and ending with arms raised and apart, both hands giving his favorite V signal as he looked out at the crowd. Then, wordlessly, he ducked inside and was out of sight. Thus ended one of the most corrupt presidencies in American history perpetrated by one of the most tormented men ever to hold the office.

Shortly after the Nixons' departure, Ford came into the East Room, was sworn into office as the thirty-eighth president, and then, as my lead story in the *Post* the next morning put it, "assured a nation torn by the ravages of the Watergate scandal, 'Our long national nightmare is over.'" Carroll Kilpatrick, writing the off-lead this time, told eloquently of the Nixon departure and long last flight into political exile in California.

I never saw Nixon in person again, but he would continue to be a source of news stories and columns for me until his death. The next big one came only a month later, when on one shining Sunday morning Ford suddenly announced that he was granting his White House predecessor a full pardon for any and all offenses he might have committed while he was president. The story rocked Washington and the country, and Ford never recovered from it. Jerry terHorst, a friend and colleague who had quit as Washington bureau chief for the *Detroit News* to become Ford's press secretary, resigned in dismay at Ford's action. Ford himself later had to face a congressional inquiry into the pardon before the furor dissipated, and the pardon was considered a major factor in significant Democratic gains in that fall's congressional elections.

The forced resignations of Agnew and Nixon and the Nixon pardon, in the wake of the government's lies and deceptions in the 1960s and 1970s about the Vietnam war, ultimately bred greater suspicions and doubts among the press corps about the behavior and trustworthiness of politicians. The result was "gotcha" journalism. Thereafter, reporters mounted more intensive quests for evidence or even just rumor of misconduct by high-level officeholders.

The mutual distrust and in some cases mutual hostility between politicians and reporters led many younger reporters to seek fame and fortune by catching the politically mighty in malfeasance, personal or legal. They yearned to be the successors of Woodward and Bernstein, who had brought down Nixon. As a result, many of us paid a price in loss or lessening of the access we had earlier enjoyed to the politicians we covered. They increasingly threw up defensive barriers against our questions and, often, just plain snooping into their private lives, pursued with disregard for the old concessions to a politician's privacy.

This phenomenon brought with it another challenge to the old, down-the-middle reporting—what came to be called "adversarial journalism." Some younger reporters sought to set the political agenda and advance their own views against issue positions and the candidates who adopted them. The flip side of the practice, openly supporting politicians and issues, became known as "advocacy journalism." To many older reporters, both were sheer heresy.

The adversarial and advocacy bugs created an epidemic of cheerleading on television and radio, as openly opinionated talk-show hosts filled the airwaves with all manner of lopsided argumentation and, ultimately, even character assassination and slander. Such palaver certainly was not new to American politics, but the scope and venomous depths of it became pervasive. These opinion mongers often were thrown in on panels with politicians and the new breed of airwave polemicists masquerading as journalists, to the degree that viewers had trouble distinguishing one from the other.

These developments heightened the imperative that consumers of political news and commentary recognize the difference between those who by training and discipline make fact gathering, reporting, and fair analysis the core of what they do, and those who peddle ideology and glibness unfiltered or restrained by fact. The advent of the radio and television shriekers and Internet bloggers given chiefly to rumormongering have made the commitment of print reporters to basic news-gathering guidelines more essential than ever before.

Although I had arrived at the *Washington Post* after Woodward, Bernstein, and others on the staff had done the heavy lifting on the Watergate story, its fallout had occupied me for most of my first year and a half on the paper. The Ervin hearings, the Nixon impeachment inquiry and resignation, and my body watch on Ford necessitated by the *Post* team's revelations kept me busy, with the Agnew investigation and resignation thrown in. Now it was time for me to turn my attention back to what had brought me to the *Post* in the first place—the pursuit of candidates pursuing the presidency.

12 Lust and Other Bumps in the Road

WITH JERRY FORD SAFELY ENSCONCED in the Oval Office and with Nelson Rockefeller as his hand-picked vice president, I was able to get back to the early jockeying for position in the 1976 presidential race. Throughout the "long national nightmare," I had been keeping my eye on some of the White House aspirants, including Senator Walter "Fritz" Mondale of Minnesota. Earlier in 1974, I had heard him deliver a strong anti-Nixon speech at a dinner in Johnstown, Pennsylvania, for Democratic congressional candidate John Murtha, after which he had been closeted with state labor leaders, making a late-night pitch for their support for a nomination that was still two years away.

After a few hours' sleep, we met at the Johnstown airport for a dawn flight to Pittsburgh, the 46-year-old senator unrecognized by the few locals on hand. Accompanying him was Sam Bregman, an old Hubert Humphrey hand who was shepherding Mondale on this early scouting expedition. Mondale told me he was following the blueprint of John F. Kennedy, who similarly had traveled the circuit with sidekick Ted Sorensen in advance of the 1960 campaign, and he left me with little doubt that he intended to follow through.

I wrote the next day:

As the small plane flew over the grays and browns of the early morning Pennsylvania countryside, Mondale sat hunched forward in the cabin and spoke with the kind of enthusiasm that infects men of ambition. It would be a long and tough road, but he was convinced this was the right time for him to travel it. Politicians looked for a man with "a hard edge," and he thought he had that, too, and had to find a way to demonstrate that. . . . [T]he plane dropped quickly to the Pittsburgh airport and Mondale kept one eye on the approaching runway as he talked about the pluses and minuses of the other Democratic prospects. He did it in a detached way, as if he were not involved. At the terminal, he climbed out and walked inside. Not a head turned in recognition. . . . A year from now, if Fritz Mondale's efforts go according to plan, heads doubtless will turn as he enters terminals, and he will not be found alone much in airports, large or small. He is walking, not running yet, but it is clear that he can hardly wait to break into a trot.

I was dead wrong. Nine months later, the "hard edge" Mondale had been sure he had seemed to have melted away in the heat of the ordeal. Unable to raise much money and, as he pithily put it, weary of the thought of another year of "sleeping in Holiday Inns," he folded his national ambitions—for the time being. I was obliged to observe in the *Post* that Mondale, "who for the past year acted like a man who wanted the presidency so much he could taste it, yesterday pushed the plate away even before the first course was served."

Mondale's decision was particularly surprising in that several weeks earlier, Senator Ted Kennedy had announced that he would not be a presidential candidate in 1976, citing family responsibilities. That decision had the opposite effect on other Democrats afflicted with Potomac fever. It opened the floodgates for them, assuring that there would be a crowded field of contenders for the party's next nomination.

I first met one of these hopefuls at the Democratic Party's off-year mini-convention in Kansas City in December 1974. As I was walking by Room 2318 of the Holiday Inn one afternoon, I spotted through the open door the little-known Governor Carter of Georgia, who called himself "Jimmy," perched on the edge of a coffee table. I heard him telling members of the New Hampshire delegation to the mini-convention: "I'll be up in New Hampshire often next year. . . . I'm going to announce for president next Thursday. I really think at this point I have as much chance as anyone else." Other delegates drifted in and out of the room as he made this seemingly ludicrous declaration.

Other Democratic prospects—Senators Lloyd Bentsen of Texas and Henry M. "Scoop" Jackson of Washington, and Representative Morris K. Udall of Arizona—were similarly courting delegates. Other prospective candidates—Senator Edmund S. Muskie of Maine, rated the early frontrunner,

Senators-elect John Glenn of Ohio and Dale Bumpers of Arkansas, George Wallace, back as governor of Alabama, and former Governor Terry Sanford of North Carolina—while not hustling support as aggressively, were part of the great mentioning game. Old standby Senator Hubert Humphrey of Minnesota, professing to be cured of presidential fever, said the chances were "one in a million" that a deadlock would lead the party to turn to him again.

Carter, true to his word, declared his candidacy on December 12. Two days later, I caught up with another long shot, Senator Fred Harris of Oklahoma, in New Hampshire implementing the same brand of political guerrilla warfare that was to make Carter famous. Harris and his wife LaDonna, for the fifth time that year, were in the state living off the land by staying with supporters overnight and sponging rides around the countryside from them. Playing off Mondale's remark that he could not face another year of "sleeping in Holiday Inns," Harris told one living-room crowd in the town of Windham where the Harrises were bedding down: "I don't blame him. I wouldn't do it either. Staying with friends is a helluva lot more enjoyable."

New Hampshire, however, was not the first priority on Carter's calendar. One day in late February 1975, he and a young sidekick named Jody Powell motored into the small town of LeMars, Iowa, just north of Sioux City, to speak at a testimonial dinner for one Marie Jahn, retiring after thirty-eight years as the Plymouth County recorder. It was the only speaking invitation he could wrangle. Powell told me later: "They may have asked a couple of other people first." For his effort, Carter was declared LeMars' Citizen of the Day by the local radio station and given a free car wash, a movie pass, and a coupon for a free pizza. The more substantial prize he had his eye on, however, was the Iowa precinct caucuses nearly a year away. In them, the first actual votes would be cast toward the ultimate selection of delegates to the Democratic National Convention in New York in the summer of 1976. Carter and Powell were getting a big jump on the rest of the field—a jump they maintained by going door-to-door across the state in what proved to be one of the great long-shot stories in American political history.

In early April, for our regular background dinner group, Carter laid out his own strategy, beyond the personal style of toting his own suit bag and making his own bed in the homes that were opened to him. As a southern alternative to George Wallace, he intended, he said, to confront him head-on, arguing that while a vote for Wallace might be a way of sending a message, it would be a wasted vote because the feisty Alabama governor could not be elected. Carter's master plan, beyond early success in Iowa, included a victory in New Hampshire over Harris and Udall, figuring that Wallace, Bentsen, and Jackson would stay out. Then, he predicted, he would dispense with Wallace in Florida, whose primary Wallace had won in 1972. After the dinner, I wrote a memo for the file with this conclusion: "The dominant characteristic of the evening's performance was Carter's repeated expressions of self-confidence, of his ability to meet all the other contenders on the issues and as a campaigner. He said he had decided two and a half years ago to run, after exposure to the 1972 candidates, who he decided were not his superiors."

At this point, Carter and several others were generally being dismissed out of hand, which I thought was premature in light of the recent history of George McGovern's nomination only four years before, after starting with only 5 percent support in the polls. I was moved to write a piece to that effect for the *Post* op-ed page, observing that it was "foolhardy to dispatch a candidate . . . when there is no clear frontrunner and the campaign is going forward in largely uncharted waters." Without mentioning Carter, I asked what would happen, for instance, if somebody beat Wallace in an early primary. "The conqueror suddenly will be 'somebody,'" I wrote; "observers will perceive a certain charisma in him that had escaped them earlier; he will be listened to more closely and voters will be astounded to learn that he has something to say. These are the dynamics of a political campaign, and each of the 'nobodies' in the race is spurred on by his knowledge that these dynamics exist, and may eventually work in his favor."

They were, indeed, to work for Carter in almost exactly that way in the approaching presidential election year. In October, his diligence in Iowa paid off with a surprising first-place finish in a straw poll at a statewide Democratic Jefferson-Jackson dinner in Ames. With Carter campaign aides packing the hall, he won 23 percent of the vote; it wasn't all that much, but it was twice as much as the next Democrat, leading me to write in the *Post* that he appeared "well along in his strategy to win recognition as the 'sleeper' Democratic candidate in advance of the first 1976 presidential primary [in New Hampshire]."

As for Wallace, even before any declaration of intent from him to run for president again, he was relishing the attention the prospect was drawing from the other Democratic hopefuls. At a National Governors Conference in New Orleans at which stopping Wallace in 1976 was much discussed, he remained aloof, staying in his Fairmont Hotel suite out of touch with fellow governors and the press. My past associations with him, however, produced an interview in which I asked how he felt about the stop-Wallace movement.

Looking out the window at the city, gripping the arm of his wheelchair with one hand and twisting a long cigar between the fingers of the other, then staring at me for a moment, he finally said: "You want to write down my reaction to that?" Pencil poised at the ready and looking down, I replied: "Yes, sir, I've got my pad out." Whereupon George Wallace just yawned. I was so intent on writing the response that I failed to see it, and in the silence that followed I looked up in puzzled anticipation. "I yawned," Wallace explained. "I just yawn at all this business." Reveling in the attention, Wallace said of the other prospective candidates: "They're stepping up the interest in beating me, and I haven't even announced yet. I must have some support out there. . . . Everybody's attacking me. Everybody's kicking my dog."

It so happened that I was at the governors' conference on a free-lance assignment for *Rolling Stone* magazine, not for the *Post,* which had assigned another reporter. But with Wallace closeted in his hotel suite as he remained the center of corridor chatter, getting the interview was a bit of a coup, so I called the *Post* national desk and inquired whether the paper wanted the story. The staffer on the desk said sure, so I filed it. Shortly afterward, I got a call-back asking whether, if the story was used, I intended to bill my expenses for the New Orleans trip to the Post. I hit the roof, saying my expenses were already being taken care of, and I didn't care whether the paper used the piece or not. In the end, it wound up on page one, but when I returned to the office I was called in with a demand that I apologize for my attitude. Sometimes, I was told, reporters tried to put one over on the national desk editors. I got irate all over again, saying that if anybody was due an apology it was me. The whole matter soon blew over, but it left a sour taste in my mouth in what otherwise already had been a very rewarding time for me at the paper.

Back on the presidential campaign beat along with two veterans, Dave Broder and Lou Cannon, I pulled occasional assignments with my traveling companion of the late Watergate days, Jerry Ford. It was routine stuff, with an occasional opportunity for comic relief as a result of one Ford verbal gaffe or another. One came on a presidential trip to Topeka for a speech to the Kansas legislature. Ford opened his remarks by observing: "Ever since I was a youngster, I have had a special feeling for Kansas, because Kansas is where Dorothy lived before she went to visit the wonderful land of Oz, where all kinds of strange, whimsical and unexpected things happened. But I'm beginning to think that if strange, whimsical and unexpected things were what Dorothy was really interested in, she wouldn't have gone to Oz. She would have come to Washington."

Here, if ever, was inspiration for a campaign song. Amid rising inflation, a gasoline crisis, and continuing turmoil in the Middle East, the scarecrow's song from the movie was revamped on the press plane. One stanza, to be sung by Ford, went:

> I could overcome inflation, put gas in every station,
> And we would feel no pain;
> I could make the Arabs cower, I could be an Eisenhower,
> If I only had a brain.

Despite frequent press denigrations of Ford's gray matter, however, the country seemed to take to his easy, old-shoe manner, and by July the first nonelected president announced his decision to seek a full term in his own right in 1976. He said nothing at the time about Rockefeller as his running mate, a question of considerable concern now to party conservatives, who also were intrigued by the formation of a Reagan-for-President committee to challenge Ford.

In early September, Ford made a trip to California during which he was scheduled to address the state legislature in Sacramento. On a typical bright Golden State morning, he left his hotel across from the state capitol building and strolled leisurely through the capitol grounds, shaking hands with onlookers and flanked by Secret Service agents, an aide or two, and a few reporters. As we all walked along beside the president, a woman standing under a huge old tree in a roped-off area and wearing a long, deep-red gown suddenly reached down under it and pulled out a .45-caliber pistol. In an instant, in full view, a Secret Service agent grabbed her and the gun as another agent seized Ford by his arm and hustled him toward the capitol building, the rest of us running along beside them. I saw Ford momentarily pause and look at the woman and then give himself up to the agent as others swarmed around him protectively. He was grim-faced but showed no panic and later delivered the speech as scheduled, dismissing the incident as a mere "distraction" to a very successful visit.

The woman was identified as Lynette Alice Fromme, 27, known as "Squeaky," a follower of Charles Manson, who had been convicted of the mass murder of seven persons in 1969. Only seventeen days later, in San Francisco, the frightening scene was replayed when a 46-year-old woman identified as Sara Jane Moore drew a revolver and actually fired at Ford as he came out of the downtown St. Francis Hotel. She missed him when a bystander knocked her arm and deflected the shot, and she was immediately disarmed and arrested. She was convicted of attempted assassination and sentenced to life imprisonment. I was in San Francisco at the time but in this case I did not witness the shooting. Dave Broder wrote the lead story, Roy Aarons of the *Post*'s local bureau reconstructed the scene, and I joined three other staffers in fleshing out the paper's extensive coverage. Suddenly I seemed to be on a presidential assassination watch.

A couple of days after the Sacramento episode, I had gone down to Los Angeles to see Ronald Reagan. At the time he was being prodded by supporters to consider challenging Ford for the 1976 Republican nomination, and some Ford backers were entertaining the thought of dissuading him by offering to make him Ford's running mate. Riding in the back seat of his red Lincoln Continental headed toward a recording studio at, appropriately, Hollywood and Vine, he wasted no time throwing cold water on playing second banana to Ford. For one thing, he told me, he didn't approve of "balancing the ticket" ideologically as a way of getting votes. A running mate, he said, "should be someone close to the philosophy of the presidential candidate so he could be an aid to him in implementing his policies."

It seemed to be a way of saying that Ford was much too moderate for him, and when I asked him point-blank what he would do if the Republican convention voted for him to be Ford's running mate, he replied: "That would depend on, could you be convinced it was the best thing for the country?" Everything he said then and later, however, made clear that he was not so convinced, and that he had a higher ambition.

At the studio, Reagan was to tape nine radio commentaries that he was selling to about 300 stations around the country. He said he was building up a good backlog, to free himself to make a political swing during which time he would finally decide whether or not to seek the presidency. But watching him and listening to him left no doubt that he had already made up his mind and was at peace with his decision.

Dressed casually in a sports shirt, slacks, and white loafers, Reagan stepped out briskly from the car at the recording studio, walking jauntily over pavement embossed with pink-pointed stars bearing the names of old silver-screen colleagues: Ann Sothern, Louis Hayward, Audrey Hepburn, Jackie Coogan. Sitting behind an overhanging microphone, he proceeded to read the commentaries he had written himself, offering, as I wrote subsequently in the *Post*, "a preview of what a 1976 Reagan campaign would be under the 11th Commandment ['Thou shalt not speak ill of another Republican.']: Not the slightest dig at President Ford, hardly a reference to Democrats even, as befits a candidate seeking independent support."

Before going on to other chores that day, Reagan went out of his way to tell me that the recent attempt on Ford's life in Sacramento was not going to deter him in any way from running. He recalled that as governor in 1968 an attempt to bomb his home while he and his wife Nancy were sleeping had been foiled. "It's just one of those things you have to accept in public life," he said. "You have to recognize it can happen, and then put it out of your mind." I had reason to recall that comment a couple of months later in Miami, and still later in Washington.

Two months later, on the day Reagan declared his challenge to Ford for the 1976 Republican nomination, I covered his speech at the National Press Club and then climbed aboard his campaign press plane for Florida. On arrival at Miami International Airport, we reporters trooped over to the nearby Ramada Inn for brief public remarks by the new candidate. He was on an elevated platform and I was standing a few feet below when a man aimed what proved to be a toy gun at him as he spoke. Not knowing the gun was a toy, Secret Service agents wrestled the man to the ground and carted him away.

At that moment, the same feeling of horror that had gripped me on witnessing the assassination of Robert Kennedy and the recent attempt on Ford in Sacramento struck me again. It drove home to me once more not only the wisdom of Lyndon Johnson's 1968 decision to assign Secret Service protection to all major candidates but also the unpredictability of presidential succession. These episodes, along with the Agnew resignation, illustrated the importance of wise choices in the selection of presidential running mates, a subject to which I would turn at greater length years later.

That matter, in fact, was much in the news at the time of the Reagan incident in Florida, as a result of a political coup by Republican conservatives against Rockefeller. From the very moment Ford picked the liberal former New York governor for the job, Republican conservative leaders had been unhappy. Still, as I wrote later in *Marathon*, "even the right-wingers saw some merit in selecting Rockefeller over George Bush, the other finalist. Everyone knowledgeable in Republican politics considered Bush incompetent to be president; one of the best-kept secrets among conservatives was how many of them, including [Mississippi state party chairman] Clarke Reed, lined up behind Rockefeller as the better alternative, for the sake of the country."

Nevertheless, by the time Rockefeller was confirmed, the party conservatives were having second thoughts. It was not only that something might happen to Ford; they didn't want Rocky using the vice presidency as a stepping stone to the next Republican presidential nomination; better to get a good conservative on the ticket in 1976. A couple of days after Ford's declaration of candidacy, his campaign manager, Howard "Bo" Callaway of Georgia, while saying it was not his intention to undercut Rockefeller, told reporters, "A lot of Reagan people are not supporters of Rockefeller, and I want it clear to them that we want their support [for Ford] whether they support Rockefeller or not." Such comments led me to write in the *Post* the next day that Callaway had "identified Vice President Rockefeller as a liability in the mission to win the broadest possible support for Mr. Ford's nomination as the Republican candidate next year."

In early November, as pressures continued on Rockefeller and his dissatisfaction with his role grew, I was obliged to write in the *Post:* "Vice President Rockefeller, pilloried from the right within his own Republican Party and ignored on major policy decisions within the Ford administration, yesterday suddenly withdrew his name from consideration as President Ford's running mate next year."

Rockefeller's decision immediately stirred speculation that Reagan might yet be dissuaded from challenging Ford and instead be his running mate. But Reagan was not changing his mind about that. He was in the Republican race to stay, even as the Democratic field continued to swell. Joining the early entries—Jimmy Carter, Fred Harris, Mo Udall, Scoop Jackson, Terry Sanford, Lloyd Bentsen—new hats were thrown into the ring: Sargent Shriver, the 1972 vice-presidential nominee; Governor Milton Shapp of

Pennsylvania, Senator Birch Bayh of Indiana, George Wallace, even Gene McCarthy.

Some of these latest entries defied logic. Shapp's candidacy particularly was a puzzlement, because he was so little known outside his own state. His modest claim to fame during two terms was the success he had achieved in settling a massive truckers' strike. When some such long shot reached for the presidency, he almost always was asked whether he wasn't really running for the vice presidency. Shapp didn't even rate that query. At a Washington press conference after getting into the race for the presidential nomination, a reporter asked him: "Aren't you really running for Secretary of Transportation?"

Shriver was another interesting case. He was very well known by now, not only as the most recent Democratic veep candidate but also as head of JFK's Peace Corps, LBJ's war on poverty, a former U.S. ambassador to Paris and, not least, husband to the former Eunice Kennedy. It was also well known that there was an unofficial pecking order in the Kennedy clan, and only with Ted Kennedy out of the running could he even think of seeking the presidency. Still, family protocol seemed to require that Shriver call on his brother-in-law, inform him that he, Ted, was the Kennedy Democrats wanted, but if he wasn't going to run, then he, Sarge, might make a stab at it. When my old friend Jim Dickenson broke the story of the meeting in the rival *Washington Star*, I went up to see Kennedy in his Senate office to learn where the matter stood. In 1968, when Robert Kennedy made his presidential bid, Shriver had turned down a campaign post to take LBJ's offer in Paris, a decision not forgotten by what I called in *Marathon* "the Family of Long Memories." So I asked Ted, "What did Sarge say to you when he came up here to see you? And what did you say to him?" Kennedy answered, "He told me he was going to run and I wished him well." Well, I asked the senator, "if Benito Mussolini walked in here and told you he was going to run, would you wish him well?" Kennedy laughed and then, grinning, shot back: "If he was married to my sister!"

Then there was Birch Bayh, a pleasant three-term Hoosier senator who played the hick from Hicksville for all it was worth. His aw-shucks manner did not do justice to his legislative record, which importantly included authorship of the Twenty-fifth Amendment providing for filling presidential and vice-presidential vacancies, successful fights against odious Nixon Supreme Court nominations, and chief sponsorship of the (unsuccessful)

Equal Rights Amendment for women. Bayh announced his candidacy on his family farm, climbing down off a tractor to do so. His boyish blue eyes all sincerity, he confessed that "I've never had a burning desire to be the President of the United States. . . . I felt closer to my God and I felt more fulfilled out in these fields than anything else I've done." A few weeks later, meeting with our dinner group, Bayh was needled unmercifully for his "closer to my God" remark. He insisted he had been speaking from the heart but said on reflection maybe it had been a mistake to say it—"at least to guys like you!"

With the 1976 presidential primaries now at hand, the *Post* political reporting team, headed by Dave Broder, was assembled; Lou Cannon, George Lardner, and I were assigned to the major primary states, and others joined in. We functioned under the direction of the managing editor for national news at the time, Harry Rosenfeld, who had been the paper's Metro editor during most of the Watergate story. We were a congenial group, and Dave was always generous in spreading around the choice assignments; he was one of the biggest of the "bigfoots" in our business but he never acted the part. He was a smart and dedicated reporter justly renowned for his integrity, balance, and fairness. Although a man of good will and good humor, on election nights he was all business until the last deadline had passed. Dave and I often labored side by side on the NBC News election night set, gratefully making use of the same network research data and results that went to the main reporting desk of our good friend John Chancellor and his sidekick David Brinkley, and the analysis of Dick Scammon and Bud Lewis, as well as being fed by *Post* reporters in the field.

When covering primaries, we mainly worked on a "zone" rather than a man-to-man basis; that is, we worked the whole state and all the candidates in it, choosing each day which of them to cover, rather than sticking to one candidate all the time. We sought thus to avoid the myopia that can result from too narrow and limited observation of one candidate whose message gets to be excessively repetitive as time goes on. I was part of the team that covered the Iowa precinct caucuses, the kickoff of the delegate selection process, and spent a good deal of time tracking Carter as well as the others.

The favorite press hangout in Des Moines was the Savery Hotel, a rather nondescript joint that when I first went to Iowa had one of those marquees usually seen on movie houses, welcoming arriving guests by name. A new owner, local real estate mogul Bill Knapp, eventually spruced it up, but not to the point that I stopped ribbing him about advertising "Rooms by the Hour" on that marquee. Knapp greatly improved the dining habits in the town by opening a restaurant named Guido's, after a chef he had met on a cruise ship and persuaded to abandon the open seas for the Heartland. Because of the caucuses, Guido became a local celebrity in his own right, reveling in nightly visits from the likes of David Brinkley, Jack Chancellor, Tom Brokaw, and Dan Rather.

The Iowa caucuses were when I began a running dialogue with Jimmy Carter over a major promise he was making on the stump, an encounter that continued through much of the 1976 campaign. Carter told voters that if elected he was going to cut the federal bureaucracy down to size with a sweeping reorganization, reducing some 1,900 federal agencies to about 200, in a move patterned on his reduction as governor of Georgia's 300 state agencies to only 22. When asked at a press conference in Sioux City one Sunday which federal agencies he would abolish, he balked. It was, he said, "impossible to say now" because he hadn't had time to study the federal apparatus, but he said no civil service employees would be fired; instead, they would be transferred or retrained.

Flying with him, Jody Powell and the pilot of a chartered two-engine propeller plane low over Iowa farmlands from Sioux City eastward to Dubuque, I pressed Carter to give me just one example of one of the 1,900 agencies that would be reduced or folded into another one. He wouldn't. "I may set up a task force after the convention," he said. "I'm not being evasive. People have common sense. They don't expect me to have all the answers." Well, I didn't expect him to have *all* the answers, just some notion of what he had in mind. With a little more prodding, he said: "For instance, there are 42 federal agencies in education. I don't know now which could be cut out. It would just be conjectural. It would just be a guess on my part." That's the way it went until the plane landed in Dubuque, and every time thereafter that I raised the matter with him.

When I discussed the issue of this Carter promise with Mo Udall in Dubuque, he told me: "There is no magic in shuffling departments around. . . . If Carter's got some secret plan in the back of his mind, he ought to tell us. And if he hasn't, he ought not to be talking this way." But such comments, and my own pestering, never budged Carter on his plan for the Great Shrinking of the Federal Bureaucracy. After his inauguration, upon publication of *Marathon*, chronicling his election, I presented him with one of the first copies, in the Oval Office (my first visit there after twenty-three years of reporting in Washington). I signed it to him, writing on the first blank page something like: "With fond recollections of our many conversations on your reorganization of the federal bureaucracy." Two White House photographs hanging over the desk in my study at home show the new president first glancing tentatively at the inscription and then breaking out in his patented toothy grin. I never did get a straight answer, and after four Carter years in the Oval Office the bureaucracy remained pretty much what it had been when he got there.

In any event, Carter won the Iowa precinct caucuses with a bit more than 27 percent of the vote, more than twice what Birch Bayh won, but considerably less than the 37 percent of participating Iowa Democrats who cast their ballots for "uncommitted." The ballot-counting on caucus night was a big thing in Des Moines, not only for the candidates and the reporters chronicling it, but also for the local gentry intrigued by all the attention from out-of-staters. Tom Whitney, the Democratic state chairman, industriously sold tickets to folks who wanted a close look at the assembled scribblers as we labored in the press room of the Des Moines Hilton across from the airport.

Iowa vaulted Carter into the nation's consciousness, bringing him heavy news media attention as the pack of candidates headed for the first primary in New Hampshire, and we reporters with them. The third-place finisher in Iowa, Fred Harris, made the most of the situation. Noting that the caucuses were looked upon to winnow out the also-rans, he optimistically declared himself "winnowed in." Next, in his native Oklahoma, he held Carter essentially to a tie, while the others who didn't show much in Iowa, Udall and Shriver, trailed and moved on to the Granite State.

From a reporter's point of view, New Hampshire was a better state to cover than Iowa. It was easier to get to, and once you were there, it was easier to travel. That year and for many thereafter, the favorite press roosting place was the Sheraton Wayfarer in Bedford, just outside Manchester. It was minutes from the local airport and only an hour from Logan Airport in Boston. You could shoot right out the front door and in a minute be on a good highway to Concord, only twenty minutes north by car, and anywhere else of note in a couple of hours—anywhere, that is, but "the North Country," a dreaded longer ride into the White Mountains, where there were few people and hence few visiting candidates. Nevertheless, an obligatory stop for all presidential hopefuls, at least once, was the largest northern city, Berlin (pronounced BURR-lin by the locals).

I remember well a flight there with Carter in a light snowfall that turned into what seemed to us, in two small chartered planes, to be a blizzard. Most of the passengers—aides, reporters, and cameramen but not an imperturbable candidate—were gripping our armrests with white knuckles as our plane ricocheted through the dismal, turbulent skies. As the engines droned on and on, Jim Wooten, then of the *New York Times* and mimic extraordinaire, finally got up and shouted over the din to his shaken colleagues: "Achtung! Your courage vill not go unrevahrded! The Fuehrer himself vill soon be leafing Berlin!" Other candidates made this scary trip once. Carter did it three times.

While we were there, Carter spoke to some small schoolchildren at St. Patrick's School. He gave them his basic sweetness-and-light spiel, only simplified for young ears, if that was possible. "I want a government always to tell the truth," he preached. "What we need is a government to be as good as our people. Wouldn't that be a great thing?" He beamed at the kids and they beamed back. It occurred to me that he was not talking down to these cherubs, nor was he treating them as adults. It was more that he treated children and adults alike as children, and they ate it up.

Udall had high hopes that his fortunes would turn in New Hampshire, but in the end the story he liked to tell voters about himself in the Granite State proved to be all too true. He would recount how he had strolled into a barber shop one morning, introducing himself: "Hi. I'm Mo Udall and I'm running for president." The barber's reply: "Yes, we were just laughing about it." As a man of unflagging good humor, Udall brushed it off and kept smiling and telling the story. But on primary night, the result was the same as in Iowa. Carter ran first with nearly 30 percent of the votes and thirteen convention delegates to 24 percent and four delegates for Udall, and the rest well behind. Later, after Udall's quest had failed, he liked to say: "The voters have spoken—the bastards!"

Carter was riding high, but there were still more than a few bumps in the road for him. In Massachusetts, he ran behind Scoop Jackson, Udall, and Wallace, giving more significance than ever to Carter's confrontation with the Alabama governor in Florida, which Wallace had carried in 1972, burying Muskie. Wallace had hoped to do the same to Carter, but by running in

Massachusetts, spending a fair amount of money there and losing, Wallace would be going into the state as a less formidable force than earlier. Further, only the weak Shapp among the liberals made a serious effort in Florida, leaving the anti-Wallace vote pretty much to Carter. And then there was Wallace's weakened physical condition. Now, whenever I ran into him, as I did in Florida, he would stick out his hand, say "Shake," and then squeeze my fingers until they hurt, asking: "Does that feel like I'm not in good physical condition?" There was nothing wrong with him, he would insist, "except I'm paralyzed."

Carter managed to beat Wallace in Florida, 34 percent to 31, and again in Illinois. Wallace retreated to North Carolina, which he hoped might be more congenial. It wasn't, nor was the weather one afternoon as I flew with Wallace on his chartered BAC-111 jet, a comfortable craft outfitted with leather seats and teak tables to the liking of his 1968 running mate, General Curtis LeMay, best remembered in politics for the casual attitude about nuclear weapons he expressed in that campaign. LeMay had insisted on a chartered Boeing 727 jet, leading Wallace, according to his campaign manager, Charlie Snider, to inquire what it was costing the campaign. "About $127,000 a week, Governor," Snider said. Wallace replied: "God damn, he's either spending all our money or dropping atomic bombs!"

On this particular windy flight from Durham to Asheville well into the Appalachians, I sat across from Wallace as he ate a late lunch of steak, potatoes, and peas smothered as usual with ketchup. I asked how he was doing. "Oh, fine," he said. "Too much flyin' in windy weather." I knew from flying with him in much less fancy planes, such as an old DC-6 Mohawk Airlines relic in his 1968 presidential bid, that there was nothing he hated and feared more than air travel in bad weather. The night before, I had been told, he had had a rough landing into Raleigh, and I asked him about it. "Comin' in, yeah," he said, puffing on his ever-present cigar between bites of steak. "This is a pretty comfortable plane, though," I offered. "Yeah, but it ain't when you have bad weather," he replied.

We talked for a while about his recent campaign losses and I inquired what would happen if he was defeated in a few more states in his southern base. He said it was harder campaigning from a wheelchair than he had expected, and when I asked him whether he was committed to going on to the Democratic convention, he answered: "If I come in any more landings like I did in Raleigh the other night . . ." Suddenly the plane lurched and dropped for a few seconds like it was falling straight down. "Damn," he muttered, "I hope we can land all right." Looking out the window, he went on: "Hell, I don't want them to land this thing if they goin' to have to land in the same kind of weather. We comin' into these mountains, you know. . . . Sheesh."

Wallace sent his press secretary, Billy Joe Camp, to the cockpit to ask the pilot what was up ahead. "If we got that kind of weather to land in like in Raleigh, just hell, turn around and land in Birmingham," Wallace said to nobody in particular. Camp reported that we were within fifteen or twenty miles of Asheville. Wallace strained from his seat to see ahead. "Asheville's in a valley? I don't know whether we're gonna get over these mountains or not." I tried the light touch. "Well, it could be raining," I said. Wallace didn't see the humor in it. "Except if it was rainin' to start with," he wailed, "we wouldn't be here."

The plane finally landed in Asheville and I could see Wallace loosening his grip on his armrests. Wallace's reaction to this bumpy flight drove home to me the sacrifice he was making to maintain his political ambitions, and the need he obviously felt for the approval of the crowds, diminished as they were. He was carried to the foot of the plane's ramp and placed in the back seat of an awaiting car. The window was rolled down and he stuck out his strong hand to shake those of well-wishers as they filed by and reached in. He was headed for another defeat in the North Carolina primary, but he wasn't quitting. It wasn't his physical condition that was doing him in, either. It was another man of the South who was countering his bluster with modulating, conciliatory tones. Carter won 54 percent of the North Carolina primary vote, to only 35 for Wallace.

There were some bumps in the road for Carter too as he pressed on relentlessly, running in some primary or caucus somewhere on every day voters went to the polls, and winning at least one contest on that day. He was almost upset in liberal Wisconsin by Udall, but votes drained away from Udall by Harris enabled Carter to prevail. Late on primary night, when it appeared that Udall had held Carter off, the *Milwaukee Sentinel* ran a banner headline: "Carter Upset by Udall." Jody Powell grabbed an early edition copy and gave it to his boss, who held it aloft for news photographers in the manner of Harry Truman gloating over the *Chicago Tribune* headline reporting his "loss" to Dewey in 1948.

Carter's real bumps were provided by the late candidacies of young Governor Jerry Brown of California and veteran Senator Frank Church of Idaho. In ten of the remaining fifteen primaries and caucuses, one or both of them beat the frontrunner, but they'd entered the race too late.

After the outcome of the Democratic contest became clear, Carter came to lunch with *Post* staff members at the home of Kay Graham. In addition to the publisher, most of the paper's key editors were present along with a few political reporters, including Broder, Haynes Johnson, and me. It was a cordial affair, with Carter holding forth about his campaign. At the end someone, I think it was Haynes, asked him how he thought he had been treated by the *Post*. He replied a bit huffily that the paper had not reported accurately on his victory in the Iowa caucuses. One of the editors, it may have been Simons, reminded him that I had been with him most of the time in Iowa. Whereupon my good friend Jimmy said, in front of my publisher and editors, that maybe that was so, but "he didn't get the story."

I was aghast. In my front-page lead from Des Moines after the caucuses I had written: "With a 2-to-1 victory over his closest challenger in the Iowa precinct caucuses, former Georgia Gov. Jimmy Carter has gained early momentum in the winnowing-out process of 1976 presidential hopefuls." I did add: "His victory is far from decisive. Nonetheless, Carter moved ahead of Democratic liberal contenders by winning 27.63 percent of the vote. . . . At the same time, however, the results were put in perspective by a large uncommitted vote—37.15 percent." Maybe it was this caveat that he didn't appreciate, although I doubt he ever saw my story. In any event, his comment cast a pall over the lunch—or at least over me.

When it was over, Carter got up and walked around the table, shaking hands with everyone. When he came to me, he stuck out his hand and gave me his famous toothy grin, saying how glad he was to see me again! So much for the man who said he wanted a government "as full of love as are the American people." Back in the *Post* newsroom later that afternoon, Mrs. Graham came over to my desk and asked me whether it was true that I hadn't gotten the story. I assured her I had filed what every other reporter there had written. She nodded kindly and that was the last I heard of it.

On the Republican side, meanwhile, Ronald Reagan, after a slow start, had offered a surprisingly strong challenge to incumbent President Ford. He got himself into hot water in New Hampshire because of a speech he had made in Chicago in which he suggested that $90 billion in federal programs could be transferred to the states. The notion was interpreted by reporters as a "plan" for a $90 billion federal budget cut, with the programs and their costs thus severed shunted onto the states, or abandoned. In New Hampshire, which had no sales or income tax and where taxes were as touchable as the third rail of a train track, the Ford campaign suggested that the scheme would require higher state taxes. Reagan eventually extricated himself by saying he had no intention of raising taxes in the Granite State, but not before we rajahs of ridicule on the press bus had turned out a little ditty to the tune of "Give Me the Simple Life." The first stanza went:

Cut ninety billion, make it a trillion,
Just call me Ron the Knife;
This old vaudevillian can save you a zillion,
I'll give you the simple life.

For all that, Reagan by sheer exuberant campaigning and his winning way came close to upsetting the sitting president in that first primary. After a series of other losses, he bounced back in the South, beating Ford in North Carolina, Texas, and several other states. But Ford regained his footing in his home state of Michigan and headed into the Republican convention in Kansas City with a modest though seemingly comfortable lead. The *New York Times* tabulation gave him 1,102 delegates, 28 short of the required majority, to 1,063 for Reagan, 67 short, with 94 uncommitted, meaning Reagan would have to pick up about two out of every three fence-sitters to win.

At the convention, I lucked into one of the best stories I ever had at the *Post*. Mississippi, one of the nation's most conservative and Republican states, was considered to be in Reagan's pocket, under the control of its state party chairman, Clarke Reed, an early Reagan advocate. I knew Reed fairly well from my travels in Mississippi, and I also had a good southern source in Harry Dent, political director in the Nixon White House, from South Carolina, who was now operating as the Ford committee's overseer of the Dixie states. To the great surprise of the Reagan camp in Kansas City, Dent managed to "steal" the bulk of Mississippi's delegates for the president in a carefully orchestrated courtship of Reed by Dent, in cahoots with Ford's chief of staff at the time, a gent named Dick Cheney.

At a White House reception in advance of the convention, Dent, after enticing Reed by telling him he could be "the kingmaker" at the convention, brought him into the Oval Office for Ford to close the sale himself. With further enticing by Dent in Kansas City, Reed began to crack. Dent confronted him with the possibility that if he didn't seize the opportunity to put Ford over the top, New York's state party chairman, Dick "Rosey" Rosenbaum, would be "the kingmaker." Dent also informed him that Reagan was going to select moderate Republican Richard Schweiker of Pennsylvania as his running mate. Reed crumbled some more, and when Ford himself got on the phone and squeezed him, Reed finally caved in.

Later, for two hours in Dent's hotel room, he spilled out the whole story to me for a page-one "tick-tock"—a play-by-play account—of how "the Battle of Mississippi" was won. The story no doubt made Dent look good. And while the wooing of Clarke Reed may not have been the decisive event in Ford's nomination, the events as reported to me by Dent and not refuted by Reed provided an insight into how political hardball was played at the highest levels.

Another game at Kansas City on a less significant level deserves retelling here. Once again it involved Johnny Apple, the *New York Times* reporter who somehow always brought out the worst in me in terms of practical jokes. It so happened that one night my sidekick, Walter Mears of the AP, and I dropped by the Savoy Grill, one of the best eateries in town, without a reservation. The maître d' stood at a small stand near the long bar, with a list of reservations in front of him. Before we could implore him for a table, he turned and walked off for a minute, giving us time to peruse the reservations list and spot a familiar name listed for that hour: "Apple." I looked at Mears and he looked at me and instantly we knew what we had to do.

When the maître d' returned we asked for the table for Apple, and he ushered us into the main dining room behind the bar. We sat down and ordered, and as we were on our first drinks—Jack Daniels straight up for Walter and Dewars with no twist and a splash of water for me—we heard a terrible uproar from the outer room. As we immediately surmised and confirmed later, the real Mr. Apple had arrived and was demanding his table. Offered one in the outer room, he erupted all the more, until a couple of waiters were seen toting a table and chairs into our room, followed by Apple and his congenial colleague from the *Times,* B. Drummond Ayres.

To make up—anonymously—for our crime, Mears and I ordered a bottle of wine sent to their table. However, bearing in mind Johnny's reputation as a wine connoisseur, we couldn't resist choosing a measly half-bottle of cheap white wine in a distinctive flat bottle. When it arrived, Apple refused to accept it, but Ayres, as he testified later, was dry as a bone and insisted on opening it. True to form, Johnny never gave us the satisfaction of acknowledging that we had put one over on him, but the story was immortalized many years later in a profile on Apple in *The New Yorker*.

Amid such shenanigans, the 1976 presidential campaign moved on to the eventual nominations of Carter and Ford. Carter selected Fritz Mondale as his running mate and Mondale accepted, recalling his earlier abhorrence of Holiday Inns by saying "I've checked and found they've all been redecorated." Ford picked Bob Dole to run with him, setting up a rather bizarre vice-presidential debate in the fall in which my friend Mears was the catalyst for Dole's implosion, by asking the question that triggered his assault on "Democrat wars."

Another bump in the road for Carter also occurred in the early fall, when the rather naïve Georgian agreed to an interview with Bob Scheer of the *Los Angeles Times* on religion, sex, and sin for, of all things, *Playboy* magazine. In it, the self-anointed Apostle of Goodness confessed to the following: "I try not to commit a deliberate sin. I recognize that I'm going to do it anyhow, because I'm human and I'm tempted. And Christ set some almost impossible standards for us. Christ said, 'I tell you that anyone who looks on a woman with lust has in his heart already committed adultery.' I've looked on a lot of women with lust. I've committed adultery in my heart many times. This is something that God recognizes I will do—and I have done it—and God forgives me for it."

In this and in uttering some sexual vulgarities like "screw" and "shack up," Carter created an uproar for a time, particularly in the press and parts of the religious community. But to our band of ersatz lyricists on the press bus, his comments were a gift from, well, if not heaven, at least from *Playboy*. On the occasion of Carter's 52nd birthday, advance man par excellence Jim King arranged a little party for him and wife Rosalyn at a motel near the Pittsburgh airport and supplied five of us with straw boaters for our routine. Donning and doffing them at appropriate times, we serenaded the Carters with our latest parody, to the tune of "Heart of My Heart":

> Lust in my heart, how I love adultery.
> Lust in my heart, that's my theology.
> When I was young, at the Plains First Baptist Church,
> I would preach and sermonize,
> But oh, how I would fantasize.

Lust in my heart, who cares if it's a sin?
Leching's a noble art.
It's okay if you shack up,
'Cause I won't get my back up.
I've got mine, I've got lust in my heart.

Lust in my heart, oh, it's bad politically,
Lust in my heart, but it brings publicity.
When I grew up, and ran for President,
A bunch of women I did screw,
But in my head, so no one knew.
Lust in my heart, I said I'd never lie.
I guess I wasn't smart.
But I'm no gay deceiver,
I'm a Christian eager-beaver.
As *Playboy* said, I've got lust in my heart.

Carter laughed heartily at our little ditty, though Rosalyn seemed less amused. We assured the candidate that such ribbing was traditional and told him of our needling Romney in song in 1968 about his observation that he had been "brainwashed" in Vietnam. Carter grinned and asked: "Have you ever written one for a winner?" We presented him a copy of *Playboy*—and with due respect for his sensitivities, we cut out all genitalia from the photographs of the naked models. We put the clippings in an envelope and gave them to Jody Powell, now Carter's press secretary, for whatever use he might find for them.

Carter seemed not to have learned any lesson in prudence, not to mention prudery. Later in the campaign he gave another interview, with novelist Norman Mailer, for the *New York Times Magazine,* in which he said he didn't intend to judge others on how they lived their personal lives. As Mailer wrote, with a delicacy not common to his other writings: "'I don't care,' he said in his quiet voice, as if the next words, while not wholly comfortable, had nonetheless to be said, 'I don't care if people say ——,' and he actually said the famous four-letter word that the *Times* has not printed in the 125 years of its publishing life."

Hamilton Jordan, Carter's campaign manager, fearful of another flap, phoned me at home a night or two after the remark appeared and asked me whether I thought the matter had blown over. I told him that the *Post* had decided it didn't warrant the kind of coverage that the *Playboy* interview had received. He was relieved.

Ford himself was not free of damaging gaffes, though not of the sexual variety. In his second debate with Carter, he stumbled badly by saying in response to a question from Max Frankel of the *New York Times*, an old schoolmate of mine at Columbia College, that "there is no Soviet domination of Eastern Europe." After the debate, turmoil reigned in the Ford entourage as Cheney and national security adviser Brent Scowcroft fended off questions from traveling reporters about the candidate's misstatement. It stopped a late Ford surge in its tracks, costing his campaign valuable days convincing him he had said something wrong and getting it back on the rails.

Later, after the election, when I asked Ford in an interview why he had said what he did, he finally had his thoughts straight. "Subjectively," he said, "the East European countries still consider themselves as a people independent. Governmentally they are not, particularly those countries that are actually occupied in part by Soviet forces. In the momentum to answer the question, I thought of it in the first sense, and not in the latter." But the fact was that Frankel had followed up by asking whether he had heard Ford correctly, and the president hadn't taken the opportunity to correct himself. The performance didn't do much to dispel Lyndon Johnson's old dig at Ford, that he couldn't "walk and chew gum at the same time."

I spent several days around this time knocking on doors to assess reaction to the campaign. In a low-income neighborhood of Pittsburgh, I asked a middle-aged woman with her hair in curlers whether she had been watching the Carter-Ford debates. "Oh, I watched a few minutes of the first one and then I turned it off," she said. "I don't want either of them influencing my vote. I want to make up my own mind." It was something like the response my friend Don Oliver of NBC got from a woman in California: "I think I'm going to vote for Ford. I voted for him the last time." That would have been quite a feat, since he wasn't on the ballot in 1972. Such was the quality of the attention being paid by many to the election that fall—a reaction frustrating to those of us who liked to think we were in the business of helping to create an "informed electorate."

There's no telling even now what did Ford in and elected Carter in the close finish that year. Some suggested it was the Eastern Europe flap; others mentioned Dole's erratic debate attack on "Democrat wars." More likely, in my opinion and that of many others, was Ford's pardon of Nixon in the first days of his presidency, which left a bad taste with voters from which he never seemed to recover. I had been with him on the takeoff of his presidential years, as body man in the months before Nixon's resignation and his ascension to the Oval Office, and on the dismal landing, as he was pushed out of it. Now I was in on Carter's takeoff and had a front row seat to witness his promised quest to create a government "as good as its people."

As the election year ended, I undertook to finish a book covering the previous four years, which had seen the fall of Nixon and Agnew, the elevation of Ford, the emergence of Carter, and much else in between. As I crashed on the project, which resulted in *Marathon: The Pursuit of the Presidency, 1972–1976*, I also considered my professional position, which had been advanced by four rewarding years at the *Washington Post* in association with such excellent reporters as Broder, Cannon, Lardner, Cohen, Bill Greider, Dick Harwood, Haynes Johnson, Helen Dewar, Bill Chapman, and many others. But another idea had been occupying my thoughts for several years, and I was now determined to embark on it.

13 The *Star* | Good Cop, Bad Cop

IN 1951, WHEN I APPLIED FOR ADMISSION to the Columbia Graduate School of Journalism, one of the questions asked on the application form was what I hoped to be doing in twenty-five years. I wrote that my goal was to be a general-assignment reporter on a major newspaper, and it was true at the time. But after many years in the trenches, and having labored under the direction of editors good and bad, it began to occur to me that reporters who stayed on the street for a long time, especially for the same newspaper, were often taken for granted. If you wanted to move up, you often had to move inside, as an editor. There were exceptions; a state house, Washington, or foreign correspondent carried a bit more clout, and so did a columnist. Getting to Washington at a relatively early age kept me feeling I was not on a treadmill to nowhere. But I came to recognize that nothing on the writing side of the business afforded one as much freedom as having one's own column.

My appetite had been whetted by those weekly, sophomoric sports columns in Hackensack in which I was allowed to indulge myself. I was further engaged by the weekly political column Casey Jones had allowed me in the Syracuse paper, and for a brief time I wrote one called "Inside the Pentagon" for a magazine called *Soldier Illustrated* for which I free-lanced.

Observing the good life enjoyed by Art Buchwald down the hall in my Newhouse Washington bureau years, I created a copy-cat column that I labeled "Washington Off Guard," which had an equally brief life in the Newhouse papers. You would have understood why it was short-lived had you read, for example, my account of an imagined Georgetown Hospital interview with newborn John F. Kennedy Jr., who was then sharing the facilities with my own newborn daughter Julie. I professed to have happened upon him "wearing a handsome crimson sweater with a large H on it . . . absorbed in Schlesinger's *Kennedy or Nixon: Does It Make Any Difference?*

Later, I began to pen another column, in a considerably more serious vein, called "In Focus" that had a somewhat longer tenure. But the management always preferred to have me digging for daily pieces and long series, so my prospects as a regular daily columnist did not seem bright.

In the 1960s, I teamed up with my best friend in the Newhouse bureau, Erwin Knoll, and we sought for more than a year to peddle to the major newspaper syndicates a reportorial column that we called "National Beat." We labored over samples, which we sent out along with some of our more ambitious joint writing projects. Although we got a lot of commendatory replies, the answer was always, "Not right now." Erwin, an excellent reporter and writer who earlier had distinguished himself at the *Washington Post*, in time left Washington to become editor of *Progressive* magazine, but I continued to harbor the ambition to be a columnist.

After twenty-eight years of writing under a solo byline, in early 1977 I joined another old friend, Jack Germond, to start our syndicated column, called "Politics Today." As basically uncompetitive rivals on the political beat, he for the Gannett newspapers and I for Newhouse, we had crossed paths, and often shared paths, for about a decade, spending countless hours in late-night saloon conversations about our mutual professional obscurity. Casting a sometimes envious eye at our old colleagues and friends, Rowland Evans and Bob Novak, and the racket they had writing their syndicated column, we would muse about the possibility of starting one ourselves.

With our eyes on the stars, at one point we came up with the grandiose scheme of trying to peddle the nonexistent column ourselves to thirty newspapers at ten bucks a week. Or maybe to ten papers at thirty bucks a week, with half the huge revenue for each of us.

By the time we got to talking more seriously about it, Germond had moved to the now-defunct *Washington Star* and I to the *Washington Post*. The *Star* at the time was struggling to stay alive under the brilliant editorship of Jim Bellows, late of the *New York Herald Tribune* and *Los Angeles Times*. Short on staff and operating budget but not on imagination and guts, Bellows had great fun professionally and personally burning Ben Bradlee, the *Post*'s editor, by picking his spots and occasionally beating the clearly superior *Post* on good stories.

The *Star* staff, Germond included, loved Bellows and the competitive underdog atmosphere he created on the paper. So when I first approached Germond, well in advance of the 1976 presidential campaign, about the idea of quitting our jobs and launching the column, he demurred. As an assistant managing editor, he had a key role in Bellows' efforts to save the paper and felt he couldn't leave.

For myself, although I had finally reached the national staff of the *Post* after my three years in the Washington bureau of the *Los Angeles Times* and loved being at the *Post*, I felt some frustration working under the thumb of editors and was determined to break out on my own. Therefore, I began casting about for another partner, approaching some of the better-known and respected reporters on the *Post* and other newspapers. I sounded out several of them who had reputations for the adventurous, but to my surprise and chagrin, they all declined to take the plunge.

Maybe it was the prospect of working with me, and having to put up with all those concocted lyrics to popular songs. Or trepidation over running the risk of failing, I don't know. In any event, I decided I'd have to wait until the end of the 1976 campaign when Germond said he might be ready. Bellows, aware of our ambitions, told him that after the campaign he would help us launch the column. Good to his word, he contacted syndicate operators and got us two offers, the better of which came from the (Chicago) Tribune Media Services, and we grabbed it. Bellows not only touted our new enterprise to other editors but gave the column—and me—a home in the *Star*, running it prominently five days a week at a payment well above the norm.

The syndicate distributed the column under the title "Politics Today." Our first effort, under a double byline, was a joint interview with President Carter in the Oval Office, which Bellows ran across the top of page one, over the masthead, headlined: "Carter Interview: The Principle and Politics of Human Rights." The column was a collaborative effort. After a long discussion between the two of us, Germond sat at the typewriter and I kibitzed. We adopted a somewhat smart-alecky tone. "As a card-carrying member of the President's union," Jack wrote, "Jimmy Carter will tell you that politics stops at the water's edge. But what is becoming apparent already is that he is relying on reaction abroad to his human rights offensive to build a coalition of support at home for his entire foreign policy." He went on to tell how Carter had crowed over the response of a delegation of Romanian officials to his granting of 5,200 visas to their countrymen. The subject was hardly up our alley as political writers, but we decided jointly that it was the most newsworthy thing Carter had told us.

The next day, still working off the Carter interview, we switched places; I manned the typewriter and Germond kibitzed. This time the column appeared on the third page under a set "Germond and Witcover" label with a headline that said: "Carter Won't Spurn the Smaller States." It related a mix-up between the new president and Indiana senator Birch Bayh, sponsor of a constitutional amendment abolishing the electoral college. Carter had said in a press conference that he favored it but wasn't sure "the ratio among the states of votes ought to be changed," which was precisely what scrapping the electoral college would do. So when we asked him whether or not he favored direct popular election of the president (as Bayh proposed and which would disadvantage smaller states), he backed off, commenting, "I'm not willing to say that yet."

This column was more clearly in our politics ballpark. We had checked with the dismayed Bayh, and concluded the piece by observing that "if the debate over direct election of presidents comes down to the need to protect the boondocks, Birch Bayh of Indiana, who likes to peddle himself as just a simple country boy, may find himself out-countried by the new kid from Plains."

In the beginning we alternated in typing and kibitzing, discussing each column thoroughly before and sometimes while committing it to paper. We had an agreement from the outset that no column would go out on the wire without both of us approving it, a deal that required the writer to read to the other by phone if one of us was out of town, which was often. After a while, each of us got to know what the other would and wouldn't tolerate, so we dispensed with that step. While our styles of writing differed somewhat, we learned how to avoid having the seams of the stitching together show too much, and we both tried to adhere to our smart-ass trademark.

Each of us had veto power, but to my recollection it was used only once in our twenty-four-year partnership, by Germond when I wrote a column about how pro football player-representatives were suspiciously released by their teams when negotiations got tough. He claimed it wasn't politics, but it seemed to me to be pretty political.

To cover the country, we divided it into four regions—Northeast, South, Midwest, and Far West. Jack took the first two and I took the second two. It was an approach that enabled us to keep and extend our sources, and we fed each other information when required. The system was sufficiently flexible that either of us could cover a story in any of the four regions, depending on where a story took us, or where one of us had especially strong background or good sources. But under this regional approach, we didn't see all that much of each other, especially during congressional, gubernatorial, and presidential campaigns, except at national and sometimes regional political conventions, where we joined forces.

The double byline format had certain benefits. First, it usually gave each of us more than a day to research a column if we needed it, though we worked on no set schedule. Occasionally, as in those first two columns based on the interview with Carter, we composed the end product together, like playing a piano duet. But more and more, one of us would write the whole column with the other offering input from sources he might have. We didn't keep count, and some weeks Germond might write two or more in a row and some weeks I would.

In a few months our client list jumped from about thirty papers to nearly a hundred, and we were in business. Each of us having written daily for more than twenty-five years, the workload wasn't a problem. But in the first year some of the columns read too much like straight reporting. It took some time, and the wise counsel from friends like Tom Winship, then editor of the *Boston Globe*, that a column needed a strong point of view, before we got on track.

It was our declared intent from the outset, however, to write a reportorial column; that is, one based on legwork rather than mere thumb-sucking. Our approach was to start on a subject with a relatively open mind, talk to people informed on that subject from various viewpoints, and then come down with our own analysis and conclusion.

This formula was easier in concept than in execution and selling to editors. We had heard editors for years complain about the predictability of columns; you could read the first paragraph, they would say, and know exactly where the column was going. We strove to escape that criticism by inquiring into a subject first, then reporting what we learned, and only then taking a position based on that inquiry.

But we found in many cases that editorial page editors, for all their complaining about predictability, wanted it. Many looked only for conservative or liberal columns, and others sought religiously to balance their pages with equal numbers of each. We might come down on one side of the spectrum on one issue and the other on another one. This unpredictability complicated the editors' lives, because they had to read all of each column when it came in over the wire to decide whether to use it or not, rather than being able to count on each day's effort delivering the desired political coloration.

Readers, too, were disappointed, and told us so when we failed to fit the mold to which they thought we belonged. Generally speaking, we did tend to reflect a liberal outlook, but that didn't stop us from criticizing liberals as well as conservatives if we decided they were wrong or lame-brained. When the circumstances of a particular story persuaded us to criticize a politician with whom we usually agreed, or take a contrary view about an issue we previously had supported, readers would write or call expressing surprise or outrage, because "we thought you were on our side."

This happened more than once with Jewish voters whose views on Israel we generally shared, when we then wrote critically of some Israeli position regarding the Palestinians. Also, feminists screamed bloody murder when, after having generally written favorably about the Equal Rights Amendment, we gently ribbed them for seeking more time to win ratification. One column observed: "We asked one of Jimmy Carter's tennis partners the other day how many sets the president usually plays. 'Well,' he said, perhaps in jest and perhaps not, 'it's two out of three, unless I win the first two. Then it's three out of five.'" The headline writer topped the column thus: "Is 'Best Three Out of Five' What ERA Partisans Need?" We also wrote that if states that had opposed the ERA could change that vote, states that had voted for it should have the right to rescind that vote if they so chose. We caught feminist hell for that, too.

With Bellows' enthusiastic support and that of other editors we knew around the country, we didn't experience the growing pains that often accompany the start of a new column. But because clients had the option of dropping a column on a month-by-month basis, for the first ten years or so our concern about losing client papers led us to write the column fifty-two weeks a year, slipping in vacation as we spelled each other. On occasions when we took vacations at the same time, we would always communicate by phone, and over at least a couple of summers we both took a couple of weeks off at Bethany Beach, Delaware, staying in separate digs with our families but meeting or at least talking by phone daily to get the column out. Only after about ten years did our syndicate folks tell us it was probably safe to interrupt the column for a couple of weeks in the summer without risking serious erosion of our client list.

Another big benefit of the double byline was that it enabled us to play good cop, bad cop. If a source didn't like what we had written, we could always say the other guy wrote it. This gambit didn't always work out to mutual advantage. Once during Carter's White House days, we collaborated on a column in the *Star* on a subject that really had nothing to do with him, but we mentioned in passing something he had done. No sooner had the paper hit the streets than Jody Powell, Carter's press secretary, called, inviting Germond, one of the first reporters to take Carter seriously as a presidential prospect back in 1975, to have a drink with the president. He went over to the White House, and Carter immediately started railing about how he knew Jack wouldn't write such a thing about him, but that I never had anything good to say about him, assuming I had written the offending comment. According to Germond, he didn't bother to play the good cop by fingering me as the bad guy. Or so he said.

In 1980, when the elder George Bush was making his first try for the Republican presidential nomination, against Ronald Reagan and others, Germond wrote a column that ran on the front page of the *Star*. Under our usual double byline, it said: "After several months of stumping the country, George Bush has declared his candidacy for the Republican presidential nomination at a time when many professionals in his Party suspect his campaign already had peaked."

It so happened that on that day I was going out with Bush on his first swing, and so he naturally concluded that I had written the piece, and coldshouldered me for the rest of the trip. I didn't disabuse him of his wrong impression. Or so I told my partner. It didn't matter that the third paragraph of the story had said: "There is, of course, no suggestion that Bush is a hopeless case. That kind of reading cannot be made about any candidate who has at least enough money to see him through the early presidential primaries next year. And George Bush has that."

We started out writing six columns a week, five on a single subject and the sixth a kind of catchall of short items. In time, we found that the sixth column alone often took as much reporting to assemble as the other five, and we dropped it. We also produced a separate weekly newsletter for about a year but bagged that also when it took up too much of our time for only modest recompense.

Although some readers compared our column with that of Evans and Novak, there were clear differences from the start. They cast a wider net than we did, delving into foreign policy with overseas reporting, and the innards of economic policy, striving always, with considerable success, for scoops, large and small. We focused more on the inside baseball of domestic politics, reporting often on who was up and who was down in various campaigns and in the parties. While we sometimes came up with a nugget of news, our emphasis was on analysis based on shoe-leather reporting in the political community. And as time went on, Rowlie and Bob reflected a more conservative bent, while we thought of ourselves as essentially centrist, leaning towards the left. Both columns felt free to criticize any sector of the political spectrum, and often did.

At the *Star*, we continued to function as political reporters as well as writing the column, working—and playing—on the campaign trail with our old mutual pal and drinking buddy, Jim Dickenson, the paper's regular political reporter. As Jack and Jim had done before my arrival at the *Star*, I now also took a certain amount of pleasure in occasionally beating what I continued to see, without disloyalty to the *Star*, as the country's best political newspaper. Germond and I calculated that in one year together we had written 600 columns and other stories for the *Star*, and neither of us considered that to be a great burden, having worked as coolies for the Gannett and Newhouse chains for so many years.

Bellows, like Bradlee at the *Post*, was an inspirational leader who, also like Ben, was a catalyst for a driving reportorial staff. Beyond that, Bellows undertook a role of dreaming up splashy layouts and promotional gimmicks designed to make up in originality for what he lacked in manpower. Jim and Ben were worthy adversaries, and it was my distinct pleasure and good fortune to have had a chance to work under each of them.

Bellows had the distinction, dubious or otherwise, of having put together both the Evans-and-Novak column years earlier and then ours. After lining up our syndication, he simply stepped back and let us get to work. We conceived the format ourselves and worked out the glitches as they inevitably arose. As a result, I never regretted leaving the powerhouse *Post* for

Washington's "second" newspaper, except in the later part of our four-year stint at the *Star*, when the owner, Joe Allbritton, sold the paper to Time Incorporated and Bellows moved on to edit the equally troubled *Los Angeles Herald-Examiner*.

I went to the *Star* from the *Post* to start the column just as Jimmy Carter was beginning his presidency, and our old friend from Plains accommodated us with that interview in the Oval Office for our maiden effort. In our first year, we focused heavily on the Carter administration, from his personal style to his greatest problems and missteps, which he seldom seemed to appreciate. We wrote about his early popularity, including his stated intention to keep in touch with the voters. On the night of St. Patrick's Day, I went to Clinton, Massachusetts, and watched him take questions for ninety minutes. I wrote then: "The audience reaction was predictably boffo. They cheered him loud and long and mobbed him when, at the close, he jumped down from the stage onto the floor to press the flesh with his Clinton friends." I'm sure that description would have pleased Jimmy.

But I also wrote: "It didn't matter that most of his answers were exact reruns of his old 1976 campaign lines. He was coming among them, and they plainly loved it. . . . Watching the whole scene from the first row of the balcony, in an uncommon mood of sobriety, was a distinguished group of Massachusetts Democrats, including Senator Ted Kennedy and Governor Michael Dukakis. As their constituents repeatedly applauded the visitor from Washington, they clapped perfunctorily, like a gang of former heavyweight champs brought to ringside to watch Muhammad Ali spar a few rounds for charity. . . . Though the President praised the notable pols in the balcony, one of the main purposes of the whole exercise was to let them know he was willing to go over their heads to their own constituents, if need be." Jimmy may not have liked that part.

Those were the days when Carter pitched energy conservation by wearing a sweater in the Oval Office, a campaign that gave us much fodder for commentary. So did the rise and fall of his Georgia banking buddy and budget director, Bert Lance, who unlike his pal in the White House never reacted negatively to what we wrote about him. After we reported that "the Bert Lance affair has become a salvage operation" with "no real hope he can function again as budget director," and he was shown the door after charges of conflict of interest had tainted Carter's goody-two-shoes image, Lance invited us over to his office for farewell pop or two. In later Lance ups and downs, too, he was always his jovial, congenial self. As they say, politics makes strange bedfellows.

In our first year of column writing, Germond and I each had opportunities to rub major politicians the wrong way on our own, with no help from our partner. One offered itself to me with the passing of Ted Kennedy's colorful and beloved driver in Massachusetts, a tough old Irish Catholic gent named Jack Crimmins. Under a column headline "A Corner Man for Kennedy," bearing the usual double byline but with my fingerprints obviously on it, I wrote, in what I thought was an affectionate manner, the following:

> Jack Crimmins, who died in Boston the other day at the age of 70, was what they call up there "a corner guy." For those who live in less civilized parts of the universe, it means somebody who hangs around the street corner, picking up the particular brand of intelligence—so valuable in politics—known as "street sense." Officially, he was Ted Kennedy's personal driver in Massachusetts, and especially during his campaigns when Kennedy worked the state as if it were one immense ward and needed a wheelman who knew every turn. But more important, he was Kennedy's ears in the streets of his city and state in a way no well-scrubbed Harvard white-shoe kid could ever have been. Crimmins was as opinionated as a cab driver with the meter running. He was all heart, but he was also all Irish and all South Boston, which meant he was also unabashed about expressing the prejudices of the community in which he lived.

I told about the time a black candidate was running against a Democratic regular for Congress and had been endorsed by the Catholic Church, "a circumstance that doubly offended Crimmins," I wrote. "He called blacks 'stove covers,' and the idea of Holy Mother the Church backing one was more than he could fathom. The morning after the election Kennedy asked him, 'Jack, did you go to the polls yesterday?' 'Yeah,' Crimmins replied, 'I was handing out [voter instruction] cards at 6:30.' 'Anybody else handing out cards?' Kennedy asked. Crimmins grimaced. 'Yeah,' he said. 'Three whores dressed up like nuns.'" I went on to record some of the less pointed Crimmins observations: "He would say of an uncooperative snob: 'He wouldn't tell you if your coat was on fire.' Of a shyster lawyer: 'He couldn't get you out of jail if your time was up.' Or, 'He couldn't fix a library card.' Of an inept public official: 'He could screw up a two-car funeral.' Of a cheap crook: 'He'd steal a hot stove.' And of a glib operator: 'He could talk a dog off a meat wagon.'" I also mentioned Crimmins' willingness to confront Kennedy when he thought he was wrong. Of Kennedy's support of welfare recipients, he would ask: "What the hell are you meeting with them welfare bums for? . . . They ought to get a job." Knowing Crimmins' deep fondness for Kennedy, I wound up the column in a way I thought the deceased would have appreciated: "Jack Crimmins was not just a guy who held Ted Kennedy's coat. He told him when it was on fire."

Kennedy, I learned from a close aide, was irate over the column and the characterization of his faithful friend. But I thought, or at least hoped, he'd see the humor and respect in it. At any rate, the next time I saw him he merely said he'd seen the piece on Crimmins. It caused me to remember another old Boston Irish expression: "Don't get mad; get even." But in the years that followed, he never tried, and I enjoyed many a laugh and fruitful interview with him thereafter.

The Crimmins column was an example of one of us working the other's "territory," because I had covered Kennedy often (as had Germond) and happened to have ridden with him on several tours with the talkative Crimmins behind the wheel. Another similar occasion was when I happened to be in Boston later, taking my daughter Julie for her opening freshman classes at Harvard. Jack had already written a column about how the Massachusetts state treasurer, Bobby Crane, a longtime Kennedy loyalist, was being leaned on by the family to step aside for young Joe Kennedy, son of the late Robert F. Kennedy, seeking a start on a political career. Crane got his back up and refused to fall on his sword. Jack called on Crane and wrote, "Bob Crane won't go quietly," quoting him: "This office isn't that much to hold onto, but there's a certain amount of pride. You know, foolish Irish pride."

Crane had held on, and when I got into Boston about three months later it occurred to me that there might be a good follow-up column on his state of mind. So I dropped by his office in the State House on Beacon Hill in the morning and found him sitting behind his desk, grinning at me. "I know why you're here," he said. He reached into a desk drawer and pulled out two tickets—for the one-game playoff that afternoon for the American League championship between the Red Sox and the Yankees! No longer being much of a baseball fan ever since the Dodgers left Brooklyn, I was only faintly aware that they were playing, and I told him I had only come to interview him on the state of his relations with Clan Kennedy. He smiled knowingly and insisted I take the pasteboards.

After I got my interview, my daughter and I headed for Fenway Park, which was packed to the rafters for what later was billed as one of the greatest games in Red Sox history, or even in the history of the game. The park was jammed with everyone from Ted Kennedy and House Speaker Tip O'Neill to the most anonymous of Beantown hoi polloi. As every Sox fan has seared in memory, the home team went into the ninth inning one run behind. The Sox loaded the bases with two outs, and local hero Carl "Yaz" Yastrzemski came to bat. While thousands held their breath as one, he took a mighty swing and sent the ball towering—over the infield! For what seemed like minutes to the faithful, Red Sox fans watched in dead silence as the ball climbed to its apex and fell—into the awaiting glove of a Yankee infielder.

A few years later, a group of us were having a few pops in the Speaker's office when he reminisced about that fateful day, and a conversation he had subsequently with the game's goat. O'Neill had just led a delegation of Boston Catholics to Vatican City for an audience with the Pope, who like Yastrzemski was Polish. When Yaz, who had not been invited, complained, word got back to the Speaker, who phoned him. As O'Neill told us the story: "I said to Yaz, 'I'm sorry, if I had known you wanted to go, I certainly would have included you.' But I told him, 'I want you to know that His Holiness asked about you.' Well, Yaz's eyes opened and he asked me, 'What did he say?' And I told him the Pope asked: 'Is it true that Yaz got up with the bases loaded and two out in the ninth and popped out?'"

I wasn't the only partner who poached on the other's territory. Through his years at Gannett, Germond had repeatedly gone to Rockford, Illinois, northwest of Chicago, to talk to voters and take soundings on the political climate there. I used to rib him that whenever I landed at the airport in Rockford I was always startled to see all the short, fat little kids running around who looked like him. Jack made a couple of incursions into Rockford in the column's first year, and while there was nothing scientific about his findings, he did sniff out a threat to that base of moderate Republicanism, then represented in the House by John B. Anderson. The fact that party bigwigs like former president Jerry Ford had come to campaign for him against a right-wing opponent for the nomination, Germond wrote, "is a symptom of something much bigger—the fear in the Republican Party that the newly energized conservative movement is going to take the whole ball of wax and reshape it in its extremist image." Anderson was renominated and reelected that year, but the specter of what came to be known as Reaganism certainly was on the horizon.

Among other things, the column gave us ample opportunity to take journalistic advantage of another version of "the gift that keeps on giving"—the utterings of Richard M. Nixon. When the first in a series of interviews with the great man by British celebrity journalist David Frost hit the television screens and revealed nothing new, we wrote: "When it comes to Richard Nixon, we're a nation of Charlie Browns. No matter how many times Lucy holds the football down for us to kick, we know she's going to yank it away at the last minute. But we take one more shot at it anyway. . . . The only difference in the ballyhooed David Frost interview is that the Napoleon of San Clemente will turn a cool million bucks on it. If the first interview proved anything at all, it's that we will always get the same combination of fancy mouthwork and maudlin fakery from Nixon he has served up without fail in the past. . . . Though no new evidence was needed, he proved afresh in the Frost interview that he remains a man of no scruples and no class."

When Nixon in another Frost interview put his personal spin on the White House–encouraged departure of Vice President Spiro Agnew, we wrote: "Spiro Agnew, meet your good friend, Richard Nixon. Spiro, you had him all wrong in October 1973 when you thought he was pushing you out the window. All he was doing, it turns out, was being 'very pragmatic' and facing the fact that your mutual enemy—the liberal press—had done you in. . . . Nixon confirmed that he had tried to help you use 'the impeachment track' . . . mainly because he believed that a vice president, like a president, should undergo the impeachment process rather than a criminal trial, and because he knew you'd never get 'a fair shake' in the courts. Isn't that rich? He never mentioned his real motivation—that he was scared stiff the criminal indictment of a vice president would set a precedent for the criminal indictment of a president."

Such blasphemous observations never went unchallenged by our unbiased readership. One admiring reader wrote:

> You vapid, bankrupt demagogues arouse the deepest contempt and disgust in anyone who has the vaguest notion of decency and honesty. Your inability to write more than a dozen words without spewing hatred, pathological and obscene, as well as fraudulent charges against President Nixon, has reached a point that reveals a dangerous impairment of your sanity. You may well believe that your warping and distortion of history may presently relegate all the evils

of the world to President Nixon, but you two cretins will fade all too soon from the scene, fortunately, and your lies with you.

And that was one of the more moderate comments. It must have been shattering to the writer that his prediction of our early demise in the columning business fell about a quarter of a century short.

Another faithful reader wrote after our comments on the Frost interviews: "By God, the slurs you two punks have hurled against this unfortunate man smack vehemently of calumny. Have you forgotten that President Nixon stopped the Vietnam war, brought home our POWs, terminated the street riots by snot-nosed dissenters?" Yes, I guess we did forget—that American forces left Vietnam under fire a year after Nixon left the White House under a different kind of fire, which was when those street riots by those snot-nosed dissenters finally ended.

Other fond memories of the column's beginnings include my having lunch with new Illinois governor Jim Thompson at Arnie's in Chicago. When I started to pay the check, Big Jim tried to stop me, saying, "I never pay here." This was the same Big Jim who never took a bribe but, being a fancier of antiques, had a shelf in his favorite shop from which citizens who wanted to show their appreciation to the governor could select an appropriate item for him.

Then there was an interview with Al Perlman, a lieutenant of Mayor Frank Rizzo of Philadelphia, in which he sang Hizzoner's praises for presiding over the nation's most crime-free major city. At one point during the interview, he crossed his legs, which raised his pants cuff, revealing a tiny pistol strapped to his ankle—hardly a testament to the City of Brotherly Love. And I remember listening to a physically broken Hubert Humphrey, returning to the Senate for an emotional farewell and speaking—at length, of course—in response to the outpouring of praise. Before sitting down, the Happy Warrior said: "I didn't intend to be that long." He paused, then added: "But that is the story of my life."

In all, it was a rich bouillabaisse that Bellows had set before Germond and me in launching our new enterprise. And there were more helpings to come.

14 Time Marches In—and Out

AFTER ONLY A YEAR in the column-writing business, I was satisfied that I had made the right choice in turning in my reporter's press card at the *Post* and striking out on an independent course. Although Germond and I were writing news stories for the *Star* along with the column, we decided ourselves where we would go, when, and what we would write about, and we served up to ourselves a rich and varied diet of assignments. While chronicling Jimmy Carter's ups and downs—mostly downs—with a skeptical Congress and carping Republican minority, we found plenty of time to get around the country for fun and profit—usually of more the former than the latter.

In the climate of Carter's tribulations, the embers of a Ted Kennedy draft continued to glow, obliging me to accompany him on occasional speaking engagements in which the question of his future intentions always came up, even as he continued to say he would not be a candidate for president in 1980. At an NAACP dinner in Detroit, a local reporter apologetically told him, "I have to ask you the same question you're always asked." To which he replied: "And I'm going to give you the same answer." At a pre-dinner reception, United Auto Workers president Doug Fraser told me he took Kennedy at his word, but if Jerry Brown were to beat Carter in an early 1980 primary, the heat would be on Kennedy to get in. Mayor Coleman Young in the same vein told me he looked at Kennedy as a buffer against Brown, described by Young as a "screwball," in one of his more delicate labels. I always remember Young's technique for avoiding being quoted directly, especially on camera. He simply inserted the ultimate four-letter word several times in every spoken sentence. It was foolproof.

There was the day I paid a call on Cleveland's boy mayor and described him thus: "The mayor of this major city sat dwarfed by the dimensions of his ornate, high-ceilinged City Hall office, his white sneakers peeking out from under a large wooden desk. It was a lazy Saturday, and diminutive Dennis Kucinich, predictably called 'Dennis the Menace' by his political foes, wore a sport shirt and sleeveless sweater that made him look no more than half his 31 years." (It may have been a heartless description, but at least I didn't say that he was out of uniform for his hometown. There, an outfit of white polyester suit, white shirt, white socks, and white shoes was known as "a full Cleveland.")

Young Kucinich was plenty fired up over an attempt to recall him for firing the city's police chief, and eventually for other acts not yet committed. "It's an unjustifiable attempted political coup spawned by poor losers," he informed me, as well as "un-American" and an "establishment Watergate" that was "denigrating the democratic process to the level of a banana republic." In this manner was I first exposed to his way with words, which I didn't encounter again until I covered his successful race for Congress in 1998, and later as, of all things, a strident anti-war, pro-peace presidential candidate in 2003–2004.

In June 1978, on the night the California legislature passed the notorious Proposition 13 backed by former governor Ronald Reagan that clamped limits on property taxes and set off a national trend, I happened to encounter him in Denver after a speech for a Republican candidate. He called the outcome "the loudest message ever sent across this country that the people realize how much government costs, they want something done about it, and they're not going to wait." Shades of the television anchorman in *Network*. Riding up in the hotel elevator, Reagan exclaimed joyously of the vote, "I hope it's really big!" As we sat in his plush suite, he regaled me with boasts of his budget surplus refunds as governor. He predicted it wouldn't be long before a constitutional amendment was passed for a federal equivalent of Prop 13. "The Democrats themselves are getting the message," he said. "We find them now making proposals they wouldn't have been caught dead making a few years ago." But, he added in a cautionary note, Carter was a politician "and he may get the word" by 1980. It was clear from this what Reagan himself had in mind for that election year.

While busily tracking the approaching 1978 off-year elections, I had occasion to check up on the whereabouts of certain Watergate figures, always good for a column. Earlier, I had located Emil "Bud" Krogh, the first Nixon White House figure to serve time for authorizing the office break-in of Daniel Ellsberg's psychiatrist, and found him living in placid Mill Valley, California, north of San Francisco, teaching public administration at Golden State University. A TV movie, *Washington Behind Closed Doors*, based on fellow Watergate figure John Ehrlichman's novel, *The Company*, had just aired, and I asked him what he thought of it. He said he hadn't watched and was busy putting the whole affair behind him.

The same was true for Ehrlichman, whom I tracked down months later at a remote adobe house on a dirt road outside Santa Fe. After being in stir himself for eighteen months, the Number 2 of Nixon's "Germans" behind Haldeman, he was not eager to be interviewed and wouldn't come out at first. But I outwaited him and he finally emerged and told me he was about to begin a daily news commentary over Mutual Radio the following month. He was sharing what amounted to a hut with Republican Congressman Pete McCloskey of California, who had challenged Nixon unsuccessfully in the 1972 Republican presidential primaries. More strange bedfellows. Ehrlichman had just finished a second Washington novel, he told me, and I wrote that he was "indeed inching his way back into the public eye. You might, in fact, call it 'a limited, modified hangout'"—an approximation of his famous description of coming partially clean on the Watergate scandal.

Other memorable moments that year included Carter's visit to Wilson, North Carolina, in the heart of tobacco country, where he pledged to maintain a strong federal loan support program, even as his Health, Education and Welfare secretary, Joe Califano, was on a rampaging crusade against smoking. Carter told two audiences he saw no "incompatibility" in the two approaches. In a classic, memorable Carterism, he declared that his cabinet member was engaged in an education and research program "to make smoking even safer than it is today." I compared that in the column, with perhaps a touch of hyperbole, to "supporting development of a new atomic bomb that is even safer for people than today's models."

On the campaign trail in September, I accompanied an underdog candidate for governor in Florida on an escapade long remembered by both of us. From Jacksonville, I reported:

As plucked chickens by the hundreds swing by him on an endless conveyer belt, Democratic gubernatorial candidate Bob Graham reaches in, pulls out the innards, deftly slices off the heart and liver with a small knife, and drops them onto another conveyer belt. Nearby, performing the same chore, Cecil Beasley, 62, a retired policeman, says of his temporary co-worker, "It's just like Walkin' Lawton Chiles [the Florida senator who walked across the state in his first campaign]. You've got to have your thing. If you ain't got a gimmick, you ain't got nothin'. Everybody knows that." State Senator Graham, dressed in blue jeans with a long plastic apron over them, is working his gimmick—nearing completion of a pledge to spend 100 work days without pay at the common labors of fellow Floridians. He has been a longshoreman, a garbage collector, an ironworker, a bellhop, a teacher of retarded children, a tomato picker, a cop and a stable boy, among dozens of other occupations.

For lack of space, I wasn't able to include details of the bellhop job, in which Graham toted the bags of a rival gubernatorial candidate, the state's attorney general, to his penthouse suite, where said rival's wife announced that her husband was taking a nap. It led to a newspaper headline the next day—"Graham Works While General Sleeps"—that may well have been a factor in Graham's upset victory. He went on to election to the U.S. Senate and, in 2003, the start of a longshot bid for the Democratic presidential nomination. When I met him for breakfast one morning at the Center of New Hampshire, Manchester's upscale Holiday Inn, I greeted him, naturally, with: "Plucked any chickens lately?"

Then there was my visit to the eighth-floor suite of George Wallace at Hilton Head, South Carolina, at the last Southern Governors Conference he would be attending as governor of Alabama. He sat in his wheelchair at the window looking down at the large swimming pool and the wide Atlantic beach below and, as I wrote, "watched quietly as lithe, bikinied bodies cavorted below. His pale blue pin-stripe suit matched the September sky. 'Sure is nice out there today,' he said."

Unable to join his fellow governors in their frolicking, Wallace reminisced softly about how he had been the voice of the middle class and how so many others had now adopted his message. "But what I said way back, isn't that what they write about so much now?" he asked, almost plaintively. "Isn't that what you used to call me radical about? Patience doesn't last forever. People can't make ends meet and if something's not done, they will become radicalized. But I'm not hunting for anything for myself. I don't claim to be any great spokesman for anyone. But even the *Washington Post* came out with an editorial to the effect that I helped bring to the fore the plight of the middle class." He paused, then added: "That was the good part of the editorial. That was before the 'but.'" He took a long draw on his cigar. "I never opted to be like someone else. I opted to be George Wallace." I believe that was the last time I saw him.

Several years later, Germond and I got a letter from him complaining about something we had written about Alabama politics. He closed the letter with this poignant observation:

> It is good to read you fellows because I enjoyed my old days with you in years past, but the bullets that I took in Maryland have taken their toll on me. I have been in bed off and on the last couple of months as a result of a hip ulcer, and your back gets weak as a result of staying in bed. However, I am going to plug on, continue to exercise, and get well. I just wanted to let you fellows know in a letter not for print that I enjoyed reading you both and remember the days we used to have personal contacts together. I wish those days could happen again. I am going to keep reading you.
>
> With kind regards, I am sincerely yours,
>
> George C. Wallace

The big developments of 1978 as far as I was concerned were the departure of Jim Bellows as editor of the *Star* and the sale of the paper by owner Joe Allbritton to Time Incorporated. When Bellows left to become editor of another ailing paper, the *Los Angeles Herald-Examiner*, it was basically because he was tired of contending with Allbritton, a Texas banker who knew nothing about newspapering. When Bellows took over the *Star* and turned it from a struggling antique to a lively, engaging, and imaginative sheet, he clearly eclipsed Allbritton the social climber, and it was only a matter of time before he walked or was pushed out the door. Not only for being the midwife of our column but as a buoyant and optimistic hands-on presence in the newsroom, I lamented his departure. Allbritton tried to make up for driving Bellows to Los Angeles by giving him a new Cadillac Seville for the trip. As I told Jim on hearing about the gift, "Being rich means never having to say you're sorry."

The sale of the paper to Time was an equally grievous offense and much more destructive. The Time bigwigs were an arrogant bunch who thought they could make a success out of the *Star* basically by turning it into a daily newsmagazine, with the emphasis on glitz, layout, and soft news. That may have worked for a publication that came out only once a week, but it was ludicrous for a daily. The personality of a sassy, in-your-face paper that Bellows had brought to the *Star* was buried in composition gimmicks, regional editions, even an effort to make it an all-day competitor to the *Post*, the city's morning powerhouse.

Brought in as editor was a veteran Time chief of correspondents named Murray Gart, a starry-eyed Time product who proceeded to antagonize much of the staff by injecting his abrasive personality and ill-informed ideas into a heretofore harmonious newsroom atmosphere. He would have lunch with one of his few political sources and come back and disgorge to Germond and me the transparent snow jobs that had been laid on him. We seldom bothered to humor him. Perhaps to humor us, he made the two of us political editors of the *Star*, which meant nothing since we were already handling the paper's political coverage along with our pal Jim Dickenson and the irreplacable self-starter, Mary McGrory, the brightest star in the paper's firmament. Our column, after having been a fixture on page one or page three of the first section under Bellows, soon was moved by Gart to the editorial page, severely cutting our readership. But what he did to the whole paper was much more serious.

One episode will suffice to illustrate the folly of Time's management of the *Star*. Gart hired a guy described as an editorial designer or some such, a tall, bearded character known in the newsroom as "The Wolfhound." Upon the election of Ronald Reagan as president, Gart and The Wolfhound got their heads together and decided, Time-like, to run a big page-one spread displaying the pictures of the Reagan cabinet. The only problem was, no cabinet members had been picked yet. The *Star*'s beat reporters were instructed nevertheless to go out and come back with the names of the likely choices. The assignment was an exercise in pure guesswork, but that didn't prevent a subsequent display of mug shots that was an embarrassment to all involved—except, perhaps, Gart and The Wolfhound.

But that is getting a bit ahead of the story. As 1979 began, we were only starting to report the early plans of the Reagan campaign to sew up the 1980 Republican presidential nomination against a large GOP field eager to take on the troubled Carter. In January, Republican leaders met in Washington and selected Detroit as the site of their next national convention, to the dismay of southern party leaders who had hoped to lure it to New Orleans or some other Dixie paradise. Clarke Reed, one of the featured players in the 1976 "Battle of Mississippi" at the previous convention, had led his region's fight for the 1980 site. As he emerged from the decisive meeting, I asked him how he felt about the choice of downtown Detroit, well-known for its heavily black population and deserted nighttime streets. "Well, there's good news and bad news," he said. "The good news is that the convention hall [Cobo Hall] is only a block away from the headquarters hotel [the Renaissance Center]. The bad news is that nobody's ever made it." The blatant racial slur was not considered very funny by others, but it reflected an attitude that still prevailed among many in the Deep South.

Although Carter was an incumbent expected to seek a second term, the sagging economy, soaring gasoline prices, and other problems fanned the continuing talk of a challenge from Ted Kennedy, despite his pointed efforts to discourage it. He fashioned a set response to questions that his aides came to call his "E, E, and I" answer—that he *expected* Carter to be renominated, that he *expected* he'd be reelected, and that he *intended* to support him. But as early as February of 1979, Kennedy and political aides and advisers had begun to meet to assess the playing field. In March, the stirrings of a draft-Kennedy movement were being heard in Iowa, and in May an old family ally, Cuyahoga County commissioner Tim Hagan, formed a draft committee in Ohio. But Kennedy continued to give the "E, E, and I" answer.

While Germond and I bird-dogged this uncertain story with the rest of the pack, we knuckled down to the certain competition for the Republican Party nomination, in which Ronald Reagan was the clear frontrunner. On the first of May, as George Bush launched his own candidacy, Jack wrote the aforementioned lead about peaking early that got us—or, rather, me—in the candidate's doghouse from the start.

I was one of twenty-eight paying reporters on the Bush charter jet, which aides said cost the campaign $18,000 for two days. They acknowledged it had been leased in part to demonstrate to reporters that their candidate was alive and well in the nomination race. With Reagan the frontrunner from the start, however, Bush had to endure repeated questions from me and others about his availability for the vice-presidential nomination. Irked at the inquiry, he devised a special response: "Take Sherman and cube it." By that, he meant the famous response of General William Tecumseh Sherman after the Civil War: "If nominated I will not accept; if elected I will not serve."

The desirability of the Republican nomination grew through 1979, and especially starting in early July when Carter canceled a speech on energy and went to Camp David to commune with himself, aides, and other advisers on how to address the problem of his sagging presidency. Over a ten-day period, a parade of nearly 150 kibitzers was summoned to counsel the president in a bizarre exercise that only underscored his leadership shortcomings. When he finally gave his speech, he said there was "a crisis of confidence" in the country "that strikes at the very heart and soul and spirit of our national will." Although he never used the word, his presentation came to be known as "the malaise speech," seeming to blame the American people for the nation's ills. The Republican hopefuls could not wait to take him on in 1980.

Carter's troubles also were stirring at least one Democrat to the notion of challenging him for reelection. In early August, when I called on Governor Jerry Brown in his Los Angeles office, he pulled a white envelope from his coat pocket and read to me what he had scribbled on the front of it. It said he was authorizing formation of an exploratory committee "to provide an alternative to the shopworn categories of political thought that are dragging the Democratic Party towards defeat." In response, in an effort to pull his leg, I told him he had it all wrong: "You're supposed to scribble on the *back* of the envelope." He looked up at me rather quizically, as if he had never heard of the story of Lincoln writing the Gettysburg Address on the back of an envelope. Oh, well.

Ted Kennedy, too, was reevaluating. In an interview for the *Star*, he said in mid-September that his earlier reluctance to challenge an incumbent Democratic president was now being outweighed by "the deepening of the problems we're facing," which were convincing him "that the divisions exist in the towns and villages and plants and factories, and not among personalities." He sounded very much like his late brother, Robert, in 1968 when he finally decided to take on another Democratic incumbent, Lyndon Johnson, and didn't want the challenge to be seen simply as a personal clash between the two men. But Ted said the two situations were not analagous because he enjoyed "a friendly relationship with the president" despite his increasing criticisms of him. Little more than a month later, he too launched a presidential exploratory committee.

Around this time, Germond and I had just obtained a contract to write a book on the 1980 presidential campaign, following on my 1976 book, *Marathon*, with the same publisher. Since we were working as a team on the column and jointly gathering string on the campaign, it was natural that we would write the book together. On the Saturday of the dedication of the John F. Kennedy Library, economist John Kenneth Galbraith held a cocktail party at his home in Cambridge, and I ran into Theodore H. White, the author of the groundbreaking "Making of the President" series. As a courtesy, since I had heard he was going to resume his series, I informed Teddy that Jack and I would be writing our book. Always cordial and encouraging to younger reporters, he replied with no trace of sarcasm: "Oh, good. You tell what happened, and I'll tell why!"

One of the things that happened that we did indeed tell about in the book, which came out in 1981 as *Blue Smoke and Mirrors: How Reagan Won and Why Carter Lost the Election of 1980*, was Kennedy's famous, or infamous, television interview with Roger Mudd, then of CBS News, in which the senator struggled unsuccessfully to answer the simple question: "Why do you want to be president?" In a long interview after the election, Mudd told me of his astonishment that Kennedy could do no better than a rambling recitation of generalities. "I sort of privately blinked," he told me. "It was like 'I want to be president because the sea is so deep and the sky is so blue.' You know, you're always a little professionally embarrassed to ask a question like that because you can read the stitches on a pitch like that. It comes across the plate about nine miles an hour."

But Kennedy couldn't hit it. As he explained later, "I spent a good deal of time thinking about running. I wasn't interested in dividing the party but I was very much concerned about the direction of the party and of the country, and I was very much concerned about what I thought would be the results if we didn't have an alternative or change. I spent time thinking of that and probably not as much time as I should have about how I'd spend the early days of the campaign, and developing and fashioning the kind of themes that I think probably would have aroused the most positive response."

In any event, as the election year approached we had a full plate before us, with competition for the 1980 presidential nominations in both parties. The political agenda was further complicated in November by an attack on the American Embassy in Teheran by young militants, protesting a decision by Carter to admit the shah of Iran into the United States from Mexico for emergency treatment of cancer and gallstones. Some 101 persons were held hostage in the opening round of a crisis that would plague Carter through the remainder of his presidency. And on top of that, in December, Soviet troops invaded Afghanistan in yet another development that placed demands on the president's time—and gave him a rationale for ducking debates with Kennedy in Iowa.

Thus was born Carter's "Rose Garden strategy," which further frustrated Kennedy's efforts to engage him in a highly visible setting and culminated in Kennedy's defeat in the Iowa caucuses and then in the New Hampshire primary. However, when Carter's attempt to rescue remaining hostages in Teheran ended in a fiasco in the desert (typically, he called it "an incomplete success"), he had to abandon the Rose Garden strategy and start campaigning. Kennedy recovered somewhat with victories in Massachusetts, New York, Connecticut, Pennsylvania, Michigan, and in five of the last eight contests, but it was too late to deny the president renomination.

Kennedy's candidacy provided the ultimate in a local angle for one of my best friends on the campaign trail, Bob Healy of the *Boston Globe*. Bob was also one of my regular tennis rivals, along with Tom Ottenad and Curtis Wilkie, as we went from one state primary to another. In Philadelphia on the night before the Pennsylvania primary, in what was not an uncommon happenstance, our little group over-indulged somewhat at the hotel bar and I foolishly bet Healy a hundred bucks on a tennis match to be played the next morning. On awakening in the morning and remembering my folly, and realizing I could never beat him in the shape in which I found myself, I contrived with the assistance of master prankster Jim Naughton of the *New York Times* to avoid the inevitable humiliation.

About half an hour before we were to meet at the court at the University of Pennsylvania, Naughton phoned Healy in his room and, introducing himself as "Agent James" of the Kennedy Secret Service detail, asked Bob to hold for a moment because the senator needed to speak to him. Bob immediately bit, turning to his wife Mary and conjecturing that Kennedy was about to pull out of the presidential race. It shaped up as a big scoop for him, so he held on. Minutes passed before "Agent James" got on the line again and told him that Kennedy had just rushed into the bathroom but asked him to hold a while longer. This went on with intermittent apologies from "Agent James" for further unavoidable delays, until it was too late for Bob to make it to the court on time. Then the ersatz agent told him that Kennedy had to leave and would call him later in the day.

When Bob finally showed up at Penn, I regretfully told him that his very tardy arrival had caused him to default the match, and that he owed me a C-note. He explained about Kennedy's call and the likelihood of the senator's dramatic withdrawal from the race, at which all assembled for the big match broke down and confessed. Healy was probably more disappointed at losing a good story than at the opportunity of winning an easy hundred, or so he assumed, from me. Thus did we relieve the grind on the trail from time to time.

The tables were turned on me shortly afterward one night when a campaign event brought Germond and me together in the same town—Austin, Texas. Catching up on our separate travels, we capped the evening with more than a few libations at the then-shabby Stephen Austin Hotel across from the sumptuous Driskill, where naturally we stayed. In the course of the evening, we were accosted by perhaps the ugliest and most repulsive hooker in all Texas, and quickly dismissed her. Hours later, after Jack and I had staggered across the street to our appointed rooms, I was aroused from my stupor by a rapping on my door.

Opening it, I discovered the same "lady" of the night. I had no idea how she had found my room. I immediately tried to close the door on her, but she pushed her way in and dashed into my bathroom. Bewildered and appalled, I demanded that she get out, and after just a moment or two she ran out again. I looked around and found that the assorted bills on my night table by the door, maybe sixty bucks or so, were gone. In testimony to my innocence, I quickly phoned the Austin cops, who arrived with dispatch to investigate. They informed me that they would check further but had little hope of catching the culprit. So I staggered back to bed to sleep off my night's consumption of booze, and this bizarre episode.

Early the next morning I was aroused again, this time by my ringing telephone. The caller was a reporter for the *Austin Statesman-American* who had checked the police blotter and wanted to know what had happened. I related the story, which seemed to get a suspicious reception on the other end of the phone. After the reporter had hung up, I realized that I might find my name in the local paper under embarrassing if innocent circumstances, so I got dressed and went down to my partner's room to seek his advice.

When Germond in a similar physical shape as myself opened the door and I related what had occurred, he broke into a huge grin. He confessed that the night before, when I had repaired briefly to the men's room of the Stephen Austin bar, he had given the hooker my room number at the Driskill and suggested I might like company. He thought the episode was hilarious until I told him about the reporter's call, whereupon with a modicum of guilt he lent me sympathetic consolation. That night after dinner we trekked to the paper at first-edition time and grabbed a copy, searching nervously through it. To my great relief, there was no story and finally we shared a laugh about the whole business—Jack's somewhat more hearty than mine.

I thought that was the end of the saga until a few nights after returning to Washington, when my office phone rang just before dinner time. A man with a distinctly Dixie twang identified himself as an officer of the Austin Police Department and said he was following up on the robbery. I told him I had given the police all the information I had, but he proceeded to ask me for my home phone number. He said he would be calling me at home in a day or two as the investigation continued. Reflexively, I asked him not to do that, but he insisted that he would have to, and hung up.

That last comment tipped me off. The story obviously had made the rounds by now. I raced out of the office and over to the Class Reunion, a press hangout near the White House. Sure enough, I found Curtis Wilkie and several other conspirators mirthfully waiting for what they expected would be my panicked arrival. But the Austin cop's voice had sounded faintly familiar, and I was able to match the voice with a face I spied as soon as I entered. It belonged to certified southern cracker Walter Isaacson, then a mere reporter for *Time*, later the magazine's managing editor and then head of CNN. His employers must have learned of his special talents.

In the final days of the 1980 primary campaign, with eight states holding contests, most self-respecting reporters, including my partner, were in sunny California. I found myself stuck in dreary Ohio along with Wilkie. Awaiting a Ted Kennedy swing through the state, we kept busy playing tennis in the mornings next to a noisy highway and watching Cleveland Indians night games in the city's dreary downtown stadium. One night the Tribe pulled off a triple play, but the stupefied fans failed to cheer because they didn't realize it had happened. To mark the occasion of our Ohio imprisonment, Curtis and I had T-shirts made for one Kennedy rally that said: "Free the Cleveland Two." Kennedy, spying us wearing them in the crowd, didn't seem to get it.

On the Republican side, the expectation was that Ronald Reagan, on the basis of his strong showing in 1976, would sweep to his party's nomination. He started out in the caucuses in Iowa, where he had launched his career in entertainment as a play-by-play announcer of Chicago Cubs baseball games via a sports news ticker coming into Des Moines. His campaign manager, John Sears, calculated on the basis of past turnout how many Reagan caucus-goers it would take to win Iowa and set about mobilizing that number. Reagan in his optimism skipped a *Des Moines Register* debate, but George Bush's Iowa manager, Rich Bond, worked diligently for a record turnout and upset Reagan in the state on caucus night. Bush prematurely claimed to have "the Big Mo"—for momentum—but instead got a jolt from an awakened Reagan campaign in the New Hampshire primary.

There Sears pulled another of his unorthodox moves by paying for what started as a televised debate in Nashua between Reagan and Bush, then at the last moment inviting the five other GOP candidates to join them, unbeknownst to Bush. In a scene marked by Reagan's firmness and Bush's petulant objection to including the five, the late invitees sullenly left the stage, and with them went Bush's hopes for the nomination. Having pulled off another inventive caper, Sears seemed to be solidly in the driver's seat of the Reagan campaign as victory in the primary beckoned.

On primary day in New Hampshire, Tom Ottenad, Germond, and I had lunch with Sears to hash over the campaign and get a heads-up on the Reagan campaign's plans for the primaries ahead. He was particularly upbeat about the scene in Nashua three nights earlier and predicted that his man would win easily. Afterward, Ottenad drove Sears back to the Holiday Inn where the Reagan party was staying. On arrival, two of Sears' chief subordinates and friends, Charlie Black and Jim Lake, were waiting and reported that Reagan wanted to see him immediately. When he went into Reagan's suite, the candidate handed him a press release announcing that Sears was "resigning" to go back to practicing law and was being replaced by Bill Casey, the former CIA director. It was a palace coup, engineered by longtime Reagan flunky Ed Meese through the candidate's wife, Nancy, and it took Black and Lake over the side with Sears. The news made an anticlimax of Reagan's primary victory that night with 50 percent of the vote to only 23 for Bush and the remaining votes scattered among the rest of the field. The three of us who had lunched with Sears had been aware of infighting in the campaign, but we never guessed such an outcome on the very day of Reagan's strong comeback, put together by Sears, who shared our surprise.

Reagan was not out of surprises that year. At the Republican National Convention in Detroit that summer, he considered the unprecedented step of choosing a former president, Gerald Ford, to be his running mate. Reagan reported later that he had broached the subject with Ford at a meeting in Palm Springs months before, at which time Ford (he said later) had told him he wasn't interested. Nevertheless, Reagan's pollster, Dick Wirthlin, took a survey testing which of a large field of prominent Republicans would most strengthen the ticket. Ford's name was thrown in and he clearly led the pack. Reagan was open to some alternative to Bush, the runner-up in the nomination fight, after the Texas transplant behaved so churlishly at their Nashua debate. So, days before the convention opened, the subject came under consideration again. When Ford in his convention speech said he didn't intend to sit out the campaign "on the sidelines" and therefore "when this convention fields the team for Governor Reagan, count me in," Reagan's strategists thought they heard a signal.

So the next day, Reagan met with Ford and asked him to be his running mate. The former president, still reluctant, said he would think it over. Soon the convention was abuzz with the idea, and when I happened to run into Reagan in a corridor of the Renaissance Center, I asked him point-blank whether it was true he was trying to get Ford to run with him. In his cordial, open way, he grinned and said: "Oh, sure. That would be the best." Well, I asked him, was there any chance of its happening? "I don't know," he said as his Secret Service agents tried to hustle him off, "I only know what he said in Palm Springs." Clearly, Reagan had a different recollection of what Ford had said there. I took his answer as confirmation that the notion was seriously in play.

It so happened that Ford had agreed to an interview with Walter Cronkite at the CBS booth in Joe Louis Arena that day. The nation's prime newscaster asked the former president about the possible deal, and to the surprise of both camps Ford began to spell out the conditions whereby he might accept. He said he wouldn't want to be confined to ceremonial tasks. "If I go to Washington, and I'm not saying that I am accepting," he said, "I have to go there with the belief that I will play a meaningful role across the board in the basic and the crucial and the important decisions" of a Reagan administration. An incredulous Cronkite asked whether he was thinking about "something like a co-presidency." Ford never used the expression himself but he didn't knock it down either. "I don't know where he got it," he told Germond and me long afterward. "It was nothing I ever said." What he had in mind then, he said later, was that "the vice president ought to be the chief operating officer as the chief of staff in the White House."

At the time, however, the term "co-presidency" sent the convention into an uproar, and nobody was more dismayed about the uproar, if not the idea, than one of Cronkite's television competitors at ABC News, Barbara Walters. She realized she had been scooped on the convention's big story. Although Ford had already given her an interview in which she hadn't brought up the subject, she raced to the CBS booth and nailed Ford as he came out. David Kennerly, Ford's photographer at the White House and afterward, gave me this eyewitness account of what was said: "She literally pleaded with him to come and do another interview with her. She said, 'Mr. President, you've got to come talk to me. You've got to.' Ford said, 'Well, Barbara, I really have to go to this other meeting.' And she says, 'Oh, Mr. President, you've got to do it . . . for old time's sake . . . for Alan's sake.'" The latter reference, Kennerly surmised, was to Alan Greenspan, the resident Washington genius on the economy and her favored date of the time. Kennerly told me he couldn't believe what he had heard. "That quote is imbedded in my mind," he said. "Begging is the only way I could put it. I wished I would have had one of those little airline barf bags, because I just about lost it. It was the single most disgusting display by a newsperson that I've ever seen in my life. And Ford said, 'Okay, Barbara.' You know the way he is."

In the end, the Ford-Reagan deal fell through, leading us to write, "What is more damaging to both Ronald Reagan and Gerald Ford is not that they couldn't make it to the altar, but that they even thought of such a shotgun marriage." I was always indebted to whoever had dreamed up the idea, though, for making possible Kennerly's memorable cameo and remark. Reagan swallowed Bush as his runnning mate, and Bush in the wink of an eye shed his previously iron-clad disavowal of interest—"Take Sherman and cube it." He not only jumped aboard the Reagan campaign like a dog leaping on a meat wagon; he embraced his ticketmate's "voodoo economics" with relish and eventually cashed the whole package in for a ticket of his own to the Oval Office eight years later.

The city of Detroit had a way of bringing out unwitting humor that political year. Democratic governor Pat Lucey of Wisconsin, chosen by independent candidate John Anderson to be his running mate, confessed at a Motor City news conference that his family car was a French Peugeot. This was a city where the United Auto Workers headquarters posted a warning sign in its parking lot that any foreign cars would be towed away to some automobile purgatory. Lucey defensively reported that his wife had bought the car and it was then five years old. "It's not a very valuable asset to the family," he apologized, "and I'm sure it's less of a valuable asset to the campaign." At the same time, it couldn't be said that the Peugeot kept Anderson out of the Oval Office.

In the fall campaign, Carter's problems with the economy and the Iranian hostage crisis proved to be too much baggage for him to overcome. The only question was whether Reagan could sell himself as a knowledgeable candidate and be kept from making damaging observations drawn from some of his half-baked notions. Stuart Spencer, his old California consultant who had worked for Ford against him in 1976, was recruited to monitor him. Reagan, as an actor accustomed to taking direction on the set, became more careful of what he said, but he always retained a natural sort of naïveté and courtliness. One day aboard the Reagan plane, I was up front in the candidate's compartment talking to Spencer when Reagan walked by to go into the section's toilet. He opened the door, then stopped. Finding a stewardess therein tidying up, he turned to Spencer with a look of horror on his face. "She's in there," he whispered in distress, "and she left the door unlocked!" He retreated to his seat, flush with embarrassment.

With the campaign over, Germond and I settled down to write our first campaign chronicle together, *Blue Smoke and Mirrors*. We divided the work according to the states we had each covered during the primary period, and then divvied up the chapters on the conventions and the fall campaign pretty much based on our sources, consulting each other more on these sections. We exchanged written chapters and commented on them and then put them together, trying to leave as few stitches showing as possible. In this and each of our succeeding three campaign books together, we crashed the project in about four months after the election, so we were able each time to bring out the first book on the subject. Meanwhile, we continued to turn out the column, a workload that made for some early mornings and late nights.

The advent of the Reagan presidency in 1981, as noted earlier, let loose some of the wretched excesses of newsmagazine journalism on the struggling daily *Star*. After the freewheeling stewardship of Jim Bellows, the uptight, formulaic approach of Gart and Time bred much disillusionment and grousing among the staff. Before long, rumors were flying that the Time bigwigs, unable to put their stamp on the paper, were looking to unload it. Over the next months I came to feel that, in their arrogance, they were concluding that if they couldn't make a go of it nobody else could, or at least they didn't want to chance that possibility. Germond talked to at least one prospective buyer and passed word of his interest to the management, but there seemed to be no desire to provide him with the basic financial information he would have needed to make a prudent decision. And so, in August of the year, the Time executives abruptly announced that they were killing Washington's illustrious old journalistic institution, which once had reigned as its undisputed best, before the impressive revitalization of the *Post* under Kay Graham and Ben Bradlee.

The excellent staff took it hard when the executioners came into the building and broke the news, their imperiousness unbent by their dismal failure. In less than five years, our column had lost its home base, and, like all the other staffers, we had to cast about for a new perch. In doing so, we were fortunate to find a Good Samaritan about thirty-five miles up the road, in Baltimore.

15 New Home, at the *Evening Sun*

WITH THE CLOSING OF the *Star* in the summer of 1981, the newsroom became an open employment agency. Newspapers around the country sent personnel officials to recruit the *Star's* considerable talent, and many of the best reporters, editors, and photographers were quickly gobbled up. Jack and I used our contacts on other papers to open a few doors for them where we could, and we pushed on a few for ourselves. We obviously hoped to move across town to the *Post*, but the decision was in the hands of Meg Greenfield, the editorial-page editor. She made clear at the outset she had no room for a pair of political junkies, with a full stable of columnists already, some of them chosen personally by her. Also, the *Star's* star, Mary McGrory, was the *Post's* first draft choice, and we certainly couldn't argue with that.

We had a memorable breakfast at the Jefferson Hotel with Ben Bradlee, who told us that as far as the *Post* was concerned, the matter was Meg's call, and I had learned from my years on the *Post* that she was not in love with the brand of inside politics we wrote about. "You guys," Ben said with customary directness, "are holding a very small pair." But he wished us well and remained a friend over the coming years.

We were determined to keep the column going and based in Washington. Soon, the *Baltimore Sun* shined on us with an offer from Jack Lemmon, managing editor of the *Evening Sun*, and we grabbed it. Lemmon was a former *Post* editor from my days there, a Germond look-alike who was an excellent and easy-going boss. He gave us a great spot at the top of page two or three on most days and full freedom to write what we chose. We also wrote news stories for the paper, which was more locally oriented than the morning *Sun* and understaffed compared to it. But the *Evening Sun* had a proud tradition going back to the days when H. L. Mencken was its famed editor and essayist, and where such protégés as William Manchester, later a best-selling nonfiction writer, learned their craft at his knee.

The *Evening Sun* under Lemmon had a scrappy personality not unlike the *Star* in the pre-Time days. It was a blue-collar newspaper in a blue-collar town, known affectionately by the locals, together with the morning sheet, as "the Sunpapers." We found a comfortable, hospitable, and accommodating home there, working out of the Washington bureau, which functioned essentially for the morning paper. The bureau chief at the time was Ernest B. "Pat" Furgurson, an old traveling companion of ours from years on the campaign trail; and the bureau had some of the best beat reporters in town, including Lyle Denniston at the Supreme Court and Charlie Corddry at the Pentagon.

While our column no longer had the Washington readership we had enjoyed at the *Star*, we retained a prestige base from which to operate and the political sources each of us had built up around the country over the years. Thanks to the latitude given us by Jack Lemmon, we picked our spots and traveled extensively, landing in the news columns nearly as often as in our regular column spot. After having spent so many years writing every day, we both still responded to the newspaper equivalent of the firehouse bell when a story broke.

Although our base paper no longer was published in the nation's capital, we continued to serve up inside baseball and analysis on national politics for our Baltimore and syndicate readers, to no complaints that ever reached us. That condition went unchanged when, in 1986, the A. S. Abell family, the Sunpapers' owner, sold it to the Times Mirror Company, publisher of the *Los Angeles Times*, putting me back in that family after nine years away. But the *Evening Sun* retained both its editorial autonomy and its personality under the new ownership, as well as its sassy underdog posture toward the morning *Sun*.

Lemmon, like Jim Bellows at the *Star* in 1977, started us off with a splash in the paper, prominently displaying the serializing of our book on the 1980 campaign five days running, and never letting up thereafter. We resumed our customary bird-dogging of political animals large and small in their lairs from Maine to California, continuing to adhere to our regular division of labor—Jack covering the Northeast and South, me handling the Midwest and West. Mayors, governors, and state and county chairmen in Germond's territory witnessed no break in their obligation to close saloons with him from Bangor to Biloxi, and those in my areas to share a modest cup or two with me from Saginaw to San Diego.

We spent 1982 keeping an eye on Reagan and Company in Washington and writing about interesting gubernatorial and congressional races around the country, as well as observing the new vice president, George "I love voodoo economics" Bush, on the campaign trail. Having not only swallowed his "Take Sherman and cube it" disavowal of ever being a second banana but also having thoroughly digested it, he was out conscientiously defending the new economic litany he now embraced.

There were other interesting about-faces that year. U.S. senator Adlai E. Stevenson III of Illinois, namesake son of the 1952 and 1956 Democratic presidential nominee and great-grandson of the vice president elected in 1892, ran for governor, disavowing any television gimmicks. I remember sitting in his Senate office listening to how he despised advertising and then seeing him run same in a failed effort to unseat Republican governor Jim Thompson. Adlai III was regarded as a bit stuffy, but he knew it. He told me about going into a Chicago bar one day and being told by a friendly bartender: "Adlai, you're a nice fella, but take some advice from me. You gotta get ridda dat 'Adlai da turd.'"

Thompson needled him as an elitist for belonging to a downtown lunch club that barred women, which Stevenson at first defended on grounds he couldn't find a place to eat at midday. At a GOP meeting in Orlando Township, I was amused to hear Thompson chide him because he couldn't "find a place to have lunch in the Loop." As he said it, I recalled that lunch I had had with the Republican governor at Arnie's steak joint, where he told me flat out that he never picked up a check there. In any event, Adlai never shucked "da turd" at the end of his name, and he lost, probably for other reasons.

In Minneapolis that same year, Eugene McCarthy, the man who chased Lyndon Johnson out of the White House with his near-miss in the New Hampshire primary in 1968 and subsequently gave up his Senate seat, also did an about-face. After two more failed presidential bids, McCarthy decided to seek his Senate seat again in the Minnesota Democratic primary, on the grounds that the country was in much worse shape than when he first bowed out.

I accompanied him one day to the cluttered newsroom of the University of Minnesota *Daily*, where a student politely noted the similarity between his comeback bid and that of perennial candidate Harold Stassen, seeking to regain the governorship he held in the 1940s. McCarthy, notorious for unwillingness to suffer fools gladly, fired back at the poor student. "That's an original thought," he said in controlled high dudgeon. "Do you want me to explain the difference, or don't you really care?"

He said, however, that Stassen had been right in 1948 as a Republican presidential candidate and could have beaten Harry Truman had he been nominated instead of Dewey, and that Stassen was right in 1956 in urging Eisenhower to dump Nixon. As for himself, McCarthy said that he could have beaten Nixon in 1968 and that in 1976 he would have made a better president than either Jimmy Carter or Gerald Ford. For the next hour and a half, McCarthy gave serious answers to all questions, though not without his usual whimsy. One solution to the arms race with the Soviet Union, he suggested, was that "if we got the Russians hooked on automobiles as we are, they would have to cut their military potential 50 percent" to afford to buy them.

That fall, I spent some time covering Jerry Brown as he sought to move from the governorship of California to the U.S. Senate, running against Republican Pete Wilson and campaigning as a foe of Reaganomics. Brown lost, and after the election I went out to Los Angeles to find out what this interesting and unorthodox politician had in mind for his next adventure. We spent an hour or so in the bar of the Holiday Inn in Brentwood as he related his idea for getting back into the political picture. He said he was going to pick a Democratic presidential candidate and back him strongly; "maybe he'll put me in his cabinet." When I asked him what cabinet position he'd like, he replied without a moment's hesitation, "I wouldn't mind NASA." I pointed out to him that the head of the National Aeronautics and Space Administration was not a cabinet position. Unfazed, the man widely derided as "Governor Moonbeam" and "the space cadet" countered, "Well, maybe he'd make it one." I didn't point out the obvious public-relations peril in such an appointment, and it didn't seem to occur to him.

The year 1983 saw the 1984 presidential hopefuls on the Democratic side competing for the honor of beating their heads against the wall in opposition to President Reagan. A decision in late 1983 by Ted Kennedy to pass up a second try for the Democratic nomination opened the gates to some early competition in party ranks, with former vice president Fritz Mondale the favorite. As usual, I focused on Iowa as custodian of the first delegate-selecting process through precinct caucuses, and Germond camped out often in New Hampshire. We also dutifully trekked to various straw-poll contests, which were, also as usual, virtually meaningless. The most fun was one in Wisconsin, where Senator Alan Cranston of California, he of the orange hair and insatiable lust for campaign funds, upset Mondale, giving us cover for superior food and drink at Milwaukee's two top German eateries, Mader's and Karl Ratsch's. It was a wake-up call for the Mondale campaign, and Cranston faded into much-warranted oblivion thereafter.

After Carter's stealth campaign for the 1976 Iowa caucuses in 1975, all the Democratic worthies had started working the state early, with us dirty-fingernail print types close behind. Most of the television gang didn't commit that early, and we still were able to travel with most of the presidential aspirants up close, sharing the back seats of their cars or vans before the reportorial onslaught that would begin in both Iowa and New Hampshire right after the start of the new year. Among the early starters were Senators John Glenn and Gary Hart, the former then considered a hot property because of his hero status as one of the original Mercury astronauts, and the latter a real longshot, known to most of us from his accessible days as George McGovern's campaign manager in 1972.

Gary, not to put too fine a point on it, was generally regarded as an inside player rather than an out-front one. He seemed at first too reserved to be an effective candidate. But we eventually came to see him in a different light as he traipsed around Iowa, quietly hitting the boondocks as other Democratic hopefuls focused on Des Moines and the state's other—you should pardon the expression—major cities. For myself, I made forays into the interior, but camped out at the Democratic hotel, the Savery, in Des Moines.

Glenn, intense but genial, simply didn't have it as a candidate. On the morning before caucus night, confirmation that he wasn't going to do well came when Tom Ottenad, Bob Healy, and I picked up his Iowa press spokesman, Larry Rasky, to play tennis, as we often did on election days. Larry came out of his hotel toting not only his tennis racquet but his bags as well, for a quick getaway.

As expected, Mondale won, with 49 percent of the vote. But the story of the night, deftly orchestrated by Keith Glaser, Hart's Iowa manager, was the meager 16.5 percent won by his candidate, the runner-up. Hart also had fled the state, to New Hampshire, but Glaser got Hart on a telephone hookup to the press room in Des Moines, over which the candidate proclaimed himself the anointed alternative to Mondale. It worked; we scribbled down his words and wrote stories about Hart's surprise showing before we ourselves packed and headed for New Hampshire the next morning. Seldom had a candidate gotten more out of less than Hart did that night. In the process, he built that small wave into a temporary tide that would sweep over Mondale in the first-in-the-nation primary only eight days later.

Hart's success in making a lot out of not much in Iowa showed itself in unexpectedly large crowds in New Hampshire. Having come from nowhere, he captured the curiosity and the attention of the locals to the point that another upset was in the air. On the Sunday morning before the primary, Tom Ottenad invited Hart to his room at the Sheraton Wayfarer to have coffee with a few of us. Hart stretched out on a bed as we discussed the seeming boomlet for him. When Bob Healy suddenly asked, "What happens if you win here?" the candidate, straight-faced until then, all at once broke into a broad grin and hearty laughter, setting off a contagion of guffaws as if all present were sharing a badly kept secret. Two days later, Hart scored a decisive 37 percent to 27 percent victory over Mondale and seemed on his way, quickly adding another upset over the former vice president in Maine as they headed for a Super Tuesday showdown of five primaries and four caucuses on a single day in mid-March.

Hart won seven of those too, but a bit of effective political spin by the Mondale campaign, with a probably unwitting assist from the television networks on election night, stole what might have been a further Hart surge toward the Democratic nomination, and saved Mondale's candidacy. The former vice president and his campaign aides got on television and crowed about beating Hart in early-reporting Alabama and Georgia, playing the results as a great comeback, and some of the network anchors and analysts bought into it. In our column, we compared Mondale to a country singer warbling "I've been down so long it looks like up to me," and concluded that winning only two of nine contests "was better than a poke in the eye with a sharp stick, but not all that much better." Nevertheless, Mondale got away with it, overshadowing what should have been another banner night for Hart.

At that, Hart's campaign was not adequately prepared to take maximum advantage of his early spurt, and the candidate himself contributed to his demise in California with a careless remark I was privileged to hear at a fund raiser shortly before the last round of primaries in June. Voters in both New Jersey and California were going to the polls on the final primary day, so Hart and his wife, Lee, decided to split the campaigning, the candidate in the Garden State and Lee in California.

On the last weekend, however, Hart joined his wife for a major fund-raising cocktail party at the sumptuous home of a prominent real-estate developer, Shelly Anderson, in the exclusive Bel Air section of Los Angeles. As the guests gazed beyond a broad patio looking out on Beverly Hills, Hart was in a whimsical mood. Referring to the division of labor with his wife, he observed: "The deal is we campaign separately. That's the bad news. The good news for her is she campaigns in California and I campaign in New Jersey."

Had Hart let it go at that, it would not have been so bad. But when his wife broke in to say that while campaigning the Golden State she had got to hold a koala, her husband blurted out: "I won't tell you what I got to hold: samples from a toxic dump." The crowd at Shelly Anderson's roared with laughter, but when word got back to New Jersey, the crack wasn't considered funny, playing as it did on New Jersey's reputation (not wholly deserved, I always contended, as a native) as a geographical armpit. On primary night, Mondale routed Hart there, winning all 117 convention delegates at stake.

In the end, Mondale managed to squeeze out enough delegate strength to declare himself the nominee going into the convention, held in San Francisco. Hart had, however, put himself in position for a serious second try in 1988 and told the convention, with no apologies to crooner Tony Bennett, "This is one Hart you will not leave in San Francisco."

The most memorable quote for me in 1984 had nothing to do with the presidential election, in which Ronald Reagan easily disposed of Mondale. It was uttered in a famous old German restaurant, Berghoff's, in Chicago's downtown Loop one lunchtime when I was covering the challenge of Democrat Paul Simon to Republican senator Charles Percy. Curtis Wilkie of the *Boston Globe*, Steve Neal of the *Chicago Sun-Times*, and I were standing at one of several high round tables having a beer and a sandwich when an advance man for Percy came up to the table next to us, occupied by some young business types. Six years earlier, Percy, seeking reelection, had run a television commercial confessing he had neglected his constituents but saying he had "got the message" and would be more attentive to their concerns in the future. Now he was in the Loop to prove it.

The conversation went something like this: "Hi. I'm with Senator Percy. He'd like to join you for a minute and hear what's on your mind." Percy then joined the little group and said: "Hi. I'm Chuck Percy. I'm running for reelection and I'll be glad to answer any questions you've got. Anything at all. And just call me 'Chuck.'" An embarrassed silence followed. Percy tried again. "Anything. Anything at all." The lunchtimers stared at each other and at their uninvited guest. Finally one said: "So, Chuck. Did they ever catch that guy who murdered your daughter?"

Stunned silence greeted the question about the notorious nighttime attack years before on one of the senator's twin daughters at his home in a Chicago suburb. Percy, gaining his composure, gave an unmemorable reply and quickly headed for the nearest exit. It was not, to be sure, funny, but it emphatically demonstrated the peril that politicians eager for votes face in soliciting questions too insistently. Some moments on the campaign trail are readily forgotten. That one never was, as Wilkie, Neal, and I always recalled it on meeting thereafter.

All in all, the 1984 campaign was nothing to write home about, but that didn't stop Germond and me from doing a book about it, this one called *Wake Us When It's Over,* a stupid title meant to convey an electorate lulled by Reagan's hypnotic effect. Instead, it seemed to suggest that the authors were so bored that the campaign was hardly worth reading about. It wasn't the title we wanted and not the one we proposed to our publisher. We wanted to call the book *Feeling No Pain,* to get across the notion that Reagan had so anesthetized the voters with his charm and conservative platitudes that Mondale had no chance. Our editors at Macmillan insisted that "feeling no pain" could only mean being drunk, and readers would not get what we were driving at! We finally relented, to our everlasting regret.

The book nevertheless demonstrated the advantage of going back to sources after an election, when they are willing to turn loose information and material they are not about to release during the campaign, lest they benefit the opposition. Once Reagan's horse was safely in the barn, we were able to get hold of a couple of internal memos that were instructive about the mind sets and strategies in each camp.

One, by Reagan strategists Lee Atwater and Stu Spencer and dubbed "The Great American Fog Machine," was written after a poor showing by

Reagan in his first debate with Mondale. "If it's clear that the President did badly," the memo said, "then it's our job to obscure the result. The single most important mission of the fog machine will be to shift the emphasis to Mondale, and to drive up his negative rating." The memo went on in great detail about how this would be done. It included a recommendation that the secretaries of state and defense be put on the campaign stump, in disregard of the longstanding tradition against politicking by them; and it specifically observed: "We should not hesitate to violate protocols by enlisting top Pentagon brass to help."

If the second debate didn't go well, the memo said, the Reagan camp could alibi that "debates can be and frequently are misleading and deceptive; winning a debate often depends more upon an effective 'cheap shot' than anything else." This from a campaign whose candidate in 1980 had demolished Jimmy Carter with his "Are you better off" question, and who would in the second 1984 debate wipe out the age issue by joking that he had no intention of using Mondale's age and inexperience against him.

The Mondale campaign also coughed up a memo after the election that shed interesting light on its debate plan. Written by strategist Pat Caddell, it proposed that Mondale use the age issue forcefully but deftly to undercut Reagan. "From the outset we must recognize that our electoral position requires not just a decisive victory but a knockout. Debate I served to loosen Reagan's political grip; Debate II must break it. The opening we were given was age. . . . The Mondale strategic imperative must be to ignite the age concern to a salient firestorm. . . . The overriding objective of this debate must be to 'break' Reagan—hurt him on age, on his lack of knowledge, on his grasp of issues. Mondale must not simply beat Reagan, he must take him apart."

Part of that effort, Caddell wrote, was to "disorient" Reagan and to suggest that he was out of it, with such rhetorical devices as "Mr. President, I don't think you understand. . . . I think you missed the point. . . . I think you are confused. . . . You've got your facts mixed up. . . ." etc. Caddell also urged Mondale to move physically toward Reagan to demonstrate his confidence and possibly unnerve the incumbent. But all this advice eventually was undone by the old movie actor when he memorably said: "I will not make age an issue in this campaign. I am not going to exploit, for political purposes, my opponent's youth and inexperience." Mondale told us later that when he heard that remark, "I knew I had lost the election."

Sifting through the ashes of a completed campaign also confirmed a bit of internal larceny by the Mondale operation that might have damaged it had it been known at the time, and had Mondale's chances not already been nearly extinct. His campaign had come upon a new dodge for beating campaign finance reform restrictions by putting money into "delegate committees"—supposedly independent paper organizations funding the election of delegates, as opposed to the candidates they supported.

It so happened, I learned after the election, that a Mondale worker in Philadelphia had been found efficiently if injudiciously keeping a written record of delegate-committee money coming illegally into the Pennsylvania campaign for Mondale. A Washington operative of the campaign thereupon was dispatched to Philadelphia, where he stole the offending notebook from the campaign's own state headquarters! I hustled to the Quaker City shortly after the campaign and confronted then District Attorney Ed Rendell, who had headed the Mondale campaign in the state, with what I had learned. He told me he had been furious when he learned of the intramural theft and demanded the notebook be returned the very next morning after it had been taken, and it was. Rendell later became chairman of the Democratic National Committee and in 2002 was elected governor of Pennsylvania. This little episode of inside baseball was stretched into two chapters of our 1984 campaign book, which may have been another reason readers interpreted the title as an invitation for them to yawn along with the authors.

No sooner was the 1984 election over than the political horses were out on the track again for 1988. I knew as early as March of 1985 that the next four years would be unusual when I was suddenly confronted with an opportunity to say something good about my favorite whipping boy, Dick Nixon. I was moved on that occasion to write: "Beating a dead horse stops being fun after a while, and so it's a welcome change to be able to say former President Richard M. Nixon is right for a change. . . . To give the devil his due, he is right in saying it costs taxpayers entirely too much to provide security for former presidents. And his decision to give up the costly Secret Service protection is a welcome surprise. That Nixon now has plenty of money to provide his own security does not take away from the gesture." In the previous year, Nixon's security had cost Uncle Sam about $12.6 million, and I wrote that "maybe Nixon's gesture will grease the way for Congress to take action in this area." It didn't.

In any event, I commended Nixon in the full knowledge that I surely would have other opportunities to rap him in the future, and I wasn't wrong about that. A year later, he popped up again on the cover of *Newsweek* with an interview in which he claimed resurrection and minimized his Watergate cover-up and other crimes by quoting Winston Churchill. "His study of history," the Rocky Balboa of American politics said with customary humility, "showed that great leaders often stumble on little things [rather] than on big things." On that occasion, I wrote in our column: "Of his own resurrection, he says that 'people see me and they think, he's risen from the dead.' He's right. The one time he was wrong was back in 1962, at that 'last press conference,' when he said, 'You won't have Nixon to kick around anymore.' Fat chance."

Sure enough, several months later Nixon showed up at a conference of Republican governors in Parsippany, New Jersey, near his East Coast abode at Upper Saddle River. He told them that the Iran-contra fiasco that was then enveloping President Reagan should be regarded as a "sideshow," and that critics should "get off his back" so he could continue to work for world peace. Like Nixon's own Watergate disaster, some sideshow.

Meanwhile, back on the political track, among the horses expected to run again in 1988 was Ted Kennedy, but he announced in late December of 1985 that for family reasons he would not. Hart, who had been trailing Kennedy, 31 percent to 45, in a Gallup Poll in July, immediately moved into frontrunner status in Democratic ranks, fanning speculation that others, like Governor Mario Cuomo of New York and Senator Joe Biden of Delaware, might now join the competition.

Hart had already been undergoing heavy scrutiny as a result of the questions raised about him—his age and his name change, from Hartpence—in his strong 1984 bid. Asked again about them around this time at a gathering of our facetiously named dinner group, Political Writers for a Democratic Society, Hart with some exasperation complained to us: "Nobody cares about all that except the press. I go all over the country and nobody ever asks me about those things except you." They had been beaten to death, he said, and weren't going to be a problem for him in the 1988 race unless we continued to hound him about them.

There were about ten of us there at Bob Healy's apartment in Washington and we knew Hart well, going back to the 1972 McGovern campaign. We all knew about the ups and downs of his marriage to Lee and so he was pressed that same night about its state. He said only that he "expected" still to be married to Lee in 1988. There had been rumors of womanizing but nobody confronted him directly about them, choosing instead the more delicate approach of inquiring about his marriage. Perhaps we were too old-school to hit him between the eyes, but the fact was we played by the standard that rumors were only rumors until proved otherwise, which I still feel is the proper yardstick for inquiry, or certainly for publication. This was so even though during the 1984 campaign some female reporters had confided in the back of the press bus that Hart had tried to romance them. But none of them was ever willing to go public with an accusation—or boast.

Over the next year and more, Hart worked diligently at strengthening his credentials as an expert on defense and foreign policy, traveling abroad often. I remember one afternoon in February of 1987 listening to him wowing about fifty New Hampshire voters in the living room of Don and Judy Schultz, in the town of Exeter, with his account of a long conversation with Mikhail Gorbachev in the Kremlin. He told of the Soviet leader's incredulity over what he saw as President Ronald Reagan's inept and uninformed discussion of nuclear arms control at their summit meeting in Reykjavik. Hart was no longer the longshot refugee from the 1972 McGovern campaign; it was not so hard to see him now as a president.

After a few more stops on the way to Boston, Hart and his young sidekick Billy Shore joined two other reporters and me for dinner at Anthony's Pier 4 restaurant, a favorite Democratic hangout in Boston Harbor. It started out as an easy social occasion and the candidate was relaxed, telling us about his recent first encounter with Nixon at a memorial service for the late Senator Jacob K. Javits of New York. Nixon, sitting next to him in the church pew, Hart recalled, kept tapping him on his knee and giving him tips on how to win the Democratic presidential nomination. He did a fair imitation of Nixon, who was dead serious all the while.

The dinner conversation, however, in time turned to Hart's own ideas about his campaign, and once again he was asked, in general terms with no reference to womanizing, what he intended to do about "the character issue." Limiting himself to the old questions about his age and his name change, he responded irritably again: "You're the only ones who ever ask me about those things. I go all over and nobody ever asks me." He said again he had nothing to hide, and when dinner was over he and Shore departed, leaving an edgy feeling around the table.

As soon as Hart formally declared his candidacy in April of 1987, however, the cat was out of the bag on the womanizing rumors. On Hart's very first campaign flight from Denver, a woman reporter told him of such rumors being floated by the Biden and Dukakis campaigns, and Hart made the mistake of relaying the report to reporters traveling with him. Thereafter the rumors haunted his every campaign event.

The whole business came to a head shortly afterward, one morning as I was on the Washington Metro en route to National Airport and New Hampshire to cover, of all things, a presidential exploration by Alexander Haig. I opened the *Washington Post* and read of the *Miami Herald*'s stakeout of Hart's Capitol Hill apartment, during which one Donna Rice was seen leaving with the candidate. I didn't wait to read all the details; I got off the Metro at the next stop and headed back into town to play catch-up on this story, which obviously was going to push everything else involving politics onto a far back burner.

At the *Sun* bureau I learned that Hart had canceled an event in New Jersey and was in Washington preparing for a speech the next day in New York before the American Newspaper Publishers Association that suddenly had taken on much greater importance. I hopped on the Metroliner to catch the event and to stick with Hart thereafter, anticipating that this story was not going to die down for quite a while. I needed no crystal ball for that observation.

Hart's appearance before the publishers was both defensive and accusatory of the *Herald* for publishing "a misleading and false story that hurt my family and other innocent people and reflected badly on my character." Present in the press gang was Tom Fiedler, the esteemed political reporter for the paper. In the hall outside the ANPA meeting after Hart's speech, Fiedler was mobbed for more details by the rest of us. It was an indication of how the press itself had become an integral part of this sensational political story. That night, I attended a Hart fund raiser at which he cast his campaign as a "crusade" that unnamed foes were trying to sabotage. "It doesn't matter if the leader is struck down in battle or with a knife in the back," he said, "because the cause goes on and the crusade continues." Donna Rice was not mentioned.

The next morning I boarded the Hart press plane to Hanover, New Hampshire, where Hart decided to face the music in a full-blown news conference at the Hanover Inn on the Dartmouth campus. My seatmate was

Paul Taylor, a sharp young reporter for the *Washington Post* who was soon to play a memorable role in the unfolding drama. Lee Hart by now had flown from Denver to join her husband in a show of solidarity.

Joe Trippi, a young Hart campaign worker in the West who accompanied Lee, told me later of her scheme of how best to handle the situation. She proposed that Hart go alone into the press conference but to say he had just learned she had arrived and was waiting for him in a room upstairs, and he would be right back. Then she would take her makeup kit and paint a black eye on her husband, whereupon he would return to the awaiting reporters and proclaim: "She loves me!" Then she would rush into the press conference and give him a big hug. But on arrival, Trippi said, when he called the campaign's resident wise men in Denver and told them of the idea, they were appalled. Before he could so inform Lee, he said, he had to get to the press conference and didn't know whether the black-eye caper would occur. It didn't, and to Trippi's relief Hart came into the room without the phony shiner.

The atmosphere in the room was electric with anticipation, and it built during what was the most tense and personally inquisitional encounter between a presidential candidate and reporters I ever witnessed. A few minutes earlier, I was told later, Hart's young press secretary, Kevin Sweeney, had held a brief prep session with the candidate, asking him likely questions, including whether he had ever had extramarital affairs in the past. Hart said then he didn't have to answer such a question. But at the press conference, after several inquiries about the stakeout at his apartment, Taylor asked him directly: "Have you ever committed adultery?" Hart responded, "I do not think that's a fair question" and proceeded to dance around the definition of the word and subsequent pointed inquiries.

Hart concluded with a plea for fairness and pressed on to the next event, where the crush of reporters and other assorted curious onlookers made clear to him he could not continue. The decision was confirmed when Taylor later that night informed Sweeney that the *Post* had an account of Hart's involvement with another woman and wanted to confront the candidate with it before possible publication.

The next morning, we all piled into the press bus and arrived at a plant gate in the town of Groveton, expecting to see Hart there. Instead, Sweeney and Trippi stood on a park bench and handed us a statement saying that the Harts were returning to Denver for a few days or weeks but that "this campaign will continue and our cause will succeed." But the next day in Denver, Hart bowed out, with another blast at the press and the political process itself. It was not his finest hour; in a way it was not unlike Dick Nixon's infamous 1962 "last press conference." And like Nixon then, Hart in time would turn up again on the presidential campaign trail, but not with the same result at all.

When Hart did get back into the race briefly in 1988, his appearance only resurrected the old questions, and his hopes that he could deliver his message were quickly dashed. After Michael Dukakis won the Democratic nomination, he also was plagued with all manner of smarmy rumors and attacks. They ranged from reports of psychiatric treatment for depression like the ones that undid Eagleton in 1972, to the famed Willie Horton ads that played on Dukakis's prisoner release program as governor, in which the convicted murderer had raped a woman while out on a weekend furlough.

All this was enough to do in Dukakis and put Reagan's vice president, George H. W. Bush, in the Oval Office. It also provided fodder for Germond and me for another campaign book, this one called *Whose Broad Stripes and Bright Stars?* in recognition of the phony struggle between Bush and Dukakis over which of them was more patriotic and flag loving. The Bush campaign hammered at Dukakis's gubernatorial veto of legislation requiring recitation of the Pledge of Allegiance in Massachusetts public schools, recommended by his legal advisers on grounds it was unconstitutional. Bush buttressed this ridiculous attack by a visit to a flag factory in Bloomfield, New Jersey, in the waning days of the campaign. The title came to me and my son Paul one weekend as we sought one that would not backfire the way the imposed *Wake Us When It's Over* had four years earlier.

Once again, the book-writing imperative of going back to our sources after the campaign yielded a fortuitous result as far as publicity was concerned. A conspicuous highlight of the fall campaign had been Bush's startling selection of lightly regarded Senator Dan Quayle as his running mate. After the Bush-Quayle ticket was elected anyway, Germond and I called on one of our old friends, Joe Canzeri, who along with Stu Spencer had been assigned to shepherd the new vice-presidential nominee, wet behind the ears in national campaigning, through the gauntlet of public and press scrutiny. Quayle had proved in need of direction from the moment he appeared on the wharf in New Orleans where Bush had disclosed his choice. Quayle proceeded to hug his benefactor like a kid who had just been told he was getting a new two-wheel bike without training wheels, as Canzeri and Spencer watched via television in their hotel room. Canzeri told us later of Spencer's reaction: "Well, we gotta correct that."

Joe, and later Stu, also related in detail the task they had in making a presentable candidate out of Quayle, which we duly recounted in the book. As they told it, Spencer was immediately summoned to the suite of Jim Baker, the Bush campaign's mastermind, after which Spencer called Canzeri and told him: "Joey, get up and get your candidate." Canzeri picked up Quayle, accompanied by his Secret Service agent, and spirited him off to another hotel, for more privacy. "He seemed to be a decent guy," Joe recalled to us, but "there was a little fear in his eyes, I saw that. . . . We filled him in on what to expect and what was going to happen and so forth. He didn't really know what he was going to do, but he liked the idea that he had a bunch of keepers or handlers."

A fusillade of questions was about to break on Quayle concerning his service in the National Guard during the Vietnam war and suspicions that his father had pulled strings to get him into the Guard, and Canzeri and Spencer were available to advise him and keep him on a short leash. Joe later gave us the full chapter and verse on how it all went, including some dynamite quotes about Quayle, such as: "You take a guy out of the Golden Gloves and throw him in the ring with Joe Louis. He took a few big hits. They weren't knockout punches but they were close to it. Then we had to take him back and do the roadwork and teach him how to box. . . . We knew we were going to have to script him." Once, when an irritable Quayle was left on his own in a speech before the City Club of Chicago and screwed up, Canzeri phoned Spencer, who was traveling with Quayle, and asked him why he had let the candidate do it. Spencer replied in his characteristically gruff way: "I want him to step on his dick, and then we'll own him again."

But the handling didn't always work, Canzeri pointed out. In preparation for Quayle's debate with Democratic vice-presidential nominee Lloyd Bentsen, he recalled, the candidate's wife, Marilyn, pushed the idea of noting that her husband had more political experience than John Kennedy did when he ran for president. But other advisers told him not to mention it. Yet, in talking about his own qualifications in the debate, Quayle observed: "I have as much experience in Congress as Jack Kennedy did when he sought the presidency." Bentsen promptly pounced, with the retort that ever after haunted Quayle: "Senator, I served with Jack Kennedy. I knew Jack

Kennedy. Jack Kennedy was a friend of mine. Senator, you are no Jack Kennedy."

With our tape recorder spinning, Canzeri also observed that Quayle had "an impatience of youth. . . . If he's interested he's interested, if he's not he's not. It's that immaturity and lack of attention. If he doesn't like it, he goes away from it. . . . He was like a kid. Ask him to turn off a light, and by the time he gets to the switch, he's forgotten what he went for."

Knowing we had hit gold, Jack and I thanked Canzeri and hustled out of his office. We sat for a moment on the steps outside, checking our notes and making sure the tape recorder had captured it all, ourselves like two giddy kids who had just filched a couple of Hershey bars from the corner candy store. A day or so later, I called Spencer, also an old friend and source, for his take on Quayle. Subsequently he told me with mock dismay: "As soon as you started, I knew you had us. I knew you had talked to Joey."

When the book came out in the spring of 1989, it was our good fortune that President Bush had a copy on Air Force One as he was flying to and from Europe. A pool reporter asked him about the quotes on Quayle and he proceeded to wave the book before television cameras on the plane, denouncing Germond and me for what we had written about Danny. We couldn't prove it, but we suspected that Bush's outburst provided the boost that lifted the book to Number 1 on the *Washington Post* best-seller list the next week. When our good friends Sara and John Mashek gave us a book party, the vice president graciously came, then stood up and proclaimed: "I knew Teddy White. Teddy White was a friend of mine. And believe me, you guys are no Teddy White." Much later, in Bush's political biography, he acknowledged he had made a mistake in choosing Quayle, but when that book came out he insisted he had been misquoted or misunderstood.

The furor at the Republican convention in New Orleans over Dan Quayle provided a welcome smoke screen for a piece I wrote for the *Baltimore Evening Sun* demonstrating that George Bush wasn't the only one whose thinking about his vice-presidential selection was bizarre. Aware of how Bush was being counseled to do something that would show he was "his own man" stepping out of Reagan's shadow, I suggested that he pick the fellow Reagan had just chosen as his new attorney general, former Pennsylvania governor Dick Thornburgh.

I conjured up the picture of a reporter asking Bush: "What does President Reagan think of your taking away the man he has just put in charge of his Justice Department?" To which the newly independent Bush would reply: "I don't know. I didn't ask him." It seemed to me like a good idea at the time—at least as good as tapping Dan Quayle for the job. So much for the folly of a reporter offering advice in print to a presidential nominee. Once again, on this subject there was a disagreement between Richard Nixon and me. The former president, after meeting with Quayle, gave him a huge boost—in his fashion—by saying he did not share the view of those who said Dan was, as Nixon delicately put it, "an intellectual midget."

In any event, Bush survived the Quayle furor and was elected, probably not so much for demonstrating he was independent of Reagan as for a general assumption that electing him was the next best thing to a third Reagan term. We were told by a key Bush aide, Peter Teeley, that his boss was not thrilled by what we had written about him in our column during the campaign and that he was declining our request for an in-person interview. But he did respond expansively to written questions we submitted for our book.

On that note, we embarked on reporting about what we never dreamed at the time would eventually come to be known as the presidency of the first George Bush.

16 Tracking Quayle and Clinton

As afternoon newspapers gradually disappeared in an era dominated by television, when workers came home to the tube rather than to their local sheet and the radio, the *Baltimore Evening Sun* was holding on. The underdog spirit of the staff kept it aggressive and lively in a way that would have given its most distinguished if sassy alumnus, H. L. Mencken, cause to rejoice. But with the closing of the rival *Baltimore News American* in 1986, it seemed a matter of time before the *Evening Sun* too would set. In the meantime, Germond and I persevered with the much-cherished independence bestowed on us by the Sunpapers editors, examining the ins and outs of the new Bush administration.

I spent a fair amount of time during this period on a Quayle "gaffe watch" —keeping an eye and ear glued to the new vice president's comings, goings, and sayings to see whether he would finally emerge from his reputation as a lightweight. For months at a time—including a trip to Eastern Europe on which I accompanied him on Air Force Two—he managed to avoid any serious missteps or misstatements. But on occasion he would slip, as when in El Salvador he declared that the United States was committed to "work toward the elimination of human rights" in the region, or when in the Pacific he called the exotic locale "Pogo Pogo." He also described the big San Francisco earthquake as "heart-rendering," not to mention his help to a spelling bee contestant on, as he put it, "p-o-t-a-t-o-e." All this lent a degree of levity to the Quayle chapter in *Crapshoot: Rolling the Dice on the Vice Presidency,* a book I did around this time, inspired in part by him.

President Bush, meanwhile, enjoyed a distinct high point in early 1991, heading a broad international coalition that drove the forces of Iraqi dictator Saddam Hussein out of Kuwait. But thereafter a seeming neglect of, or disinterest in, a deep economic downturn at home bred public disaffection. A flip-flop on his convention acceptance speech pledge of "no new taxes" led many in the conservative faithful to abandon him. They may have voted for a third Reagan term but they felt they weren't getting it.

In early 1992, Quayle was dispatched to New Hampshire to assure the locals, hard hit by recession, that Bush had not forgotten them, and I went along to see how he handled the task. His message was received coolly, because they felt that the president should have brought it himself, especially after they had been instrumental in the 1988 primary in getting his presidential campaign on track. When Bush finally did come, he woodenly—and incredibly—read from a cue card that said "Message: I care."

The 1992 New Hampshire primary presented a new experience for me— seeing a longtime personal friend and sometimes fellow radio commentator, Pat Buchanan, running for the lofty office of president of the United States. I went to the state capital, Concord, to watch and listen to him declare his candidacy, and I looked in on him from time to time over the next few months as he threw a scare into Bush. On primary day, when early-afternoon exit polls showed Buchanan running even with Bush, euphoria struck the challenger's camp and panic hit the incumbent's strategists. Although Bush finally won 57 percent of the primary vote to 37 for Buchanan, the old Nixon speechwriter was exuberant at a "victory party" that had the Sheraton Wayfarer jumping. (Among the customers at the bar was Gene McCarthy, recalling his own celebration in the same hotel twenty-four years earlier after his historic moral victory over Lyndon Johnson.)

The more significant, and dramatic, story in New Hampshire then, however, was in the Democratic presidential primary. A year-long saga about womanizing by Arkansas governor Bill Clinton and other assorted political headaches for him had surfaced in mid-January. I happened to be at the Sheraton Tara in Nashua with Wilkie when Clinton arrived for a conference on health care. He was surrounded by reporters asking him about a story in the national tabloid *Star* concerning an old Arkansas lawsuit containing allegations of sexual hanky-panky against him. Clinton dismissed it as "old news" and "totally bogus" and went on his way, seemingly unruffled.

But the genie was out of the bottle. In a subsequent televised debate among the Democratic candidates, moderator Cokie Roberts asked him about concerns in the party that "allegations of womanizing" could cost him the women's vote. He blamed the talk on the Republicans. But a few days later back in New Hampshire the roof fell in on him. One morning I was in the lobby of the Center of New Hampshire, the Holiday Inn in Manchester, about to set off on a day's campaigning with Clinton, when an ABC News producer, Mark Halperin, took him aside and told him something. Clinton went up to his room, resulting in a late start for the day, nothing unusual for him, so those of us going with him thought little of it at the time.

Halperin had informed him about another, more damaging story about to appear in the same tabloid, a first-person account by a Little Rock singer named Gennifer Flowers headlined "They Made Love All Over Her Apartment." Clinton decided to go on with the day's campaigning, and we reporters piled into press vans and headed for Claremont, on the western side of the state.

It was miserable weather that got gloomier as the day wore on. The press vans arrived at a paint brush manufacturing plant before Clinton did. By this time, some photocopies of the story were being handed around among us, and the candidate on arrival was trapped in the plant's entry way and bombarded with questions. "The story is not accurate, the story is just not true," he insisted, accusing Flowers of taking money for it. He admitted he had received calls of distress from her but said he had told her "to just tell the truth."

Surprisingly, Clinton then went on the scheduled plant tour, delivering his standard stump speech to the employees before quickly disappearing up a set of stairs to the plant's offices, with aides George Stephanopoulos and Paul Begala close behind. We reporters were left below trying to decide what to do with the story and queuing up at the lone pay phone to contact our editors. For once, the circumstances left no room for discussion about whether it was proper to pursue such a story broken by what our mainstream business regularly dismissed as the "gossip" or "supermarket" press. A development had interrupted a presidential candidate's campaign; that was a fact. Failure to report it would be a cover-up at the least.

The decision to file the story was made easier by the fact that Clinton aides began distributing a copy of a year-old letter, faxed to the Claremont factory by the campaign headquarters, from Flowers' lawyer to a Little Rock radio station. It charged that one of its talk show hosts had "wrongfully and untruthfully alleged an affair" between his client and Clinton. This exercise in damage control by the Clinton campaign had to be reported along with the candidate's denial.

Most newspapers, including my own, played the story prominently the next day, though the *New York Times* ran only eight inches and relegated it to an inside page. But the prime television station in New Hampshire, WMUR in Manchester, showed the fiasco in Claremont on its late evening news show. ABC News, whose diligence had forced the story out, surprisingly didn't report it on its evening news. The network chose instead to back into it by using it as the basis for an analysis of news ethics later on its showcase *Nightline* program.

Clinton and entourage halted campaigning and retreated to Little Rock to brainstorm the next move. The upshot was acceptance of an invitation to the Clintons to appear the coming Sunday night on *Sixty Minutes*, right after the Super Bowl, before an estimated audience of 34 million viewers. On the show, Clinton again denied a relationship with Flowers and went only so far as to say he had been responsible for unspecified "wrongdoing," and for "causing pain in my marriage." Wife Hillary Clinton stood by him.

Back in New Hampshire shortly afterward, Clinton walked into the lobby of the Sheraton Tara in Nashua another morning and was confronted by a press mob asking him about a story in that day's *Wall Street Journal*. A retired army recruiter was quoted as saying that Clinton in 1969 had signed up for the ROTC program at the University of Arkansas Law School to avoid the draft, and was then "able to manipulate things so that he didn't have to go in" during the Vietnam war. ABC News soon got hold of a letter Clinton had written to the recruiter thanking him "for saving me from the draft" and explaining he had finally subjected himself to it "to maintain my political viability within the system" with an eye to a future "political life." This time Clinton went on *Nightline* and explained that he had finally given up his deferment and entered the draft as an act of conscience, but drew a high lottery number and was never called up.

He thereupon plunged back into campaigning with even greater vigor and determination. One night Germond and I were riding with Clinton in his car as he was heading to WMUR for another television appearance. As we approached the station, housed in an old textile mill in downtown Manchester, we asked him point-blank whether there was anything more in his personal past that could surface and deepen his political problems. Sitting in the front seat next to the driver, he turned to us and said flatly he was certain there was not. All he could do now, he told us, was try to reach as many voters as he could and answer all questions posed to him. The answer was no surprise, but we felt we had to ask. We both had been around Clinton long enough to be aware of his penchant for dissembling. He spoke this reassurance with a conviction we would come to recognize was also part of his political arsenal.

Clinton and his strategists knew he was in trouble in New Hampshire, slipping in the polls against the regional favorite, Senator Paul Tsongas of neighboring Massachusetts. They concocted an approach that cast him as the underdog, and when he finished a fairly distant second to Tsongas in the primary—33 percent to 25, but well ahead of Nebraska's Senator Bob Kerrey at 11—he proclaimed himself on primary night to be "The Comeback Kid." Thus both Clinton on the Democratic side and Buchanan on the Republican were claiming victories not borne out by the numbers. Buchanan plodded on through the California primary in June as a lost cause, but Clinton used his second-place finish somehow to propel himself back into the thick of the Democratic race. His superior talent as a campaigner carried him through in a relatively weak field that also included Senator Tom Harkin of Iowa, labor's favorite, and Jerry Brown, more an irritant now than a threat.

Clinton's political talent was a mixture of knowledgeable elucidation of the issues and old-fashioned schmoozing. For me, it was pointedly illustrated during the Michigan primary when I watched and heard him operate one afternoon in Macomb County, celebrated home of "the Reagan Democrats," and then the next morning before a black congregation in Detroit. First he went to the nearly lily-white middle-class suburbs where Reagan had reigned, just north of heavily black Detroit, and pleaded for racial harmony and conciliation. "I do not believe we have any hope of doing what we have to do in America," he said at Macomb County Community College, "unless we come together across racial lines again. This is a crisis of economic values. It has nothing to do with race." Somebody, he said, had to tell the Reagan Democrats, "Look, I'll give you your values back, but you've got to say, 'Okay, let's do it with everybody in this country.'" The crowd responded warmly.

The next morning Clinton went to the Pleasant Grove Baptist Church in Detroit and repeated basically the same message he had given the Reagan Democrats. But he added: "I come here to challenge you to reach out your hand to them, for we have been divided for too long. . . . Tell the people of Macomb County, 'If you'll give up your race feelings, we'll say we want empowerment, not entitlement; we want opportunity but we accept responsibility; we're going to help be a part of the change.'"

The message was that if the lily-whites in Reagan country would lay off their racial biases, and if the blacks in Detroit would eschew handouts, grasp new opportunities, and be responsible for their own lives, everybody would be better off. On primary night, Clinton walked off with the Reagan Democrats, who had defected from the party for eight years, and got a heavy black vote in Detroit as well, fashioning a 51 percent majority in Michigan.

With Clinton moving steadily toward nomination and Bush doing the same on the Republican side, their quests were being complicated by a wild card in the person of a Texas gadfly named Ross Perot. Though distinctly short in the saddle, the little man with ego and ambition as big as all outdoors had gone on the Larry King television show and launched a crusade of the politically disaffected into a self-created "draft" that he pledged to answer and finance if sufficiently urged.

Perot's surge induced me to make a pilgrimage to Dallas before the Democratic convention, for an interview with the man who was taking it upon himself to save the country for his only "bosses," the American people. I called on him, after excessive preliminaries, at his office, which was replete with Remington sculptures of cowboys, bucking broncos, and other reproductions of life in the Wild West, and found him to be a living extension of all that. He guardedly suffered my intrusion and all I got for the effort was a regurgitation of the boiler-plate I had already heard in his Larry King appearances. He sounded like a man determined to fight to the finish for his "bosses," so I was surprised along with everyone else when, in the midst of the Democratic convention in New York, he bugged out of the race, on the mystifying grounds that the Democrats had suddenly gotten their act together.

Later he argued ridiculously that vague harassments of his second daughter's wedding by the Republicans had forced his hand. This nonsense led us to write in our column from the convention: "If Ross Perot were Pinocchio, his nose would be growing all the way from Dallas to here after the whopper he unleashed on the country to explain why he was leaving millions of dedicated volunteers in the lurch."

That bombshell overshadowed all else at the convention, but Clinton quickly regained the story line with an innovative and entertaining campaign novelty. He and his choice of a running mate, fellow southerner Al Gore of Tennessee, left directly from the convention on a highly publicized bus tour of the Midwest, the first of several, that captured the news media spotlight and held it for weeks. It was the brainchild of a couple of Democratic staffers, Steve Rosenthal of the Democratic National Committee and Carter Wilkie, a young Clinton aide in Indiana and son of my traveling press companion, Curtis Wilkie. Young Wilkie touted the notion that local reporters whose small news organizations could not afford the expensive jet-planing of national entourages would use the bus tour to get a taste of being "the boys on the bus" as the tour moved through their bailiwicks. A Clinton volunteer, Mort Engelberg, a successful Hollywood producer with such films as *Smokey and the Bandit* under his belt who advanced Democratic campaigns for the fun of it, chimed in with the same notion. I went along for parts of the ride.

The exercise proved to be a serendipitous bonding of Clinton and Gore, two strapping men of the same generation and similar political leanings. Each had his own bus, trailed by several press buses, and the candidates worked up a routine marked by levity, good cheer, and healthy doses of Republican-bashing before crowds that gathered in small towns and highway crossroads. Clinton's talents on the stump were well known, but Gore, with a reputation as a somber, super-serious stiff, was unveiled as the possessor of a dry humor and the timing to go with it.

Gore would warm up the crowd before introducing Clinton by intoning in mock high dudgeon: "Bush and Quayle have run out of ideas. They've run out of energy. They've run out of gas, and with your help come November, they're going to be run out of office!" He would conclude by shouting, "It's time for Bush and Quayle to go!" Then he would sternly inquire of the crowd, "What time is it?" And he would lead the mob in the roared reply: "It's time for them to go!"

Each time, Clinton would throw his large head back and laugh uproariously, as if he had been bowled over by his running mate for the first time. Then he would gesture toward Gore and say: "I made a pretty good decision, didn't I?" Sometimes, as he did at a stop in Wilmington, Ohio, he would add: "It would suit me for this election to be based on the first decision George Bush made [of Quayle as his running mate] and on the first decision I made." It was a not-so-subtle reminder of possible succession, and sometimes he would spell it out. But mostly he didn't break the mood of good fun that marked the dog-and-pony show at these campaign stops.

There was more than entertainment involved, however. Increasingly, these two good old boys would get together on Clinton's bus, talking politics and schmoozing by the hour, no matter how late it was. We reporters would be left by the roadside late into the night waiting for them to emerge. At Gore warm-ups beyond the witching hour, when he would ask the crowd, "What time is it?" weary voices from the press section would shout back: "It's time for us to go!" One night as we waited for another Clinton-Gore schmooze to end so we all could go to the appointed overnight hotel and get a few hours' sleep, aides started rocking Clinton's lead bus back and forth to shake them loose from their talkathon.

While Clinton and Gore no doubt strategized en route, heavy thinking was also going on back in Little Rock, at the Clinton headquarters in the ballyhooed "war room" directed by the frenetic but shrewd James Carville. I had first encountered this human skyrocket in Pennsylvania in 1991 when he and his sidekick Paul Begala orchestrated the upset Senate victory of Harris Wofford over former Republican governor and Reagan attorney general Richard Thornburgh in a special election. I decided now to break off from the campaign trail briefly to check out the Little Rock operation, and Carville put aside his frenzied tasks for a few moments to explain it to me. We talked within view of the famous instructional sign on the war room wall, only one third of which became famous: "Change vs. more of the same. The economy, stupid. Don't forget health care."

I had hoped also to see Paul Tully, the brilliant, energetic, and jovial brains of many other Democratic campaigns I had covered over the years, who was now camping out in Little Rock, giving twenty-five hours a day to the Clinton cause. But Paul was out of town that day, so I just left word that I was sorry I had missed him and would catch him the next time. Sadly, there was no next time, because shortly afterward, the full-speed-ahead Tully, after a big dinner and much good political talk with his campaign colleagues, turned in for the night and never woke up. Of all the hundreds of politicians Germond and I had encountered over the years, none was more knowledgeable nor more interesting and good-spirited in conveying his special insider's political code than the big-hearted old Yale football player, Paul Tully. When we wrote our 1992 campaign book, we naturally dedicated it to his memory.

While Clinton and Gore campaigned by bus in close fellowship, Bush and Quayle went their separate ways by design, which we all took as an acknowledgment that the head of the ticket wanted to put as much distance as possible between himself and the old spelling-bee champ. At the same time, Perot, apparently feeling his daughters were safe from Republican threats and having decided that the Democrats really hadn't been rehabilitated at all, jumped back into the race just in time to get a spot in the campaign debates with Bush and Clinton. But it was too little and too late for him. As for Bush, he was no match on his feet for Clinton. Aside from the substance of the debates, Bush's body English did him in. In the key debate in Richmond, the camera caught him glancing at his watch, as if he couldn't wait until it was over. Audible gasps went up in the press room as reporters glued to the television screens caught the damaging moment. It was also noticed with dismay, I was later told by Bush aides, in their staff viewing room.

In the final days, Bush favored the old campaigning stand-by of whistle-stopping by train, and that was entertaining, but not always intentionally. Late polling was suggesting that Clinton's sizable lead over Bush was shrinking, and as the incumbent president's adrenaline appeared to be pumping faster, his speech became zanier. In Macomb County, Michigan, he disjointedly needled Gore for his laments about the shrinking ozone layer and environmental threats of all sorts: "You know why I call him Ozone Man? This guy is so far off in the environmental extreme, we'll be up to our necks in owls and out of work for every American. This guy's crazy. He is way out, far out. Far out, man!"

In Columbus, Ohio, the next day, it was more of the same: "Governor Clinton and Ozone, all they do is talk of change." Charging Clinton with waffling on issues, Bush declared: "You cannot have a lot of buts sitting there in the Oval Office." Was that pun intentional? Who knew? It got laughs from the crowd as Bush delivered his lop-sided grin at the reaction. Later, he took to calling Clinton and Gore "bozos," leading aides to suggest privately to him that such language was not "presidential."

On the final weekend of the campaign, I was handed an unexpected local angle for the *Baltimore Sun*. Who had showed up in St. Louis to give Bush a totally unexpected endorsement but Democratic governor William Donald Schaefer of Maryland, at war with his own party at home. It was particularly surprising in that solidly Democratic Maryland was a shoo-in for Clinton, but at this point Bush was happy to get help from whatever quarter.

On October 31—Halloween—I hopped aboard Bush's last whistle-stop train, through Wisconsin on an old freight line, obviously chosen as a magnet for the television cameras. Bush, buoyed by the train ride and large depot crowds, geared his pitch to the occasion, in his fashion. "Today is Halloween, our opponents' favorite holiday," he proclaimed. "They're literally trying to scare America." If Clinton was elected, he said, "every day is going to be Halloween. Fright and terror!" In Oshkosh, he repeated the warning, ending with: "Fright and terror! Witches and devils everywhere!" This from the president of the United States. But as the train stopped in Burlington, a single-propeller plane flew over trailing a sign that said: "Iran-contra haunts you."

By the Stevens Point stop, Bush was dismissing as "part of a Democratic witch hunt" a new indictment of his secretary of defense, Caspar Weinberger, for false testimony in the Iran-contra affair. But at the same time he was clearly enjoying the hoopla. Mary Matalin, one of his longtime aides on the trip, told me about a local radio reporter, shuttled in for a quick interview, who asked Bush how he felt about the big turnout. Bush, she said, beamed and answered: "Great! I've only been mooned once!"

After the election, in connection with writing our 1992 campaign book, I tracked down the three voters in the Richmond area who had questioned the candidates most sharply in the critical second debate. They all agreed they had been impressed by Clinton and were surprised at how inept the president of the United States had seemed. For all the personal hurdles that Clinton had to overcome, his ability to think and talk on his feet more than compensated in the clutch, especially against an incumbent president who failed to convey a sufficient depth of concern about the problems of average Americans in hard economic times.

As the election year ended, I had to take some personal stock of my own. The hurly-burly of covering national politics had taken a toll on my life. After the 1988 campaign, Marian and I had decided in an amicable fashion to separate after thirty-six years of marriage in which my work absences did not help. In this time she had completed a successful career as a much-admired and revered grade-school teacher and had returned to journalism as an esteemed editor of business newsletters. Our children, Paul, Amy, and Julie, were all grown, successfully through college and on their own. Paul, a graduate of William and Mary, was now a budding fantasy-fiction writer and editor in New York, about to publish his first, and well-received, novel. Amy, a graduate of Randolph-Macon College, was now a computer specialist, wife, and mother of our two grandchildren, Corin and Macey, in Yorktown, Virginia. And Julie, a graduate of Harvard and the Johns Hopkins School of Advanced International Studies, was working in Washington and visiting foreign lands assessing nutritional needs in the developing world. All of them were sources of great pride and satisfaction to us.

I moved from our comfortable home in the Northern Virginia suburb of Reston and into a small apartment in Washington. In 1991 we divorced, again amicably. At this time, I also became involved in the adoption of an infant boy from Bulgaria, Peter, who has remained a close and equally cherished part of my family ever since. Meanwhile, I continued on the campaign trail, doing the daily column at the *Evening Sun* with my partner and writing political books as opportunity and interest dictated, at the dawn of the Bill Clinton era.

That era did not start as auspiciously as the Democrats had hoped. Instead of launching his presidency with some proposal that had wide public and congressional approval, such as his plan for volunteer national service, for some unfathomable reason he elected to push for protection against abuse of homosexuals in the military. The gay community itself was not particularly agitating for such action, but Clinton decided to press for it anyway. For a man who already was in bad odor within the military for his draft-dodging antics during the Vietnam war, this aggressive proposal was a formula for political disaster.

Senate Republican leader Bob Dole, a seriously wounded veteran of combat in Italy during World War II, observed bitingly that a man who had never shared a foxhole with anyone couldn't understand what this proposal would do to military morale. Advancing it deprived the new president of much of the honeymoon period that traditionally greets the new occupant of the Oval Office. A compromise, in a "don't ask, don't tell" policy, finally cooled off the controversy, but didn't do anything to help Clinton's tepid relationship with the military brass.

A second proclaimed objective, to appoint a cabinet that "looks like America," with diversity in race, ethnicity, and particularly gender, produced a chaotic and embarrassing search for females for top jobs. In Clinton's determination to appoint a woman as his attorney general, his first two choices bowed out as a result of having hired for domestic work immigrants who lacked proper papers or for whom Social Security payments were not made.

Clinton and his wife Hillary were also plagued from the start by a number of mini-scandals, including an attempted purge of the White House travel office staff to make way for cronies in the travel business in Arkansas. Such stories raised speculation about staff incompetence and personal image problems, to the point that Clinton brought in one of Washington's most prominent spin doctors, the ideologically ambidextrous David Gergen, to polish up the Clintons' public faces. I compared him in the column at the time to "the geography teacher job applicant" who when asked about the shape of the world replied he "could teach it round or flat."

The appointment of Gergen, a sometime newsmagazine editor and television commentator, gave me an opportunity to air one of my particular gripes—about political switch-hitters who not only can move from one party to another but also from the political world to journalism as if only a revolving door separated the two. "This should be an easy task for Gergen," I wrote, "who successfully transformed himself from propagandist not only for Reagan but also for Richard Nixon, Gerald Ford, and George Bush into a journalist, taking to the printed word and the television screen wrapped in the trapping of what is supposed to pass for objectivity in journalism these days." I noted that "having participated in the selling of the Ronald Reagan tax cuts and runaway deficits in that Republican administration," Gergen had "signed on with the gang that is pledged to roll back those policies."

I quoted his statement in a CNN interview at the time that "the lines between politics and journalism sometimes get a little blurred," without crediting himself with helping to blur them. He said he had to ask himself, regarding journalism and friendship with politicians, "Where does one start and the other stop." He never said whether he'd found that line. I wrote that Gergen and other professional switch-hitters certainly had the right to do whatever they could get away with, "including talking editors and television producers into giving them voices with which to put forward their partisan views in nonpartisan journalistic settings." I ended by ranting that "there was a simpler time when politicians functioned as politicians and journalists did their thing, which was to report on what politicians did, and you could tell one without a scorecard. But life is no longer so simple, any more than the world is flat."

But Clinton's biggest problems in his first two presidential years were beyond image repair by any spin doctor. Most serious was the effort of the new president and his policy-oriented wife to craft, largely behind closed doors, an ambitious plan of universal health care coverage. It ran into a buzz saw that not even an army of David Gergens could have blunted, and that plagued the Clintons into the next year. When our little dinner group had Hillary Clinton as our guest one night at the home of Judy Woodruff and Al Hunt, and she commented how she thought Gergen would improve the climate with the press, the guffaws around the table seemed to surprise her.

Then there were the old womanizing stories again, with reports that Arkansas state troopers were saying they had ferried Clinton to various trysts and observed others around the governor's mansion before he became a presidential candidate. A woman named Paula Jones brought suit against Clinton, charging that as governor he had propositioned her in 1991 at a Little Rock hotel. And under way were the beginnings of a marathon investigation into an old Arkansas land development deal known as Whitewater, in which the Clintons insisted they had taken a financial bath.

But the biggest threat to the president was a rival push for power by the Republican conservative ideologue, House Minority Whip Newt Gingrich. By focusing on Clinton personally and his early difficulties, Gingrich succeeded in "nationalizing" the off-year congressional elections of 1994 and achieving Republican control of the House for the first time in forty years. Gingrich and allies sold what they called their "Contract With America," an agenda of right-wing issues, to the voters. But Gingrich himself was a ticking time bomb of self-destruction. Even before he became House Speaker, he had elevated his talent for character assassination by saying on television that "up to a quarter of the [Clinton] White House staff when they first came in had used drugs in the last four or five years." His "proof" was something an unnamed "senior law-enforcement official" said was true, "in his judgment." It prompted us to write that in addition to implementing the "Contract," the House Republicans needed to "put a muzzle on" Gingrich.

They failed to do either one, and in so failing they overreached throughout 1995, making themselves vulnerable to a deft Clinton counterattack. At year's end they tried to trap him in a budget squeeze and he squeezed back, by permitting two government shutdowns that deprived Americans of desired services, for which Clinton successfully blamed Gingrich and the Republicans in Congress.

To help him recover his earlier public support, Clinton called on the services of a political consultant who had helped engineer an earlier comeback in Arkansas after the young governor had lost his first bid for reelection in 1980. The strategist, Dick Morris, had won a certain notoriety by working both sides of the political street, having also counseled the likes of Republican senator Trent Lott. He persuaded Clinton to raise money for an extensive television advertising campaign that helped restore his popularity in advance of a 1996 reelection bid that now seemed much more hopeful than he could have imagined only two years earlier.

So Germond and I geared up for yet another campaign in the back of the bus. By now, though, many of the old faces there were gone—into retirement or to their ultimate reward. It was getting to be much less fun without them but we persevered, once more responding to the old firehouse bell, like a pair of aging nags conditioned to keep plodding around the political track.

17 The *Sun* | Endings and Beginnings

ON SEPTEMBER 15, 1995, ALL OF US on the *Evening Sun* were saddened when the bigwigs and green-eyeshade types decided to close down our locally oriented and venerable underdog newspaper. With the rival *News American* gone and the arithmetic of declining afternoon circulation dictating economies, the *Evening Sun* was put to bed for the last time. The paper went out with a good-humored bang. An eight-column banner bid farewell to Baltimore in humorous colloquial fashion. Using the famed vernacular of the city's always hospitable waitresses, and with a nod to the surviving a.m. *Sun*, it proclaimed: "GOOD NIGHT, HON; WILL YOU LOVE US IN THE MORNING?"

Thereafter our column was switched to the morning *Sun*, where we continued to enjoy a free hand under editor John Carroll, a man of quiet but decisive authority. When, in 2000, the *Chicago Tribune* bought the *Los Angeles Times* and the *Sun*, Carroll was transferred to Los Angeles as editor of the *Times*. Replacing him at the *Sun* was the similarly even-tempered Bill Marimow, who likewise left us on our own, welcoming our doing double duty as reporters as well as political columnists.

The death of the afternoon sheet proved to have more than professional significance for me. A few days before the *Evening Sun* went down for the last time, the Newseum, the museum of news in Arlington, Virginia, that was the brainchild of retired Gannett Newspapers' dynamo Al Neuharth, held a lunch that coincided with the paper's closing. Being one of the paper's two representatives in Washington, I decided to attend. The featured speaker was the program director at the Newseum, then researching a biography on the *Evening Sun*'s most famous and illustrious alumnus, the biting essayist and satirist, H. L. Mencken. Her name was Marion Elizabeth Rodgers. I had never heard of her, but she had my attention from her first word, and not only because she was a font of inside information on the great Mencken. She also was a striking brunette with a radiant smile and an unusually mellifluous voice with just a touch of some South American accent.

After her speech, I went up and asked her a question about a favorite quote of mine that I suspected was from Mencken, famously unwed for most of his life. It was the line that "a bachelor is a man who does not make the same mistake once." Ms. Rodgers smilingly said she didn't believe it came from Mencken. While I was at it, I told her I was writing a book about what was wrong with the way we selected our presidents (later published as *No Way to Pick a President*) and asked whether she knew of any good Mencken quotes that would be appropriate. She said she was sure there were some and would let me know if she came across any. I assumed she didn't, because I didn't hear from her—until seven months later.

Then one day a bulky package came in the mail with a host of clippings about Mencken and his prose. The rest, as they say, is history. We soon encountered each other at various Newseum functions, including the annual Robert F. Kennedy Journalism Awards. Nearly a year later we were married, in the garden of what became our home in Georgetown, by Martin Tornallyay, one of the Hungarian refugees I had helped resettle in Syracuse in 1956. My decision to show the *Evening Sun* flag at that farewell Mencken lunch at the Newseum turned out to be most serendipitous for me, as it has been ever since. Marion's biography, published by Oxford University Press, is called *Mencken, the American Iconoclast: The Life and Times of the Bad Boy of Baltimore.*

As the 1996 presidential campaign got under way, a new managing editor asked Germond and me to take on additional reporting duties for the paper beyond our regular column. Both of us having done so at the *Star* and the *Evening Sun*, we readily agreed. The increased workload led to another frenetic election year for us, but we reveled in it as in the past. Once again Jack took chief responsibility for covering the New Hampshire primary and I camped out in Iowa, with each of us occasionally working the other's side of the street to keep informed about the overall shape of the campaign.

In this particular cycle, however, I was obliged to leave Des Moines and Davenport behind for a short time to cover a departure in the usual delegate-selection calendar. Louisiana's Republicans decided to hold a sort of bootleg presidential caucus day in advance of the traditional Iowa kickoff. With such New Orleans eateries as Galatoire's, Antoine's, Brennan's, and Commander's Palace beckoning, it was a sacrifice I consented to without quarrel. As a bonus, my friend Curtis Wilkie was now based in The Big Easy for the *Boston Globe*—a coup in itself—and we were able to team up in working and eating our way through the new (and ultimately short-lived) Louisiana caucuses.

Iowa Republicans were outraged at the effrontery of their Louisiana cousins in stealing a march on their first-in-the-nation-caucus tradition, which always brought candidates, and free-spending newsgatherers, to their state. Making it worse as far as the Iowans were concerned, the planned Louisiana caucuses were in name only. As set up, they more resembled a primary, which by tradition was always first held in New Hampshire.

Iowa's Republican governor, Terry Branstad, tried to short-circuit the Louisiana caucus "steal" by calling on all the GOP presidential candidates to boycott it. All but three did—Senator Phil Gramm of Texas, television commentator Pat Buchanan, and conservative Alan Keyes, a defeated Maryland senatorial nominee. Gramm, running well behind Senator Bob Dole in Iowa, saw Louisiana as a chance for an early victory, inasmuch as he had won 72 percent of a straw poll at a state party convention there a year earlier. Buchanan had other ideas; by campaigning hard and with his customary bombast, he saw an opportunity to give Gramm a black eye and strengthen his own position on the party's right. I have no idea what Keyes was about, other than finding another road on his usual ego trip to nowhere. Although a Marylander, he was one "local angle" who was so outlandish that I never felt tempted to write much about him.

(Branstad, a boyish textbook conservative held in minimum high regard by the Iowa press corps, was the brunt of a memorable skit at the Iowa version of the Washington Gridiron dinner. In a spin-off of the old Johnny Carson routine of a great mind-reader, an Iowa reporter playing the seer was given the answer "Dolly Parton and Terry Branstad" and had to divine what the question was. The question, he replied, was: "Name three boobs." From the ensuing laughter, he clearly was judged to have gotten it right.)

Buchanan threw himself into the Louisiana "caucuses" with gusto, and Wilkie and I dutifully traipsed in his shadow on a couple of occasions. The caucuses were clearly a makeshift operation run like a state primary. There were no election-night gatherings of voters in private homes and church basements to discuss the issues and candidates, as in the Iowa caucuses. Instead, the Louisiana GOP hurriedly and haphazardly set up polling places in only forty-two sites across the state, resulting in a paltry turnout of 21,500 voters, only about 5 percent of the state's registered Republicans.

Wilkie and I dropped by one at a firehouse in New Orleans and it was a joke. The firemen sat around waiting for an alarm to sound as one or two lonely voters sauntered in and others gaped at the scene, more out of curiosity than interest in this latest innovation of democracy at work. Buchanan did indeed upset Gramm, sending the Texan's presidential aspirations down the drain. Only a few national reporters were on hand in Baton Rouge on election night, most others writing off the Louisiana event and staying in Des Moines. So Wilkie, these few other colleagues, and I had in the Gramm disaster what is known in our trade as "a technical exclusive"—one that nobody else bothered to go after. We also ate much better every night than did our brethren at Guido's in Des Moines.

On the heels of Buchanan's upset of Gramm in Louisiana, he came within three percentage points of beating Dole in Iowa and moved into New Hampshire with a full head of steam. There, memories were fresh among Republicans of the scare he had thrown into Bush in the 1992 primary. It seemed strange to me, after having sat across a microphone from Pat in our early radio shows, now to be sitting and interviewing him as an emerging serious candidate for the presidency.

On primary night, Buchanan scored another upset over Dole, and at a genuine victory party in Manchester he continued to cast his campaign as a crusade for the little guy, increasingly in militaristic terms. To his cheering troops, he played the field general, thundering: "Do not wait for orders from headquarters, everybody! Mount up and ride to the sound of the guns!"

Buchanan's success sent me winging out to Arizona, which he saw as his next opportunity. He bragged about igniting a "wildfire" among the independent-minded, often gun-toting descendants of the Old West. One Sunday he showed up at a gun show in Phoenix wearing a black cowboy hat and western string tie and hoisting a shotgun over his head, as assembled customers cheered wildly at his defense of the Second Amendment. The array of weaponry on display for sale at the show was truly staggering to a New Jersey boy like me who had never fired a gun in anger or in any other state. In the end, however, the bankroll of self-starting candidate Steve

Forbes, heir to the magazine empire, bought enough television advertising to overcome Buchanan's emotional appeal, and Forbes won the primary, dousing Pat's "wildfire" in Arizona.

But Dole the loyal party workhorse, who argued that it was his "turn," survived both Forbes and Buchanan. In nailing down the Republican nomination, he earned the right to take on President Clinton, who had sailed through his own party's primaries with no heavy lifting.

The end of the 1996 primary season brought a brief and welcome breathing spell for all of us on the campaign trail, but it was marked by a sad occasion for many of us in both print and television. My old friend, John Chancellor, called Jack by those who knew him best, was struck down by cancer and passed away in July, two days short of his 69th birthday. We were all aware of his struggle, and in fact many fellow reporters months earlier had attended a magnificent dinner in his honor at the University of Pennsylvania in Philadelphia at which the first John Chancellor Award was bestowed on a most worthy recipient, Bill Minor, a longtime chronicler of Deep South politics. In April, Walter Mears, who had authored a couple of books on the news business with Chancellor, and I drove up to Trenton to have what turned out to be a final lunch with him. In old reporter's fashion, we interviewed New Jersey governor Christie Whitman at the state capitol to cover our expenses and then had a long session of reminiscences with our old friend at a nearby pub. He was in good spirits and talked about enjoying his new surroundings in Princeton. That was the last time either of us saw him.

Chancellor, for all his success and fame as a television reporter and commentator, always had a warm spot in his heart for us print guys, out of his early experience as a city news service reporter in Chicago. Although ultimately ensconced in a New York television studio five nights a week, during campaigns he would often spend his free weekends on the campaign trail, just to soak up the atmosphere and to join us nightly in the best restaurants and bars at hand.

Self-effacing as he was, he confessed discomfort at the public recognition he drew on campaigns; it sometimes equaled that given the candidates he covered. Once, in Los Angeles, as a local politician was about to introduce the candidate, the pol turned to the press pen and drew the crowd's attention to what he called "a living legend" standing there among us grunts. Thereafter, Chancellor had to suffer often being addressed by his pals as

"Living Legend." On another occasion, in Portland, Maine, at a Gary Hart rally, a sweet young thing, looking in his direction, suddenly shouted: "There he is! The guy on television!" Thereupon she rushed toward him— and right past to a local television anchorman. Chancellor was reminded of that scene, too, more than once by his print cronies.

I wrote in a farewell column to him: "It is no secret that many newspapermen look down their noses at their television counterparts. Sometimes it may be out of envy of their celebrity and salaries. More often it is out of limited regard for the depth and breadth of their reporting. John Chancellor never engendered that attitude. Always he extended the same courtly friendliness toward his print colleagues as he did toward those in his own medium, and exhibited the highest integrity and ethics in his work and personal life." What I didn't write was that he was a great traveling and drinking companion who closed many a bar without ever showing the slightest sign of his prodigious alcoholic intake. He was a great philosopher of life and people, marked by gentleness and a wry sense of humor, and an endless source of wise counsel in all matters professional and personal.

The Democratic convention in Chicago, the first there since the riotous calamity in 1968, was a lavish affair for which Democratic mayor Richard M. Daley, son of the man who had set the city's police on demonstrators twenty-eight years earlier, pulled out all the stops. His brother, Bill, one of my best sources and oldest friends there, presided over a joyous welcoming party on the storied Navy Pier, but the convention itself was another coronation—a routine nomination of an incumbent president.

All went smoothly and it seemed there would be little out of the ordinary to write about. One day, our little reporters' dinner group met in the Marriott suite of Al Hunt of the *Wall Street Journal* and his wife, Judy Woodruff, of CNN for lunch. Our guest was Clinton political consultant Dick Morris, whose timely television ad campaign had played a major role in the president's resurrection after the 1994 debacle of the Gingrich revolution. Morris was riding high as the self-proclaimed architect of the strategy of "triangulation"—positioning Clinton between and above congressional Republicans on the right and Democrats on the left, out of the line of fire from each.

The lunch was a pleasant interlude marked by heavy doses of Morris's false modesty and his patronizing of the assembled senior political reporters. At one point, Morris excused himself from the large round table that had been wheeled into the suite and went into the bedroom to make a call. If we assumed the purpose was to convey some urgent advice to the president of the United States, that would have been all right with Morris, who was basking in the spotlight as one of the men who had put Clinton on the verge of a second term that earlier had been considered much in question.

It was only shortly later that word spread through the convention that Morris suddenly was out as Clinton's political swami. It turned out that he had been found to have engaged in certain indiscretions and sexual play with a prostitute. The most notorious were permitting the lady to listen in to phone conversations he was having with the president, and surrendering to what was described as a foot fetish. In retrospect we all wondered about that phone call during our lunch with him. Was it from Clinton or from the lady in question? We never found out, and Morris recovered sufficiently to have a book published that not surprisingly cast himself as the president's political savior. Eventually he became a newspaper columnist of sorts in yet another manifestation of the motto of certain other former political operatives: If you can't hoodwink 'em, join 'em.

Clinton easily survived the Morris embarrassment and won reelection against the overmatched Dole, one of the least-understood of major American political figures of the time. Reputed to be a mean-spirited man, a charge seemingly confirmed by occasional outbursts of anger as in his "Democrat wars" remark in his 1976 debate with Mondale, Dole in reality was a barrel of laughs most of the time. Nobody I ever encountered had a quicker wit, often aimed at others but also at himself.

One of his favorite targets was Nixon. Dole was chairman of the Republican National Committee during Watergate, and he always maintained that the break-in had occurred on his night off. One year when Dole was up for reelection, he was asked whether he wanted the beleaguered Nixon to campaign for him in Kansas. "I'd settle for a flyover in Air Force One," he cracked. My favorite Dole dig was when he was a guest at a dinner of the print journalists' Gridiron Club shortly after the assassination of Egyptian president Anwar Sadat. Noting that President Ronald Reagan had just appointed as his representatives at the funeral the three living former presidents, Jerry Ford, Jimmy Carter, and Nixon, Dole described them as "See no evil, speak no evil, and—evil."

In 1988, when the senior George Bush tapped Quayle as his running mate rather than Dole or his wife Elizabeth, both of whom were on the short list, Bush phoned him to explain and then asked to speak to Elizabeth. Dole told us later: "I think he was trying to save a dime. I said, 'No, I'll have her call you back.'" But he also never forgot how Bush had run an ad in New Hampshire accusing him of "straddling" on tax increases, after which Dole told Tom Brokaw on election night to tell Bush to "stop lying about my record." Near the end of his own presidential campaign in 1996, when Dole tripped and fell off a platform, he bounced up with another wisecrack.

It was, however, a somewhat desperate Bob Dole who was unable to get a good handle on Clinton as an opponent. At one point, Dole compared with Watergate the disclosure that the FBI had conducted background reports on some leading Republicans, on a list for Secret Service clearance. Resurrecting Watergate was a tired old trick that had been used repeatedly by Republicans to suggest that every subsequent Democratic screw-up was just as bad.

Indeed, as I wrote during the 1996 campaign about one prominent Nixon apologist, *New York Times* columnist William Safire: "Mr. Safire, who professes to have a reverence for language, has been polluting ours ever since he left Richard Nixon's employ as a speechwriter and began coining 'gates'— starting with Billygate and Lancegate in the Jimmy Carter years. [The obvious references were to the shady business dealings of Carter's loose-cannon brother Billy and Georgia banker Bert Lance.] He and others have produced inanities like Koreagate, Contragate, Nannygate, Troopergate and now Travelgate, as if any of these screw-ups came close to Watergate." (Troopergate referred to Arkansas state troopers reporting on Clinton's womanizing as governor; Travelgate referred to Clinton's 1993 purging of the White House travel office to make way for Arkansas cronies in the travel business. Contragate, however, referred to a Republican fiasco—the 1987 swapping of arms for aid to the Contra rebels in Nicaragua under Reagan.)

Clinton weathered his mini-scandals, as well as a full-blown investigation by the FBI and one by an independent counsel of his and Hillary's investment in the land development deal known as Whitewater. (Miraculously, as far as I can remember, it did not come to be known as Whitewatergate.) Clinton cast his reelection campaign in terms of crossing a "bridge into the twenty-first century," and his second term began more optimistically than the first. But those clouds of scandal and possible misconduct continued to hang over both him and his wife.

Once again, the old specter of womanizing reappeared against the president. The woman named Paula Jones, who earlier had charged that Clinton as governor had tried to compromise her at a Little Rock hotel, had filed a sexual harassment suit against him. He denied the charge and his lawyers tried to detour or postpone the suit, on grounds that responding to it would interfere with the president's ability to concentrate on his job. But the Supreme Court in a remarkably near-sighted, stupid decision said the case would not hinder him and could go forward.

In September of 1997 reports floated that Clinton's lawyers were considering settling the suit for $700,000 just to get rid of it. I wrote at the time that doing so seemed "either preposterous or imbecilic" and "totally senseless," and would be seen as an admission of guilt. "Among other things, a payoff might well encourage new allegations by opportunistic women," the column suggested, "motivated by anything from monetary reward to national publicity or desire to do more political damage to him." It wasn't the money itself, I noted. Although Clinton was already burdened with heavy legal bills, "former presidents don't go on welfare; numerous money-making schemes with no heavy lifting are thrown their way." For this last, I needed no crystal ball; the post–White House bonanzas of predecessors Ford and Reagan had already demonstrated this fact of current culture.

Whether or not to pay off Paula Jones would soon seem a minor problem, as Clinton's earlier alleged womanizing would pale in comparison to the bombshell that burst on him, and the country, in January of 1998. It was disclosed, first on the Internet and then in the *Washington Post* and other major newspapers, that the president of the United States had engaged in personal misconduct of a sexual nature with a young White House intern named Monica Lewinsky. Bizarrely, as I wrote in the *Sun* at the time, while the substance was not the same, there were notable similarities between this matter and Watergate. For once, maybe the label slapped on it— Monicagate—might have been appropriate in certain respects.

I wrote that, like Nixon, "another president is facing allegations of a different sort that raise the specter of his presidency also coming to a premature end." The charges that Clinton "had an affair with a young White House intern and then tried to get her to lie about it under oath" would, "like the Watergate case . . . constitute conspiracy to obstruct justice—a cover-up and an impeachable crime." I noted that in each affair "taped conversations were and are at the core of the allegations; both presidents had won landslide reelections despite disclosures of potentially damaging information. . . . Both those landslides were driven by excessive zeal [Nixon's for collecting damaging information about the Democrats, Clinton's for record campaign fund raising] to win what were perceived as easy reelections for them." Both also had secretaries (Rose Mary Woods for Nixon and Betty Currie for Clinton) who played key roles in the sagas.

While a "smoking gun" tape in which Nixon discussed using the CIA to block an FBI investigation of the Watergate break-in finally got him, I noted, Clinton's case rested thus far on which of the players would be believed. With no crystal ball at hand, I concluded: "Unless there are unforeseen developments that broaden the allegations against Clinton beyond marital infidelity, lying about it and urging the woman in question to do the same, impeachment and removal from office may seem to most Americans too high a price to pay."

After thousands more words written on the subject, and a long year of further investigations and Clinton dissemblings, that speculation proved half right and half wrong. The president was indeed impeached through the determined, often impassioned, insistence of the Republican majority in the House of Representatives. But the action, rebuffed by the Democratic minority and a few Republicans in the Senate who held their noses and voted to acquit him, fell short of the two-thirds required for conviction.

The decision was in keeping with the public's opinion, as gauged by most polls, that removal from office did "seem to most Americans too high a price to pay" for Clinton's self-indulgent and careless behavior. I personally felt, after seeing how Agnew had thumbed his nose at his prosecutors in avoiding impeachment by resignation, that Clinton deserved to be impeached for lying under oath to a grand jury in the case. I felt such action would underscore that not even a president was, in the memorable words of yet another White House secretary, Fawn Hall, in the Iran-contra case, "above the law." As for Clinton's acquittal, I felt it was no less partisan, with more than enough Democrats in the Senate to block conviction, than was the vigorous and venomous prosecution by Republicans in the House that impeached him. In a history of the Democratic Party, *Party of the People*, published later, I said so. In retrospect, perhaps the outcome—impeachment but acquittal—did serve the public interest. Clinton's insistence thereafter that he had defended the Constitution in fighting for his political life showed, however, that his capacity for shamelessly making lemonade out of one huge lemon remained infinite.

The whole distasteful matter was hardly the send-off that Clinton's chosen heir-apparent, Vice President Al Gore, needed as he embarked on his own campaign for the Democratic nomination in 2000. When he stood on the White House lawn after Clinton's impeachment and showed solidarity along with other Democratic leaders, it was understandable. But when he went on, gratuitously using the occasion to say that Clinton would go down in history as one of America's greatest presidents, that attempt at making more lemonade left a particularly sour taste in my mouth.

Gore faced a dilemma regarding Clinton as he focused more intensely on his bid to be the standard-bearer in 2000. He had an emphatic endorsement from the departing president, who several times called him the best vice president in American history and the best prepared to assume the presidency. At the same time, because Clinton had become such a controversial figure and anathema to Americans who deplored his personal behavior in the White House, Gore had to figure out whether Clinton would on balance be a plus or a minus for his own campaign. His resulting ambivalence injected an element not usually seen in a campaign in which the baton of leadership is handed from president to vice president or other personally anointed successor.

Besides, Gore was not going to have a free ride to the party's nomination. Poised to challenge him was a prominent Democrat with celebrity status in the world of sports—former Senator Bill Bradley of New Jersey, an All-American basketball star at Princeton and then a professional standout for the New York Knicks. I had covered Bradley's initiation into politics in 1978 when he was elected to the U.S. Senate in his first bid for public office, and had tracked him occasionally thereafter. As a politician, he was a likeable but somewhat aloof figure, perhaps as a result of the aura of acclaim in which he had always functioned as a sports celebrity. He also was a man of intellect and curiosity but tempered by a caution that did not always serve him well in the world of politics.

As he had been a strong competitor on the basketball court, this caution always seemed incongruous to me. At a major fund-raising event in East Brunswick, New Jersey, in March of 1999, I heard his wife Ernestine amuse the large crowd by describing her first impressions of him as he played for the Knicks in Madison Square Garden. In an obvious allusion to his toughness behind an often benign demeanor, she told of how he could take care of himself in the rough and tumble of the pro game. She called him "the man with the elbows," for the way he warded off opposing players in tussles for the ball under the basket. But in the game of politics, particularly in his competition with Gore in the Iowa caucuses of 2000, the man with the elbows suffered for failing to flail them with the same abandon as when his opponents were the Boston Celtics.

The demise of Bradley's presidential ambitions actually began before the voting in Iowa, at the state's annual Democratic Jefferson-Jackson dinner in early October of 1999, attended by both Democratic hopefuls. Bradley made a conciliatory appeal for a friendly competition between the two, patterned after the ongoing home-run hitting contest between sluggers Sammy Sosa and Mark McGwire, pushing each other to greater accomplishments. "Why can't it be Vice President Gore pushing Bill Bradley and Bill Bradley pushing Vice President Gore?" the former senator asked. In answer, Gore reiterated an earlier challenge of weekly debates. As Bradley sat quietly, Gore demanded: "What about it, Bill? If you agree, stand up!" Bradley simply smiled and did not stir. No sharp elbows would be thrown by him that night, but Gore tossed a few, chiding his opponent for having voted for the deep Reagan budget cuts of 1981 in child anti-poverty and other funds and for retiring from the Senate rather than confronting the subsequent Newt Gingrich onslaught.

The critical Gore attack came in mid-January 2000 about ten days before the caucuses, in a debate televised statewide. What the Gore camp yielded in passion and compassion to the Bradley team it more than made up in preparation and "elbows." A Gore researcher found an obscure Bradley vote in the Senate in 1993 against a flood relief effort that would have benefited Iowans. Bradley earlier had voted for the main relief legislation but had followed his Senate party leadership against the amendment. An Iowa farmer, Chris Peterson, whose farm had lost 300 acres to the 1993 flooding, was located by the Gore campaign and placed in the debate audience.

Gore confronted Bradley with that vote and pointedly introduced Peterson, while saying to Bradley there were "many other disasters facing farmers where you were one of a handful who didn't help the farmers." Bradley, clearly unprepared for the attack, lamely responded that "this is not about the past; this is about the future. This is about what we're going to do to change the agriculture policy we've had the last eight to ten years." The answer was flat and dismissive, almost like turning the other cheek rather than throwing an elbow. Bradley may have wanted to make the campaign about the future, but Gore, I wrote afterward, "whether Bradley likes it or not, is making it about the past."

Later that afternoon, I ran into Bradley in an elevator at the Fort Des Moines Hotel, where both of us were staying. He asked how I thought he had done. Evasively, I said he had done okay. Afterward, I debated with myself whether I should have leveled with him, but I took the easy way out, telling myself it wasn't my place to offer advice to candidates. But it was my place to write assessments, and the next day I told my readers what I thought about the ambush Gore had sprung on Bradley, and about his weak response. For me, that debate encounter told it all about the Gore-Bradley contest that year.

After pledging a positive, issues-based campaign, Bradley a few days later, in warning some grade school kids about the perils of cigarette smoking, took note that Gore had voted in 1988 against curbs on tobacco advertising, and in 1995 against efforts to prevent a tobacco tax cut. Gore blithely responded that Bradley's comment "smacks of desperate, negative campaigning" that "sounds like he's gone back 15 years to pick out some amendment that had other things connected to it." When it came to sharp elbows, it was Al Gore who was the professional.

Gore handily won the Iowa caucuses and the competition moved on to the New Hampshire primary, in which Bradley had been running a much stronger race. There, Bradley grew increasingly exasperated at Gore's penchant for distorting his record and began tagging Gore as untrustworthy. The allegation didn't save Bradley's candidacy but it did cling to Gore the rest of the year. "Why should we believe that you will tell the truth as president," Bradley repeatedly asked, "if you don't tell the truth as a candidate?" Soon Gore's exaggerations, such as implying that he had invented the Internet, became the brunt of late-night talk show jokes, always a barometer of a candidate's troubles. Bradley, too, joined in. "When Al accuses me of negative campaigning he reminds me of Richard Nixon," he would say. "He would chop down a tree, stand on a stump and give a speech about conservation." But Gore beat him again in New Hampshire and Bradley's campaign petered out thereafter.

In the Republican nomination race, money didn't simply talk; it shouted. As early as 1995, Phil Gramm, single-mindedly raising cash for the 1996 race, had proclaimed at a Texas fund raiser: "The best friend you can have in politics is ready money." He had raised $20 million that year, but it was-n't enough to overcome his lackluster campaign and personality. But the message proved to be true in 2000 for Texas governor George W. Bush, son of the former president. He raised so much money through what could be called fat-cat bundling—getting wealthy donors to solicit their rich friends in his behalf—that most of the dozen or so GOP challengers dropped by the wayside well before he clinched the nomination.

At a massive candidate cattle show in Ames, Iowa, in August of 1999, Bush won 31 percent of a straw poll vote among nine Republicans and went on from there. The independently wealthy Steve Forbes, running for a sec-ond time on his own nickel, or, rather his own mountain of them, one-upped Bush and the others, who had put up hospitality tents under a broiling sun. He installed a massive air-conditioning system in his. He finished second in the poll, with 21 percent, but it was all downhill from there.

Each of the candidates addressed the crowd at the spacious Hilton Coliseum, and Forbes' appearance was marked by a large indoor fireworks display that somehow got past the fire marshals. As he started speaking, a horde of red, white, and blue balloons descended on the crowd—or more specifically on the Pat Buchanan cheering section, where the balloons were eagerly popped, drowning out Forbes' opening remarks. "It was a rare case," I wrote that night, "of Steve Forbes' wretched excess backfiring on him. He left the podium to the jarring explosion of more fireworks, wearing his usual look of oblivious self-satisfaction." In the end, his personal bankroll was no match for Bush's campaign treasury and strong support from the Republican establishment, including his fellow governors.

Bush's only serious competition for his party's nomination came from Senator John McCain of Arizona, who skipped the Iowa caucuses, won handily by Bush, and focused on the New Hampshire primary. By dint of more energetic campaigning and a strong pitch to independent voters as a reformer, McCain upset Bush and forced the Texas governor to revamp his own image. Bush strategists cooked up a new slogan, "A Reformer With Results," that was all rhetoric with no substantial results to claim. But with it Bush somehow proceeded to cut McCain down in the next major primary, in South Carolina, with personal smears on McCain's stability and on his family.

Along with many others, I took a couple of turns riding on the now-famous "Straight Talk Express" bus, wherein McCain spent hours schmoozing with reporters crowded into the back section fitted out with a couple of easy chairs. His campaign strategist, Mike Murphy, a survivor of many other campaigns I had covered, took the other chair and joined in the kibitzing. McCain was remarkably candid and gave us so much to write about that we were awash with quotes before the day was out.

I had covered McCain in his first campaign for the Senate and often thereafter, including when he successfully overcame bad publicity as one of five senators who had given a helping hand to a notorious constituent in the savings-and-loan scandal of the 1980s. McCain took perverse pleasure in needling me about the fact that I was older than he was, although the debilitations of his long imprisonment as a naval officer during the Vietnam war made him look my senior by a number of years. Every time I boarded the Straight Talk Express I had to endure his urging some other reporter to give the old man his seat.

McCain was a top-notch campaigner. His problem was that once he left New Hampshire, he started running out of independent voters who could cast ballots in Republican primaries. It probably cost him South Carolina, whose closed primary descended into mud-slinging on both sides. Although he won in Michigan where independents could vote, as the campaign moved westward McCain's reputation as a maverick in his own party basically did him in. He and Bush eventually made peace in a Pittsburgh meeting that had all the trappings of a Cold War summit, but their relations remained icy long afterward.

The fall campaign between Bush and Gore was complicated, in ways not fully anticipated, by the candidacy on the Green Party ticket of longtime reformer Ralph Nader. He along with Pat Buchanan, who by now had abandoned his longstanding commitment to the Republican Party and seized the nomination of what remained of Ross Perot's Reform Party, provided a couple of sideshows to the main event, with Nader's turning out to be critical.

Nader toured the country insisting in an echo of George Wallace that there was no difference between the Republican and Democratic candidates and hence it didn't matter which of them was elected. He resisted the pleas of Democrats who argued he would take votes away from Gore in key states, which proved only too true later in Florida.

As usual, Germond and I trooped separately from state to state through the fall taking the public and political pulse wherever we went. We seldom traveled with the candidates but instead caught their acts as they came through wherever we were. We had long before decided that this modus operandi yielded more information for us than riding the candidates' insulated campaign and press planes, though occasionally we still did that, too. As usual, we kept in touch by phone on what columns to write and who would write them.

We teamed up only at the presidential debates. Gore, off the strength of earlier debates against Quayle and Perot, entered the 2000 confrontations with much higher expectations than Bush, who already was being subjected to criticism as an intellectual lightweight and disadvantaged speaker. His lack of foreign-policy knowledge had been highlighted early in the campaign, when a Boston television reporter asked him to name three fairly obscure foreign leaders and he flunked. At the time it seemed a cheap shot to say that he was a dummy in that realm, but the episode unwittingly helped lower expectations for Bush when he met Gore in debate on foreign policy.

In an earlier debate, Gore had taken such a condescending attitude toward Bush's generalized and poorly articulated answers that he lost points in post-debate analyses by raising his eyebrows and sighing, turning Bush into a sympathetic character. Bush's managers so deftly played the low expectations game going in to the foreign-policy debate that many observers later even declared him the winner. That debate in time would warrant recollection, for his firm disavowal of American "nation-building" and any role as the world's policeman.

Perhaps the most interesting information I culled from my travels that fall was the attitude of state campaign managers for Gore about bringing Clinton in to stump for him. As the Gore campaign seemed stalled and sluggish, Democratic voters who had stood by Clinton through his impeachment ordeal asked why Gore wasn't using him more. But Clinton's vice president, determined to be his "own man" after eight years under Clinton's shadow, seemed to go out of his way to separate himself from the administration in which he had played an unprecedentedly large part for a vice president. On the trail, Gore would go so far as to say he didn't want people to vote for him on the basis of what the Clinton-Gore administration had done but for what he proposed to do as president in his own right. It seemed to me a pretty foolish approach, like offering himself as a pig in a poke.

But as election day neared, I learned from campaign managers in key battleground states like Wisconsin that they didn't want Clinton coming in.

They insisted that internal polls indicated that the outgoing president, because of his personal behavior, so inflamed Republican and many independent voters that his presence might swell the turnout against the Democratic candidate to the point of causing him to lose their states. Gore wound up carrying Wisconsin without Clinton, but Democratic postmortems in traditionally Democratic states lost to Bush, like West Virginia, agonized about whether Gore could have carried them with a boost from Clinton, one of the best campaigners in either party in years.

As Democrats will never forget, the election came down to winning Florida's twenty-five electoral votes, or at least playing the inside game better there—not easy with the Republican candidate's younger brother, Jeb, holding forth as governor and fellow GOP officeholders like Secretary of State Katherine Harris doing all they could to deliver the state to him. Because of various vote-counting problems, the decision was passed on to the U.S. Supreme Court.

On the morning before its decision was handed down giving the election to Bush on a 5–4 vote that ran against the Court's precedent of leaving matters of state elections to the state courts, I went up to the Court. There, on the sidewalk in front of the majestic marble edifice bearing the motto "Equal Justice Under Law," I listened to the comments of assembled, mostly hostile, voters who clearly wanted the justices to keep their cotton-picking hands off the election. Signs held aloft proclaimed "Gore Got More" and "Impeach Scalia!" When one pro-Gore group began singing, in a rephrasing of the old Vietnam plea, "All We Are Saying Is Count All the Votes," a pro-Bush group tried to drown out the refrain with "No More Gore!"

In the crunch that night, the Republicans on the bench bent themselves out of shape to put Bush in the White House. I wrote the next day: "In the end, for all the legalistic legerdemain, a conservative majority of the U.S. Supreme Court may not have elected George W. Bush president, but it certainly anointed him. Its artful, unsigned ruling to 'remand' the vote count controversy to the Florida justices who tried to give Gore one last shot to prove he won was a weakly transparent effort at avoiding the appearance of finality—while assuring it by providing neither the time for a remedy nor any inclination to entertain one."

The five who made up the majority insisted that "none stand more in admiration of the Constitution's design to leave the selection of the Presi-

dent to the people, through their legislatures, and to the political sphere." They could have demonstrated that admiration, I wrote, "by declining to enter the case on the grounds used many times in the past—that elections are state matters, to be left to them and, if necessary, to their courts." Instead, the five Republicans simply cut Gore off, while stipulating, remarkably, that the decision should not be taken as a precedent, saying "our consideration is limited to the present circumstances, for the problem of equal protection in election processes [their grounds for barring further recounts] generally presents many complexities."

The whole fiasco was particularly galling to me because in my book *No Way to Pick a President*, published just before the start of the 2000 election, I had included a chapter called "An Accident Waiting to Happen." It warned that just as had occurred at least three times before and maybe four, the prospect loomed for a candidate who got the most votes not being elected. It noted that Andrew Jackson in 1824, Samuel Tilden in 1876 and Grover Cleveland in 1888 all won a plurality of the popular vote but lost out in the electoral college. In the fourth instance, use of a certain popular-vote calculation in Alabama would have given Nixon more popular votes than Kennedy.

After reviewing the origins of the electoral college and the pros and cons of it, I cited a 1956 Senate floor debate between Senators John Kennedy and John Pastore of Rhode Island. Kennedy, defending the electoral college, pointed out to Pastore that his little state was over-represented in it by virtue of having two senators in spite of its population. He asked whether his colleague would be willing to lose the two electors to which Rhode Island was then entitled. Pastore replied: "I would do away with the whole electoral college. I would do away with it completely. I would have the people elect the President of the United States on election day. I would not care where the candidates came from, whether they came from the North, the South, the West or the East. They are all Americans. We are all one country. I say let us vote for the best man. It is as simple as that. That is my idea of representative government. Everything else beyond that is a gimmick."

I ended the chapter by observing: "Gimmick or not, the electoral college remains in existence today, a 'Rube Goldberg mechanism' that few Americans know about or understand, whose chief contribution to our political system is its way of making possible the installation of a person whom a majority of Americans don't want. This particular college should close its doors."

A year later, after the U.S. Supreme Court had decided to substitute its will for that of the voters, I felt all the more strongly about that judgment, which I still hold, regardless of which party would benefit from the change. In any event, it was a hell of a way to end an election year—and, as it turned out, the columning team of Germond and Witcover.

18 On My Own Again

THE YEAR 2001 BROUGHT not only a change at the White House but also in the byline that had run over our column for twenty-four years, first at the *Washington Star* for four years and then for the next twenty at the *Baltimore Evening* and then morning *Sun*s.

My longtime partner, Jack Germond, had decided earlier in the election year to retire at its conclusion. The decision surprised me, inasmuch as I had always regarded him as much more of a political junkie than I was. Earlier, when people would ask him how much longer he would continue chasing politicians around, he would always reply, "Until they get it right." Therefore, in a farewell column to him under my single byline, I wrote: "So are we to conclude from his retirement that he thinks they got it right this time around, with the Florida fiasco and the Supreme Court doing a good imitation of Tammany Hall? You'll have to ask him, if you can find him in the hills of West Virginia or in the clubhouse at Charles Town." He and his wife, Alice, were retiring to a country house there, hard by the little track at which he could continue his love affair with swift four-legged creatures.

Looking back at our twenty-four years in harness, I mused in the same column on the advantages of our "good cop, bad cop" routine and on our harmonious partnership. "In all the years we toiled under the double byline," I recalled, "we never kept track of how many columns each of us wrote. Over the 24 years, I figure we did 6,912 of them, or 3,956 apiece. Except there was that time Jack went to Hawaii to make a speech, which means I wrote 3,957 and he wrote 3,955. But who's counting?"

I also related the secret that Germond "doesn't like it known, because it doesn't square with his tough-guy image, but he's really a religious man. Like another well-known religious figure, he also was born in a stable—at Pimlico. Or so it often seemed to hear him go on about the ponies."

Keeping to the same theme, I continued: "His own stable of political sources is legendary. When he wants to write about Democratic politics, he calls Bob Strauss. When he wants to write about Republican or third-party politics, he calls Bob Strauss. Once, I called the great man and asked him if he really had told Germond such-and-so. He replied: 'Who is this Germond?'"

Turning to his little-known athletic prowess, I reported: "You might be surprised to learn that Jack used to play tennis. Once we challenged our friendly competitors, Rowland Evans, an excellent player, and Bob Novak, who doesn't know which end of the racquet to hold, to a high-stakes match. But we pulled out on learning that Bob intended to substitute his wife, Geraldine, a pretty fair player. Jack could have held his own against her, but I was no match for Rowlie."

I also observed that "outside the news business, Germond is best known as a television talking head, but within the print community his claim to fame is 'the Germond rule.' At dinner, the check is always split equally among the diners, no matter how much you eat and drink. This naturally leads to the corollary of ordering 'defensively.' That is, consume as much as Jack does, or come out on the short end."

Even with Germond out to pasture, his restaurant rule lived on, at least among the declining number of old fogies brought up on eating and drinking defensively. Some younger reporters thought the idea tiresome, requiring their re-education about acceptable behavior on the campaign trail. As time went on, however, I found I was often recommended a netherworld destination if I insisted too long or loudly on compliance.

Buckling down to business on my own, I spent a number of columns early in that first year as a solo act ranting about the folly of the electoral college and calling for reform. Germond and I as a duo had sometimes got on a soap box, but more often we had hewed to a format of reporting and analyzing. Part of the reason was because that approach had been drilled into each of us in long years as more or less objective reporters. Another reason was that, in keeping with our agreement that we agree or at least acquiesce on everything that went out under our double byline, there occasionally was a tendency to shy from extremes in our conclusions. So, writing on my own again was in a sense liberating. It no longer was necessary to have almost daily consultations on what was to be written and how strongly. Also, under a single byline you were out there by yourself, encouraging a bit more freedom and leeway in expressing personal as opposed to shared or collective opinions.

My views against the electoral college and other matters therefore tended to produce a different editorial "voice" than had come out of the partnership of two reporters who had generally compatible notions but sometimes divergences in emphasis or level of concern. Thus, commenting on the period after award of the election to Bush, when Republican leaders called on Democrats to "get over it," I wrote that the legitimacy of Bush's constitutional claim to the Oval Office could not be questioned, but, if the GOP leaders "mean the country should docilely tolerate the process and election machinery that produced that result, they are asking for a whitewash." Congressional reviews, I said, "are imperative if the country is to be spared another disgrace like the 2000 election fiasco." Not surprising to me, that free advice was summarily ignored with nothing done by Congress to deal with an electoral college that had so dismally served the public interest.

One thing I did learn in that first year back on my own. It was not enough simply to hit and run on a topic that I believed warranted further discussion; I had to pursue it, even at the risk of being considered a crank or a bore by a share of the column's readers. Accordingly, I continued to raise the electoral college issue and to press for reform of that anachronism. I drew attention to a bill sponsored by Republican Representative Jim Leach of Iowa to abolish the college but keep electors in a way that would ensure election of the popular-vote winner. The bill got nowhere but I felt it deserved an airing.

I covered House and Senate hearings on election reform, and when they focused on the evils of hanging and dimpled "chads" I took those occasions to remind readers of the electoral college. When a voting reform bill finally came up for a vote in the House, its authors declined to include any change in the college on the grounds that small-state members of Congress would never agree. Nevertheless I urged its passage, but with the caveat: "How many more such results have to occur before these self-proclaimed reformers decide even to face up to this travesty?" It was a meaningless rhetorical question and I knew it, but still I felt it was worth repeating if the column was to have any backbone at all.

Likewise, I continued to nag at the failure of Congress to pass the modest campaign finance reform of banning unregulated "soft" money to the national political parties. And after covering the boot-licking performance of just-defeated-senator John Ashcroft of Missouri at his confirmation hearing to be Bush's attorney general, full of promises to abandon his fierce opposition to legal abortion, gun control, and other right-wing issues, I tracked through the year his contemptuous acts and comments that gave the lie to his assurances before his old colleagues.

I also returned often to the power bestowed in the new administration upon Vice President Dick Cheney by a president who seemed to defer to him. I did not, however, write about or even recognize for some time his role in a little high-level administration group whose members would soon emerge as the architects of a radical new path for American foreign policy. To me then, he was still the benign, soft-spoken gent that John Mashek and I had played doubles tennis against a few times before he had reached his eventual eminence.

As for the Democrats, I repeatedly chided their congressional leaders for going along with Bush's huge, destructive tax cut in the face of a sliding economy. I sought to be an equal-opportunity critic, but with the ball in the Republicans' court, they became my more frequent targets in the column.

When Bush's early popularity showed signs of slipping along with the economy, I began to think he was on a glide path to a one-term presidency. It was a slow news time in which the big story was the mysterious disappearance of a young congressional intern working for Representative Gary Condit of California.

In mid-August, in the course of covering a National Governors Conference in Providence, Rhode Island, I was able to make a sentimental journey to the city where in the early 1950s I had tasted my first real daily newspaper experience, on the *Journal*. I stayed at the remodeled Biltmore Hotel where the *Journal* had put me up when I had a week's internship at the paper during Easter week recess from the Columbia Journalism School. True to form for a columnist always looking for raw material, I wrote about my nostalgic return: "No doubt the Providence of half a century ago was nothing to brag about, but through the eyes of a greenhorn reporter kicked off the dock for the first time, it looked pretty good then. And for all the glossy urban renewal since, the recollections of how it was still bring back the old town, and the fun of starting a lifelong adventure here, making a living by the printed word."

In the summer lull, Marion temporarily put aside her labors on her Mencken biography and we slipped off to Europe on vacation. Then came September 11. We were about to tour Versailles when we saw on French television the hijacked planes plowing into the twin towers of the World Trade Center in New York and into the Pentagon. We packed up and headed into Paris, seeking the earliest plane home. I felt guilty being abroad at this shocking time, and wrote from there: "Near the end of a lethargic summer in Washington in which the primary public concern seemed to be the whereabouts and fate of one missing federal intern, it seemed like a good time to escape abroad for vacation. Talk about bad timing."

I went on to describe the scene at Paris's sprawling Charles de Gaulle Airport where we futilely undertook pursuit of a flight home, amid mobs of nervous and demanding tourists. We joined, I related, "staggeringly long lines of travelers in a babel of anxious voices [who] suddenly fell quiet upon the signal of a public-address announcement" that a period of silence observed across Europe "was about to begin. Travelers and ticket agents alike of all nationalities and races stood still, with heads bowed in prayer, for the 180 seconds of utter mid-day hush that seemed in a previously bustling airport to last much longer. Later, on French television, similar scenes flashed from around the world, underscoring the sense that what had happened in New York and Washington was not merely an American tragedy but a worldwide awareness that a new and fearful era had begun. It suddenly erased the American assumption of security that had set America apart from the rest of the world until that fateful morning."

It took us several days to snare a Washington flight, getting no sympathy from friends who saw little grounds for it in a delay that obliged us to spend extra autumn days in the beautiful City of Light. But we were particularly anxious about a favorite nephew who was a New Jersey firefighter exhaustively involved in the first rescue efforts at the World Trade Center. He was okay, but thereafter suffered major respiratory and some psychological problems before eventual recovery.

Shortly after our return, I went up to New York to see for myself what the terrorists had wrought there. I reported in the column that for all the immense destruction and shock to the city, its citizens seemed to have responded remarkably quickly to Bush's urging that they "get back to normal."

It is not normal in New York, to be sure, for taxi drivers to take it easy on their horns or for pedestrians to say "Excuse me" when they inadvertently jostle a stranger on the always bustling sidewalks. But in other ways, particularly in the pursuit of commerce, the city that never sleeps does seem to be getting back into the hurly-burly rhythm for which it is famous. Yet perceptible differences do cling. The signs and the air of unabashed patriotism are everywhere, from the epidemic of American flags looking down from skyscrapers that escaped the fate of the twin towers, to the flag lapel pins that have sprouted here like shamrocks on St. Patrick's Day. Never mind that they are being hawked relentlessly for profit at nearly every corner, especially around what now is known to everybody as Ground Zero. Hey, as they say here, ya gotta make a living.

One clearly political ramification of September 11 was that partisanship was put on hold. President Bush, after a somewhat uncertain and shaky beginning, grasped the immense significance and implications of the attacks and rallied the country to what he declared was "a war on terrorism" and its perpetrators. He called on Congress for support, and both parties responded by authorizing him to use the force necessary against "nations, organizations or persons he determines planned, authorized, committed or aided the terrorist attacks . . . or harbored such organizations or persons, in order to prevent any future acts of international terrorism" by them. The legislation was carefully worded to focus such use of force against the perpetrators of September 11. The authors obviously had in mind the Gulf of Tonkin resolution of 1964, which had given Lyndon Johnson a blank check to broaden the war in Vietnam as he chose. Al Gore, who before the attacks had been preparing to emerge from relative quiet with a critical speech at the annual Iowa Jefferson-Jackson dinner, opted instead to pledge his support to Bush in waging that war.

The mayhem of 9/11, as the date quickly came to be abbreviated, was soon attributed to a widespread terrorist organization, al Qaeda, masterminded by Osama bin Laden from camps in Afghanistan and protected by the ruling Taliban regime. Bush sent in American forces, who routed the Taliban and the camps but failed to seize bin Laden. The president vowed in Wild West rhetoric to get him "dead or alive," but bin Laden continued to direct his terrorist network from hideaways.

It was in this atmosphere of uncertainty that I concluded my first year of writing the column on my own. It had been a year of new challenges in a critical period of change that included the passing of three friends at the *Washington Post* who had strengthened my commitment to the news business by their examples—Dick Harwood, fellow reporter on the campaign trail and later my national editor, the incomparable cartoonist Herb Block, always the nicest guy in the newsroom, and Katharine Graham, the generous and unassuming publisher. I wrote about each of them with an appreciation of their great contributions to our craft, and their help to me.

The next year, the second of the George W. Bush administration, marked a distinct turn in the focus of the column, certainly since I had started writing it alone. In the wake of September 11, Bush's political fortunes had shot skyward as he cast himself as a wartime president with a mission to make his country and the world safe from terrorism. Unknown or at least unnoticed by the nation at large, the small group of neoconservative theorists in and close to the Bush administration, including Cheney, had been musing about the more ambitious and decisive role they thought the United States could and should play as the remaining superpower, through a more muscular use of its military and economic strength. Within days of the terrorist attacks, Secretary of Defense Donald Rumsfeld and his deputy, Paul Wolfowitz, reportedly approached Bush about the possibility or even the imperative of military action against the dictatorial regime of Saddam Hussein in Iraq as part of the war on terrorism, although there was no convincing evidence that he had played any role in those attacks.

In his 2002 State of the Union address, Bush significantly broadened his targets in the war on terrorism, specifically listing three rogue nations, Iraq, Iran, and North Korea, as an "axis of evil" imperiling the rest of the world. Up to then, I had generally supported Bush's anti-terror actions, which in Afghanistan clearly qualified as self-defense after the September 11 attacks. But now I became concerned about his belligerent cowboy rhetoric toward Iraq. An attack on that country without its having had a connection to those attacks was not, as far as I could see, authorized by Congress in its narrow approval of military action.

In late April of 2002, I looked in on a sparsely attended Senate subcommittee hearing called by Democrat Russell Feingold of Wisconsin that examined the scope of the War Powers Act of 1973 and the president's constitutional powers in war making. The act had been passed in reaction to

LBJ's seizing on the Tonkin Gulf Resolution to take whatever military action he chose in Vietnam.

Feingold said he didn't intend to raise the specific question of a potential U.S. attack on Iraq. But his clear purpose was to provide underpinning for his view that Congress could not be bypassed in initiating a war. He assembled a panel of constitutional scholars whose consensus was that only Congress had the explicit power to "declare war" under Article I, Section 8 of the Constitution. Georgetown law professor Jane E. Stromseth quoted James Madison: "In no part of the constitution is more wisdom to be found than in the clause which confides the question of war and peace to the legislature, and not to the executive department."

Other panelists challenged the emerging doctrine of "anticipatory self-defense" whereby, I wrote, "Bush could argue that every nation has the right to defend itself under attack, and that the development or possession of weapons of mass destruction by a hostile country would justify not waiting for an attack." An administration spokesman, Deputy Assistant Attorney General John Yoo, contended that the president in any event could act on his own, under his constitutional powers as "commander-in-chief," without congressional authorization, though Bush would prefer to have it. After that earful in the committee room, I wrote: "This is an issue that cries out for further exploration now, before the president confronts Congress with a fait accompli in an unauthorized attack on Iraq of indeterminate ramifications."

In subsequent columns, I raised questions about Congress's failure to invoke the War Powers Act, which requires congressional action and imposes a limit on how long troops can be deployed in the target country, and about the new theory of preemptive war, under which it could be launched unilaterally if so decided by the president. In two days of hearings, the Senate Foreign Relations Committee sought to assess the threat of weapons of mass destruction from Iraq and the likely aftermath of what now was being called "regime change," a softer pseudonym for ousting Saddam Hussein from Baghdad or killing him. I quoted Republican senator Richard Lugar of Indiana, among the most respected men in Congress, calling for a public debate to build "public support for actions that will require great sacrifices from the American people." I added: "If the debate inconveniences our tough-talking president, so be it."

Bush finally did call on the United Nations to produce a new resolution demanding that Saddam Hussein give up his alleged weapons of mass destruction. But he indicated at the same time that he was determined to go it alone with military force if necessary if there was no swift compliance. I wrote then: "The question other UN members continue to ask is: Why now? The specter of nuclear weapons in Baghdad or environs doesn't seem to spook them as it does the American president. Unless he does a better job convincing them, he may have to do without that UN resolution—which, after all, may be all right with him."

Later in September, I joined those relatively few voices in the columning business attempting to draw attention to the president's new "National Security Strategy" paper. I wrote: "It serves notice that he intends his prospective actions in Iraq not to be some one-shot gambit but rather the opening volley of an ongoing superpower policy against terrorism and purveyors of weapons of mass destruction in a new, more perilous world." I followed that observation a few days later with this: "What's the rush? Why is this country plunging pell-mell toward a war at such haste that a full-blown public debate on the merits or folly of the exercise must be sacrificed?"

As an equal-opportunity critic, in an October column I chided the Democratic leaders in the House and Senate, Dick Gephardt and Tom Daschle, for urging their party colleagues to pass another Bush war resolution. They apparently acted on the foolhardy assumption that in doing so they would get the Iraq issue off the table before the approaching congressional elections. That way, they had reasoned naïvely, Republican candidates would be vulnerable on the crumbling economy. But Bush continued to wrap himself in the flag, and the Republicans kept control of both houses. "Now that the midterm elections are over," I wrote, "maybe the country can get back to considering the wisdom of President Bush's determination to launch America on a preemptive first strike against Iraq. But maybe not." My crystal ball was clear enough on that.

In those elections, I found the issue of Iraq coming up only rarely. One Democrat who voted against the Bush war resolution, Senator Paul Wellstone of Minnesota, hammered hard against the notion of preemptive war as he toured his state seeking reelection. In Daddy-O's Cafe in the little town of Elk River north of Minneapolis one afternoon, I wrote later, "as usual he was in high dudgeon about everything from the threatened war in Iraq to unmet social and economic needs at home. Only 30 or so Minnesotans were on hand, but he gave them the full Wellstone treatment, pounding his fist in the air as he spoke. 'We need to be wise as to when we use military force and when we don't,' he said. 'It's the last option, never the first option.' Men and women in work clothes came up, exchanging handshakes and hugs. Several said, simply, 'Thank you, Paul, for your vote.' They didn't elaborate and didn't have to."

As Wellstone left the little café, we arranged to get together to talk the next day, when I was to pick up his campaign again. That was the last time I saw him. The following morning, the small plane carrying him, his ever-present campaign partner and wife, Sheila, daughter Marcia, three campaign aides, and two pilots crashed in a thickly wooded area and all perished. Among the voices raised against the invasion of Iraq, none was louder and more persuasive than that of this diminutive former college wrestler and professor, who met his constituents on a personal level and identified with their needs and desires more effectively than any other politician I had ever encountered.

I heard the news while interviewing the campaign manager of Wellstone's Republican challenger, Norman Coleman, the former mayor of St. Paul. I raced back to the Wellstone headquarters, where former vice president Walter Mondale, Senator Ted Kennedy, in the state to campaign for Wellstone, and other party luminaries sorrowfully hugged stunned campaign workers, all of whom habitually called their candidate "Paul," at his insistence from their first meeting. Mondale shortly afterward was prevailed upon to run in his place, but a huge memorial service for Wellstone so overflowed with support for the departed senator that it unwisely turned into a raucous political rally. Angered Republicans and other Minnesotans, for all their esteem for both Wellstone and Mondale, elected Coleman to the Senate seat.

Meanwhile, the Bush administration pressed on in its determination to bring Saddam Hussein to heel, with or without UN sanction and support. The president through his secretary of state, Colin Powell, pushed the United Nations Security Council into passing a resolution authorizing resumption of inspectors in Iraq to look for weapons of mass destruction, while pressing Saddam Hussein to comply with prior resolutions demanding disarmament.

In attempting to make the case that Hussein had such weapons, Powell in his presentation to the UN offered merely artists' simulations of supposed mobile laboratories wherein chemical and biological agents were being manufactured. I wondered at the time why, with the U.S. government's vaunted photographic equipment that allegedly could spot a pimple on a man's nose, Powell wasn't able to produce actual photos of the mobile labs. But the mock-ups apparently served their purpose.

Hussein continued to insist he had no weapons of mass destruction, and in December, I wrote: "The Bush administration appears to hope that he will continue to deny their existence even if strong evidence is discovered, thus vindicating the administration's sweeping allegations and providing the green light for American military action, with or without UN sanction and assistance."

The stormy year ended with the administration poised to invade Iraq, but, apparently in deference to Powell, it waited to see whether the international body would finally run out of patience with the Iraqi leader and yield to the bully boy in the White House.

The new year sent me back onto the presidential campaign trail, what with the long list of Democratic hopefuls embarking on their quest for funds raised in the year prior to the election, which would be matchable by Uncle Sam. Some of them, rolling over on the war issue, continued to hold fast to the weak economy as their ticket to beating Bush. But others, like former Vermont governor Howard Dean, Senator Bob Graham of Florida, and avowed peacenik Representative Dennis Kucinich of Ohio, challenged the president directly on his war plans. I aired their dissents in the column.

One of those who had voted for the war resolution, Senator John Kerry of Massachusetts, had done so with an artful hedge, warning Bush not to "rush to war" without solid support and sanction from the United Nations. In late January, I heard him explain his position in a long speech at Georgetown University. In the question-and-answer period, a student called him on the hedge, saying "perhaps this middle-ground position will get you elected president, but . . . you would still send our brothers and sons to war against an enemy who represents no proven threat to the United States." Kerry replied that he recognized Saddam Hussein as a threat but had cast what he called "a 'but' vote . . . yes, but I want to make sure you're going to the UN." It was a position that was destined to cause him much difficulty in the months ahead, as Bush, after reluctantly going back to the world body again, was rebuffed by France, Germany, Russia, and other major UN members.

As I had been doing through the previous year, I continued in the column to question Bush's policy and demeanor. I did so to a degree that clearly agitated a substantial number of readers, judging from the increase in critical and hostile e-mail messages that were being fired at me. When the president charged that the UN was flirting with becoming "irrelevant" by failing to support his plans to invade Iraq, I wrote that the French and German leaders were in fact "making a last effort to preserve the relevance of the United Nations in choosing further diplomacy over bullets and missiles. . . . No amount of Bush administration rhetorical bullying is likely to change the view in the United Nations and in most parts of the world that an invasion of Iraq is not commensurate to any imminent threat from Baghdad. Hussein by general acknowledgment is a monster. But to those still opposing war, the case of imminent threat is still to be made. Insisting that it be made can demonstrate the relevance of the United Nations, not the contrary."

When I wrote that Bush's efforts to pressure the UN to buy into his advanced plans for invasion "can only be described as an unmitigated fiasco, born of President Bush's determination to act against Iraq with or without the world body," I was buried in a flood of bitter e-mails. I printed excerpts from some of them in a subsequent column. "The e-mails," I reported, "lend considerable backing to one succinct personal assessment: 'You, my friend, are a complete moron.'" Another ventured: "Saddam loves your kind. He relishes the fact that there are those in America writing such harsh opinion pieces of President Bush. . . . Brownshirts are alive and well in America, where you're free to dissent; sadly, in Iraq they are not." And I also quoted "a lady from Texas" who sweetly offered: "Blame Bush, my butt—you don't like our president so you have to blame him for the inactive boobs who sit on an irrelevant Security Council somewhere in New York. That bunch of socialists is what's wrong with the world, not President Bush. . . . I'm sick and tired of my money going to a bunch of idiots who want to sit on their butts and criticize America."

From San Diego, I was assessed as "a sad example of an American, continually bashing our president, while for eight years giving the immoral Bill Clinton a pass [this after I'd written that his impeachment was warranted for his lying to a grand jury]. I'm proud that Mr. Bush is moving to oust the Hitler of the Mideast. You would have been the darling of the British 'Chamberlains' who allowed the Third Reich to flourish and kill millions of people." And from Georgia, a "Proud Citizen" wondered: "I will cast my lot with my country. How about you?" A North Carolinian advised: "You should have labeled your column 'Blame America,' because that is what you are doing. Oh, you try to disguise it, but your disdain for this country and what it stands for shines through." I also received suggestions for future travel plans, such as: "America, love it or leave it."

There were a few e-mails supportive of what I had written, but they were greatly outnumbered by those that found my comments wanting. Interesting to me, however, was that as the drama moved on, the sentiments in the e-mails eventually turned around. The critics essentially fell quiet and readers who shared or came to share my observations on Bush's Iraq adventure increasingly expressed their views, in somewhat less personal terms.

When the president finally asserted that he was about out of patience with the UN foot-draggers, I wrote in another column: "Now that our own Gary Cooper has declared High Noon and given Saddam Hussein 48 hours to get out of Dodge, it's being said that diplomacy has failed. Closer to the truth is that it was ambushed before it ran its course." Nevertheless, with only Great Britain and a handful of minor UN members supporting him, Bush launched his preemptive invasion, still insisting that Saddam Hussein posed a real threat to the West, especially the United States, with those alleged weapons of mass destruction.

Once the invasion began, I put my own personal marker down. "Now that the bombs are falling on Iraq," I wrote, "there can be no question that full support at home is due the American troops in the field, in the air and at sea." But I added:

> The onset of the war and American support for it, however, need not silence legitimate questions at home about the wisdom of initiating hostilities before international solidarity was achieved. Nor does the start of the conflict suspend the right, or the obligation, of Americans to question and challenge the new Bush doctrine of preemptive war to prevent possible threats down the road. At a time when the government is imposing almost unprecedented restrictions on certain civil liberties and detentions in the name of homeland security, it is all the more important that voices of responsible dissent be heard. . . . So the war begins, with support in this corner always for the men and women risking their lives and their quest for military success, without surrendering the right and need to question the policy that obliges them to do so.

The swift fall of Saddam Hussein (but not his immediate capture) achieved one justification for Bush's invasion, but not the one so heavily peddled before the shooting started in the failed effort to win UN sanction for it. In early April, I wrote: "Now that regime change in Baghdad is at hand, does it matter whether those weapons of mass destruction that posed an 'imminent' threat to us are found?" I argued that it did. "It remains important as buttressing of American credibility in the basic decision to go into Iraq," I said in the column, but "discovery is not likely, however, to end the broader question of the wisdom and the constitutional and international legality of preemptive invasion." And shortly afterward: "You have to wonder why the administration felt it had to warn the American people of an imminent threat of weapons of mass destruction when it now seems clear its main objective was regime change in Iraq." And this: "There will remain, nevertheless, the whole dispute over the White House national security strategy paper of last fall that declares preemptive war to be a legitimate act of self-defense. What is being urgently preempted in the absence of an imminent threat?"

Finally, there was the hyping of intelligence to justify the invasion. By June I was writing: "At the beginning in the galaxy of Republican presidents, there was Abraham Lincoln as the Great Emancipator. Then we had Ronald Reagan as the Great Communicator. Now, in George W. Bush, we have the Great Justifier."

It was around this time that my e-mails really began to turn from vitriolic attacks on me to questions about Bush. "You ask whether Bush's case was built on deception," one *Baltimore Sun* reader wrote. "Do Marylanders like crab cakes? It is abundantly clear from recent remarks by Secretary Rumsfeld that the whole WMD argument was a gigantic fraud. He is now left to arguing that the Iraqis may have destroyed them. . . . These people just lie. Why don't you just come out and say it?" Another wrote: "I find it odd that you do not utter the word 'impeach' in your articles. . . . If the Republicans were right to hound and clamor for impeachment of President Clinton because he 'lied' about his personal life, lying about reasons for going to war and putting many lives at risk is so much more egregious and deserving of impeachment. Why the silence?" Suddenly I was being accused of being too soft on Bush.

For all this seeming shift in public opinion, the Democratic candidates in Congress who had supported the war resolution mostly continued to do so. But after Saddam Hussein was toppled and what had been advertised by the Bush administration as a "liberation" disintegrated into an American-British occupation of Iraq with hordes of U.S. casualties, they became critical of Bush's postinvasion policies. Kerry, whose support of the war resolution came with the caveat that Bush continue to seek more UN support, found himself cast by Dean and Democratic competitors for the party's nomination as "ambiguous" on the war. Kerry fell in the polls compared to Dean, who was forcefully continuing his categorical opposition to any invasion of Iraq.

Sometime later, I caught up with Kerry at a rally in Dover, New Hampshire, and, reminding him of that earlier exchange at Georgetown, asked him whether that "yes, but" answer could sustain him against Dean's assaults. He said he felt confident: "It holds up completely." But in formally declaring his candidacy, Kerry found it necessary to explain that position all over again.

While Kerry was struggling to overcome the perception that he was trying to have it both ways on the war in Iraq, his chief accuser, Howard Dean, was surging as a result of his all-out assault on Bush on that war. His advance was certified not only by polls but in the immense amount of money and volunteer support he was generating by way of the Internet in national politics' first major demonstration of that medium's pulling power.

In August I went up to Dean's campaign headquarters in Burlington, Vermont (a beautiful drive that was more than worth the effort to reach this rural outpost), to see for myself how it was being done and to talk to the candidate. There I found an old friend and source from the Mondale and Hart campaigns running the show. Joe Trippi, an affable guy I had first met when he was a young second- or even third-tier political operative in those earlier campaigns, was now managing the effort with a generational appreciation of the new wonder-tool of the computer world. By that time, Trippi was laying claim to 83,000 cash contributors for this heretofore obscure former governor of this small state, with an astounding goal of reaching 900,000 by year's end. Much of this support was being fueled by Dean's unremitting pounding of Bush on the war. Dean himself was not nearly as intense one-on-one as he was on the stump, and was pretty laid back given the remarkable early success he was enjoying and having apparently read accurately the Democratic voters' mood on Bush and the war.

"The premise on which the country went to war," he told me, "turned out not to have been true. Saddam Hussein was never a danger to the United States. We're in more danger now than we were before the president went into Iraq." And he gloated mildly about the dilemma now faced by the other Democratic candidates who had voted for the Bush war resolution—Kerry, Dick Gephardt, Joe Lieberman, and John Edwards.

"The job of president means you have to really make tough decisions and clear-eyed decisions," Dean said. "So I think the four guys who supported the war have got some explaining to do, because they basically swallowed all the evidence that the president was dishing them up, the major proportion of which turned out to be exaggerated or simply not true."

I wrote after the interview: "In any event, it's clear from listening to Dean that he's enjoying the squirming of the pro-war Democratic candidates, and the opportunity their stance gives him to counter the charge that a former governor of a tiny state such as Vermont doesn't know enough about foreign policy to be president." As the morass in Iraq dragged on, those four Democratic candidates continued to seek traction on an issue that Dean had already made his own. Entry into the Democratic race in September by retired General Wesley Clark, working the same side of the street, posed new competition to Dean for the anti-war vote.

Since the start of Bush's focus on Iraq, I had shifted my own focus in the column from pure domestic politics to what I considered a major and dangerous new course in the conduct of American foreign policy. Now, with that new course becoming a centerpiece of the Democratic presidential campaign for the 2004 nomination, I found the two critical aspects of domestic and foreign policy coming together as I resumed my travels on the campaign trail.

For years the column had more often emphasized its reportorial and analytical aspects; its "voice" had now become more opinionated. Part of the reason, obviously, was that I was writing the column under a single byline, which gave me more freedom to say exactly what was on my mind. But also greatly driving the tone of that voice was my growing feeling that more than any time in the half a century I had been writing, the country's leadership was taking it down a disastrous path, both at home and abroad. In all those fifty years, I had not encountered such a wrongheaded, intently ideological view that it was America's destiny to go it alone, nor such arrogance in doing so to get its way. I felt strongly that now was the time to step up to the plate and say so, and to do my best to present whatever evidence and thoughts I could assemble to justify speaking out in that fashion. So after half a century of seeing myself as a wise-guy reporter, I had, alas, started to turn into a wise-guy pontificator.

19 One More Campaign

GOING INTO 2004 I WAS EMBARKING on my twelfth presidential campaign, amid personal dismay over the war in Iraq, a stagnant economy at home, and an ever-stronger sense that the country was going in the wrong direction in both spheres. While resuming my customary candidate-chasing, I felt compelled more than ever before to express my concern about these matters in the column. I continued to harp especially on the folly of a war undertaken in arrogance and deception, at great cost to America's reputation and standing in the Western community of nations, followed by an ill-conceived and botched occupation.

In the eleven previous presidential elections, dating back to the Kennedy-Nixon campaign of 1960, I had always undertaken as my prime responsibility recounting daily events as a reporter in the journalistic trenches, adding column-writing in 1977 at the *Washington Star* and then, in 1981, at the *Baltimore Sun*. But for the 2004 campaign, the *Sun*'s editorial page editor, Dianne Donovan, decided I should confine my efforts to the column, expressing fear that readers might be confused by getting my straight reporting and analytical column writing simultaneously. I had enjoyed the dual task and received no editorial complaints at the *Star* or until then at the *Sun*, and I felt that my long experience in political reporting was being wasted by the decision, but I complied.

Since early 2002, I had been expressing, for me, unusually strong opinions in the column about what I saw as President Bush's blatant abuse of presidential power in planning for and launching his war of choice. The tenor of the column, and the voter reactions to it, made the decision to keep me out of straight reporting more understandable, although no one ever tried to temper my criticisms or cited their often contentious tone as the reason for barring me from writing for the news columns. Still believing, however, in the wisdom of going where the story was and seeing it for myself, immediately after the New Year I headed out for Iowa and the campaign's first contest for convention delegates. President Bush was unchallenged in the Republican caucuses but eight of the ten declared candidates on the Democratic side were competing.

Senator Joseph Lieberman, after an early venture into Iowa that only demonstrated his weakness there, elected to bypass the caucuses and concentrate on the first primary, in New Hampshire, as did late-starting retired general Wesley Clark. Howard Dean came into Iowa with a full head of steam, but before long his aggressive, bombastic campaign style and some erratic observations, as well as relentless attacks from some of the other Democrats, began to eat at his support.

I must confess that I misread the effectiveness of the army of Dean foot soldiers that poured into Iowa to make an unprecedented grass-roots assault on the state's electorate. At the same time, the quiet, below-the-radar mobilization on behalf of John Kerry failed to impress me. The Massachusetts senator's high expectations in New Hampshire had been eroding as the new year began, leading to a major staff shake-up and a decision to shift resources to Iowa.

Dean's phenomenal early success in fund raising, volunteer recruiting, and in the polls led competing Democrats and the White House to target him in an Anybody-But-Dean effort that came unusually early in the election cycle. The former Vermont governor responded by chiding his fellow Democrats, especially Kerry, for having supported Bush's war resolution in Congress, and intensifying his attacks on the Republican president, which to many came off as too angry and ill-tempered. Also, upon the capture of Iraqi president Saddam Hussein, Dean observed with considerable reason but not much political savvy that finding him didn't make the United States safer. Such observations compounded the impression that Dean if nominated would be an easy target for Bush.

The 2004 campaign was the first under the new McCain-Feingold campaign finance reforms, which prohibited unregulated contributions, or "soft money," directly to federal candidates, their campaigns, or the national and state political parties. Passage of the reforms in 2004 was considered a great boon to clean politics and reducing the influence of money in the nomination and election process, but it proved to be at best a partial solution. Soon, however, political strategists found a huge loophole in the income tax code. An obscure item, Section 527, permitted such soft money contributions if made not directly to the candidates or their campaigns but for activities beneficial to them. These "527 committees" were required to act independently of the candidates, campaigns, and the parties, but that very fact made it easy for the beneficiaries to disavow them if doing so served their political interests.

In a presidential campaign that was at least a match for any previous one I had covered in its negative tone, the 527 committees did much of the dirty work while the candidates and their campaigns could insist they were remaining on the high road. The 527s got warmed up in the Democratic primaries as the Anybody-But-Dean effort took its toll on the bombastic Vermonter. But they really kicked in and played a more critical role in the general election that fall.

When Dean began to slip in Iowa, Kerry was quick to take advantage of the shift, and to benefit as well from a disappointing showing by Missouri congressman Dick Gephardt, the 1988 caucus winner in Iowa, who was saying flat-out that he had to win in his neighboring state to remain in the race. He too had supported the war resolution and had urged fellow House Democrats to do the same.

As the campaign heated up, I was finding writing only my column three times a week during a campaign, and no news stories, less than satisfying. I undertook occasional longer analytical pieces for the *Sun*'s Sunday "Perspective" section, but it was depressing not being required anymore as a reportorial firehorse to come racing out of the station when the bell clanged. Among the columnist fraternity, only a few colleagues, such as Dave Broder of the *Washington Post* and Ron Brownstein of the *Los Angeles Times*, seemed to continue the double duty.

Despite my now-limited output and my new focus on a disastrous foreign adventure that was emerging as the likely key issue of the election, the lure of the campaign trail remained. Early in January, in Boone, Iowa, I caught up with a new face in presidential politics whose chances seemed on paper to be nil—a freshman southern senator who looked like he could be right out of college. But the minute 50-year-old John Edwards of North Carolina strode, grinning from ear to ear, into the Ericson Public Library and capti-

vated sixty Iowa farmers in heavy wool lumberjack shirts and wide suspenders, it was clear I was in the presence of a political phenomenon. I decided right there in Boone to keep my eye on Edwards, a conclusion increasingly reached by other reporters in Iowa. But the fund-raising and poll numbers for Dean were so dazzling that not only Edwards but also Kerry seemed
lost in the rush to anoint the hot candidate from Vermont.

On caucus night in Iowa, though, Kerry surprisingly swept past Dean, an
outcome marked shockingly by Dean's bellowing, seemingly out-of-control
pep talk to his disappointed followers, an unpresidential surge of enthusiasm from which he never recovered. Watching it in the press filing room in
the Des Moines Convention Center that night, many of us declared Dean,
who finished third behind newcomer Edwards, dead on the spot. We hastened to bang out Dean's political obituary on our laptop computers as what
came to be known as "the Dean scream" flashed repeatedly on the television
monitors throughout the room.

The next morning the campaign traveling circus moved on to New
Hampshire, where only weeks earlier the other Democratic campaigns were
openly acknowledging that they were running to finish second to Dean.
Now it was all Kerry as the restored New England favorite son. When he
subsequently raced toward the Democratic nomination by winning five of
seven primary and caucus contests in early February, I wrote: "He can probably thank the erratic performance of former Gov. Howard Dean of Vermont
in the Iowa caucuses and thereafter. Dean's overheated and angry attacks
not only on Bush but also on his Democratic rivals left many voters with the
impression that he is too hot to handle."

Edwards made the most of his second-place finish in Iowa by offering
himself as a kind of Jimmy Carter goody two-shoes, vowing to hew to the
high campaign road and not criticize his opponents. I noted also in early
February that Kerry could thank Edwards too "for cooling off the intraparty
rhetoric," which seemed to "reflect a general Democratic desire to get past
the delegate-selection period with a minimum of division, the better to
achieve a united front afterward in the prime party objective of getting Bush
out of the White House."

Edwards tapered off in New Hampshire but bounced back by winning
the primary in his native South Carolina, where Kerry competed just to
demonstrate he was a national candidate running everywhere. The contest
provided me an excuse to make a long-delayed pilgrimage with my three

grown offspring—Paul, Amy, and Julie—to our tenuous Dixie roots. Between Kerry and Edwards campaign stops, we journeyed to the little town of Marion, where my father had spent his early childhood. We tracked down Witcover Street, a nondescript two-block stretch with a signpost that provided an ideal prop for a family photo. Then it was back to the campaign, by way of picturesque Charleston and a sampling of the local fare. I was able to impress—or, rather, amuse—my clan when a South Carolinian came up to me at an Edwards rally, shook my hand, and said how thrilled he was to meet . . . Daniel Schorr.

Edwards finished a close second to Kerry in Wisconsin, but Kerry carried Ohio. With the Democratic presidential nomination thus decided by early March, I abandoned my usual practice of traipsing around the country with the candidates all through the preconvention period, electing to stay in Washington covering the political ramifications of a war turning ever uglier. The president, while campaigning diligently as a "wartime president" and playing the patriotism card for all he was worth, was running into increasing resistance; American troops were encountering armed insurgents on Iraqi streets, where the liberation had become a clearly unwanted occupation.

On top of that, Bush was facing accelerating public, press, and Democratic criticism over his administration's failure to find the weapons of mass destruction whose alleged presence had been his prime justification for invading Iraq. At the same time, developments in Iraq were so dire that they were pushing the presidential campaign, usually the dominant issue before the country every four years, into the shadows. Kerry and Bush continued to speak and to raise money, but the campaign seemed unable to get traction with the American public because of what was going on in Iraq. So, writing about the war and its ramifications became the most realistic way to address the presidential campaign itself.

As the two major-party nominees slogged toward their national conventions, I was confronted with a major distraction at the *Sun*. The powers at the parent *Chicago Tribune*, which in 2000 had swallowed up the *Sun* along with its previous absentee owner, the *Los Angeles Times*, undertook "voluntary" staff buyouts at both papers. Bill Marimow, the *Sun*'s highly regarded editor, had already been summarily fired, apparently for being an impediment to the *Tribune*-installed publisher's plans to sacrifice the paper's quality editorial content to the financial bottom line. Marimow was replaced as editor by a young *Tribune* alumnus named Tim Franklin. In the midst of my presidential election coverage, he summoned me to Baltimore and urged me to volunteer for an insultingly meager buyout, after twenty-three years as a featured *Sun* columnist. Franklin tried to put a better face on the squeeze by saying, "in fairness to you," that I should know that the editorial pages were to be redesigned and use of my column would be cut from three a week to one after the election. He also kindly pointed out that, although the *Sun's* medical care plan for retirees was being scrapped, if I accepted the payoff I would remain eligible. I managed to restrain any expression of gratitude for his thoughtfulness.

As a further sweetener for this sour pill, Franklin offered me a one-year contract to continue the column on a one-a-week basis, for about a third of my salary. With no intention of retiring anytime soon, I asked for a longer contract period, but he said it was the company's policy to give only one-year contracts. However, in the presence of then–managing editor Tony Barbieri, he said that renewing would be no problem, and he wanted my byline to stay in the paper. Donovan, the editorial page editor and *Tribune* import who earlier had ordered that I stop writing news stories, also told me that the most she could offer was one column a week. It was, as Don Corleone might have said, an offer I couldn't refuse, so I swallowed the pill.

Once the 2004 election was over, Donovan decided to run the column twice a week—for the same pay the contract provided for using it once a week. Later, the contract would be amended to convert my very small travel allowance to additional salary, thus keeping me off the road for the rest of the contract year. I naïvely consoled myself that when it came time for the contract to be renewed, the finances would be adjusted to compensate me fairly and allow me to resume modest travel.

These contract developments took the edge off much, but not all, of my enthusiasm for covering the rest of the campaign. On a very limited travel budget, I found myself almost back to the system instilled in me by my old Washington bureau chief at Newhouse—hunting for the best bargains on airfares and hotels to stretch my budget as far as I could. But by this time I was so concerned about the outcome of the election, and what four more years of George W. Bush might mean for the country, that I wanted to see the campaign through, and I did.

Through all this period, the Democrats were taking great advantage of the 527 loophole in the income tax code, pouring soft money into voter identification and registration drives and into television commercials benefiting the Kerry campaign. The Republicans were slower to enter the 527 competition, but in the summer one supporting group manufactured a Kerry vulnerability that proved critical to the election's outcome.

In the summer, a group of Vietnam veterans called Swift Boat Veterans for Truth, ostensibly acting on their own initiative, purchased an ad that questioned Kerry's entitlement to the Silver and Bronze Stars and three Purple Hearts awarded him in Vietnam. The ad also played on the report that upon return home, Kerry had thrown away his awards in protest against the Vietnam war. The charges were particularly obnoxious inasmuch as they were made to benefit the candidacy of Bush, who had joined the Texas Air National Guard, managed to avoid service in Vietnam, and left the Guard under suspicious circumstances.

At the Democratic National Convention in Boston, the Kerry campaign pointedly limited its criticism of Bush and made no appreciable defense of Kerry on the swift boat group's charges until later in the campaign. The smears effectively took the focus off Bush's ill-conceived invasion of Iraq and its chaotic aftermath, and for weeks made Kerry's service in Vietnam thirty-five years earlier the hot issue.

After the Democrats had nominated Kerry and Edwards as their ticket, I joined the bus caravan undertaken by the pair out of Boston through New York State, Pennsylvania, West Virginia, and Ohio, for the specific purpose of comparing it with the previous bus tour of Bill Clinton and Al Gore in 1992. That earlier excursion marked a close bonding of the two Democrats that brought energy, color, and humor to their campaign and in my judgment had been an important factor in their appeal and ultimate election.

The Kerry-Edwards combination was lively and warm but did not reach the level of that earlier Democratic duo. Kerry's seemingly natural aloofness bent but didn't break in the presence of Edwards' infectious optimism, and in my mind the pair did not click as Clinton and Gore had twelve years earlier. Kerry, in light of his ambivalent position on the Iraq war, could have used a more effective defense on that issue from his running mate. But Edwards, while persuasive in attacking Bush's domestic priorities, lacked the experience in foreign policy to give much support to Kerry on that front. In retrospect, I came to feel that Senator Bob Graham of Florida, one of that critical state's biggest vote-getters and a sharp and knowledgeable critic of the Iraq war, would have made a stronger running mate.

The Bush campaign hammered relentlessly at what it called Kerry's flip-flopping on the war and other issues, and damaged him with challenges to his patriotism, strongly underpinned by the swift boat veterans' assault on his Vietnam service. That diversion inevitably also focused further attention on Bush's own stateside service in the Air National Guard. It all led to my writing:

> The relative merits of the Bush and Kerry military service during the Vietnam war obviously go to questions of character and patriotism, and should be aired. But . . . it's past time when Kerry must push Bush to defend the results in Iraq of his vaunted leadership skills. It has become a cliché in this campaign that Kerry's strongest argument for election is that he is not George W. Bush. In the remaining weeks of the campaign, he isn't likely to make voters feel much better about himself. So he needs to give voters the reasons Bush must go, and the best one is not that he didn't serve in Vietnam, but that he got the country into a war it didn't have to fight, and has made a costly mess of it.

In September, I visited such key swing states as Florida, Ohio, Michigan, and New Hampshire, catching the principal candidates as they came through. I always found that approach to be not only more economical but also more educational than traveling with them and being subjected to repeated servings of their boilerplate remarks.

Both Bush and Kerry drew extremely large crowds, signaling possibly record turnouts on Election Day. The president's rallies were notably controlled, for reasons of security and politics. Attendees had to obtain tickets from local Republican party offices, and Bush, at the events I witnessed, took only questions about which he had been briefed, from prepped voters selected by the campaign in advance. On at least one occasion, when Bush threw a cue to a questioner and she didn't pick up on it, he prompted her like a teacher helping a student who had forgotten her lines. Kerry's rallies were more open and the questions more spontaneous. I believe this is one reason Bush was less prepared and less comfortable in his first debate with Kerry and it showed.

In early October I dutifully schlepped from Miami to Cleveland to St. Louis to Phoenix, covering the debates in the fashion their organizers allowed. That is, I joined the army of reporters herded at each debate site into the isolation of a huge press center into which the ninety-minute confrontation was televised. Those of us who made the trek saw only what we could have witnessed sitting in our own living rooms. We had the added thrill of being subjected to an invasion of campaign spinmeisters even before the debating candidates had left the stage, telling us how and why their man won. They marched into the press center followed by minions holding large identifying signs aloft, just in case the reporters couldn't tell Bush master strategist Karl Rove from Kerry strategist Tad Devine.

After the debates, I returned to Ohio and Florida, generally deemed by this time as likely to decide the election's outcome and identified by the polls as extremely tight. In light of the 2000 election, an important part of covering this campaign would be monitoring what was being done to assure fair and honest voting, and Florida particularly was under intense scrutiny.

In an interview, Howard L. Simon, executive director of the American Civil Liberties Union of Florida, summed up the local sentiment thus: "It's shaping up again to be a real close election, and if so officials here will get down on their knees and pray, 'Lord, please don't let there be a recount!'"

After the vote-counting debacle in 2000, Congress had passed the Help America Vote Act, authorizing millions of dollars to the states to upgrade their voting machines and install other safeguards. But the states resisted calls for uniformity in voting machines, and as a result another hodge-podge of methodologies threatened continued confusion. In Florida, about half the voters were to use new optical-scanner machines, affording easy recount, while the other half were to cast their ballot by touch screen, which had no recount capability without printers, which were not attached. In Ohio, it was potentially worse; the state was still using punch-card ballots of the sort so discredited in Florida in 2000.

The new law provided for provisional ballots, whereby a voter whose registration was questioned at the polls could cast a ballot that would be counted if the voter's eligibility was later confirmed. In both Ohio and Florida, the ranking election officials ruled that if a voter showed up in a precinct for which he or she was not registered, no provisional ballot could be cast. With many voters having moved from one precinct to another since 2000, this was an invitation to turmoil and complaint.

Many states including Florida also provided for early voting in 2004, producing huge lines outside limited special polling places, another indication of a record turnout. Spurring that outcome were unprecedented registration and get-out-the-vote campaigns by both parties and by the supposedly unaffiliated 527 committees, raising millions of dollars of soft money in an end run around the recently passed McCain-Feingold reforms.

Beyond all these developments feeding the potential for another round of mischief in Florida, the voting process was again being supervised by a strong supporter of President Bush appointed by his brother, Governor Jeb Bush. Katherine Harris, the Florida secretary of state who was, depending on one's bias, either the heroine or the villain in the 2000 Florida recount, had been elected to Congress. Jeb Bush replaced her with a political clone named Glenda Hood, whose restrictive ruling on provisional balloting set the Democrats to screaming foul. No less an expert than global fair-election champion President Jimmy Carter wrote in the *Washington Post* that "the same strong bias" shown by Harris in 2000 had "become evident in her successor."

On my final visit to Florida, I brought along my 13-year-old son Peter to give him a taste of what his old man had been doing all year and perhaps to interest him in the newspaper game, since he, like my other son Paul, was a good writer. We heard an interesting speech by Kerry in Fort Lauderdale that got little press attention in which he made a late bid to combat another diversion lobbed by the Bush campaign—his supposed deficiency in religiosity because he supported abortion rights in conflict with the position of his own Catholic Church. Kerry delivered an impressive defense that was reminiscent of John F. Kennedy's famous speech to a Baptist convention in 1960.

In an effort to neutralize somewhat Bush's advantage with fundamentalist and evangelical churchgoers, Kerry quoted the Bible several times to make his point that it was more Christian to pursue the teachings of Christ in one's own life than simply to declare one's faith. "In the Book of James," Kerry said at one point, "we are taught: 'It is not enough, my brother, to say you have faith when there are no deeds. Faith without works is dead.'"

Making the same point about the role of a Catholic politician made by JFK forty-four years earlier, Kerry said: "My task, as I see it, is not to write every doctrine into law. That is not possible or right in a pluralistic society. But my faith does give me values to live by and apply to the decisions I make." The message was not destined to work for Kerry, though, as it had for Kennedy in winning over non-Catholic churchgoers. Election post-mortems later indicated that an outpouring of Bush votes from the religious right everywhere was a major factor in the outcome.

On this trip, Peter was able to see and hear a live former president for the first time, when Bill Clinton delivered a spontaneous stem-winder in behalf of Kerry to an overflow outdoor crowd one night in downtown Miami. Peter was impressed by Clinton, but my hopes that the speech might light a spark in a future reporter were dimmed by the fact that Clinton characteristically was a couple of hours late, and we had not had dinner yet.

Through all this, I continued in the column to focus on the Bush foreign-policy adventure as the critical matter before the American voter. On Election Day I wrote:

Amid a presidential campaign that has seen such diversions as the Vietnam War records of President Bush and Sen. John Kerry and a blizzard of negative, distorting television ads from both sides, one issue should remain paramount as voters go to the polls today. More than any other, the war in Iraq—how it started and how it has been conducted—requires a judgment from the American electorate on the man who launched the invasion on faulty and mis-leading information, and wound up with a bloody and chaotic aftermath.

Through a combination of arrogance and incompetence, President Bush stumbled into a foreign-policy calamity at great cost in American lives and treasure for which no clear escape is in view. Every reelection bid by a sitting president should by definition be a referendum on his first-term performance, rewarding him with a second term if it so merits, turning him out if it doesn't. This incumbent would prefer to remind voters of his commendable early response to the Sept. 11 attacks rather than answer for what has happened since then, as a result of his reckless pursuit of policies that more than ever have divided America.

Voters today may well cast their ballots on any of the other issues, legitimate or phony, that have filled so much of the candidates' rhetoric and television and radio airwaves in the long campaign reaching its conclusion today. But if they do so, they will be dodging their responsibility to weigh in on the one critical issue that will determine the course of this country for the next four years and probably beyond. If you're satisfied with a president who has set the country on a radical new course that has enmeshed it in a botched war of choice, who hasn't leveled with you before or since it began, and says he won't change what he's been doing if he is given another four years, then vote for George W. Bush.

In this fashion did I dodge making an endorsement, as an oldtime objective reporter is supposed to do. In any event, I had never judged John Kerry to be a particularly effective candidate in his own right. In my mind, he was the available vehicle for opposing the reckless and arrogant incumbent whom I judged to be the worst and most dangerous president in my lifetime. Kerry was the Un-Bush of 2004, and as such he was not quite strong enough to prevent the president from becoming the clear if narrow majority choice of the American people. So much for my two-year effort to make the case against him and, in my thinking, against his disastrous policies at home and abroad.

By selling Bush as a wartime president and a born-again Christian who was not a liberal from Massachusetts, Bush guru Karl Rove fashioned a winning margin in a second close election, this one with both a popular-vote and electoral-college majority, but hardly a resounding mandate for the war or other Bush policies. That did not stop the reelected president from declaring one, which was no surprise, inasmuch as the first time around, when he lost the popular vote by more than half a million ballots, he still governed from the start as if he had such a mandate.

As in 2000, the 2004 election turned on the electoral votes in one state, this time Ohio rather than Florida. Whereas the 2000 result was stained by widespread evidence of fraud or incredible incompetence in Florida that discriminated against certain categories of voters, the Ohio result, in which Bush won by 118,000 ballots after a statewide recount, saw more subtle shenanigans. In many heavily Democratic precincts, reported shortages of voting machines appeared to cut down on participation, as voters had to endure waits of several hours, often in heavy rain, while ample machines were on hand in heavily Republican precincts, facilitating swift casting of ballots.

The election campaign of 2004 nevertheless was a demonstration of how the parties and the unaffiliated "527 committees," by sheer energy and innovation and in spite of the supposedly dampening effect of negative advertising, were able to generate the largest turnouts in history in both parties. By percentage of eligible voters, it did not approach many earlier elections I had covered including the classic Kennedy-Nixon race of 1960. But the size of opposing forces, one rallying around the born-again wartime president and the other fiercely determined to turn him out of office, revealed a vitality challenging the cliché that voters had given up on trying to influence the government decisions that affected their lives.

The new technological developments in mass communication, highlighted by the Internet as a vehicle for grass-roots organizing, fund raising, and the stimulation of debate, were understood and seized by both parties and by individual voters as well. With the disappearance of hometown campaign storefronts and torchlight political parades, a new form of citizen participation—in cyberspace—had begun to rejuvenate participatory democracy within the confines of millions of American homes.

As the Republicans retained the White House and enlarged their majorities in both House and Senate, GOP optimists talked of the 2004 election as a defining one, introducing an era of Republican dominance. But I remembered similar projections by the Democrats after Lyndon Johnson's landslide defeat of Republican Barry Goldwater in 1964, which was followed four years later by the election of Richard Nixon. It is always dangerous in politics to look very far ahead. There was still a war on, with no clear resolution in sight.

In my first column after the election, I again wrote of Bush's war of choice, which I had opposed so strenuously:

> With the United States so thoroughly and extensively engaged, Americans in all quarters must hope that the reelected president can now focus on achieving stability in Iraq as expeditiously as possible, and with it the political solutions that will enable the return of U.S. military forces with a minimum of further casualties.
>
> Until that happens, all those who continue to believe his pre-emptive war is destructive to America's position in the world community, and see his efforts to shape the politics of another region of the world coming at much too high a price in American lives and treasure, have the obligation to keep on saying so.

And that's what I continued to do.

20 The Way We Were, and Are

THE END OF THE 2004 ELECTION was a natural time of reflection for me, after more than half a century of writing about politics. My interest in events and the people who shaped them was still high and my opinions still strongly held. But I found that a lot of nostalgia had begun to creep in, often turning my thoughts and observations to the good old days, which may not have been as good, after all, as I liked to remember.

Much of this turn of mind could be attributed to the loss or disappearance of many of my fellow travelers on the campaign trail, in politics and the news business. Those who were the stars of the analysis business when I broke into it, the likes of Teddy White, Joe Alsop, Mark Childs, and Joe Kraft, all were gone. Of my own generation in national political reporting, only my old friends Dave Broder of the *Washington Post* and Bob Novak, the Prince of Darkness, continued regularly to pound the beat around the country from Washington.

What I recalled as the long days of comradely frivolity and laughter at the back of the bus seemed to have diminished, along with the endless nights of good talk and drink at countless saloons from Des Moines to Manchester and on out to San Francisco and back. More and more I was being approached by young reporters asking me somewhat incredulously, "Mr. [too often now] Witcover, is it true you were around in the seventies?" In fact, I had now been on the trail for one newspaper or another since the fifties. I had a hard time believing it myself.

In the intervening time, some of my oldest traveling buddies, like Bruce Biossat, Jack Chancellor, Tom Ottenad, and Warren Weaver, had passed away. Others had put their old portables in storage and retired: Germond, Mears, my *Boston Globe* pals Bob Healy, John Mashek, Curtis Wilkie, Jim Doyle, Marty Nolan, and Dave Nyhan; Jim Dickenson of the *Washington Star*, Pat Furgurson of the *Baltimore Sun*, Dan Rapoport of UPI, Loye Miller of *Time*, Jim Perry of the *Wall Street Journal*, and Jon Margolis of the *Chicago Tribune*. Still others had stayed in the business but had pretty much moved out of political reporting, such as Roger Mudd, Sam Donaldson, and Johnny Apple, and I seldom saw them anymore.

It didn't help my tennis game any that there were no longer players of my generation on the circuit willing to tote a racquet around and get up at sunrise to swat the ball before undertaking the day's reporting chores. There weren't as frequent opportunities, either, to eat defensively under the Germond Rule as in the past; solitary dinners rather than crowded tables and seats at the bar became customary. And afterward I no longer had to bolt from the restaurant at full throttle to assure a seat in the back of the cab, to beat the Weaver Rule on paying taxi fares.

But the changes were in much more than the reportorial guard. On the positive side, the mechanics of the job had in many ways become easier. Writing and filing by computer was faster and more efficient than pounding out stories on a portable Olivetti on the back of a bouncing bus, then dictating or hunting down the nearest Western Union office—if one existed. Getting off a bus or train and racing house to house looking for a phone, pleading to a startled housewife for the use of her line, may sound quaint now. But it was a necessary if frenetic and undependable way of getting the story to your paper. Misspelled names in print were frequent, despite our laboriously spelling them out to harassed dictationists at the home office (including, at the *Star*, an ambitious youngster named Maureen Dowd, who eventually found more rewarding work).

The tape recorder, which was just coming into general use by reporters when I started, was a great boon for accuracy in quoting interviewees and speechifying candidates. But it was at the price of turning us into traveling stenographers, often obliging us to spend much time debating over a word or two on a scratchy tape when it would have been more fruitfully spent analyzing the significance of what had been said. And the tape recorder often had an intimidating effect on candidates and other politicians interviewed. It could make them more wary of what they said than they had been in the days when they were confronted only by pencil and pad.

During our little private dinners with presidential candidates and other key politicians, our standard rule was no tape recorders or even notepads were to be used, the better to encourage candor and relaxed exchanges. Only after the guest had departed would we pull out our pencils and pads and collectively reconstruct the most important things said. Since it was all on background, not to be attributed directly to the guest, this procedure always served us well. What we might write from the dinner conversation necessarily was broad and interpretative, but the purpose was always to get a better feeling and understanding of the guest, not to nail him for a slip of the tongue that might produce a snappy one-day yarn.

The mechanics have indeed greatly improved, as with the cell phone, which enables one to talk directly to one's editor from the back of the bus, cutting down on those mad dashes and searches for phones of yore. But the continuing key element in reporting—access to candidates and other principal sources—has sharply diminished. Sources have become more defensive and hence less available, curtailing our opportunities to demonstrate how eminently trustworthy we are.

The advent of the satellite dish has brought about a quantum leap in the number of local television anchormen covering presidential campaigns, usually on the fly and necessarily, because of their local news obligations, with limited knowledge of the beat they are dropping in on. They often don't know the candidates or much background about the sophisticated issues involved in presidential campaigns, and thus they wing it, popping obvious and unproductive questions. Physically, they can turn the most casual exchange with a candidate into a mob scene in their endless quest for the often innocuous or silly sound bite by which they make their living.

The central role of television in presidential campaigns today also has given birth to the army of professional technocrats who now dominate the political culture and community, increasingly elevating consultants, pollsters, and media magicians in importance, wealth, and visibility. It happens to the degree that candidates often must guard against losing control of their own campaigns. Many don't, and themselves become so enraptured with the specialized talents and persuasive powers of this new generation of political pros that, as in the movie of the same name, they let the tail wag the dog.

This phenomenon on one hand produces many more campaign sources for the diligent reporter. But on the other, it often creates a layer of protection shielding the candidate from reporters, reducing their access. Press secretaries, demeaned as "flacks" who were meant to be seen and not heard, now are elevated as "communications directors." They not uncommonly seek to field reporters' questions on their own or at least to hold the reporters at bay until the candidate's brain trust can come up with the proper self-serving answer.

The old days of the one-horse jockey—the relative, friend, or business associate of the candidate who joined one campaign for one presidential aspirant out of loyalty or a conviction that the object of his efforts would make an outstanding public servant—are largely gone. There are few Ted Sorensens, who labored for John Kennedy, served in his administration, and then essentially got out of campaign politics. Now the running of campaigns is a high-income, round-the-clock profession in which practitioners take on multiple candidates and often, as with Dick Morris of foot-fetish fame, will work for either party. The loyalty to candidate and party of old timers like Democrat Ray Strother and Republican Stu Spencer at the higher levels has yielded to a compulsion to go for the money.

At the same time, death has claimed some of the straightest arrows in the business, whose labors gave the lie to the old press cliché that the best way to look at a politician is down. Two of the best who passed on in 2004 were pollster Bob Teeter and media consultant and strategist John Deardourff, who collaborated on many highly ethical Republican campaigns and through the years unfailingly parceled out to reporters honest information and insight along with good humor and personal good will. They made nice livings out of politics, but neither struck it rich; they were motivated more by helping candidates who, as they themselves always did, strove to give public service a good name.

For the consultant breed in general, however, television as an essential ingredient has greatly upped the ante in a winning campaign, and losing ones as well. The high cost of buying television time and of hiring the swamis who are masters in its use has converted many politicians into fundraising machines. I well remember "covering" a couple of real experts in the art of dunning contributors, Senator Alan Cranston of California, Democrat, and Senator Rudy Boschwitz of Minnesota, Republican. Each assignment consisted of sitting in the senator's outer office while he dialed for dollars by the hour. What's more, both of them seemed to revel in the chore.

Aspirants with unlimited bankrolls of their own, such as political novices Ross Perot and Steve Forbes, literally buy their way into the presidential election process with no other visible qualification for running than their checkbooks. Still others, like George W. Bush, have an army of fat-cat friends and thus are able to bypass the federal campaign finance laws designed to limit the influence of money. They simply get their deep-pocketed pals to bundle contributions to such a degree that such candidates can decline the federal subsidy intended to buy their cooperation in slowing the flow of dough.

Also adding to the mountain of money that towers over presidential politics today is the Internet, a fund-raising as well as grass-roots organizing tool. The early long-shot campaign of Howard Dean for the 2004 Democratic nomination was largely constructed by the imaginative and aggressive use of the Internet, creating and sustaining a campaign treasury and a network of supporters that left the other candidates in the dust.

Dean's success in using the Internet as a campaign weapon was overseen by an innovative political veteran of the Mondale and Hart campaigns of the 1980s, his campaign manager, Joe Trippi. He took note of the technological revolution in politics around him and adapted it most effectively to the grass-roots techniques of his early years in the game.

The Dean campaign's Internet fund raising was so successful, in fact, that the former small-state governor, not a wealthy person, was able in time to join President Bush in forgoing the federal campaign finance subsidy. One competitor for the Democratic nomination, John Kerry, a man of independent means (with a wealthy wife), soon did the same, putting the other Democratic contenders at a distinct disadvantage—and casting a heavy shadow over the efforts of reformers to create a level playing field in elections.

The Internet has also built an immense echo chamber of public interest and voter participation through the blogging phenomenon, of benefit to candidates and often to political writers as well. For columnists, it can be a royal pain to open your e-mail each morning and be flooded with unsolicited comment, advice, and, often, invective. But it can also be rewarding to get direct feedback from readers, positive or negative, about what you have written.

One of the boosts I used to get when I worked in the towns where my work was published—Hackensack, Providence, Newark, and Washington— was encountering live readers who had something to say, good or bad, about my product. Working in Washington for papers read in Syracuse, Huntsville, Los Angeles, Baltimore, and syndicate client cities elsewhere, figuratively stuffing my pieces in a bottle and tossing them into the ocean, wasn't the same in terms of instant, personal reaction.

The arrival of the Internet during my years at the *Sun* and in syndication, however, opened up a whole new audience that could not only sample my wares but also instantly fire back at me agreements or, more frequently, dissents. Quite often these have come in colorful language, assessing my degree of intelligence, patriotism, and balance. Having this daily response has further enlivened my own interest in the issues and people about which I write. Thanks to e-mail, I no longer feel like some shipwrecked sailor on a desert island, stuffing that bottle and tossing it into the sea each day. I now have a running conversation with readers beyond their occasional letters to the editor. As hostile as some of what comes back at me is, some of it also is enlightening, and I feel much more engaged now than I did in the days of one-way communication with voiceless readers. My incoming e-mail keeps me in better touch with sentiment out there in the great void of cyberspace, as my contemporary travel companions call it, and gives me a ready opportunity to reply when the mood strikes.

Many people currently doing political reporting for newspapers find their own satisfying connection with the public by taking their views and personalities directly to television, for celebrity or profit or both. That has not been my thing, although I have appeared on the tube from time to time, usually shamelessly flacking one of my books. I've always felt there was a contradiction between the newspaper discipline of considering carefully what you want to say and then writing it with precision, and going on television and saying the first thing that pops into your head. Obviously not all the opinion-peddlers and "celebrity journalists" on television talk shows are guilty of glibness, but no doubt you can think of one or two who qualify.

I confess that I come from the earlier news-business world that was divided between "us" and "them." "Us" were the old newspaper toilers who wrote for print and saw ourselves as the guardians of the highest standards of our craft. "Them" were the television types we saw as majoring in the flippant and superficial. I've known too many distinguished print reporters and too many outstanding television practitioners not to appreciate how simplistic that comparison can be. But I still adhere to the notion that print reporters who go back and forth from the one discipline to the other, like going through a revolving door, often undermine the credibility of their first calling in pursuit of fame and fortune in the second.

In my mind, the best of the political reporters who have succeeded my own generation are those who, although they may sometimes appear on television, concentrate on putting one carefully considered word after another in print. These include, first, Dan Balz and money-in-politics specialist Tom Edsall of the *Washington Post* and Ron Brownstein of the *Los Angeles Times,* who seem to be everywhere all the time with lucid and well-considered reporting and analysis; Ron Fournier of the AP, often the first with the most and best, in his wire service's tradition; John Harwood of the *Wall Street Journal*; Jill Lawrence and Susan Page of *USA Today*; Dick Polman of the *Philadelphia Inquirer,* Carl Leubsdorf of the *Dallas Morning News,* and my colleague Paul West of the *Baltimore Sun,* among many others.

Meanwhile, as in the long past, Dave Broder of the *Post* continues to set the standard for integrity, dependability, and insight for these younger fellers and gals who have come along. Dave exercises his influence through his widely recognized fairness and scholarship. On the rare occasion when he expresses a sharply critical opinion, it carries the weight of the Pope speaking *ex cathedra* on some matter of ecclesiastical law. And the other Washington-based long-distance runner, Bob Novak, remains the model for old-fashioned enterprise, with a fearsome countenance that belies a warm heart. It's a rare combination not readily perceived by those who don't know him, as Bob seems to prefer.

All in all, the business of writing about national politics is in as good, if perhaps more sober, hands as it was in my earlier days. Today's crew is probably better educated in various aspects of political science than my gang was, but maybe not quite so well versed in the art of having a helluva good time in the process of writing about it. I like to recall the story, perhaps apocryphal, about the new-generation reporter from the *Wall Street Journal* who was sent to New Hampshire early to cover the presidential primary. The first thing he did, the story goes, was join a bridge club. In my day, we would have reserved a permanent seat at the bar in the Sheraton Wayfarer. And so it goes. Maybe it's just that when the others start calling you Mister, or worse yet ask at the back of the bus who that older guy is, you have to face that you are no longer one of the hard-drinking, carousing boys you used to be.

Finally, I can't conclude this chronicle without expressing my concern about the corruption, or even hijacking, of the news business by a new generation of television and radio entertainers, especially those with a hard ideological bias, who pay little or no homage to journalistic standards of accuracy and fairness. The growth of this political propaganda industry on the airwaves, along with the epidemic of blogging on the Internet, spreading unproved or questionable rumor as it often did during the 2004 campaign, poses a serious additional challenge to newspapers and television newsrooms.

It no longer seems sufficient for traditional news organizations to report news straight and true; they must now also deal with these viruses of inaccurate, slanted talk-show palaver and unsubstantiated conspiracy-theory blogs infecting the information bloodstream of the country. The mere repetition of such information gives it a maddening credibility, as in the continued belief among many voters, according to polls, that Saddam Hussein was involved in the terrorist attacks of 9/11 and that weapons of mass destruction were found in Iraq, when neither has been proved true.

There have always been kibitzers in the news business and rabble-rousing Walter Winchells who have thrived on gossip and hearsay to titillate readers, listeners, and viewers. Complaining now about talk radio and Internet blogging invites ridicule that one is hopelessly out of date. Neither the TV and radio ranters nor the bloggers are going to disappear, and self-starting Internet sleuths challenging public and press statements can be constructive, if the sleuthing is conducted in a responsible way, as it often is. Newspaper people are notoriously thin-skinned. We don't take much to having our faults pointed out to us, especially by people we often deride as "googoos," good-government types who from time to time call for the press to monitor itself or face outside monitoring of its ethical and other shortcomings. But we can't expect to be given a free ride when we fall short of our own standards. At the same time, the Internet is a megaphone to the world with no muffler on it, and it seems fruitless to expect voluntary restraint by those who decide to use it irresponsibly. These, however, are challenges for the next generation.

In June of 2005, as the end of my one-year contract with the *Sun* approached, I was well aware of a provision whereby the column would "automatically renew for one year" unless, at least sixty days before the year was up, either party terminated the deal in writing. So I wasn't too surprised, just a few days before the cutoff deadline, to receive by Federal Express a curt two-line letter notifying me that the contract would not be extended, with no explanation whatever. It came, not from Franklin, the editor who had assured me a year earlier that there would be no problem in renewing, nor from Donovan, my immediate boss on the editorial pages, but from the *Sun*'s head bean-counter, another *Tribune* import. The letter concluded with this heartfelt sentiment: "We appreciate your many years of service to *The Sun* and its readers and wish you well in all of your future endeavors." It was nothing personal—just the impersonal action of the newspaper's absentee ownership in the process of remaking one of its chattels in its own image.

Mine was hardly the only body tossed overboard from a demoralized *Sun* editorial ship that was leaking fast. Beyond all those veterans who had taken the "voluntary" buyout, some with more time on the paper than I, reporters who saw what was happening to the *Sun* were now deserting in droves for jobs elsewhere. In the Washington Bureau, which had nearly twenty reporters and editors when I first joined it in 1981, maybe half a dozen were left. The front section of the proud old *Sun* was now awash with bylines from the *Tribune* and its other newspaper "properties," as my acquisitive former boss S. I. Newhouse would have put it.

My principal regret in all this was that the focus of my column since early 2002—holding George W. Bush to account for his reckless and in my mind illegal scheme of invading a country that was not a threat to us—would be absent from the *Sun*. But I vowed to persevere, using my three-a-week newspaper syndication around the country. I was further fortified by the knowledge that the column was accessible on the Internet, which would continue to provide it wide readership.

As I parted company with the *Baltimore Sun* on this discordant note after twenty-four years, I took comfort in a quote from H. L. Mencken that covers one wall of the paper's refurbished front lobby on Calvert Street: "As I look back on a misspent life, I find myself more and more convinced that I had more fun doing news reporting than in any other enterprise. It is really the life of kings."

I don't agree with a lot of what the old boy wrote and said, but he sure had it right there. From my days of writing sophomoric sports pieces in college and sorting football contest entries at the *New York Daily News* to becoming an anonymous rider on the campaign trail, I have never regretted the choice I made so long ago—to become an ink-stained wretch. I've found that when you dip long enough into the inkwell, it doesn't wash off.

Index

About the Author

Jules Witcover has been a reporter, syndicated columnist, and author of a host of books on American politics and history since 1949, when he started out on a weekly newspaper in New Jersey. He moved to the *Providence (Rhode Island) Journal* in 1951, to the *Newark (New Jersey) Star-Ledger* in 1953, and in 1954 to Washington, where he has written on politics and government ever since, for the Newhouse Newspapers, the *Los Angeles Times*, the *Washington Post*, the *Washington Star*, and finally for the *Baltimore Evening Sun* beginning in 1977 and the morning *Sun* in 1981.

His political books have covered the 1968 presidential campaigns of Robert Kennedy and Richard Nixon and every presidential election from 1976, when his *Marathon: The Pursuit of the Presidency, 1972–1976* was a Book-of-the-Month Club Main Selection, through 1992, after which he dissected the electoral process in *No Way to Pick a President: How Money and Hired Guns Have Debased American Elections*, published in 1999. This was followed in 2003 by *Party of the People: A History of the Democrats*. Over these years he has often criticized how his own business has met its responsibilities, views that find their way into this volume.